Mary on the Eve of the Second Vatican Council

EDITED BY

John C. Cavadini

AND

Danielle M. Peters

Mary ON THE EVE OF

THE SECOND VATICAN COUNCIL

UNIVERSITY OF NOTRE DAME PRESS

NOTRE DAME, INDIANA

University of Notre Dame Press
Notre Dame, Indiana 46556
www.undpress.nd.edu
Copyright © 2017 by the University of Notre Dame

The Press gratefully acknowledges the support of the Institute for Scholarship in the Liberal Arts, University of Notre Dame, in the publication of this book.

Published in the United States of America

Library of Congress Cataloging-in-Publication Data

Names: Cavadini, John C., editor.
Title: Mary on the eve of the Second Vatican Council /
    edited by John C. Cavadini and Danielle M. Peters.
Description: Notre Dame : University of Notre Dame Press, 2017. |
    Includes index.
Identifiers: LCCN 2017001229 (print) | LCCN 2017010059 (ebook) |
    ISBN 9780268101589 (hardcover : alk. paper) | ISBN 0268101582
    (hardcover : alk. paper) | ISBN 9780268101596 (pbk. : alk. paper) |
    ISBN 0268101590 (pbk. : alk. paper) | ISBN 9780268101602 (pdf) |
    ISBN 9780268101619 (epub)
Subjects: LCSH: Mary, Blessed Virgin, Saint. | Vatican Council
    (2nd : 1962–1965 : Basilica di San Pietro in Vaticano). De Beata Maria
    Virgine Deipara in mysterio Christi et ecclesiae.
Classification: LCC BT613 .M37 2017 (print) | LCC BT613 (ebook) |
    DDC 232.9109/04—dc23
LC record available at https://lccn.loc.gov/2017001229

∞ *This paper meets the requirements of ANSI/NISO Z39.48-1992
(Permanence of Paper).*

Dedicated to Father Edward D. O'Connor, C.S.C.

CONTENTS

ILLUSTRATIONS

Illustrations are found in chapter 3. All except the Hollywood Madonna (public domain) are copyright © The Marian Library/International Marian Research Institute, University of Dayton, and are reprinted with permission.

ACKNOWLEDGMENTS

The editors express their gratitude to those whose assistance made this book possible. Professors Ann Astell, Lawrence Cunningham, and Cyril O'Regan and Fr. James Phalan, C.S.C, helped plan the original conference at which many of the papers that form the bases of the chapters in this volume were given in their earliest form. Major funding for this conference came from two couples who are benefactors of the Institute for Church Life: Lou and Michele Gentine and Dick and Linda Green. Without their support, neither the conference nor this subsequent collection of essays would have been possible. Staff at the McGrath Institute for Church Life were involved at every step of the way, especially Brian R. Shappell, business manager; Valerie McCance, coordinator of central office activities; Betsy Karnes, administrative assistant; and, at an earlier stage, Jennifer Monahan, assistant director. The staff at the University of Notre Dame Press are always professional, patient, and altogether praiseworthy for their good counsel and efficient operation. John Sehorn and later Gregory Cruess offered valuable editorial assistance with characteristic good scholarly judgment. Fr. Edward O'Connor, C.S.C., was an inspiring spirit. This book is dedicated to him.

September 24, 2014,
Commemoration of Our Lady of Mercy

John C. Cavadini
Danielle M. Peters

Introduction

John C. Cavadini

This book has the aim of an invitation. I wonder if there is any person more uniquely associated with Catholicism than Mary, the Mother of Jesus. I do not mean to imply that Mary is the most important person in Catholic teaching, belief, or practice. The person of Jesus Christ would take that place. But Jesus is not uniquely associated with Catholicism: all Christians believe in Jesus in some central way, and even some non-Christian religions find a place for him. But if one wants to use the image of a person to call to mind on a poster, on the cover of a book, in a film, something Catholic without using the word "Catholic," Mary is the most likely candidate. In polemics against the Church, in the Church's own imagination as expressed in art and theology, the Catholic Church is uniquely associated with Mary. Mary remains the person whose name or image will bring to mind Catholicism most readily.

It is ironic that this should be the case since, after the Second Vatican Council, the level of devotion to Mary, at least in the Catholicism of much of Europe and North America, plummeted and remains very low, so low that the eminent theologian Karl Rahner bemoaned the state of Marian devotion in a famous essay that one of our contributors, Peter Joseph Fritz, brings to our attention. Of course she holds her place in the

I

liturgy, and yet, to judge by the comments of another contributor, Fr. James Phelan, homilies on Mary are rarely heard, sometimes not even on Marian feast days. And "Mariology," if by that is meant the theological study of Mary, has all but vanished from the theological mainstream and from theological curricula. It is an irony, then, that Mary persists in the cultural imagination as the person most uniquely associated with Catholicism. It is an even further irony that Mariology was one of the most flourishing of theological disciplines in the decades on the "eve" of the Second Vatican Council, and indeed had been flourishing for about one hundred years before. Both theology and devotion had so prospered in the "long" century between the declaration of the Immaculate Conception as dogma by Pius IX (1854) and the declaration of the Assumption as dogma by Pius XII (1950) and the subsequent opening of the Council (1962).

The invitation extended by this book is to study the Marian theology of this long century and to begin to find ways to take up some of its strands and cultivate them anew. There are so many, as it were, beautifully colored threads of reflection on Mary that have been simply left behind. Some of them were woven into the tapestry of chapter 8 of *Lumen Gentium* (LG), the Council's Dogmatic Constitution on the Church. Some of them were not. All of them were dropped, seemingly, after the Council. Perhaps it is time to pick some of them up and weave them anew. Perhaps after a distance of nearly sixty years we can look at the various theologies without feeling quite so keenly the controversies out of which they arose and to which they contributed, and that may allow us to see golden threads of continuity that we had not seen before. It may allow us to refuse some of the dichotomies that seemed so urgent in some of those decades, for example, between the so-called Marian maximalism and the so-called minimalism; refuse them, at least, as defining features of the story of Marian theology in the long Marian century preceding the Council. From the perspective of the present dearth, even the "minimalism" of the 1950s can look fairly maximalist!

The volume begins with a section on historical highlights of the period we consider. The first chapter is a retrospect of the development of Marian theology by Fr. Brian E. Daley, who looks back from the perspective of *Lumen Gentium* to the earliest beginnings. Fifty years after the Council, we are, he says, "still trying to discern what features of preconciliar Catholic life were of permanent importance, in need now of refreshment or even reconstruction, and what were just part of a world that has properly evolved away." This applies to the theology of the "Marian Age," as the whole modern era of Catholicism could be called because of its increasing focus on Mary, culminating in the two Marian dogmatic definitions of 1854 and 1950. Perhaps the most crucial development in the ancient Church was the affirmation of Mary as "Mother of God" at Ephesus in 431, with the efflorescence of Marian devotion everywhere in the Church. Ironically this devotion flourished regardless of whether the Chalcedonian definition of the person of Christ, with its reaffirmation of the title "Mother of God," was accepted or not. Liturgical devotion to Mary was a constant throughout a church that was divided on other (related) issues, and even the non-Chalcedonian churches accepted the Dormition, or, as it became known in the West, the Assumption, of Mary. In the West, two developments in Marian theology were to have a long history of development themselves, all the way into the twentieth century. These were Bernard of Clairvaux's idea that Mary is "the 'aqueduct,' the channel through whom all God's grace flows to a parched humanity"—a precursor of the idea that Mary is "Mediatrix" of all graces—and the development of the doctrine of the Immaculate Conception, which achieved its most precise and persuasive early form under John Duns Scotus. The theology of the Marian Age focused on the development of these and other "privileges" of Mary, sometimes veering into enthusiasms that seem "to have shifted the emphasis of Christian belief and piety from Jesus to Mary," as with de Montfort, who, Daley writes, "draws on the tradition of her channeling God's grace to the world . . . and alters it into an image of her complete control of that grace," to the extent that "Christianity seems to have been transformed into 'Marianity.'"

In reaction to such enthusiasm, to be sure, but also to Catholic theology even in less enthusiastic versions, we find, for example, Karl Barth's 1938 rejection of Catholic Mariology as "the critical, central dogma of the Roman Catholic Church, . . . the one heresy . . . which explains all the rest . . . the principle, type, and essence of the human creature cooperating . . . in its own redemption," and thus "the principle, type and essence of the Church." Meanwhile, Catholic theology in the 1930s had begun to experience the new movement that came to be called *ressourcement*: a "return to the sources of theology," which "attempted to move away from the deductive, apologetic rationalism" and "looked for historical development, continuities, and influences within a changing but organically growing tradition, inspired by a new encounter with the Church Fathers" and, through them, the Bible. Taking Barth at his word, in a way, these theologians began to focus on what de Lubac (1937) called "a single Mystery: the Mystery of Christ and the Church." Otto Semmelroth in 1950 explicitly and systematically inserts Mary into this "single mystery" as "both the personal center and the symbol of what God has brought to fulfillment in the Church: as Bride." In a sense, he accepts Barth's critique and attempts to draw out the biblical and patristic dimensions of Mary's place in this "single mystery," precisely so that the mystery is not divided, as Barth feared. Yves Congar follows suit in 1952 with *Christ, Our Lady and the Church*, both attempting to reconnect, as de Lubac had done, the theology of Mary with the theology of Christ and the Church—agreeing with Barth, in a sense, that something had gone awry—and yet defending Catholic teaching on Mary and the Church by insisting on the crucial role of the humanity of Christ in redemption, and thus on the roles of Mary and the Church, who are both intimately associated with it. Barth's critique, from Congar's point of view, represents a rejection, implicitly, of the "mediating role of Christ's humanity," an irony, since Barth's objection was precisely to the way in which he believed Catholic theology to have displaced this mediating role in favor of Mary and the Church. Hugo Rahner's book *Our Lady and the Church*, published the year before, follows the same idea of Mary as a "type" of the Church. In 1956 his brother Karl Rahner argued along distinct, although related, lines for the integration of Mary into the economy of biblical faith. For Karl Rahner, the "fundamental principle of Mariology" is realized in the Assumption of Mary, that is, the acknowledgment of Mary as the most perfectly redeemed of all human beings.

Thus, on the eve of the Second Vatican Council we had, in the theology developed by the *ressourcement* theologians, a Mariology that was tied integrally to the history of salvation, made possible by "a renewed, historically grounded, liturgically centered, scripturally expressed, understanding of the *Church*" (emphasis in original). When the Council was announced in 1959, the older themes of the Marian Age, concentrating especially on the relationship of Mary and Jesus and the privileges flowing from this relationship—for example, her status as Mediatrix—which glorify her "as singular, as different from the rest of us," were understood by a number of more traditional theologians as a way of glorifying, not of detracting from, Christ the Lord. From this perspective, it was argued that the Council should have a separate document on Mary. The perspective developed by the *ressourcement* theologians, however, was behind an alternative proposal presented to the Council, namely, that Mary be included as part of the Council's statement on ecclesiology. By a narrow vote, the Council fathers approved the latter proposal. "The resulting final section of *Lumen Gentium*," as Daley writes, "is in many ways one of the most complete summations we have of modern Catholic Marian doctrine," one that folds Marian theology formally into the theology of the Church and yet manages to integrate into this theology, and thereby contextualize within it, the privileges strand of the Marian Age, including her role as Mediatrix, which appears as "an expression of her continuing motherhood." Daley's essay concludes with a brief look at the development of Marian theology in the writings of Popes Paul VI, John Paul II, and Francis as commentary on and development of the synthesis of *Lumen Gentium*.

The second chapter in the volume, by Fr. Thomas A. Thompson, offers the reader a second retrospect of Catholic Marian theology from the perspective of *Lumen Gentium*, this time paying special attention to the theme of Mary's *faith* as the golden thread that helps us to narrate the history of this theology. In figures as early as Justin Martyr and Irenaeus, Mary's faith is contrasted to the unbelief and disobedience of Eve. In Ambrose the theme of Mary's faith becomes a link to the faith of all believers, all of whom, like Mary, can conceive and give birth to the Word of God. For Ambrose, Mary serves as a *type* of the Church, both of whom give birth to believers. As such, Mary is also the mother of believers. Augustine develops the idea more fully: "For Augustine, Mary's maternity was an encompassing mystery transcending temporal succession; it was an illustration of the *Totus Christus*, that is, the inseparability of the physical body of the Christ from the body of the members." Mary's faith preceded her conception of Christ physically, as the conception of Christ in her heart and, presumably, all of his members.

This Augustinian tradition continues in Bede and other monastic teachers in the West, but in the "Marian revival" featuring Bernard of Clairvaux and the development of the "Hail Mary" in the twelfth century and moving on to Albert the Great and Thomas, there are no references to the faith of Mary. Apart from Albert the Great, the Mary–Church relation is hardly present, and after him it "appears to have fallen into oblivion." Marian theology picks up after the Council of Trent, and the word "Mariology" appears for the first time in a treatise from 1602, but it is in the nineteenth century that we find an acceleration of Marian teaching and, though itself critiqued for an overly rationalistic methodology, "the Scholastic revival in Italy was a response to rationalism and modern philosophy." But the renewal of liturgical, biblical, and patristic theology beginning in the nineteenth century and the early twentieth eventually reached Mariology through the *ressourcement* theologians, and the deductive method of the Neo-Scholastic handbooks was left behind, even though the search for a "fundamental principle" for Mariology persisted in this new style of theology. "Yet to be written," Thompson notes, "is the history of the Marian *ressourcement*, which at Vatican II was responsible for an image of the Virgin Mary different from the one that was found in the early twentieth-century manuals." He writes, "First recovered" from the early centuries was "the Mary–Church relationship" and "then the Virgin Mary's integration into Scripture and salvation history." Thompson summarizes the contributions of Hugo Rahner, Alois Müller, Heinrich Köster, René Laurentin, and Otto Semmelroth as well as the contributions of the Mariological societies that evolved in the first half of the twentieth century.

Lumen Gentium chapter 8 presents Mary within the *one* mystery of Christ and the Church, reconciling and integrating a Christocentric or Christotypical view of Mary and an ecclesiotypical view. Thompson writes that that document proclaims that "within the Church, Mary's relation to Christ is fully intact" in all its various dimensions, and within this one mystery, Mary's place in salvation history is elaborated under four Old Testament types: the promised Woman (cf. Gen. 3.15, where the Latin text has a feminine subject); the virgin who shall conceive (Isa. 7:14; Mic. 5:2–3; Matt. 1:22–23); the humble and poor of the Lord; and Daughter of Sion. Mary's faith, mentioned in the second of the blessings that Elizabeth directs to her: "Blessed are you among women, and blest is the fruit of your womb; Blest is she who believed that there would be a fulfillment of what was spoken to her by the Lord" (Luke 1:38, 1:45), bridges the two testaments. Perhaps, Thompson suggests, this second blessing, highlighted by John Paul II in his encyclical *Redemptoris Mater*, could also be added to the Hail Mary, along with the first.

The next chapter in the collection also offers an overview of the period, in this case a kind of parallel overview tracing developments in Marian representation against developments in theology. Without trying to claim too close a correspondence that would seem forced on the art, the chapter of Fr. Johann G. Roten demonstrates certain resonances between Marian theology and Marian art, even as it keeps our eyes on some of the larger cultural developments that affected both art and theology at the same time. Devotional art associated with the village of Epinal in northeast France had a popular character and was most closely associated with the "Christotypical" or "Marian privilege" theology that emphasized Mary's role as Mediatrix or Co-redemptrix. Devotional art was also closely influenced by the nineteenth- and twentieth-century apparition tradition. Insofar as the "Marian century" was a century of upheaval, with two horrific world wars in its latter half, to which corresponded both the art and the privilege theology, "There was a terrible need for redemption from the tragedies and consequences of two world wars, and thus an urgent call for trustworthy mediation between heaven and earth." Accordingly, the Epinal representations often depict Mary with a unique combination of compassion and strength: "The overall message is one of mercy and power." The popular images did undergo development, partly in response to the so-called realism of Hollywood and partly in reaction against what came to be perceived as their own previous sentimentality. Yet these somewhat iconoclastic trends did not succeed in displacing the popular images but were rather taken up into a still recognizably iconic style. The more "artistic" or high-culture representation of Mary evinced trends that in some ways broke sharply with the sentiments of religion in general, not just popular religion, as can be seen in the developments leading up to Max Ernst's *The Virgin Spanks the Son of Man before Three Witnesses* of 1926. A transition had taken place from religion triumphing in the arts to art triumphing over religion, which art observed without celebrating. In terms of more religious, high-culture art, we find a transition from Romanticism to expressionism associated with Plateau d'Assy. Despite all of the changes in the representation of Mary in the Marian Age, up to the eve of the Second Vatican Council the fundamental image remained that of Mother and Child: "Whether sacred or secular, kitsch and popular or of genuine artistic quality but seemingly non-Christian, whether of pious inspiration or for aesthetic enjoyment only—there remains the abiding and irreversible reality of Mother and Child," the "foundational expression" of Marian art that serves as a kind of summary of the Gospel and of all of revelation, which renders it irreplaceable. It should be noted that Fr. Roten's endnotes provide the reader with a wonderful annotated bibliography, in effect, for anyone wishing to pursue this topic further.

The chapters in the second section of the book take up individual theologians, beginning with Yves Congar. Christopher Ruddy's chapter analyzes the contribution of Congar by tracking his opposition to two opposed tendencies, namely, the "maximalist Mariology" of certain Catholic theologians and the extreme minimalism of neoorthodox Protestantism. For Congar, the maximalist strain of Mariology was, as we have already seen from our overview essays, dialectical or deductive in character, separated from the rest of theology and so an "isolated maximalism" that tended to "work by deduction from atemporal principles." Congar's approach was that of the *ressourcement*, recovering the way in which the Fathers placed the mystery of Mary within the mystery of the Church and the latter within the mystery of the divine economy of salvation. Ruddy writes: "This tethering or integration of Mary to ecclesiology and soteriology is the foundation of Congar's Mariology." At the same time, for Congar, Protestant minimalism with regard to Mary was simply a function of Protestant minimalism with regard to the salvific role of Christ's humanity and thus to the role of human cooperation in God's gracious saving work. Ruddy explains Congar's view: "Jesus's conception and birth, in this view, are not something that Mary does but something that she receives; she has no active role, save that of her *fiat*, which 'receives and recognizes that God is at work in her.'" Congar, on the other hand, would want to recognize an active role of cooperation in both Mary and the Church. As he writes: "In setting up this union of heaven and earth accomplished in person by Jesus Christ, a share is also to be attributed to our Lady through her cooperation in the mystery of the Incarnation, and to the Church because it communicates to us the effects that flow from the Incarnation." As Ruddy writes, for Congar "Mary and the Church are . . . 'one and the same mystery in two moments,'" with Mary's virginal motherhood being a type of the Church's virginal motherhood. Ruddy's assessment of Congar's contribution to Mariology recognizes his positive contributions, including his role in reconnecting Mary to the Church and to salvation history, but also notes the drawbacks that Congar's Mariology had, as its aim was "less to open up or to explore a theology of Mary than to correct theological and devotional excesses" and as such was "more reactive than constructive, more concerned with corralling than cultivating," and less willing to emphasize Mary's unique dignity among all creatures. There is "a decided coolness in Congar's Marian thought" as a result, and Ruddy wonders whether one of Congar's "unintended" legacies was "postconciliar Catholic ecclesiology's relative neglect of Mary"—whether, in other words, once the mystery of Mary was subsumed by the mystery of the Church, it became an optional afterthought in ecclesiology, following the minimizing "trajectory" and energy of Congar's Mariology rather than the positive claims it makes. Ruddy concludes with an observation that could almost be the motto of this whole collection: "It is no slight . . . to suggest that a new work of integration, *ressourcement*, and discernment is needed today if Mary is to reclaim her rightful place in the mysteries of Christ and the Church."

Ruddy's chapter raises this question: as Mariology moved away from the trope of "Mary's privileges" to contextualizing Mary in another theological framework such as that of the Church, how do we avoid rendering Mary just another example of that framework, even if the preeminent example, such that there is no longer a point to Mariology, except as the preeminent illustration of a category? This seems to be what happened with Congar's trajectory, if Ruddy is correct.

Next is Matthew Levering's chapter, which examines three theologians' writing in the 1950s, exactly on the "eve" of the Second Vatican Council. By studying writings of René Laurentin, Otto Semmelroth, and Karl Rahner, all written in close proximity to each other (1953, 1954, and 1956, respectively), Levering examines whether and to what extent each theologian attended to the relationship between Mary and the Holy Spirit as it is stated explicitly or implicitly in Scripture. He takes as a cue for his analysis comments by Congar that, on the one hand, "it is very important to remain conscious of the deep bond that exists between the Virgin Mary and the Spirit" and, on the other hand, to guard against a tendency to "functionally replace the Holy Spirit with Mary." Levering shows that of the three theologians he studies, only Laurentin attended to the relationship between Mary and the Spirit, and, further, he did so by following the "biblical portraiture," which shows, among other things, that "the Holy Spirit did not simply make the infant Christ present in [Mary's] womb; rather the Holy Spirit also consecrated her and assimilated her to her Son so that she could fulfill her unique vocation as mother of her Son." Again, Levering writes, "Laurentin's approach takes us through Mary's life and shows how deeply her unique relationship with the Holy Spirit marks her vocation." This approach, Levering suggests, preserves a sense of Mary's uniqueness, her "privileges," without detaching her from the biblical story of redemption. The approaches of Semmelroth and Rahner, by contrast, begin to bleach out Mary's distinctiveness in favor of Mary as a type of the Church (Semmelroth) or as an exemplar of God's grace (Rahner). Semmelroth preserved more of a connection between Mary and the Holy Spirit than did Rahner; nevertheless, "he [Semmelroth] generally studied the mysteries of Mary in order to show something about the Church." In the sermons of Rahner that Levering studies, "the particular details of Mary's life and the specific person of the Holy Spirit do not have much of a role." More important is that "she exemplifies what grace is and what humans are," and Mary seems almost collapsed into theological anthropology as the most important exemplar of God's grace, extended to all human beings. It was Laurentin, "even more than Semmelroth or Rahner," who "anticipated the achievements of *Lumen Gentium*, which clearly states that Mary is "the beloved daughter of the Father and the temple of the Holy Spirit," as befits her reception of "the high office and dignity of Mother of the Son of God" (citing LG 53).

The following chapter, by Peter Joseph Fritz, focuses on Karl Rahner alone. Rahner appears in Fritz's lucid essay as the self-described "minimalist" that he is, and yet we find that his minimalism has a "maximalist" twist. In fact, the very words "maximalist" and "minimalist" seem somewhat problematic since they do not exhaust the debates in Mariology that arose in the Marian Age and to some extent may continue in the present. Fritz shows that Rahner attacks the maximalism of certain mid-century Mariologies precisely because they seem to be "centrifugal," that is, they seem to be ways of refusing to deal with attacks on the central claims of the Christian message, such as those of atheism, and so are "escape hatches" that actually end up evacuating Mary of the very significance they so hoped to attach to her. Rahner's minimalism was for him a way to reintegrate Mary into the very story of salvation that makes her meaningful to us. What Fritz calls his "fundamental principle" for Marian theology was not her motherhood, therefore, which for Rahner "connotes privatization," Fritz says, but rather "the fact that Mary is one human person among many, . . . blessed *among* women" (emphasis in original), because—and this is Rahner's fundamental principle—she is the person who is, in his words, "redeemed in the most perfect way." As Rahner saw it, this minimalist position actually maximizes Mary's significance to us. Fritz explains: "Rahner's stress on Mary's belonging to the human race ends up underscoring her constitutive place in the salvific economy. Minimizing her personal privilege maximizes her salvation-historical significance." Combining his fundamental principle with his brother Hugo's ecclesiotypical view of Mary, Rahner argues that it is precisely as the most perfectly redeemed person that Mary *is* the "type of the Church": as Fritz writes, Mary's "giving of the Spirit through the enfleshed Word" shows that the true apostolic life is not what Rahner calls a "spirit of anarchy" but one that results in a "bounded ecclesiology," to use Fritz's term, that has, in Rahner's words, "the courage to submit to flesh, to concrete precisions." Near the end of Rahner's life, this courage appears in a new form in the title of an essay from 1983, "Courage for Devotion to Mary." This essay laments the loss of Marian devotion in many countries of the Western world in favor of New Age spiritualities or meditative practices associated with Eastern religions. Rahner's attack on a certain kind of Marian maximalism was not intended to distance the Church from traditional Marian devotions such as the rosary; it was intended to draw out their full significance rather than to risk the centrifugal theological moves that would ultimately seem to cut them off as peripheral spiritual phenomena. Fritz regards this essay as ranking "among the most significant Rahner ever wrote." It exhibits Rahner's minimalism as giving very little court to the minimalistic "progressives" who have given up Marian devotions "in the name of progress." In closing, Fritz notes that "Rahner teaches us that if we ever feel inclined to minimize our words about Mary, the resulting minimalism should manifest itself as the simplicity of traditional Marian prayer."

The study by Troy A. Stefano takes up the task of describing the Mariology of someone who never wrote a particular work on Mary but whose work is nevertheless suffused with mariological reflection, namely, Henri de Lubac, perhaps the *ressourcement* theologian par excellence. De Lubac's success in Mariology, in fact, may be due to the dispersed character of his reflections. He was out not to combat the maximalism or the minimalism of other Mariologists or indeed to engage in a separate subject called Mariology but to present a compelling account of the Catholic faith steeped in the biblical tradition as it had been inherited from the Fathers of the Church. This requires (as for Congar) a profound appreciation of the Incarnation. De Lubac seems to be able to hold together the Christotypical emphasis in Mariology—associated with the uniqueness of Mary and her "privileges"—with the ecclesiotypical emphasis in Mariology, which was increasingly associated with Marian minimalism as the Council approached. De Lubac's use of the Marian titles "Immaculate Spouse," "Virgin Mother," and "Mother of the Church" is key to his unique approach. All three, taken together, preserve the integrity of an "incarnational logic" that honors Mary's uniqueness (perhaps more than the approaches of Congar and Rahner?) even as it integrates Mary fully into the economy of salvation history. The key here is to realize that the economy is constituted by God's self-emptying love, fully accomplished in the Incarnation, and that this self-emptying moment is never taken back; "God, thus bodily mediated, is never consequently received unmediated apart from Christ's body," as Stefano writes. God's self-emptying love is the ultimate mystery. Mary's role in mediating that love to us through her motherhood of Christ is unique and irreplaceable. To try to minimize it is, in effect, to turn the Incarnation into an abstraction instead of remembering that Jesus is a person and, we could add, following Origen (in *On First Principles* 2.6.2), that he came into the world as a baby who cried just like any other baby. To minimize Mary's role is to defeat the purpose of confessing the Incarnation and to vitiate the fullness of one's confession of the economy of salvation. Under each of the three titles, Mary at once advances and recapitulates, in Christ, the economy of salvation. As Immaculate Spouse, Mary's unique relationship to the Word fully discloses the spousal love of God for Israel and brings it to fulfillment in her role as Virgin Mother. Here the spousal dimension, "following Scheeben," is prioritized because it emphasizes the perfection of Mary in grace as a perfection for a true cooperation *as* beloved spouse "to ensure that Mary as Virgin Mother cannot be turned into an abstraction by seeing her as solely an instrument for the Incarnation," in Stefano's words. This seems to be an important difference from the views of all of the theologians studied so far except, perhaps, for Laurentin. As Virgin Mother, according to de Lubac, Mary thus becomes the "sacrament" of Christ. As Stefano writes: "The structure of Christ's own historicity is the 'form' of his mediation; if Christ's condescension to adapt to our weakness came through Mary, Christ's 'form' remains as the Incarnate One through Mary. Christ is *forever* from Mary's womb" (emphasis in original). Mary is a "type of the Church" not simply as a representative, or even as *the* representative member, but because she is the Mother of the Church. Her "hour" comes when Christ's hour comes and she is given as mother to the Beloved Disciple. The moment when her spousal and maternal identity passes over into the Church, who is Spouse and Virgin Mother, is the moment when the fullness of the significance of her status as Mother of the Incarnate Word is revealed. Only by calling Mary "Mother" do we fully realize our identity as members of the Church, members of Christ's body, and fully confess the mystery of the Incarnation, universalizing it without abstracting it. Therefore, as Stefano writes: "To invoke Mary as our mother . . . is to say that the spousal and maternal mediations of the Church are themselves derivative of the concrete relation between Christ and Mary." If calling Mary the "type" of the Church deemphasizes the priority of Mary, the result will be an abstraction of the body of Christ, the Church, into an impersonal structure, no longer "wholly personal," no longer "she," no longer the "continuation" of the Incarnation but a displacement of it into the past.

The next chapter, by Msgr. Michael Heintz, presents another *res-sourcement* theologian writing on Mary in the decade before Vatican II, Louis Bouyer, whose theology, as Heintz analyzes it, presents the same concern as that of de Lubac for exhibiting Mary's integration into the economy of salvation precisely by preserving her irreducible uniqueness. In other words, the "ecclesiotypical" theology depends on the "Christo-typical," and the Christotypical is prevented from becoming isolated (as Rahner feared) from the rest of theology because it is oriented precisely toward the ecclesiotypical. In agreement with Rahner's approach, Bouyer writes: "Our Lady shows forth what is, *par excellence*, the Gospel teach-ing, namely, how our human nature is raised by grace to a degree corre-sponding to the closeness of the bond that unites us to Christ. . . . In her we are able to discern, realized in time, all that the divine Wisdom held in store for us." In a striking phrase that reminds us even more of Rahner, Heintz notes that, in a way, "Mariology *is* theological anthropology." And yet Bouyer has many safeguards in place that keep Mariology from collapsing into theological anthropology, such that Mary is distin-guished from us only by degree, not by an irreducibly unique role. Mary is not only a member, the most redeemed member, of the Church but also the "link" between Christ and the Church. More particularly, it is Mary's faith that is the link, as the perfect coming together of predesti-nation and human freedom. As Bouyer states: "From the standpoint of God's initiative, of predestination, we may say that it was because the moment had come when the Word had decided to take flesh that faith flowered in Mary. But from the standpoint of saving human freedom, it is equally true to say that the Word became incarnate at that moment rather than at any other because he had at last found a soul of entire faith, wholly disposed to receive him." Christ is "above faith" because, though his human nature is fully human, it is taken up by a divine person and established in the beatific vision, yet "Christ's humanity, though pos-sessed by a divine person, yet remains ours, because it first belonged to the person of Mary," and thus our humanity is united to Christ's human-ity "through" the humanity of Mary. She thus serves as the link between Christ and the Church. Her utter uniqueness does not isolate her but in fact makes her "the masterpiece of grace," and her fiat is "arguably the freest choice ever made by a human person." Though she is a member of the Church, she can never be collapsed fully into it because that would destroy the link that connects the Church to Christ. Mary's "privileges"—her maternity and her holiness, for example—in one sense will be fully extended to the Church eschatologically, and yet, in another sense, the conditions for the extension of these privileges would be destroyed if they did not persist in Mary uniquely. Thus, if Mary is a "type" of the Church, it is not because she foreshadows the Church by containing already the perfection that the Church eventually will have; rather, it is the other way around. Heintz writes that "ecclesial maternity," for example, "is first and foremost Marian, and the Church, Bouyer asserts, can be called 'Mother' only by being a 'continuation' of Mary's own maternity." Mary's virginal motherhood is, in Bouyer's words, "the condition of possibility for the Church's motherhood." If Mary is the Seat of Wisdom, it is the Wisdom of the "mystery" of God's self-emptying love made manifest in Christ. She is, Heintz says, the "Seat of *this* Wisdom" (my emphasis) and cannot be dissolved fully into the Church without undoing the Wisdom that made the Church.

The third section of the book gives us a glimpse of Mary on the eve of the Second Vatican Council as she entered into preaching and into the spirituality of monastic and secular institutes and movements. The first chapter in this section, by Fr. Kevin Grove, takes up the earliest example in the book, one close to the heart of the University of Notre Dame, namely, the Marian preaching of Basil Moreau, founder of the Congregation of Holy Cross, which founded the university. As he introduces us to the pastoral concerns of Moreau's preaching, Grove demonstrates conclusively that the characterization of the Mary of the doctrine of the Immaculate Conception on offer in such scholarly works as the essay "Immaculate and Powerful," by Barbara Corrado Pope, is a caricature. According to this and similar views, the doctrine portrays a Mary who is not scriptural, in Pope's words a "pure and passive vessel" who is anything but a disciple. The Mary of Scripture disappears into this doctrine, which seems to be little more than a papal ideology in support of what Grove calls "conservative government ideals against postrevolution secular, or modern, values." The Mary of the doctrine becomes isolated even from other doctrinal contexts—Trinitarian, Christological, and ecclesiological—becoming, "both in popular preaching and in theological discussion . . . a more and more autonomous figure." Grove comments that such scholarly claims "are often leveraged without any support" and that "at least in the singular example of Moreau"—who, as an Ultra-montanist, could be expected to exhibit the worst of the ideological tendencies alleged here—"we see the paradigmatic opposite." Preaching on the Immaculate Heart of Mary, Moreau draws a picture fully determined by the portraiture of Scripture (to use the expression of Levering in a different context), of someone who is anything but passive in her "daily and mutual" sharing in the life of Jesus. The Incarnation is central, revealing the influence of the earlier "French School" of theology, but precisely as self-emptied into the realities of daily life. "What appears here is a Mary who—at the level of experience and perhaps without full comprehension—must have been working through the human aspect of raising a Son who was the Word having assumed her flesh." She is as such not only a disciple but "the model of discipleship, more so than the twelve," more than Thomas and Peter, and more even than the Beloved Disciple. She is not a passive instrument, disconnected from the Trinity, but the "minister" of the Father's designs and as such a "cooperator" in the sufferings of her Son and in the plan of salvation. One difference: the Father, who gave up His Only Begotten Son, is impassible by nature, but Mary, as a human mother, is able to suffer and, insofar as she gives up her innocent Son, she suffers with him and in a sense is martyred herself on Calvary. In the suffering of Mary, Grove states, Moreau is "exploring the depths of sorrow as complete configuration to the redemption wrought in Jesus Christ" and therefore to the depths of human compassion. The Immaculate Heart of Mary, far from the distant "powerful" Mary of the caricature, "bears forth the mystery of the Incarnation" in her willingness to accept sorrow on our behalf and in "pondering in her heart" her own sorrows, which are the sorrows of her Son, which in turn are the sorrows of all human hearts. Here is again a characteristic of the French School spirituality initiated by Pierre de Bérulle in the early seventeenth century and eclipsed by the French Revolution, which attempted to replace Mary with the Goddess of Reason. If Moreau is attempting to recover a tradition, it is this one in which the "privileges" of Mary are hers only in service of her larger mission of compassion in the economy of redemption. Grove sums up his chapter with a brief reflection on the famous "Golden Dome" of the University of Notre Dame, on top of which is an image of Mary of the Immaculate Conception: "Such a gilded icon of doctrine might seem the ultimate evacuation of the historical Mary in favor of what has become 'immaculate and powerful.' But there might be a more charitable and indeed more probable reading possible. For a thinker like Moreau it would have been impossible to enshrine a doctrine *qua* doctrine in gold, but so decorating a mother who teaches how to relate to Christ—and opens up the imagination to all points of Jesus's life—would be a worthwhile pondering."

The following chapter is also on the Immaculate Conception, but this time as the focus of a collection of scholarly essays for a conference held at the University of Notre Dame in 1954, edited by Fr. Ed O'Connor and published in 1958, just four years before the opening of the Council. Some of the participants were present at the Council or otherwise actively involved. Ann W. Astell's chapter pays tribute to the volume, published by the University of Notre Dame Press nearly fifty years ago and still "the most cited, most comprehensive collection on the development of the doctrine in the English language." Peter Fritz's essay reminded us that Karl Rahner had called for a pluralist Catholic conversation regarding Mariology in which so-called maximalists and minimalists could receive each other's perspectives and perhaps realize that the conversation was more cohesive than it first might seem. The volume edited by O'Connor bears out that insight, as noticed by no less an ecclesiologist than Cardinal Avery Dulles, who called the volume "a skillful and prudent compromise between two tendencies in modern Catholic theology, one of which would emphasize Mary's unique connection with Christ the Redeemer; the other, her close connection with the Church and all the redeemed." That is, "if," as Astell adds parenthetically, compromise "is indeed the appropriate word," suggesting that it is not. Astell's chapter suggests instead that the volume is a particular spiritual penetration into the mystery from which the essays arise, one that is performed in the essays themselves, as well as in their editorial integration, which allows and in fact even insists that these perspectives be integrated. "Indeed," she writes, "O'Connor's 'Preface' to [the] volume consistently conjoins them, admitting no contradiction between them," and more, integrating the mystery of the Immaculate Conception with the other mysteries of the faith, ameliorating the isolation with which Mariology, especially of the maximalist sort, had so often been charged. What is interesting is that the integration it achieves is achieved not from the minimalist perspective of Rahner, which could sponsor a pluralist conversation but not envision the integration of the perspectives (as he himself admitted) but from a more Christotypical perspective. As Astell writes: "It begins with Mary and extends into ecclesiology a historical narrative of a mysterious, personal, Marian redemption effected in, with, and through Christ." From the point of view of proximate history, Astell observes, this "'particular outlook' that holds together the Christotypical and ecclesiotypical features in a single, specifically soteriological 'point of balance'" is on the losing trajectory. O'Connor clearly thought, and hoped, that the Church was on the way "towards a definition of Mary's co-redemption and mediation of graces." This is the opposite trajectory from the one that the Church has actually taken, but it is also the opposite trajectory from the one that Chris Ruddy invited us to consider as Congar's. Perhaps there is a reason, beyond the solidity of the scholarship in this collection, that it has endured as a live resource for so many years, even given some of the shortcomings that Astell also notes.

It is as though the collection has a spiritual heart at its center, as though the collection transcends its character as a collection and communicates this spiritual heart, proceeding from a spiritual transformation proceeding directly from the mystery of the Immaculate Conception herself. "We are enveloped in mystery," the patrologist Jouassard writes at the end of his chapter, "a mystery that God allows our dull minds to penetrate slowly." The *ressourcement* style of historical study, fully allowing for and documenting in a rigorous scholarly way the development of doctrine in the Church, arises from a spiritual conviction. Astell writes: "What gives coherence to the book as a whole—apart from the contributors' shared devotion to Mary Immaculate—is the constantly reiterated witness to, and expectation of, doctrinal development, as a proof of the Holy Spirit's presence in, and guidance of, the Church in its understanding of Mary and thus of itself as Christ's bride." O'Connor's own chapter on the "spirituality of the Blessed Virgin" is in a way the soul of the collection, taking up this spirituality with reference both to Mary's "personal life and to the lives of others insofar as they are influenced by her," including the witness of such saints as John Eudes, C.J.M., and

Louis-Marie Grignion de Montfort, from the French School of spirituality introduced by Kevin Grove's chapter. The collection presents us with a historical approach that is not historicizing because of this "soul" living in the book, balancing "the *nouvelle théologie* of the historians with the Neo-Thomism of dogmatic theologians, joining history with significance" instead of playing them off against each other.

Astell's chapter also gives us a clue as to the origin of this "soul" animating the book, itself a life that was influenced by and penetrated with the mystery of Mary, in the many-layered way that such influence often comes about. It turns out that there is a connection between O'Connor's chapter and L'Arche, founded in 1964 by Jean Vanier, who had given his project to aid the mentally handicapped this Marian title ("Ark"). Père Thomas Philippe, O.P., who was the chaplain of L'Arche from its foundation, was master of studies at the Dominican House of Studies outside of Paris, the Saulchoir, when O'Connor studied there. Philippe had succeeded Marie-Dominique Chenu, O.P., whom Philippe had been charged by the Holy Office to remove in 1942. Philippe was himself removed in 1952, criticized for his unorthodoxy and exaggerated Marian mysticism, which was based on an experience he had in prayer in 1937. He spent ten years under ecclesiastical censure but emerged from that to take his place in the L'Arche movement. Astell notes: "Neo-Thomist in his Mariology, Marian in his mysticism, Père Thomas had a heart that was drawn into the crucible of all the vital intellectual movements of his day, into the deep mysteries of human beauty and affliction, and the charitable practices demanded by them." O'Connor repeatedly cites Philippe, even though at the time he was still under censure. Astell writes that we have in this collection an enactment of what Philippe called true Marian spirituality, namely, "a close union of doctrine and practice, . . . objective, because based directly on the dogmas of the Church . . . at the same time a spirituality of littleness . . . of personal intimacy with Jesus and Mary [and of service to the poor]." For anyone "who has the patience to discover it," there is perhaps a pedagogy in this collection for the trajectory of Marian theology that may show a path forward.

The next two chapters, each in its own way, continue the demonstration that at the heart of major ecclesial movements in the twentieth-century Church there is a Marian spirituality whose trajectory has yet to be fully realized. Both chapters suggest that a key to the success of the movements described is the creative interpretation of Marian doctrine achieved in an enterprise in which there is a close union between doctrine and practice. Danielle M. Peters explores the contribution of the founder of the international Schoenstatt Movement, Fr. Joseph Kentenich. Fr. Kentenich, who was apprehended by the Gestapo in 1941 and imprisoned at Dachau until 1945, knew firsthand what he called the "anthropological heresy" of his day, a heresy that he said "refers directly to human nature." He thought the symptoms of this heresy include "a rapidly increasing secularization accompanied by an equally accelerated dehumanization"; at once a "flight from God" and "an alarming inability to build community and to love"; and "individualism and nihilism." Fr. Kentenich commented, "Personhood is combated. Human freedom, the whole structure of human nature as it is created by God, is increasingly ruined" in favor of mass manipulation of the human psyche and even, he predicted in 1948, human cloning. As a response to the anthropological heresy, Fr. Kentenich worked toward a vision of "the new person in the new community," as Peters writes, and he placed it under the protection of Mary, who, as Mother of God, Fr. Kentenich wrote, "is, as it were the point of intersection between nature and supernature." He very self-consciously focused on the Church's teaching on Mary in order to discover what Peters refers to as its "anthropological and pedagogical corollary for the Christian life." Working theologically off of insights found in the writings of M. Scheeben, Fr. Kentenich's Mariology was always "Christ-centered . . . even when Vatican II and post–Vatican II theology stressed an ecclesiotypical and anthropocentric" Mariology that seemed to be following another trajectory. Thus Fr. Kentenich would be placed on the "higher" end of Mariology, if one were comparing overall, and yet he was critical of the dominant, "privilege"-centered Mariology of the theology and piety on the eve of the Council, not because it had centered on Mary's privileges but because it seemed, in retrospect, to have had so little effect. It seemed isolated from the rest of Catholic faith and life: "See how little depth it had!," Fr. Kentenich exclaimed. "What is left of it today? . . . How little it had taken root in the subconscious life of the soul!"

The solution lay not in deemphasizing Mary's "Christotypical" profile but in using it, exploiting its potential to connect to the rest of Christian teaching and to Christian life. Thus, for example, Peters writes that for Fr. Kentenich, "Psychologically and pedagogically the dogma of the Immaculate Conception is the most significant of all Marian dogmas for our time because it draws attention to the dignity and value of the human person." The solemn proclamation of the dogma of the Assumption was a "pedagogical event," Fr. Kentenich thought, and, in a way that recalls both Rahner and Bouyer, a "synthesis of anthropology." In particular, like the dogma of the Immaculate Conception, it responds to the anthropological heresies of the day by reminding us of the heavenly glory to which each human body is called, the very body that, today, he wrote, is both "maltreated and on the other hand . . . adored." No doubt the "maltreated" reflected his time in the concentration camp. Again, Peters writes, Mary's fiat is not simply a private act but is a "representative act and the expression of humanity's self-surrender to the Son of God." It is crucial to keep the proper balance, though: Mary's fiat as a private act does not dissolve into an abstract representation. As Peters writes: "The 'Yes' of the individual to Christ simultaneously is therefore, though not always consciously, the individual's alignment with Mary's 'Yes,'" which remains unique not just as a model but as a unique participation in the mystery of Christ into which we are invited. Just as Christ entrusted himself to Mary in a unique way, as his Mother, and as Mother was his first and primary Educator, so Mary is, Peters writes, "Mother and Educator of the whole Body of Christ," and Christian devotion to Mary is an incorporation into her pedagogy, into the "school of Mary," as John Paul II later characterized it. Mary's unique cooperation in redemption through her wholly graced and wholly free "Yes" is the pedagogy that can respond to the anthropological heresies of the age because the dignity of the creature is recovered, not in competition with divine initiative but at that initiative itself. Mary is the most perfectly redeemed creature, as Rahner suggested, but in order to preserve her significance as such, her unique relation to Christ must be maintained as a starting and ending point; otherwise, the implication seems to be, one has no answer to the dehumanizing and depersonalizing "heresies" against human nature in our time. Peters closes by suggesting that a trajectory from Vatican II that picks up on the trajectory laid out by Schoenstatt, as Fr. Kentenich inspired it, has been laid out by Popes Paul VI, John Paul II, and, incipiently, Francis.

The theme of the integration of doctrine and practice is continued in Peter Casarella's examination of the "Marian profiles" of two prominent twentieth-century Catholic women, both of whom initiated lay movements in the Church, Adrienne von Speyr and her younger contemporary Chiara Lubich. Yves Congar's notion of analogy provides the key here to an understanding of how Mary, with her irreducibly unique relationship to Christ, has become ecclesiotypical without being collapsed into the doctrine of the Church or of theological anthropology. The notion of a Marian "profile" for the Church and for movements within the Church is intended to carry this insight of the primacy of analogy. For Adrienne von Speyr, the image of Mary, Virgin Mother of Mercy, predominates, along with the image used to express it, that is, the image of the poor and all the needy (all of us!) gathered under Mary's protective mantle. Casarella points out that Mary's own contemplation of the mysteries in which she was so uniquely involved changed from a more "abstract" mode to one that, "after pregnancy and giving birth, after standing at the foot of the Cross . . . becomes a model of contemplative prayer that is in touch with the anguish of the human heart." Christ alone suffers "actively," but Mary, in communion with John, "goes into labor" as a passive recipient of that suffering. It forms her, and she becomes the Mother of the Church, the Virgin Mother of Mercy, and the Church, by analogy and by participation in her unique "labor," acquires a Marian profile of active lay works of mercy. As von Balthasar put it, based on the insights of von Speyr, Mary "is seen as spreading her protective cloak over the whole of Christendom, and making some part of her stainlessness flow out over the bride, the Church." As Casarella writes, she becomes in this way (and echoing what we have learned from Fr. Kentenich), "the teacher of the fecundity of contemplative prayer that is in solidarity with the suffering of the world."

Chiara Lubich, the founder of Focolare, "exemplifies a woman entrusted with the gift of the Holy Spirit to go forth like Mary from the foot of the Cross without forgetting the total significance of the event she has witnessed," Casarella notes and credits her with unique and profound Marian insights that created the spirituality associated with Focolare. "One idea closely tied to [Chiara's] Marian origins is that Jesus Forsaken is a key to a Christian understanding of unity," and associated with the concrete specificity of Jesus forsaken on the cross is *"Maria desolata,"* Mary, desolate from having witnessed the death of her Son. Her desolation in solidarity with her Son, however, is not simply desolation at his death but a unique solidarity with his forsakenness. Lubich understands Jesus's delivery of Mary to be the Mother of the Church in the person of the Beloved Disciple as a desolation because accepting this act, consummated with Jesus's death, means renouncing her unique Motherhood of Jesus, in her words, "faced with the passage from one Maternity to another which Jesus indicated to her. . . . In that moment Jesus had neither Mother nor Father. He was nothingness born of nothingness. And Mary was also suspended in nothingness. Her greatness had been her divine Maternity. Now it had been taken away from her." Commenting on this passage from Lubich, Casarella notes: "In sum, through Mary's renunciation of maternity she became mother of us all." Paradoxically, one can think of this renunciation as one of Mary's unique privileges. No one else can make it. The Marian profile that it creates is one of a "radical openness to the Spirit," a participation in the forsakenness of Jesus that is uniquely hers but is itself available to participate in. Do we hear an echo of the way in which Fr. Kentenich believed a Marian spirituality to be the answer to the anthropological heresies of our day? If Mary in the Spirit is, one could almost say, co-forsaken, exhibiting a kind of cooperation in the desolation of Jesus, this free and loving renunciation is also a free and loving cooperation in love, a radical stance of welcome. Casarella writes: "The same Spirit has given life to the movement to proclaim the notion of 'mutual interdependence' to a multicultural, multiethnic world threatened by the atomizing, deracinating effects of unrestrained globalization." The analogy between Jesus and Mary's interdependence, God and the creatures' interdependence—in both cases wholly dependent on the first term in the pair—is obvious. Lubich even extended the spirituality to an ideal practice of the means of communication in the media.

Finally in this section of the book we have the chapter of Lawrence S. Cunningham, whose contribution ensures that our collection at least touches on the issue of Mary in monasticism on the eve of the Council. Thomas Merton, "himself predisposed to a deep devotion to Our Lady," applied the image of the Visitation to the contemplative.

Like John, who waited in darkness and could not physically see anything, the true contemplative is, in Cunningham's words, an "eschatological watcher standing in hope for the coming of the Word." He comes to the contemplative, equally in darkness, equally hidden, and, as was Christ to John, equally "mediated to him by Mary." There is also a corresponding hiddenness of Mary herself: "All that has been written about the Virgin Mother of God proves to me that hers is the most hidden of sanctities," Merton writes. It is hidden in her humility and her poverty, and the one who can "see" this humility and poverty is the one who can see the God bearer, and thus the Christ she bears. Merton adds: "No one has ever more perfectly contained the light of God than Mary who by the perfection of her purity and humility is, as it were, completely identified with truth like the clean window pane which vanishes entirely into the light which it transmits." We receive the contemplative illumination of Christ through Mary.

In the epilogue we have a brief pastoral reflection by Fr. James H. Phalan, who invites us to think about the place of Mary in the new evangelization. In a way, this returns us to the opening theme of our introduction. We find our expectations for a standard narrative of Marian theology and devotion unsettled even if we turn to countries and regions where Marian devotion is still vigorous. Fr. Phalan's observations are that even in such places, preaching about Mary is rare: "I learned that very rarely priests and religious preach about her" and that "they do not do so because they have never studied her." Here we find a different kind of gap between theology and devotion, perhaps not the gap between a theology of Mary and its application but a devotion that seems to leave no trace in theology. "It would seem fairly obvious," Phalan comments, that such intense popular devotion as he had witnessed in Mexico and Brazil "would be a powerful source of energy for the New Evangelization; yet I have come to understand," he goes on to observe, "that this energy is relatively untapped." Phalan also observes that there are "no formal and extensive studies . . . of Marian devotion" in contemporary America and that such an undertaking might reveal that the decline in Marian devotion in this country is "correlative with a general decline in daily devotion and prayer on the part of Catholics over the past fifty years." It would be interesting to know if Marian devotion would be a key element in the New Evangelization in Western countries, too, where, even at Marian pilgrimage places, homilies on the Blessed Mother seem noticeable by their absence. "What are we to make of this great Marian silence?" Phalan asks.

Again the question of trajectory surfaces. The decision of the Council to include Mary in the Dogmatic Constitution on the Church rather than to treat her in her own separate document, just because it was a change, seemed to many to be a change that was consistent with the trajectory that Chris Ruddy associated with Congar. Phalan observes that "the apparent change in emphasis given to the Blessed Virgin contributed to some extent to what became the full-scale collapse of Mariology." Ironically, this includes *Lumen Gentium* chapter 8 itself! Phalan writes: "This text has, by and large, been insufficiently studied and deserves much more attention in order to orient Marian devotion today," as well as, he adds, Marian theological reflection.

So we return to the invitation we hope to issue with the publication of this collection, an invitation to begin to study more deeply the Mariology that was so vibrant in the Marian Age before the Council and then collapsed to the point where, seemingly, Catholic preachers feel ill at ease in speaking of Mary. Perhaps the place to begin is indeed *Lumen Gentium* itself. Perhaps it is time to see what it looks like when it is released from seeming to be the *terminus ad quem* of a trajectory of minimization. Phalan notes: "Although Mary does not have 'her own text' [in the Council documents], she does occupy the final chapter of the fundamental dogmatic text on the Church. As in the case of other topics in other magisterial documents, this final turn to Our Lady was meant to stress her fundamental importance." Perhaps this chapter of *Lumen Gentium* was actually part of a larger trajectory that we have not as yet discerned very well. If there can be a minimalism that is actually a maximalism, as Peter Fritz suggests of Rahner's theology, perhaps there is also a maximalism that can be a minimalism, that is, a theology that, precisely by retaining the unique and irreducible role of Mary, is able to preserve and enrich our understanding of the whole economy of salvation in which she plays a part— a crucial part. Perhaps that was the trajectory of which *Lumen Gentium* was itself a part. But we will never know unless we begin ourselves to enter that trajectory and to play our parts in forming it. The editors are aware that a chapter on Hugo Rahner (1900–1968) under the rubric "Ressourcement Theologians and Response," and a contribution on some major representatives of a Christotypical Mariology—like Carlo Balić, O.F.M. (1899–1977), and Gabriele M. Roschini, O.S.M. (1900–1977)—could have further enhanced this volume. Hence the invitation to study and to explore tendered by this collection.

Results and paradoxes arising from the chapters of this book include the following:

1. One could imagine that ecumenical interests, certainly a feature of some preconciliar Mariology, might have prompted a more biblically based Mariology as well as one that was more minimalist. But the renewed emphasis on the study of Scripture in the twentieth century did not necessarily result in a richer Mariology, even where there seems to have been warrant for it and even where it might have dovetailed with a more minimalist theology. Fr. Thompson's chapter shows how the biblical theme of the faith of Mary was never taken up into devotion or into theology. Matthew Levering's chapter shows how the theme of the Holy Spirit's relationship to Mary, a prominent scriptural theme, was only unevenly developed on the eve of Vatican II, even by the self-avowed minimalist Karl Rahner, at least in the sermons that Levering has presented for study here. Was the Marian movement ever entirely "in sync" with the biblical and liturgical movements, as Phalan wonders? Or did the biblical and liturgical movements eventually become so "historicizing" that they left theology behind, even as Marian theology could not assimilate these pervasively historicizing tendencies?

2. The "direction," "spirit," or "vector" of a particular Mariology may be just as important as what it actually says. As rich as Congar's Mariology could be, it seemed, in the words of Chris Ruddy, to be somewhat "cold," not really minimalist but with a governing interest of minimizing. Could it be that one future tack for Mariology might be to take up Congar's Mariology and infuse it with a different trajectory: one of development rather than of keeping in check?

3. Perhaps instead of the categories "maximalist" and "minimalist," which Peter Fritz's chapter shows have serious and perhaps fatal limitations, new categories are needed: mystery versus rationalism or reductionism, as Troy Stefano's chapter might suggest, or even mystery versus positivist historicism. The search for a Marian "principle" may have been misguided in the first place, as it turned a person, in herself irreducibly a mystery *as a person*, inadvertently into a principle.

4. Areas for further study might include contemporary Marian homiletics, to the extent that this can be determined. Also, devotion to Mary did not decrease (seemingly) in the global South, or so it seems. This should be studied. Phalan's chapter brings up the issue for contemporary preaching, and Kevin Grove's chapter shows conclusively, in a historical mode, that a study of Marian sermons can bear rich fruit theologically and can serve to undercut caricatures of Marian cult and culture. If it can work for the nineteenth century, perhaps it can work for today.

5. Fr. Roten's chapter shows us the need to engage in a theologically sophisticated study of Marian art and to begin to notice what questions—perhaps questions coming on the one hand from devotion and prayer or, on the other, from the surrounding culture—it raises.

6. Finally, all of the chapters show that the most creative Mariology of this period, whatever its supposed "maximalist" or "minimalist" stripe, tried to emphasize connections: in particular, the three-way connections between theology, devotion, and Christian life and discipleship. It seems that the surest result of these chapters is that the kind of "maximalism" that is to be avoided is the one that results in the isolation of Mariology to its own independent "science" in effect; and the kind of "minimalism" to be avoided is the one that so collapses Mary into a theological category that Mariology makes no sense anymore and devotion either collapses, or, if it continues, has no theological reception.

HISTORICAL
HIGHLIGHTS

CHAPTER 1

Sign and Source of the Church

Mary in the Ressourcement *and at Vatican II*

BRIAN E. DALEY, S.J.

A lot of things in the Catholic Church changed at the Second Vatican Council. Whether they involved Church doctrine or pastoral practice, whether they were substantial or rhetorical, whether we should receive the Council's documents today with what have been typified as the "hermeneutics of change" or the "hermeneutics of continuity," the documents the Council left us—to say nothing of their interpretation and application during the fifty years that have followed since the Council's close—have certainly turned out to be very different from what Catholics in the immediate preconciliar years hoped or feared. When I was a high-school sophomore, for example, in 1955, Fr. William Leonard, S.J., a liturgical scholar at Boston College who was generally known then as a "progressive" (as people who called themselves "liturgists" in those days tended to be), suggested in a lecture that it would be *possible*, surely, for the Western Church to begin celebrating the Mass in vernacular languages again, as it had in antiquity; this would take a long time to develop, he cautioned—perhaps a century, surely not in any of *our* lifetimes—but it could happen, nonetheless! Friday abstinence, tight restrictions on marriage with non-Catholics, religious habits for sisters, official discouragement of theological and spiritual contact with other Christians, and a host of other familiar features of daily life for Catholics seemed, in the 1950s, to be engraved in the stone face of Peter's rock. It was just the way Catholics were. Yet ten years later, as the Council came to a close in 1965, these and a host of other defining details, large and small, were suddenly open to reconsideration; within a few years, many had started to change in what seemed to be radical ways. The earthquake, inside and outside the Church, had begun, and all of us, fifty years later, are still trying to discern what features of the structure of preconciliar Catholic life were of permanent importance, in need now of refreshment or even reconstruction, and what were just part of a world that has properly evolved away.

Mary was certainly a central part of preconciliar Catholic life. Historians of modern theology sometimes speak of a "Marian movement" that dominated the rhythms of Catholic theology and devotional life in the nineteenth and twentieth centuries, and that led some historians to call the modern era of Catholicism a "Marian Age." The spiritual, intellectual, and aesthetic energies of the Catholic world seemed to be increasingly focused on Mary. The first two solemn and self-conscious acts of papal dogmatic definition, which formally claimed to teach with the Spirit-governed infallibility of the Church's faith itself, were Pius IX's proclamation of the dogma of Mary's lifelong sinlessness, her Immaculate Conception, in 1854, and Pius XII's proclamation in 1950 of her final glorification as a whole human person, her Assumption—body and soul— into heaven to stand alongside her glorified incarnate Son. Since the reports of Mary's apparition to two French peasant children at La Salette in 1846 and to Bernadette Soubirous at Lourdes in 1858, Marian apparitions have increasingly become a feature of Catholic life and have left an increasingly strong mark on the devotional life and even the faith of ordinary Catholics. Partly as a result of interest in these apparitions, Marian devotions played an increasingly large part in the life of the ordinary Catholic and the Catholic parish in the nineteenth and twentieth centuries; books and articles on Mary suddenly took a large role in Catholic theological literature, new Marian associations were formed, Marian theological congresses were held, and Marian journals were founded in several Western languages. Along with all these things, new theological theories on Mary's involvement in the salvation of Christians were developed: theories about her unique but genuine priesthood, her co-presence with the glorified Jesus in the Blessed Sacrament, her "congruous merit" with that of Jesus in the work of redemption, the role of her Immaculate Heart in longing for the return of sinful humanity to God. Popes began issuing encyclicals promoting the rosary and other Marian devotions, notably Leo XIII in the 1890s and Pius XII in the 1940s and 1950s. Mary had clearly moved to the center of the Catholic devotional and theological consciousness.

ORIGINS OF MARIOLOGY

Lively interest in Mary, engaging the hearts of Christian disciples as much as their minds, was of course nothing new in the life of the Church. As early as the mid–second century, the celebrated narrative of Mary's birth and childhood, known as the *Book of James* or (from the Renaissance on) the *Protoevangelium of James*, with an extended narration of the events of Jesus's conception and birth as they are presented in the Gospels of Matthew and Luke, seems to have been put together in a context of deep Judeo-Christian piety, probably in multicultural Syria, with the aim of showing, by midrash-style storytelling, how holy and observant the human family of Jesus was in terms of Jewish law. Irenaeus of Lyon, writing at the end of the second century, sounds a theme echoed by several of his contemporaries in portraying Mary, the obedient virgin, as the counterpart of Eve in the story of the fall; just as Eve heard the voice of the tempter and turned away from God's will, Mary heard another angelic voice, calling her to obedience and trust, and said yes to it; so a new age in human history began. Syriac poets of the fourth and fifth century, beginning with the great lyric theologian Ephrem, celebrated Mary for holding in her own body, and in her own trusting faith, the whole unfathomable mystery of human salvation. Latin theologians in the late fourth century, as part of a growing controversy over the value of asceticism and celibacy in the Christian community, argued over whether or not Mary and Joseph, the parents in "the holy family," to use our modern phrase, actually went on, after the miraculous birth of Jesus, to have normal sexual relations, and other children, afterward; St. Jerome's position that they did not, defended with characteristic learning and acerbity, became the accepted tradition of the Catholic Church. The so-called *Protoevangelium* (about AD 150) is the first Christian document we know to affirm Mary's virginity *in partu* (chapter 20). Clement of Alexandria, in *Stromateis* 7.16.93 (about AD 190), refers to this idea as credible, though contested, and uses it as a figure for the "virginal" generation of faith by the Scriptures in the minds of believers.[1]

In the fifth century, different ways of conceiving and expressing the union of God the Son with the man Jesus, defended notably by Nestorius, bishop of Constantinople, and Cyril, bishop of Alexandria, led to the famous controversy over the appropriateness of using the title *Theotokos*, "Mother of God," for Mary, the mother of Jesus, a title that had deep roots in Alexandrian piety and liturgical prayer. The immediate controversy was resolved by common agreement between Cyril and his Antiochene critics early in AD 433. The title, paradoxical as it sounds, does indeed capture the Church's faith in who the Son of Mary really is. As a result the focus on Mary as worthy of veneration and joyful attention in her own right suddenly skyrocketed: within twenty years, major churches specifically in her honor were built, or rededicated, in Rome, Constantinople, and Jerusalem. A new style of rhetoric celebrating Mary as the inner meaning of a long list of familiar Old Testament objects—for example, Moses's burning bush, Aaron's flowering rod, Gideon's miraculously dampened fleece—took a central role in the sermons of such accomplished preachers as Proclus of Constantinople, Cyril of Alexandria, and Hesychius of Jerusalem; as a kind of devotional by-product, the litany came into being. Mary came to be celebrated, in fifth- and sixth-century hymnody, preaching, and iconography, as a royal figure enthroned as Queen along with her glorified Son. And by the early sixth century, in a process that is still not clear in all its details, the conviction grew in virtually all the churches of the East, both those that accepted the Chalcedonian formulation of the mystery of Christ and those that did not, that rumors of her resurrection, her bodily entry even during the present age into the glory of her risen Son (which the West calls her "Assumption") after a peaceful and happy death (which the East calls her "Dormition" or "falling asleep"), are in fact *true*, the first promise of a salvation in fullness that will eventually include all the faithful.

In the Middle Ages in the West, this focus on the unique privileges and powerful presence in sacred history of Mary, the human mother of the Lord, continued to grow. St. Bernard, the powerful preacher and monastic reformer of the early twelfth century, emphasized the world-changing humility and obedience of Mary, who accepted her role as Mother of God at the angel's invitation. Bernard emphasizes with new force that Mary is thus not simply the human channel through whom the Savior has come among us but is herself a *mediator* between God and humanity, endowed with the approachable human qualities of a mother: "A truly faithful and powerful 'Mediator of God and men is the Man Jesus Christ' (1 Tim. 2:5), but the Majesty of his Godhead inspires mortals with fear. His manhood seems to be swallowed up in his divinity. . . . So great a Mediator is Christ that we have need of another to mediate between him and us, and for this we can find none so qualified as Mary. . . . Why should human fragility fear to have recourse to Mary? In her is found nothing austere, nothing to terrify: everything about her is full of sweetness."[2]

So Bernard was the first in the West to develop for Mary's role in history the image of the "aqueduct," the channel through whom all God's grace flows to a parched humanity; by God's own choice, he suggests, all the transforming and deifying power of Christ within us is communicated through Mary's body and her collaborative will.[3]

A second crucial development in the medieval Western understanding of Mary was the suggestion, made first in the mid–twelfth century by the monk Eadmer of Canterbury (d. 1126), that she was not only a supremely holy person, by God's grace—*panagia*, i.e., all-holy, as some later Greek patristic authors had named her—but that her holiness began at the first moment of her existence, when she was conceived in the womb. By the redemptive grace of Christ, the heritage of sin that burdens all of Adam's descendants not only was removed but in fact never touched her. Eadmer was probably giving voice to popular religious traditions in England at the time. Almost two hundred years later, the Scottish Franciscan John Duns Scotus developed an elaborate theological argument for this belief, what we now know as Mary's Immaculate Conception, based on the assumption that while Mary, like all human beings, needed to be redeemed from the power of sin by the work of her Son, it was appropriate that she should be redeemed in the most perfect imaginable way, through a preventive rather than simply a curative liberation from the curse of Adam. After arguing at some length that God can heal a person from the power of sin by preventing its occurrence, as well as by healing its effects—either more or less instantaneously or after a longer period of time—Scotus offered elaborate philosophical refutations of the usual criticisms raised against such an idea. He sums up his own position in strikingly modest terms: "Which of these three positions is factually the case, God knows—but if the authority of the Church or the authority of Scripture does not contradict such, it seems probable that what is more excellent should be attributed to Mary."[4]

This cautious if carefully argued suggestion of Scotus, as we know, gathered force through the succeeding centuries, although it was also resisted, mainly by the Dominicans and others who followed Thomas Aquinas, for the reason that it seemed to suggest that Mary did not really need to be saved by Christ from the heritage of Adam. In 1477 Pope Sixtus IV, himself originally a Franciscan, approved the hitherto local celebration of Mary's Immaculate Conception on December 8 as a liturgical feast for the whole Latin Church. With the feast, the idea behind it gradually became a central feature of popular devotion to Mary, and it seems to have spurred on the iconographic practice, especially in sixteenth- and seventeenth-century Spain, of representing her as *la Immaculada*, a beautiful young woman aloft in the clouds, surrounded by angels, an idealized form of perfect humanity. Mary's Immaculate Conception became common teaching and an accepted part of Catholic piety. Finally, as we know, in 1854, after elaborate consultation with bishops and theologians, Pope Pius IX solemnly declared Mary's Immaculate Conception, her freedom from sin throughout her whole existence, as generally affirmed in popular Catholic devotion, to be part of the revealed faith of the Church.

A revealing presentation of the growing focus of many post-Reformation Catholics on the centrality of Mary in God's plan of salvation is the treatise of the French rural missionary priest Louis Grignion de Montfort, *True Devotion to the Blessed Virgin*, from the early eighteenth century; Grignion de Montfort died in 1716, but the manuscript of this work, really an extended invitation to Catholics to consecrate themselves, with all the merit and value of their lives, trustingly to Mary, was discovered, incomplete and unedited, and published only in 1842. A later representative of the "French School" of spirituality, which stressed the supreme importance of devotion to the ordinary humanity of Jesus, in whom we find salvation, de Montfort here extends this emphasis to include Mary, his fully human mother. To the modern reader, much in the treatise can sound exaggerated, even bizarre, as an example of Christian spiritual instruction: the center of the committed Christian's life seems to be an unconditional commitment to Mary, to whom God providentially committed his own Son, rather than simply a commitment to Jesus. "It was through the most holy Virgin Mary that Jesus came into the world," he begins, "and it is also through her that He has to reign in the world."[5]

> She is the sanctuary and resting-place of the blessed Trinity, where God dwells in greater and more divine splendor than anywhere else in the universe, not excluding his "dwelling above the cherubim" and seraphim [par. 5]. . . . Every day, from one end of the earth to the other, in the highest heaven and in the lowest abyss, all things preach, all things proclaim the wondrous Virgin Mary [par. 8]. . . . The whole world is filled with her glory [par. 9]. . . . Finally, we must say in the words of the apostle Paul, "Eye has not seen, nor has ear heard, nor has the heart of man understood" the beauty, the grandeur, the excellence of Mary, who is indeed a miracle of miracles of grace, of nature, of glory. "If you wish to understand the Mother," says a saint [unidentified], "then understand the Son" [par. 12].

There is a level of enthusiasm here that seems to have shifted the emphasis of Christian belief and piety from Jesus to Mary; the presence of her Son in the world and the providence of God are instruments to justify devotion to her. So de Montfort draws on the tradition of her channeling God's grace to the world, expressed centuries before by Bernard, and alters it into an image of her complete control of that grace: "God the Holy Spirit entrusted his wondrous gifts to Mary, his faithful spouse, and chose her as the dispenser of all he possesses, so that she distributes all his gifts and graces to whom she wills, as much as she wills, how she wills and when she wills. No heavenly gift is given to men which does not pass through her virginal hands."[6]

Mary's providential, pivotal role in the economy of salvation has here been shifted into her being herself the final, controlling agent of providence. *She* dwells in the souls of the elect (par. 35); *she* is queen of all things, by grace, just as Jesus is king "by conquest" (par. 37). *Her Kingdom* is about to be revealed in the end times (pars. 49–50). Christianity seems to have been transformed into "Marianity!" It is true that de Montfort recognizes a possible tension between his earlier emphasis on the centrality of Mary for authentic faith and the long Christian tradition, so he adds later in the work: "If devotion to our Lady distracted us from our Lord, we would have to reject it as an illusion of the devil" (par. 62). In his mind, authentic devotion to Mary "is only in order to establish devotion to our Lord more perfectly, by providing a smooth and certain way of reaching Jesus Christ" (ibid.). In the minds of many twentieth-century theologians, however, the tension remained.[7]

It is precisely this emphasis on Mary's role in the life of faith by Catholic theologians and devotional writers, present in some ways since early Christian centuries but increasingly proclaimed in modernity, that prompted Karl Barth, in the *Church Dogmatics* I/2 (1938), to protest against the Catholic doctrinal and devotional tradition on Mary in the strongest terms. In the context of his own theology of revelation, as the unique entry of God into human history and discourse in Jesus, Barth rejects Catholic Mariology as "an attack upon the miracle of revelation" and "a false doctrine . . . a diseased construct of theological thought."[8] He explains:

> Marian dogma is neither more nor less than the critical, central dogma of the Roman Catholic Church, the dogma from which all their important positions are to be regarded, and by which they stand or fall. . . . In the doctrine and worship of Mary there is disclosed the one heresy of the Roman Catholic Church which explains all the rest. The "mother of God" of Roman Catholic Marian dogma is quite simply the principle, type, and essence of the human creature cooperating servant-like (*ministerialiter*) in its own redemption on the basis of prevenient grace, and to that extent the principle, type and essence of the Church.[9]

For Barth and those who share his view of Christianity, this approach to interpreting the Gospel of grace is radically distorted:

> Jesus Christ, the Word of God, exists, reigns, and rules in as sovereign a way within the created world as he does from eternity with his

Father, no doubt over and in man, no doubt in his Church and by it, but in such a way that at every point he is always himself the Lord, and man, like the Church, can give honor only to him and never, however indirectly to himself as well. There can be no thought of any reciprocity or mutual efficacy, even with the most careful precautions. Faith in particular is not an act of reciprocity, but the act of renouncing all reciprocity, the act of acknowledging the one Mediator, besides whom there is no other.[10]

MARY AND THE *RESSOURCEMENT*

Barth's critique of Catholic Marian theology and devotion, along with that of many other serious Protestant thinkers, certainly played a role in leading twentieth-century Catholic theologians to reexamine the role Mary had played in forming the Catholic synthesis through the centuries: not to reject her role but to seek new ways of integrating it with the larger field of Christian revelation and teaching. Through this critique and other criticisms of Marian piety and doctrine, Catholic theologians came more and more to realize that their understanding of human involvement in the working of God's grace is indeed different from that of the Reformers and their heirs.[11] But the context for this realization was changing, from polemical opposition to a spirit of dialogue based on common Christian origins. Alongside the Marian Movement we referred to before, the Catholic Church, in Europe especially, had experienced in its thought the stirrings of several other movements in the decades after the First World War, which came to full expression during the pontificate of Pius XII: the *liturgical* movement, aimed at reaffirming the central role of liturgical prayer in the spiritual life of the Church and seeking to make possible a more focused participation of all its members in liturgical celebration;[12] the *biblical* movement, which aimed at affirming more clearly the scriptural foundation of Catholic theology, grounding Catholic biblical studies in the best contemporary critical scholarship and making the Scriptures more easily available to laypeople;[13] and the *ecumenical* movement, in which Catholic experts were gradually, at first somewhat tentatively, encouraged to seek common ground with representatives of other churches in the hope of finding ways of moving toward mutual recognition and full communion.[14]

Along with these new perspectives and interests, the Catholic Church in the 1930s experienced a less formally articulated but perhaps still more influential intellectual movement that came to be known as *ressourcement*. This "return to the sources" of theology signaled a style of studying and teaching the Church's doctrine and speculation that attempted to move away from the deductive, apologetic rationalism of many nineteenth- and early twentieth-century writers. Instead it looked for historical development, continuities, and influences within a changing but organically growing tradition inspired by a new encounter with the Church Fathers. The life and thought of the first several centuries of Christian history seemed to offer a promising key to the full understanding of later theological tradition and to conceiving the parameters of what might now be an acceptable change. This style of theology, practiced first in France and Germany by a number of younger theologians, including leading figures like the Dominicans Marie-Dominique Chenu and Yves Congar and the Jesuits Henri de Lubac, Hans Urs von Balthasar, Jean Daniélou, and Henri Bouillard, was at first met with suspicion among Church authorities as relativistic and lacking in rigor.[15] Yet by the mid-1950s it had become the predominant style of theological thought among Catholic theologians in Europe and North America. Under Pope Pius XII, in fact, the stage was set for what was to transpire at the Second Vatican Council.

These new movements in Catholic thought converged, by at least the late 1930s, in a new emphasis on the central importance of both Christ and the Church for doctrine and devotion. The unifying link was the emerging sense that God saves and transforms the human race in and through its common history and its institutions, not simply by working inwardly and invisibly in individual believers. In his great programmatic work *Catholicisme*, first published in 1937 as an attempt to reconceive the Church itself in social, humanly engaged terms, the forty-one-year-old Henri de Lubac insisted that "God acts in history and reveals himself through history. Or rather, God inserts himself in history and so bestows on it a 'religious consecration' which compels us to treat it with due respect. . . . The Bible, which contains the revelation of salvation, contains, too, in its own way the history of the world. . . . It was in this way that the Bible was read by the Fathers of the Church."[16]

For classic Christian exegesis, de Lubac goes on to argue, this meant that in Scripture God is always revealing to us the continuous story of his two covenants with the human race, accomplishing through time "a single Mystery: the Mystery of Christ and the Church. . . . For the whole of the Old Testament is habitually seen by the Fathers as one comprehensive and extensive prophecy, and the subject of the prophecy is no less than the mystery of Christ, which would not be complete were it not also the Mystery of the Church."[17]

De Lubac then goes on to list all the objects and persons in the Old Testament that the Fathers, from time to time, took as figures of the Church. Included were almost all the women who are prominently mentioned there, all of whom suggest that Jewish-Gentile people would one day be, in their collectivity, the Bride of Christ: "In the privileged history of the patriarchs and the faithful people they saw the long betrothal of Christ with his Church which preceded the mystic marriage of Nazareth and Calvary."[18] From the perspective of renewed interest in patristic exegesis of the Bible, it was just a short step for theologians to see in the daughter of Israel, Mary of Nazareth, the figure of the bridal Church par excellence.

That step was taken explicitly in 1950 by Otto Semmelroth, a thirty-eight-year-old German Jesuit, who argued in his first book, *Urbild der Kirche*, that Mary's real role and identity in the early and medieval Church was not so much an object of personal devotion as "the representative of a theological idea. The mystery of the divine economy of salvation is both enclosed and expressed within her."[19]

In this context of a new appreciation of the Church itself as the true Body of Christ, present in history as the beginning of the final stage in God's plan of salvation, Mary can be seen as both the personal center and the symbol of what God has brought to fulfillment in the Church: as the Bride; as the Mother of God, who begets him in his human form; as mediator between God, who is the source of all grace, and the realization of his grace in our own freedom from sin; as the new Eve, the beginning of renewed humanity.[20] All of these figures are seen, from the Church Fathers on, as images properly applied to Mary. "Fittingly is she espoused [to Joseph]," Ambrose remarks, "but a Virgin because she prefigures the Church, which is undefiled yet wed. A Virgin conceived us by the Spirit; a Virgin brings us forth without travail."[21] Thus these figures are realized fully, Semmelroth argues, in the Church, which Clement of Alexandria calls our "Virgin Mother."[22] Even the more modern and radical thesis that Mary is co-redeemer of humanity along with her Son, usually explained in terms of her compassion and patient suffering on Calvary, contains an element of truth, Semmelroth says, if this is seen as part of her typological relationship to the Church, which must itself be seen, despite Barth's objections, as a collaborator in the work of redemption. Semmelroth writes:

> In the theology of Christ's Redemption, there is a tacit—or admitted—assumption that sinful man cannot save himself by his own strength alone. . . . Yet such emphasis must not leave the door open to the one-sided view that Redemption is only the deed of a God who gives. God's giving consists precisely in the fact that it presents man with the opportunity to be active himself. Man co-redeems because he is redeemed. The inverse of the proposition is just as true: man is redeemed because he co-redeems. [And, quoting Maurice de la Taille, Semmelroth adds:] "The more the Church herself is redeemed, the more she is co-redeemer."[23]

Semmelroth sums up his own position by saying:

> The basic mystery of Mariology is that which brings Mary closer to the center of the economy of salvation, which is the Church. This coming-together, however, does not take place through the mystery of the mere fact that she is mother of God; rather, it takes place through the divine motherhood specified as a bridal relationship, because this is here revealed as a specifically bridal assent to the advent and work of the Savior. . . . Mary as Archetype is in closest union with the Church, because she is the germ of the Church, because she bears within herself the *pleroma* of grace that will be poured from her into the Church that unfolds in time and space.[24]

In 1952 the Paris Dominican Yves Congar, among other things a pioneer in Catholic efforts toward greater ecumenical understanding and dialogue, published a short, densely argued work titled, in the English translation, *Christ, Our Lady, and the Church*.[25] Written to commemorate the fifteenth centenary of the Council of Chalcedon in 451, where the two complete natures in which the one hypostasis or individual Jesus Christ subsists were formally defined, Congar's argument is that the Catholic tradition of Marian doctrine and the Catholic understanding of the Church are closely linked, as Semmelroth had insisted a few years earlier, and that both are rooted in the Chalcedonian understanding of the role of the humanity of Christ in working our salvation. To insist, as Luther and Karl Barth did, that the salvation of humanity is wholly and immediately worked in us by God and that human cooperation plays no role whatever in the process is to misunderstand what redeemed and deified humanity is. Christ, Mary, and the Church, Congar suggests, as theological themes, are "intimately connected, and their connection depends upon a single principle which must be applied, with due qualification, in each of the three cases: the principle, that is, that human nature plays its part in the work of salvation, yet equally clearly the total power of effecting that salvation comes from God." He continues:

> Protestants are critical of our idea of the Church, and still more of our Mariology and the devotion it inspires. But they fail to understand them because they fail to trace them to the truths in which they are rooted; to the dogmas of Christology and to the role of Christ's humanity in the economy of salvation. The sacred humanity united to the divinity without confusion or division is the instrument of our salvation, and the means by which all grace is communicated to us. This is why our Lady, by her intimate association with the sacred humanity, and the Church in consequence of it, play the part our teaching assigns to them.[26]

Congar argues that Barth's objection to human cooperation in the revelation and work of God in the world, and thus his insistence that both Catholic Mariology and Catholic sacramental ecclesiology are fundamentally misguided, is simply a misunderstanding of what the Bible and the tradition of faith assert about how God works in our midst and an implicit abandonment of the mediating role of Christ's humanity.

The previous year (1951), Hugo Rahner, S.J., published his own little book on Mary and the Church, specifically to meet the demand for a simple way to understand the wider significance of the dogma of Mary's

Assumption, which had been proclaimed by Pope Pius XII in 1950.[27] Hugo Rahner's book is a set of straightforward reflections on Mary as a type of the Church, mainly drawn from the Church Fathers and laid out systematically to elucidate the main events and mysteries of her life, from her conception to her assumption into glory. In the foreword he explains his reason for undertaking the task: to connect Marian piety and doctrines with the new twentieth-century Catholic emphases on liturgy and sacraments:

> The most important formative element in Catholic piety today is probably the newly found understanding of the life-giving power of our holy mother the Church in her sacraments and her liturgy. But at the same time there have been during the last hundred years such remarkable dogmatic developments, bringing out ever more clearly the place of our Lady in the system of Catholic thought. Now there are some Christians—including profound thinkers [is he thinking of Barth?] and earnestly striving souls—who feel that these two trends are in contradiction; perhaps their eyes are still "held" (Luke 24:16), so that they cannot yet recognize the heavenly mystery when they look at the earthly features of the Church, and it is not yet granted to them to see in the simple earthly life of Mary the Mother of God the highest mystery of all the Bible and theology, in the birth of God from a human virgin the very nature of the Church, and in the Mystery of the Church itself the profoundest element in our spiritual formation. It is the purpose of this book to collect and unite these ideas. We must learn to see the Church in our Lady, and our Lady in the Church.[28]

In 1956 Hugo Rahner's younger brother, Karl, also published a book of reflections on Mary based on a series of homilies he had given three years earlier, during May devotions in the University Church in Innsbruck and titled *Mary, Mother of the Lord*.[29] Karl Rahner, too, is concerned with bringing the Catholic Church's long history of Marian theology and devotion together in a way that shows its coherence with the whole of biblical faith. For him, however, the organizing principle, the "fundamental principle of Mariology" that binds the whole together,[30] is not so much Mary's role through the centuries as "archetype of the Church" but the belief of Catholic Christians that she is the most perfectly redeemed of all human beings: she is "full of grace" in order that Jesus, the cause and form of God's grace in human history, might be born of her. Mary is most perfectly redeemed so that we also might be redeemed.[31] She is important for us because the transcendent, redeeming God touches us most closely through her in the person of her Son, the incarnate agent of our redemption. Karl Rahner writes, in the introduction to his book, implicitly countering Protestant critiques of Mariology as his earlier *ressourcement* colleagues had done:

> If, then, God is the one who forms with us a history of salvation, and if we must speak of this God, in faith and theology, as Lord of this single history of salvation and destruction within this one human race, then we must say again: because God has so arranged this history with human beings that in it one human is to be meaningful for another, then in our proclamation of faith and in our articulation of theology—which tell the story of God's saving acts toward us—we must speak once again of the human person. This is for the simple reason that God has willed that the salvation he works in us be accomplished by him through human beings. Therefore, too, in this explication of faith, and of the theology of the importance of human persons in God's history, we must also speak of Mary, the Blessed Virgin. She, after all, is the mother of the one on whom our whole salvation is founded, because he is God and a human being in a single person. . . . This is the reason that theology must speak of her.[32]

If salvation, as the Scriptures narrate, is a historical process, it must work not just through the independent encounters of individuals with the God who is wholly other but through the people and things and events that surround us all in time and space, which form a community of grace: through the prophets and laws and sacrifices of ancient Israel; through the witness of the Apostles and the life and sacraments of the Church founded on them; through the saints of every age who lived in fidelity to this saving God; and above all through Christ, God's Word made flesh, who lives in the midst of his people. Mary's paramount importance for the Church is that she stands nearest, in this sacred history, to Christ our Redeemer.

THE SECOND VATICAN COUNCIL AND MARY

Through the gradual shifts in perspective that Catholic theology had been undergoing since the 1920s, Mary was thus coming to be understood by many in a new way. The new emphasis on God's saving work among us as shaping a *history of salvation*, which stretched from the election of Abraham to the coming of the Holy Spirit on the Twelve to form the Church of disciples; the new Catholic openness to biblical criticism and concern for making the text of the Bible more easily accessible to the faithful; a new emphasis on the sacraments, particularly on the Eucharistic *liturgy*, as forming the proper core of Catholic spirituality; and the consequent implications for a renewed, historically grounded, liturgically centered, scripturally expressed understanding of the *Church*—all of these themes were worked out in detail by the *ressourcement* school of theologians. They were given cautious but significant approval in the writings and actions of Pope Pius XII and formed the intellectual and religious backdrop for the debates and documents of the Second Vatican Council, for which Pope John XXIII announced his plans to an astonished world in January 1959, a little over four months after his election to the See of Peter.

These new perspectives were to leave an indelible mark on how the Council would speak of Mary. In the time between Pope John's surprise announcement in January 1959 and the Council's formal opening in October 1962, commissions were formed to prepare schemata or drafts of possible documents. Chief among them was the Theological Commission, chaired by Cardinal Alfredo Ottaviani, whose members and consulters included some of the most eminent theologians and Scripture scholars of the day. Mary obviously had an important place on their list of themes for the Council to consider. Some six hundred bishops from around the world had signed a petition to the pope in the year before the Council's opening, calling for a special document on Mary that would sum up her central role in Catholic life. Some hoped for a new dogmatic definition, possibly focused on naming her Mediatrix of all Grace or Co-redemptrix in the divine plan of salvation. Others, aware of the concerns for ecumenical understanding that had grown under Pius XII and was now central to the thought of John XXIII, urged moderation. They campaigned for a document that would integrate Mary within a broader theological perspective.

The schema on Mary that was prepared by the Theological Commission before the Council and offered to the Central Preparatory Commission in June 1962 was fairly brief and was mainly focused on Mary's unique relationship to Christ the Savior (par. 1).[33] Because of her involvement in the mystery of salvation, she is the "singular exemplar of the Church." But beyond this, the Church believes that God chose to redeem her from sin "in a more sublime way" than the rest of humanity. Citing nineteenth- and twentieth-century popes, as well as St. John of Damascus, the document continues: "By her consent, Mary, the daughter of Adam, became not only the mother of Jesus, the unique divine Mediator, but also associated (*consociavit*) her work with him and under him in effecting the redemption of the human race."[34] This partnership, the document continues, is the reason for Mary's Immaculate Conception and comes to its perfection in her letting herself be joined with her Son's sacrifice on the cross by grief, a *generosa socia* in the plan of salvation to the last (par. 2). Because she is so centrally involved in the work of redemption in Christ, Mary is also "not without justification" called "mediatrix." By her prayer and her maternal love for the faithful, and without in any way obscuring the unique mediation of Christ, "she is present (*adsit*) in the conferring of all graces on human beings" (par. 3). The document then goes on to explain how the Catholic Church understands the two modern dogmas concerning Mary, her Immaculate Conception and her bodily Assumption, as well as her virginal motherhood. In glorifying her as singular, as different from the rest of us, the Church glorifies Christ the Lord (par. 4). Finally, the document encourages traditional Catholic devotion to Mary (par. 5) and expresses the hope that this love and esteem for her will work as a force for the conversion of nonbelievers and for Christian unity (par. 6).

The draft was not discussed during the first session of the Council in the fall of 1962. However, during preliminary discussions of the schema on the Church in the closing days of that session, seven bishops suggested that a revised version of the draft on Mary might better be included as a final section of what the Council would say on ecclesiology. Revisions were made to the existing draft during the intersession. But the Theological Commission, meeting on October 9, 1963, just before the second session began, suggested, by a small margin, that what the Council was going to say about Mary be located in an enlarged document on the Church. This suggestion was controversial enough, and deemed significant enough, that part of a day's meeting during the second plenary session, on October 24, 1963, was set aside to allow the Council fathers to hear both sides of the question.[35]

Cardinal Rufino Santos of Manila, speaking on behalf of those who still hoped for a separate document on Mary, argued (a) that many might see it as detracting from Mary's dignity to include treatment of her role in the document on the Church; (b) that it would be difficult, in the context of a larger decree, to do full justice to all that the Church believes about her; and (c) that such an inclusion might also make the Council's presentation of the Church appear less acceptable to our non-Catholic brothers and sisters. Representing the other side, Cardinal Franz König of Vienna argued (a) that all that the Catholic Church says about Mary really flows from our vision of the Church itself, both as it is now *in via* and in its eschatological fulfillment; (b) that because of the divine economy, both Mary and the Church are "instruments of redemption, working together actively, in the hand of Christ, for our salvation";[36] (c) that the biblical foundation for our understanding of Mary's privileges is, above all, the vision of the "woman crowned with twelve stars" in Revelation 12, which can be applied equally to Mary and to the early Jerusalem community; (d) that, pastorally, it is important to communicate to the faithful *why* we honor Mary as we do as a type of the Church in its perfection; and (e) that, ecumenically, it is also important to indicate the fundamental reasons for Catholic Marian doctrine to our Orthodox and Protestant brethren. And all of this would be determined, first of all, by the context in which the Council would choose to speak of her. As they say about real estate, "location is everything!"

Cardinal Santos had urged that the Council fathers be given some time to pray and reflect about where to put the draft on Mary, and that was done. Five days later, on October 29, a vote on the placement of the document on Mary was taken, which turned out to be one of the closest of the entire Council: of 2,193 bishops present, 1,114 voted in favor of including a revised Marian draft in the Dogmatic Constitution on the Church, and 1,074 voted against it, with a majority of about 53.5 percent. The decision held, nonetheless, and two respected members of the Theological Commission were appointed to revise the schema: Msgr. Gerard Philips, a well-known ecclesiologist from the University of Leuven, and Fr. Carlo Balić, a Croatian Franciscan who was one of the editors of the works of John Duns Scotus. Their work during the intersession of 1963/64 led the way, after further debate on the Council floor the following September 16–18, 1964, to the somewhat more ample document we know as chapter 8 of *Lumen Gentium*, Vatican II's Dogmatic Constitution on the Church.

This resulting final section of *Lumen Gentium* is in many ways one of the most complete summations we have of modern Catholic Marian doctrine: terse, amply documented from Scripture and the long theological tradition, yet carefully conscious of the implications of a theology of Mary for how the Catholic Church wants to live in today's world. Beginning from the mystery of the Incarnation, which is "revealed and continued in the Church" (52), it points to the singular place of Mary in the history of salvation, as "Mother of the Son of God." Because she is graced above all other creatures, "she is hailed as pre-eminent and as a wholly unique member of the Church, and as its type and outstanding model in faith and charity" (53). Carefully insisting that the Council does not intend to define further any doctrines on Mary, or to solve any open questions (54), the chapter goes on to offer a summary of what one can say about Mary in scriptural terms (55–59), then turns to discuss her role as Mediatrix, really the crux of twentieth-century theological debates about her, largely as an expression of her continuing motherhood: "Mary's function as mother of men in no way obscures or diminishes the unique mediation of Christ, but rather shows its power. But the Blessed Virgin's saving influence on humanity originates not in any inner necessity but in the disposition of God. It flows forth from the superabundance of the merits of Christ, rests on his mediation, depends entirely on it, and draws all its power from it. It does not hinder in any way the immediate union of the faithful with Christ, but on the contrary fosters it" (60).

After summarizing briefly the Church's beliefs on Mary's Immaculate Conception, her virginal motherhood of Christ, her share in his saving work, and her entry into glory (61–62), the document admits that it "does not hesitate to profess the subordinate role of Mary" (62); it then embraces St. Ambrose's phrase, designating her as "a type of the church" (63). "For in the Mystery of the church, which is itself rightly called mother and virgin, the Blessed Virgin stands out in eminent and singular fashion, presenting us with the exemplar of both virgin and mother" (63). This directly affects the way Christians feel themselves related to Mary: "While in the most Blessed Virgin the Church has already reached that perfection whereby she exists without spot or wrinkle, the faithful still strive to conquer sin and increase in holiness. And so they turn to Mary, who shines forth for the whole community as the model of virtues" (65). For the Church as a community, she embodies what we are called to *be*; in her role as Virgin Mother of Christ, she reminds us of what we are called to *do* apostolically in the world: bring the "whole Christ" to new reality (65).

Finally, the document offers both encouragement and guiding norms for Catholic Marian devotion, which is essentially different from our adoration of God. It is to be centered on Christ; it is to be shaped by the guidelines approved by the Church, especially those laid down for the liturgy; it is to avoid both exaggeration and minimalism; it is to be rooted in Scripture, the language of the Fathers, and the Church's Magisterium; it should be carefully expressed in order to avoid scandalizing our "separated brethren." It should, in other words, be relocated within the broader priorities of twentieth-century Catholic theology and of the Council's teaching (67). With a prayer for Mary's patronage of the Council's broader enterprise (67–68), this wide-ranging Constitution, embodying a traditional, yet revolutionary and breathtakingly comprehensive, vision of the Church, comes to a close.

It is no exaggeration, I think, to suggest that the Catholic Church's official approach to thinking about Mary, to praying to and with her, still remains within the framework of *Lumen Gentium* chapter 8 today, fifty years later, and so within the language and thought patterns of the theologians and movements that influenced its shaping. The two main papal documents that have addressed the role of Mary in Catholic life and thought since then are really efforts to show how the seeds of a renewed yet traditional understanding of Mary's relation to all of us, sown in *Lumen Gentium*, might grow and bear fruit in a healthy way. Paul VI's great apostolic exhortation *Marialis Cultus* of 1974 outlines the principles for celebrating Mary's role in the Church's life in liturgy and personal prayer. John Paul II's monumental meditation on Mary, *Redemptoris Mater* of 1987, is both a detailed commentary on *Lumen Gentium* chapter 8 and a further reflection on its discussion of Mary's maternal mediation between Christ and the Church.

In his interview of August 2013 with Fr. Antonio Spadaro, S.J., published in a variety of Jesuit journals, Pope Francis reflected much more informally on this central, still growing, insight of Vatican II into who Mary really is meant to be for us: she is one of us, and she brings us to God with her.[37] Reflecting on what it means to him to "think with the Church," in Ignatius of Loyola's phrase, and to live at the Church's heart, Pope Francis remarks:

> The image of the Church I like is that of the holy, faithful people of God. This is the definition I often use, and then this is the image in the Second Vatican Council's Dogmatic Constitution on the Church (12). Belonging to a people has a strong theological value. In the history of salvation, God has saved a people. There is no full identity without belonging to a people. No one is saved alone (20). . . . And the Church is the people of God on a journey through history, with joys and sorrows. Thinking with the Church, therefore, is my way of being a part of this people. . . . This is how it is with Mary. If you want to know who she is, you ask theologians; if you want to know how to love her, you have to ask the people (22).

Both of those activities, the pope seems to be saying—*acting* in faith and loving, walking with our brothers and sisters on pilgrimage, and *contemplating* God alone with rapt attention—are central parts of the life of this Church, which we are together. It is these things that bring us, together, closer to salvation. And Mary, that "great sign" given to the Church since its earliest days, still walks in the midst of us, showing both our minds and our hearts what it means to be the people of God.

NOTES

1. "Perpetual virginity" is usually understood to mean virginity *ante partum* (before the actual birth of Jesus, or virginal *conception*), virginity *in partu* (continuing physical virginity in the actual event of Jesus's birth), and virginity *post partum* (virginity after the birth of Jesus). Only the first of these is affirmed directly by the New Testament. The second begins to be affirmed early—in the *Protevangelium*—and is alluded to here, in a somewhat noncommittal way, by Clement. The third is not clearly affirmed until the controversies over asceticism in the late fourth century. All three are part of the generally affirmed view of Mary and are in that sense Catholic teaching. While it is true that the perpetual virginity of Mary has not been solemnly defined, it is, however, widely considered to be *de fide* mainly because Mary is called *beata Maria semper virgo* in officially approved liturgical prayers (e.g., the Confiteor, Eucharistic Prayer No. 1, etc.), and by the ordinary and universal Magisterium (cf. Lateran IV [*Enchiridion Symbolorum* 801]; *Lumen Gentium*, pars. 52, 57, 69; *Catechism of the Catholic Church*, 499–500).

2. St. Bernard, *Sermons on the Blessed Virgin Mary* (Chulmleigh, England: Augustine, 1984), 207–8.

3. Ibid., 86, 103.

4. Joannes Duns Scotus, "Ordinatio III, Dist. 3, q. 1," in John Duns Scotus, *Four Questions on Mary*, trans. Allan Wolter, O.F.M. (St. Bonaventure, NY: Franciscan Institute, 2000), 45.

5. Grignion de Montfort, *True Devotion to the Blessed Virgin Mary* (Bay Shore, NY: Montfort Fathers, 1941), par. 1.

6. Ibid., par. 25; cf. par. 44. Several popes have spoken of Mary as the Dispensatrix or Mediatrix of all graces. For example, St. Pius X, Encyclical Letter *Ad Diem Illum* (1904), 12; Pius XII, Encyclical Letter *Ad Caeli Reginam* (1954), 39; St. John Paul II, Address to the General Chapter of the Mercedarian Sisters of Charity (June 28, 1996), *Inseg* 19, no. 1 (1996): 1638; Benedict XVI, Letter to Archbishop Zimowski (January 10, 2013). Vatican II, *Lumen Gentium*, 62, refers to Mary as "Mediatrix," as a description of her continuing, uninterrupted "motherhood in the economy of grace," as St. John Paul II emphasizes in his encyclical *Redemptoris Mater* (March 25, 1987), 23–24.

7. It should be noted that the Marian doctrine of de Montfort has received some endorsement from central Catholic authorities—even after Vatican II. For example, on January 6, 1980, the Congregation for Catholic Education issued a *Circular Letter Concerning Some of the More Urgent Aspects of Spiritual Formation in Seminaries*. This letter underscores the importance of Marian doctrine and devotion in seminary formation, and—in addition to *Lumen Gentium* and Paul VI's *Marialis Cultus* (1974)—it recommends the writings of St. Louis Grignion de Montfort (II, 4). St. John Paul II, who took his papal motto "*Totus*

tuus" from a prayer composed by de Montfort, also expressed his pleasure (*gaudemus*) in knowing that "even in our times new manifestations of this spirituality [of de Montfort] and devotion are not lacking" (*Redemptoris Mater*, 48).

8. Karl Barth, *Church Dogmatics* I/2 (Edinburgh: T. and T. Clark, 1960), 140, 139.

9. Ibid., 143. See also 145: "For it is to the creature creatively cooperating in the work of God that there really applies the irresistible ascription to Mary of that dignity, of those privileges, of those assertions about her *co-operatio* in our salvation, which involve a relative rivalry with Christ. The exact equivalent of this creature is the Roman Catholic concept of the Church."

10. Ibid., 146.

11. See Henri de Lubac's comment on similar critical passages in Barth's work: "Setting on one side the value judgments that go with it, we can accept the Barthian analysis." *The Splendor of the Church*, trans. Michael Mason (New York: Sheed and Ward, 1956), 239.

12. The Catholic liturgical movement was given official encouragement and a theological rationale in Pius XII's encyclical *Mediator Dei* of November 1947.

13. After forty years of opposition or grudging toleration, modern biblical scholarship was encouraged, and even held out as central to the Church's approach to theology, by Pius XII in his encyclical *Divino Afflante Spiritu* of September 30, 1943.

14. Although Catholics were forbidden in Pope Pius XI's encyclical *Mortalium Animos* (1928) to engage in any kind of discussion with non-Catholics that might seem to promote mutual recognition, an instruction of the Holy Office under Pius XII in 1947, titled *Ecclesia Catholica*, recognized the modern ecumenical movement as a divine blessing.

15. Some at the time interpreted Pius XII's encyclical *Humani Generis* of 1950 as implicitly directed against this movement because of the encyclical's general opposition to any emphasis on growth or evolution in our understanding of truth.

16. Henri de Lubac, *Catholicism: Christ and the Common Destiny of Man*, trans. Lancelot Sheppard and Elizabeth Englund, O.C.D. (San Francisco: Ignatius, 1988), 165.

17. Ibid., 176, 183–84.

18. Ibid., 190.

19. Otto Semmelroth, *Urbild der Kirche: Organischer Aufbau des Mariengeheimnisses* (Würzburg: Echter, 1950), trans. as *Mary, Archetype of the Church* by Maria von Eroes and John Devlin (New York: Sheed and Ward, 1963).

20. Ibid., 10–24.

21. Otto Semmelroth, *Exposition of the Gospel According to St. Luke 2.7*, trans. Theodosia Tomkinson (Erna, CA: Center for Traditionalist Orthodox Studies, 1998), 36.

22. Clement of Alexandria, *Paedagogos* 1.6.

23. Semmelroth, *Mary, Archetype of the Church*, 63, citing Maurice de la Taille, *Mysterium fidei* (Paris: G. Beauchesne, 1924), 648.

24. Ibid., 54–55 (translation corrected from original).

25. Yves Congar, *Le Christ, Marie, et l'Eglise* (Bruges: Desclée de Brouwer, 1952); *Christ, Our Lady, and the Church: A Study in Eirenic Theology*, trans. Henry St. John (London: Longmans, Green, 1957).

26. Ibid., 31.

27. Hugo Rahner, *Maria und die Kirche* (Innsbruck: Tyrolia, 1951), trans. as *Our Lady and the Church* by Sebastian Bullough, O.P. (London: Darton, Longman and Todd, 1961).

28. Ibid., vii–viii.

29. Karl Rahner, "Maria, Mutter des Herrn," in *Karl Rahner: Sämtliche Werke* 9 (Freiburg: Herder, 2004), 515–66, trans. as *Mary, Mother of the Lord: Theological Meditations* by W. J. O'Hara (New York: Herder, 1963).

30. On the need for such a "fundamental principle," see also Semmelroth, *Mary, Archetype of the Church*, 13–15.

31. Karl Rahner, *Maria, Mutter des Herrn*, 532.

32. Ibid., 526. Translation by the author.

33. *Acta Synodalia Sacrosancti Concilii Oecumenici Vaticani II Volumen I Periodus Prima Pars IV* (Vatican City, 1971), 92–98. Translation by the author.

34. "Schema of the Dogmatic Constitution on the Blessed Virgin Mary, Mother of God and Mother of Men (1962, in Latin and English)," English translation of the *Acta Synodalia* by Rev. James T. O'Connor in *Marian Studies* 37 (1986): 201. Translation slightly modified from the original.

35. For the original texts of the reports made in this discussion, see *Acta Synodalia* II/2/3, 299–345.

36. Ibid., 344.

37. Antonio Spadaro, S.J., "A Big Heart Open to God: The Exclusive Interview with Pope Francis," *America*, September 30, 2013, 12, 20–22.

CHAPTER 2

Recovering Mary's Faith and Her Role in the Church

THOMAS A. THOMPSON, S.M.

This presentation on Mary's faith and her role in the Church was developed during the Year of Faith, 2012–13, commemorating the fiftieth anniversary of the opening of the Second Vatican Council. The first part is a historical survey related to chapter 8 of *Lumen Gentium* (LG), dealing with the early authors who spoke of Mary's faith and her relation to the Church (Irenaeus, Ambrose, and Augustine). The survey continues with the developments (not treated in LG) that contributed to the eventual disappearance of references to Mary's faith and her role in the Church. Next, the mid–twentieth century's Marian *ressourcement* includes short profiles of theologians who contributed to the "recovery," and the final section deals with the ecclesiological character of Vatican II, with a summary outlining Mary's faith and her role in the Church as found in the conciliar and postconciliar documents.

HISTORICAL PERSPECTIVES: MARY'S FAITH
AND ROLE IN THE CHURCH

The Early Centuries

The Virgin Mary was not prominent in the literature of the first three centuries; some references can be found in the Apocrypha and commentaries on Scripture. But there were no separate Marian treatises or feasts. In the first two centuries, the dominant image was Christ and the Church (especially as prefigured in the Old Testament).[1]

Justin Martyr (ca. 155) was the first to make a comparison between Mary and Eve. Sin entered the world through Adam (1 Cor. 15:21–22) and life through Christ. Justin wrote: "For Eve, who was virgin and undefiled, gave birth to disobedience and death after listening to the serpent's words. But the Virgin Mary conceived in faith and joy; for when the angel Gabriel brought her the glad tidings that the Holy Spirit would come upon her, so that the Holy One born of her would be the Son of God, she answered, 'Let it be done to me according to your word'" (Luke 1:38).[2]

Against the Gnostics, who denied the true humanity of Christ, Irenaeus of Lyon (d. 177), disciple of St. Polycarp, insisted that Christ, Son of God, was also true man: "He, God's Word, came down from the Father and became flesh; he abased himself even unto death and brought the economy of our salvation to its completion."[3] Christ, the new head of humanity, replaced the "old" Adam by a type of recapitulation (*anakephalaiosis*; Eph. 1:10, Rom. 5:12ff.). The new Adam was accompanied by Mary, the New Eve: "By disobeying, she [Eve] became the cause of death for herself and for the whole human race. In the same way, Mary . . . by obeying became the cause of salvation for herself and for the whole human race." The restoration was an "undoing" of the events leading to the fall. "The knot of Eve's disobedience was untied by Mary's obedience. What Eve bound through her unbelief, Mary loosed by her faith."[4]

In *On the Apostolic Preaching*, Irenaeus wrote that all Scripture is oriented toward Christ and God's plan of salvation (*oeconomia*). Within this plan, Christ's incarnation was needed to restore and overcome the deeds of Adam and Eve. Here Christ was accompanied by Mary, the advocate of Eve: "Adam had to be recapitulated in Christ, so that mortality might be swallowed up in immortality, and Eve in Mary, so that a virgin being an advocate for a virgin might undo and destroy the virginal disobedience by virginal obedience."[5] God's plan, interrupted by Adam, associated with Eve, is resumed and brought to its completion by Christ, associated with Mary.

Ambrose and Augustine

In the fourth century, a new stage of awareness about the role of Mary opened in the West with Ambrose and Augustine. More positive, less cautious, it may have been influenced by writings from the East and popular devotion but certainly by interest in Christian virginity. Both Ambrose and Augustine wrote treatises on virginity and treatises addressed to virgins, in which frequent reference was made to the Virgin Mary. Ambrose spoke of Mary's virtues—humility, prudence, temperance, charity—thus: "This woman is the model of virginity. For such was Mary, that the life of this one woman may be an example for all."[6] He invited his people to identify with and share Mary's faith: "You see that Mary did not doubt, but believed and received the fruit of her faith. To you, blessed ones, who hear and believe, take note, any soul who believes, both conceives and gives birth to the word of God and recognizes his work."[7]

Ambrose also referred to Mary as *typus* of the Church: "Wedded but virgin, because she is type of the Church, which is wedded and immaculate." In conceiving Christ, Mary conceived and gave birth to the members of Christ's body: "She conceived us in the Spirit and gave birth to us."[8] Mary continues her maternal relationship to the Church and assists the members: "Mary is the branch; the flower of Mary is Christ, who, like the fruit of a good tree, according to our progress in virtue, now flowers, bears fruit in us, and is reborn through the Resurrection that returns life to his body."[9]

Augustine developed themes found in Ambrose. Augustine insists on the human origins of Mary: "If Mary is from Adam and Adam is from the earth, therefore Mary is from the earth."[10] Mary was a member of the Church: "As holy, Mary is blessed, but the Church is better than the Virgin Mary. Why? Because Mary is part of the Church, a holy member, an outstanding member, a super eminent member, but a member of the whole body nonetheless. If she is a member of the whole body, the body is undoubtedly greater than one of its members."[11]

For Augustine, Mary's maternity was an encompassing mystery transcending temporal succession; it was an illustration of the *Totus Christus*, that is, the inseparability of the physical body of the Christ from the body of the members. Of Mary he wrote: "She is Mother in the Spirit, but not of our Head, the Savior himself, for it is she who was spiritually born from him, since all who believe in him, among whom she too is to be counted, are rightly called children of the Bridegroom. Rather, she is clearly the Mother of his members; that is, of ourselves, because she cooperated by her charity, so that faithful Christians, members of the Head, might be born in the Church. As for the body (in the flesh), she is Mother of its Head."[12]

Because of Mary's physical maternity of Christ and spiritual maternity of the Church's members, the Church and Mary are inseparable. The Church who gives birth to Christ in the sacraments and in the faithful is an image of Mary: "But what is much more difficult to see, yet nonetheless true, is that the Church is Christ's Mother. How, I ask you, is Mary Christ's Mother, if not because she gives birth to his members, and you, to whom I am now speaking, are Christ's members. And who gave birth to you? I can already hear the answer that comes from your hearts: our mother the Church. She is then the holy and glorious mother, who is like to Mary, who is both virgin and mother, who gives birth to Christ—and you are Christ's members."[13]

In his homilies Augustine referred to Mary's faith, which preceded her conception of Christ: "Mary full of faith conceived Christ first in her heart before conceiving him in her womb."[14] She was first the believing disciple and then the Mother of God.[15] "Mary believed and what she believed was accomplished in her."[16] Mary's attentiveness to the word made her a member of Christ's spiritual family. Commenting on Matthew 12:50, Augustine said, "Holy virgins, with Mary you are (also) mothers, if you do the will of the heavenly Father: Mary in a most laudable and praiseworthy way is the mother of Christ, according to the text 'Whoever does the will of my father in heaven is brother and sister and mother to me.' In doing the will of God, Mary may be the mother of God in her body, but spiritually she is both sister and mother of Christ."[17]

Lumen Gentium drew upon Ambrose and Augustine to speak of Mary's motherhood reflected in and as part of the Church's character: "The Church, moreover, contemplating Mary's mysterious sanctity, imitating her charity, and faithfully fulfilling the Father's will, becomes herself a mother by accepting God's word in faith. For by her preaching and by baptism she brings forth to a new and immortal life children who are conceived of the Holy Spirit and born of God" (LG 64).

The Council of Ephesus in 431

Augustine had been invited to Ephesus but died before the Council was held. The immediate cause of the Council was a homily given by Proclus of Constantinople (about 428) in which he referred to the Virgin Mary as *Theotokos* (God-bearer), in the presence of Nestorius, patriarch of Constantinople, who rejected the title. Under the leadership of Cyril of Alexandria, the Council at Ephesus condemned the teaching of Nestorius.[18]

The conciliar declaration had great influence on Marian devotion: churches were dedicated to Mary, and Marian feasts were instituted. In popular piety, especially in the East, Mary's identification as *Theotokos* and the angel's greeting at the Annunciation were enshrined in sermons, hymns, and prayers that provided a pattern and a vocabulary that influenced both East and West.

At Ephesus, Cyril of Alexandria delivered what is sometimes called "the most famous Marian sermon of antiquity."[19] In Byzantine homiletic style, with extended phrases, he addressed the *Theotokos*: "We hail you, *Theotokos*, venerable treasure of the entire world, inextinguishable lamp, crown of virginity, scepter of orthodoxy, imperishable temple containing him who cannot be contained." His conclusion includes a reference to Mary and the Church: "Let us give glory to Mary, ever virgin, that is to the holy Church, and her son and immaculate spouse."[20]

A similar style was part of the sixth-century *Akathist* hymn, called "the most beautiful, the most profound, the most ancient Marian hymn of all Christian literature."[21] Mary was the "restoration of the fallen Adam . . . the Star that causes the Sun to appear . . . the ransom of all the world . . . the unfailing well spring of the living Water."[22] The *Akathist*, translated into Latin around the year 800, influenced the litanies and prayers that developed in the West. The titles by which Mary was addressed may originally have had an ecclesial or Christological dimension, but there is little indication that this orientation was perceived in the West.

The Mary-Church Relation in the Middle Ages

The Augustinian view of Mary's maternal relation to the members of the Church was continued in the Western monastic tradition. In his commentary on Luke, Bede the Venerable (d. 735) speaks of the union between Mary, the Church, and the believer:

> From today and until the end of the world the Lord does not cease to be conceived in Nazareth and to be born in Bethlehem, since upon receiving the flower of truth each one of His hearers makes himself the house of eternal bread. Daily in a virginal womb, that is, in the mind of believers, He is conceived by faith. He is born through Baptism. Daily the Church, Mother of God, following her teacher and ascending from the way of worldly commerce, which Galilee represents, to the city Juda, city of religions and praise, pays the tribute of her devotion to the eternal king.[23]

One of the last witnesses to the Mary–Church relation was the Cistercian Isaac of Stella (d. 1169): "Both [Mary and the Church] are the mother of Christ, but neither of the two gives birth to Christ without the other." He also spoke of the mutual relation of the Church, Mary, and the individual believer: "What is said about the Church (*universaliter*) is applicable to the Virgin Mary in a special way (*specialiter*), but also to the individual believer (*personaliter*)."[24]

In the Marian revival in the West in the eleventh and twelfth centuries, Bernard of Clairvaux was a major figure; he expressed his love and devotion in personal and dramatic ways: "If the storms of temptations arise, if you crash against the rocks of tribulation, look to the star, call upon Mary. If you are tossed about on the waves of pride, of ambition, of slander, of hostility, look to the star, call upon Mary."[25] In his "Sermon on the Aqueduct," Bernard speaks of Mary as the channel, the aqueduct, who by her desire, fervor, and prayer brought God's mercy to earth.[26] At times Bernard refers to Mary as a merciful mediator who approaches on our behalf her Son, who is the just judge. Bernard's language at times reflects titles from medieval chivalry: "Our Queen has preceded us, and has been so gloriously received that her servants can follow their Lady."[27] For Bernard, Mary was Queen (*regina*) or Lady (*domina*). Although he attributed a motherly heart to Mary, he never spoke of her as "our" or "my" mother.[28]

The "Hail Mary" and the great Marian antiphons (*Salve Regina, Regina Caeli, Ave Regina Caelorum, Alma Redemptoris Mater*) originated about the twelfth century, and all are types of greetings to Mary, containing profound and eloquent references to the divine maternity and the virginity of Mary. There is no reference to Mary's response of faith or to the Church.[29]

Early Scholasticism had no treatises dealing with the Church or the Virgin Mary. In the *Summa Theologica* (ST), Thomas Aquinas writes of the Virgin Mary in the *Tertia Pars*, with four questions related to Christ's coming into the world (qu. 27–30). He presents the Incarnation as a type of spiritual marriage between the Son of God and humanity, on whose behalf Mary offered her consent: *loco totius humanae naturae* (ST III, 30, 1). Earlier he had concluded: "The Blessed Virgin from the fact that she is the Mother of God has a kind of infinite dignity from the infinite good which is God" (ST I, 25, a6, ad. 4).

St. Albert the Great was noted for his Marian devotion, and, although none of his works was dedicated to Mary, his writings contain many Marian references. There are a few references to Mary and the Church: "Mary is a type of the Church as she conceives and brings forth new members. Her son is the image of those who have been born again." And, in another place, "And so, as Ambrose says, she is the model of holy Church, just as Joseph is the model of the prelates of the Church.[30] After Albert, the Mary–Church relation appears to have fallen into oblivion.[31]

Pseudo-Albert and the Knowledge of Mary

The Epistle to the Hebrews refers to Christ as "the leader and perfecter of faith" (Heb. 12:1), but there is no reference in Scripture to the faith of Christ. When speaking of the knowledge of Christ, the Scholastics made several distinctions: acquired, infused, beatific (*per se* or *per accidens*). Soon these distinctions were applied to the Virgin Mary's knowledge. In the thirteenth century a work appeared, attributed to St. Albert the Great, which influenced the image of Mary for centuries: *Mariale supra Missus est Angelus*. According to the author, Mary's "fullness of grace" conferred on her a certain "omnicompetence" involving spiritual gifts: the beatific vision (*propinquissima*); knowledge of angels, souls, and demons; and perfect knowledge of all created things. Mary was said to possess in the highest degree all individual and universal blessings.

Because the work was attributed to Albert (and was included in the published editions of his works), it occupied a pinnacle that ensured that, even in the early twentieth century, scholars had to take it into consideration.[32] A section on Mary's knowledge became a part of Marian treatises. However, in 1952 it was established that the *Mariale* was the work not of Albert the Great but of an anonymous author now designated Pseudo-Albert.[33] Writing on Mary's knowledge in 1955, Francis J. Connell stated: "It would be impossible to cite even a small number of the numerous theological books and articles which treat of Mary's knowledge."[34]

Early Modern Catholicism

The Council of Trent made few references to the Virgin Mary, but immediately after the Council there was a great increase in Marian devotion, fostered by the victory at the Battle of Lepanto, the approval of the rosary, and interest in the Immaculate Conception. The sixteenth-century Jesuit theologians, frequently identified as founders of the mariological movement, were also apologists involved in the controversies with the Protestant Reformers. Francisco Suarez (d. 1617), "the founder of the systematic or scholastic Mariology," composed a commentary on the *Tertia Pars* of the *Summa* of St. Thomas Aquinas, "On the Mysteries of the Life of Christ." He stated that "mysteries of grace, which God wrought in the Virgin, are not to be measured by ordinary laws, but by divine omnipotence, with due respect for the propriety of the matter and in the absence of contradiction and inconsistency in the Scriptures."[35] On the Virgin Mary he wrote that "the knowledge of the faith of Mary exceeded that of all the apostles and theologians." Against Erasmus, who had written that Mary was not aware of the divinity of her Son, he replied, "This opinion is impious and heretical, against the tradition of the Church."[36] In his massive work *De Maria Incomparabili*, Peter Canisius, the "Second Apostle to Germany," devoted two chapters to refuting errors, such as that Mary did not know the divinity of her son.[37]

The word "Mariology" appeared for the first time in the *Summae sacrae mariologiae pars prima* (1602) by Placido Nigido.[38] The work consisted of "questions and responses that might be easily transmitted for use against heresy." *Mariologia* was defined as *"doctrina de Beata Virgine Maria."* Mariology was to be a separate treatise insofar as it represented Mary's relation with God, but it was not to be separate from theology. Marian doctrine was related to Aristotle's "four causes" (final, efficient, material, formal).[39]

The Missal of the Council of Trent contained one of the few references in the liturgy of the Roman rite to the faith of Mary; it was in the eighth-century antiphon *Cunctas Haereses* (with Mary termed "the conqueror of heresy"): "Rejoice O Virgin Mary, for you alone have destroyed all heresies: You believed the words of the Archangel Gabriel."[40]

In the seventeenth and eighteenth centuries, dogmatic theology, influenced by philosophical currents, waned, and with a few exceptions, such as Lawrence of Brindisi, little appears on Mary. However, in that same period there are references to the person of Mary, to her love and faith, in the ascetical and devotional literature, especially in the French School of spirituality (Cardinal Pierre de Bérulle, St. John Eudes, St. Louis Grignion de Montfort, and Jean-Jacques Olier), and in the "most widely distributed book on Our Lady in modern times," the *Glories of Mary* of St. Alphonsus de Liguori.[41]

The Nineteenth-Century Mariological Movement

In the second half of the nineteenth century, several factors combined to produce a Catholic theological revival in which doctrine figured prominently. The Scholastic revival in Italy was a response to rationalism and modern philosophy. The declaration of the dogma of the Immaculate Conception in 1854 and the apparitions at Lourdes in 1858 (seen as a confirmation of the papal pronouncement) would predispose Marian devotees to esteem doctrinal pronouncement. Other factors were Vatican I's *Dei Filius* (Constitution on Catholic Faith, 1869), *Pastor Aeternus* (the declaration of papal infallibility, 1870), and the Neo-Scholastic revival promoted by Leo XIII's encyclical *Aeterni Patris* (1879).

Vatican I spoke of the role of the Church in defining precisely *what* is to be believed: "All those things are to be believed with divine and Catholic faith which are contained in the word of God, written or handed down, and which, by the Church, either in solemn judgment or through her ordinary and universal teaching office, are proposed for belief as having been divinely revealed."[42] A prevalent trend was that those doctrines defined by the Church were considered more significant than those not defined and that the highest dignity that a "revealed truth could attain would be to be defined by the pope or an ecumenical council."[43] This tendency was present in all sectors of Catholic theology, but especially in Mariology, characterized as "unquestionably the most active area in dogmatic theology."[44]

Much as in the other areas of theology, the early twentieth-century manuals of Mariology followed the deductive method, that is, the thesis was stated and then proved by a listing of sources, with high place given to the statements of the Magisterium. (René Laurentin was among the first to part from the deductive method. He acknowledged that the method responded to the need for unity and simplicity but that, at the same time, it omitted much. A statement was placed in a timeless context: "Too frequently it was delivering fragmentary pieces and not entering into the whole design of God."[45])

Since Mariology was a "science" in the Neo-Scholastic sense, there was a need for "a fundamental truth which furnished the ultimate reason for the various theses of a given science . . . a basic proposition, accepted by all, which alone gives organic coherence and logical *nexus* to the treatise."[46] The divine maternity was usually the fundamental principle, but also proposed were Mary as Co-redemptrix, the plenitude of grace (Alois Müller), the bridal maternity of Mary (M. J. Scheeben), and Mary as Archetype of the Church (Otto Semmelroth).

A major figure in the mariological movement in the early twentieth century was Joseph Désiré Cardinal Mercier, the archbishop of Malines and primate of Belgium. He was admired for his conduct during World

War I and regarded as a pioneer in relating Thomistic philosophy to modern thought. In 1913, and again after World War I, he began a movement for the liturgical celebration and papal definition of Mary as Mediatrix of all Grace, "to be believed as part of Catholic faith." He enlisted the support of the bishops of Belgium, about four hundred bishops worldwide, and theologians from the Louvain.

A congress to promote the papal declaration of Mary as Mediatrix was held in Malines in 1921, and in 1931 Joseph Bittremieux, a distinguished professor at the Louvain and associate of Cardinal Mercier, was instrumental in founding what would be the first national mariological society, the Flemish "Journées Mariales" (*Mariale Dagen*), in 1931. The French mariological society was founded by B.-M. Morineau in 1935; the Spanish, by Narciso García Garcés in 1941; and the American, by Juniper Carol in 1949. These mariological societies dealt with Marian doctrines defined or approaching definition, excluding consideration of Marian devotion. Frequent topics of study were the Assumption, Mary as Mediatrix of Grace, Mary as Co-redemptrix, and the Queenship of Mary.[47] In 1946 the Pontifical Marian Academy was founded, in part to coordinate the national mariological societies. At the conclusion of the First International Mariological Congress in Rome, a *votum* was submitted to the Holy See requesting the definition of Mary as "true collaborator in the work of redemption, spiritual mother of all, intercessor and dispenser of graces, in a word, universal Mediatress of God and man."[48]

The 1950s represented the apex of doctrinal and privilege-centered Mariology. In 1950 Pius XII proclaimed the dogma of the Assumption; the definition spoke of the "privileges which the most provident God has lavished upon this loving associate of our Redeemer, privileges which reach such an exalted plane that, except for her, nothing created by God other than the human nature of Jesus Christ has ever reached this level."[49] To commemorate the centenary of the proclamation of the dogma of the Immaculate Conception, Pius XII designated 1954 a Marian Year, and in *Fulgens Corona* he referred to the Immaculate Conception and the Assumption as "two singular privileges bestowed upon the Virgin Mother of God."[50] He instituted the feast of the Queenship of the Virgin Mary, popularly viewed as the "crowning," confirming Mary's position alongside Christ the King.[51]

MID-TWENTIETH-CENTURY MARIAN *RESSOURCEMENT*

Yet to be written is the history of the Marian *ressourcement*, which at Vatican II was responsible for an image of the Virgin Mary different from the one that was found in the early twentieth-century manuals. The Marian *ressourcement* did not begin in the nineteenth or early twentieth century as did the great liturgical, biblical, and patristic movements. It was during the years immediately following World War II that those scholars involved with Marian studies (especially in Germany) called for a broader, more historical, less scholastic approach. And, as shall be seen, the Marian renewal benefited much from the recoveries of patristic, liturgical, and scriptural movements. The *ressourcement* first recovered the Mary–Church relationship of the early centuries and then the Virgin Mary's integration into Scripture and salvation history. The following short profiles present a few of the significant voices from this era.

Hugo Rahner

Hugo Rahner began his *Mary and the Church* with words of Romano Guardini: "A new religious movement has begun, whose effects will be far-reaching beyond measure: souls have become aware of the Church." Rahner noted two contemporary trends: an awakening of love for the Church as our mother and a remarkable development of the Church's teaching on the Virgin Mary. He lamented that "the strong Marian movement of our day seems to have little connection with the theology of the Church, and even perhaps to run counter to it."[52] The Church is inseparably bound up with the mystery of Mary. The chapters of his book are titles applicable to both Mary and the Church: "Immaculata," "Ever-Virgin," "Mother of God," "Mother of the Faithful," "Mary at the Font, "Growth in Holiness," *"Mulier Fortis,"* "Pledge of the Spirit," "Woman of the Apocalypse," and "Queen Assumed into Heaven."

Alois Müller

In 1951 Alois Müller completed a dissertation at the University of Fribourg on the unity between Mary and the Church as found in patristic sources. In the introduction he stated that the very title of his work

(*Ecclesia–Maria: Die Einheit Marias und der Kirche*) would be incomprehensible to mariologists and could not fit into any current treatise. Yet in the early Church Mariology and ecclesiology were virtually synonymous. Müller suggested that mariologists turn to the basic themes of Scripture, such as the covenant and the marital relation between God and humanity. A characteristic of much ancient literature and the Scriptures was "collective personalities," that is, individuals who personify the principal themes. The spousal relationship is well expressed in the figure of the Daughter of Sion (Isa. 54:5–6, Jer. 2:2, Bar. 48, John 3:28–30).[53]

Heinrich Köster

In 1946 Heinrich Köster wrote that dogma alone presented a limited representation of Mary. Modern movements were seeking images with which people could identify. Köster said that what was needed was an image of Mary as a person with independence, polarity, personality, and identity within salvation history. For him, salvation history embraced the grand themes and aspirations of sacred and human history, and these themes were personified in specific persons, such as Abraham, Moses, Jacob, Paul. He saw the Virgin Mary as the apex (*personale Spitze*) of humanity and representative of all that it hopes for: "What salvation history presents, an independent and personal encounter between God and humanity in the covenant, reaches its highest expression in motherhood."[54]

At the 1958 International Mariological Congress at Lourdes, Köster introduced two complementary ways of considering the role of the Virgin Mary. The first, the Christotypical, was founded on Mary's relation with Christ (frequently expressed in the figure of the New Eve); the second, the ecclesiotypical, was derived from Mary's relation to the Church and to the history of salvation. Köster defined salvation history as "one continuous and progressive totality initiated by God whose purpose is the union of God with humanity similar to the marital union."[55]

René Laurentin

After receiving doctorates from the Sorbonne and the Institut Catholique, René Laurentin wrote in 1953 *Court traité de théologie mariale*, later edited and revised several times. He stated clearly what is obvious but at times forgotten: "The fundamental mission of Mary is to unite (*rattacher*) the Savior to humanity."[56] Rather than following the deductive method, he presented the person of Mary within Scripture, the Church, and salvation history. His position on the knowledge of Mary differed from that found in earlier Marian treatises: Mary was truly a Jewish woman of the Old Testament when she received the revelation of the mystery of the Incarnation. She was not ignorant of what God was going to accomplish, but neither did she possess the concepts and the formulas that were later used to explain the mystery of Christ.

Most significant were Laurentin's works of biblical exegesis: the first devoted to the structure and theology of the first two chapters of Luke's gospel and the second to Luke 2:48–50, Jesus in the Temple, the Paschal Mystery and the Faith of Mary.[57] With Stanislaus Lyonnet he is credited with identifying the Virgin Mary as the Daughter of Sion, principally because the Lucan greeting to Mary, "Rejoice" (Luke 1:28) appears in the Septuagint as an announcement of messianic joy addressed to Sion (Zeph. 3:14–17, Joel 2:21–27, Zech. 9:9–10, Lam. 4:22). In Luke's infancy narrative he noted references and stylistic similarities to the Hebrew Scriptures, making the Lucan narrative a type of "midrash" of Hebrew texts to serve as a completion of or bridge between the two covenants.

Otto Semmelroth

In 1950 Otto Semmelroth entered the discussion of the fundamental principle of Mariology.[58] The early Christian writers pointed to Mary in God's plan of salvation. It is only within the Church that Mary's role of mother and associate of Christ can be understood. Semmelroth points out that the image of the Church is disparate without Mary. "Both [the Church's] invisible, spiritual core and the totality of her external unity call for a type to personify her and make her present to us." As bride and mother, Mary is the Archetype (*Urbild*) of the Church, that is, the living person who represents the innermost essence of the Church. Mary is the "personification" of the Church; the spiritual reality has become the fundamental part of the person.

Another significant work that contributed to the pre–Vatican II Marian *ressourcement* was Albert Gelin's *The Poor of Yaweh*, with a section on the Virgin Mary's identification with the *anawim* (or the "poor" as described in the Old Testament): Gelin writes that in the Magnificat "we hear the woman who has so identified herself with anawim, that conscious of the newness of the Incarnation, she has become their perfect and living expression."[59] Other works of note were Max Thurian's *Mother of the Lord: Figure of the Church*, with a section on "Mary, Daughter of Sion," and Lucien Deiss's *Mary, Daughter of Sion*.[60]

In 1951, two mariological societies in Europe took a significant turn, leaving aside their programs dealing with doctrine. After three annual programs devoted to the study of the doctrine of the Assumption, the French Mariological Society (*Societé francaise d'études mariales*) undertook a three-year program (1951–53) devoted to Mary and the Church.[61] The German Mariological Society (*Mariologische Arbeitsgemeinschaft deutscher Theologen*) began a two-year program on Mary in salvation history in 1952.[62]

VATICAN II AND THE VIRGIN MARY

Vatican II's Ecclesiological Character

In his first announcement of a council (1959), John XXIII indicated that the Church was to be the theme of the Council. In 1963 Paul VI also indicated that the Council was to give a "clearer and fuller definition of the mystery of the Church." At the closing of the second session, Paul VI expressed the wish that the Council would continue its consideration of the schema on the Virgin Mary, "whom the Church recognizes as the Mother of God, who occupies the place highest after Christ, and the closest to us, and is rightly acknowledged as Mother of the Church."[63]

Before the Council began, Cardinal Domenico Tardini had requested of the world's bishops and theological faculties suggestions for topics to be considered at the Council. Of the 2,000 replies there were about 600 requests for a statement on Mary; 382 requested a statement on Mary's mediation; and about 280 wished a dogmatic definition of Mary as Mediatrix. At the beginning of the Council, Carlo Balić, O.F.M., founder of the International Pontifical Marian Academy, had submitted a schema for the Council's statement on the Virgin Mary: it was six pages of text and twenty-four pages of the *Praenotanda*, explaining that all the statements could be found in papal documents and listing the errors concerning Mary's virginity and her knowledge of the divinity of her Son at the time of the Annunciation, as well as mistakes made by both "maximalists and mimimalists."[64] However, the question remained of whether the Council's statement on Mary would be integrated into a major conciliar pronouncement or be a separate document.

On October 1, 1963, at the second session of the Council, Cardinal Raúl Silva Henríquez of Santiago, Chile, in a short intervention on behalf of forty Latin American bishops, spoke in favor of including the Marian schema in the document of the Church. He regretted that forms of Marian devotion seemed apart from the mystery of Christ and the Church: "We think it is of great importance and general interest, from both the ecumenical and pastoral viewpoints, that the Marian doctrine does not appear as a sort of independent theological overgrowth, but takes its place in the whole complex of the message of salvation."[65] The "debate" that occurred on October 24, 1963, between Cardinal Rufino Santos of Manila and Cardinal Franz König of Vienna, dealt with whether the schema on the Virgin Mary should be part of the document *De Ecclesia* or constitute a separate document.[66] The vote that occurred on October 29, 1963, with 1,114 in favor and 1,074 opposed, passed by a margin of seventeen votes. As Cardinal Ratzinger later wrote, it was an "intellectual watershed," a decision with enormous consequences.[67]

Mary in the One Mystery of Christ and the Church

Vatican II's first document, *Sacrosanctum Concilium* (SC), established "mystery" as the basis for understanding the Church and the liturgy. The Constitution on the Liturgy speaks of God's saving plan and the wonderful deeds of God in the Old Testament, which culminate in the paschal mystery: the death, resurrection, and ascension of Christ (SC 5). The document contains at least twenty-three references to the "mystery" celebrated in liturgy: for example, the mystery of Christ, the mystery of redemption, the mystery of salvation, the paschal mystery. The single but significant reference to Mary is this: "In celebrating this annual cycle of Christ's mysteries, the Church honors with a special love the Blessed Virgin Mary, Mother of God, who is joined by an inseparable bond (*indissolubili nexu*) to the saving work of Christ" (SC 103).

The title of *Lumen Gentium*'s chapter 1 is "The Mystery of the Church," and that of its eighth chapter is "Mary in the Mystery of Christ and the Church." Within this one mystery, Christ, the Church, and Mary are related. In the apostolic exhortation *Marialis cultus* (MC, 1974), Paul VI wrote that Marian devotion is one part, a most noble part, of Christocentric worship and that every consideration of Christ and the Church begins with the saving plan of God. When the Church considers its own identity, it eventually leads to "the same figure of a Woman: the Virgin Mary, Mother of Christ and Mother of the Church" (MC Intro), and when the Church reflects on the Virgin Mary, it looks to Mary as its hope and culmination.

Lumen Gentium says that within the Church, Mary's relation to Christ is fully intact; she is honored as "truly the Mother of God and of the Redeemer," as the Mother of God's Son, "and so is also the favorite daughter of the Father as well as the sanctuary of the Holy Spirit" (LG 53). Mary was "enriched from the first instant of her conception with splendor of an entirely unique holiness" that came wholly from Christ; she is "redeemed in a more exalted fashion, by reason of the merits of her Son" (LG 53). The union between Mother and Son is manifested from the time of his virginal conception until his death (LG 57). Mary was the singularly generous associate and humble handmaid of the Lord. At the end of her life, she was assumed into heavenly glory in body and soul to be more closely conformed to her risen Son (LG 59).

In the mystery of the Church, Mary is a woman, daughter of Adam, "a preeminent and altogether singular member of the Church" (LG 53). In conceiving Christ, she is the mother of Christ's members, "because she cooperated in bringing about the birth of the faithful in the Church, who are the members of the Head" (LG 53). Mary's motherhood of grace, begun at the Annunciation, continues in the Church uninterruptedly until all reach their heavenly home.

Mary's exemplarity for the Church is derived from her nature and her activity. She is a "type" of the Church in the order of faith, charity, and perfect union with Christ and the model of the Church, virgin and mother. She brought forth Christ with a faith unsullied by any doubt (LG 63). She is the model of virtue for the members of the Church. Contemplating Mary in the light of the Word made man, the Church enters the mystery of the Incarnation (LG 65).

Mary is also the eschatological model and fulfillment of the Church. She precedes the Church as a sure sign of hope and confidence to the Church in its pilgrimage of faith (LG 68). "In the most holy Virgin, the Church has already reached that perfection whereby she exists without spot or wrinkle" (LG 65; cf. Eph. 5:27). In the words of *Sacrosanctum Concilium*, "In her, the Church admires and exalts the most excellent fruit of redemption, and joyfully contemplates, as in a faultless image, that which she herself desires and hopes wholly to be" (SC 103).

Mary in Salvation History

Salvation history is God's plan of salvation (*oeconomia*) centered in Christ and the Church (Eph. 3:9). In *Lumen Gentium* we read, "The Sacred Scriptures of the Old and New Testaments and the Tradition show forth the role of the Mother of the Savior in the economy of salvation in an ever clearer light. . . . The Old Testament was preparation for the coming of Christ into the world, and, read in the light of later revelation, it reveals the figure of a woman" (LG 55).

Lumen Gentium gives four examples of the Virgin Mary prefigured in the Old Testament. The first example is "the promised Woman" (Gen. 3:15). The Latin text (*ipsa conteret caput tuum*) greatly influenced the "living tradition of the universal Church and the analogy of faith," according to Vatican II's Dogmatic Constitution on Divine Revelation, *Dei Verbum* (12). In Pope Pius IX's apostolic constitution on the Immaculate Conception, *Ineffabilis Deus* (December 8, 1854), along with the liturgical tradition, this phrase from Genesis is the sole scriptural reference cited for the dogma of the Immaculate Conception.

The second typological prefiguration is "the Virgin who shall conceive and bear a Son whose name is Emmanuel" (Isa. 7:14, Mic. 5:2–3), a text that Matthew saw as referring to the Virgin Mary (Matt. 1:22–23).

Mary is also prefigured among the humble and poor of the Lord, who, with trust, hope for and accept salvation from him. Mary's Magnificat is her and the Church's identification with the humble and poor: the Magnificat is "the song both of the Mother of God and the Church, the song of the Daughter of Sion and the new People of God."[68]

The final typological prefiguration is Mary as Daughter of Sion. Here Mary is prefigured, and particularly applicable here is the note in *Lumen Gentium* that she has also "deeply entered into salvation history and unites in herself and radiates the most important teachings of the faith" (LG 65). She is the Daughter of Sion, who, in the "fullness of time," gave birth to the Son of God and inaugurated the New Covenant. "Finally, with Her, the outstanding Daughter of Sion, after a long expectation of the promise, the times are fulfilled and the new Economy (*nova instauratur Oeconomia*) is established, when the Son of God assumed human nature from her so that, by the mysteries of his flesh, he might free us from sin" (LG 55). Mary is the personification of Sion, the one with whom God establishes the Covenant with humanity,[69] and John Paul II noted that it is significant that it is a woman who accomplishes this feat.[70]

Mary's role in the inauguration of the New Covenant, together with the many references to Abraham in Luke's Annunciation narrative, was developed in John Paul's *Redemptoris Mater*: "Mary's faith can also be compared to that of Abraham, whom St. Paul calls 'our father in faith' (cf. Rom. 4:12). In the salvific economy of God's revelation, Abraham's faith constitutes the beginning of the Old Covenant; Mary's faith at the Annunciation inaugurates the New Covenant."[71]

The Abraham–Mary comparison is developed in the *Catechism of the Catholic Church*. The response to the self-revelation of God can be only "the obedience of faith," that is, listening and submitting freely to the word that has been heard: "Abraham is model of such obedience in the Sacred Scripture. The Virgin Mary is its most perfect embodiment."[72]

A key text on Mary's faith is the second of Elizabeth's blessings directed to Mary. At the Visitation scene Elizabeth first said, "Blest are you among women, and blest is the fruit of your womb" (Luke 1:38). This first blessing was included in the "Hail Mary," the prayer of the Church for many centuries. But Elizabeth's second blessing, which John Paul II called the key to Mary's innermost reality, which reached its apex at the cross, could also become part of that prayer.[73] Elizabeth said, "Blest is she who believed (*hē pisteusasa*) that there would be a fulfillment of what was spoken to her by the Lord" (Luke 1:45). Mary's response: "From now on, all generations will call me blest" (Luke 1:48).

NOTES

1. Yves M.-J. Congar, "Marie et l'Église dans la pensée patristique," *Revue des Sciences Philosophiques et Théologiques* 38 (1954): 4.

2. Justin, *Dialogue with Trypho*, 100, in *Patrologia Graeca* (PG) 6, 709–12; Luigi Gambero, *Mary and the Fathers of the Church: The Blessed Virgin Mary in Patristic Thought*, trans. Thomas Buffer (San Francisco: Ignatius, 1999), 47.

3. Irenaeus, *Against the Heresies* 3, 18; Gambero, *Mary and the Fathers*, 53.

4. Irenaeus, *Against the Heresies* 3, 22; Gambero, *Mary and the Fathers*, 54–55.

5. Irenaeus, *On the Apostolic Preaching*, trans. John Behr (Crestwood, NY: St. Vladimir Seminary Press, 1997), 61.

6. Ambrose, *De virginibus* 2, 15, in *Patrologia Latina* (PL) 16, 210; Gambero, *Mary and the Fathers*, 191.

7. Ambrose, *Expositio Evangelii secundum Lucam* 2, 26, in *Corpus Scriptorum Ecclesiasticorum Latinorum* (CSEL) 32, IV, 55; PL 15, 1562: 83–84.

8. Ambrose, *Expositio Evangelii secundum Lucam* 2, 5–9, in CSEL 32, IV, 45; LG 63; PL 15, 5555; Gambero, *Mary and the Fathers*, 198.

9. Ambrose, *Expositio Evangelii secundum Lucam* 2, 24, in CSEL 32, IV, 54 (PL 15, 1641–42); Gambero, *Mary and the Fathers*, 199.

10. Augustine, *Sermo IV*, in *Enchiridion Marianum biblicum patristicum*, ed. Dominic Casagrande (Rome: Cor Unum, 1973), 585; CSEL 41, 237.

11. Augustine, Sermon (Denis) 25, 7, in *Miscellanea Agostiniana: Testi e Studi*, ed. Germain Morin and Antonio Casamassa, vol. 1 (Rome: Tipografia poliglotta vaticana, 1930), 163.

12. Augustine, *De sancta virginitate* 6; CSEL 41, 240; Gambero, *Mary and the Fathers*, 223.

13. Augustine, Sermon (Denis) 25, 8, in *Miscellanea agostiniana*, ed. Morin and Casamassa, 163.

14. Augustine, Sermon 215, 4: "Illa [Maria] fide plena et Christum prius mente quam ventre concipiens" (PL 38, 1074).

15. Augustine, Sermon (Denis) 25, 7, in *Miscellanea agostiniana*, ed. Morin and Casamassa, 162: "Et ideo plus est Mariae, discipulam fuisse Christi, quam matrem fuisse Christi; plus est felicius discipulam fuisse Christi, quam matrem fuisse Christi." See also, Casagrande, *Enchiridion Marianum*, 620.

16. Augustine, Sermon 215, 4: "Credidit Maria et in ea quod credidit factum est" (PL 38, 1074).

17. Augustine, *De Sancta Virginitate* V, 5; CSEL 41, 239: "Maria ergo faciens voluntatem Dei corporaliter Christi tantummodo mater est, spiritualiter autem et soror et mater."

18. Josef Neuner and Jacques Dupuis, *The Christian Faith in the Doctrinal Documents of the Catholic Church*, rev. ed. (New York: Alba House, 1982), no. 606.

19. Johannes Quasten, *Patrology III* (Utrecht and Antwerp: Spectrum, 1963), 131.

20. "Cyril of Alexandria," in Michael O'Carroll, *Theotokos: A Theological Encyclopedia of the Blessed Virgin Mary* (Collegeville, MN: Liturgical Press, 1990), 111–14.

21. O'Carroll, *Theotokos*, 8.

22. Holy Transfiguration Monastery, *The Service of the Akathist Hymn* (Boston, 1991), 55–58.

23. Venerable Bede, *In Luce evangelium expositio*, vol. 1, 2, in PL 92, 330.

24. Isaac of Stella, *Sermo 51 in Assumptione*, in PL 194, 1862–63, 1865: "Utraque Christi mater, sed neutra sine altera totum parit"; Luigi Gambero, *Mary in the Middle Ages* (San Francisco: Ignatius, 2000), 171.

25. Hilda C. Graef, *Mary: A History of Doctrine and Devotion* (Notre Dame, IN: Christian Classics, 2009), 186, citing *Homiliae Super Missus Est* 2, 7, in PL 183, 55–88; Gambero, *Mary in the Middle Ages*, 133.

26. *De aquaeducta* 4–5, in PL 183, 440; Gambero, *Mary in the Middle Ages*, 135, n. 3.

27. Graef, *Mary: A History*, 188.

28. Gambero, *Mary in the Middle Ages*, 136; Theodore Koehler, "Maternité spirituelle de Marie," in *Maria: Études sur la Saint Vierge*, ed. Hubert du Manoir (Paris: Beauchesne, 1949–71), 1:575.

29. Although there may be little evidence of the Mary–Church relation in the theological tradition, it was present in the Gothic cathedrals dedicated to Our Lady, with architecture frequently symbolizing the relation between Mary and the Church. The high points of the liturgy of Chartres were Advent, the Nativity of Mary, and the anniversary of the Dedication of the Church. See Margot Fassler, *The Virgin of Chartres: Making History through Liturgy and the Arts* (New Haven, CT: Yale University Press, 2010).

30. Gambero, *Mary in the Middle Ages*, 230, citing *B. Alberti Magni Opera omnia*, ed. Augusti Borgnet, 38 vols. (Paris: L. Vivès, 1890–99), 22:197.

31. Alois Müller, *Ecclesia–Maria: Die Einheit Marias und der Kirche* (Freiburg, Schweiz: Universitätsverlag, 1955), 1, 5, 207; Cyril Vollert, "Mary and the Church," in *Mariology*, 3 vols., ed. J. B. Carol (Milwaukee: Bruce, 1955–61), vol. 2, 551.

32. See Enrico dal Covolo and Aristide Serra, eds., *Storia della Mariologia 1: Dal modello biblico al modello letterario* (Rome: Citta Nuovo Editrice, 2009), 586–88 (on the *Mariale*), esp. 587, n. 104, citing an article by René Laurentin, "Que reste-t-il de l'oeuvre mariale d'Albert le Grand?" and *B. Alberti Magni Opera*, ed. Borgnet, 37:1–362.

33. O'Carroll, "Pseudo-Albert," in *Marienlexikon*, ed. Remigius Bäumer and Leo Scheffczyk (St. Ottilien, Germany: EOS, 1988–94), vol. 3, 365–66; Graef, *Mary: A History*, 217, n. 65, citing Fries.

34. Francis J. Connell, "Our Lady's Knowledge," in *Mariology*, 3 vols., ed. J. B. Carol (Milwaukee: Bruce, 1955–61), vol. 2, 313–24. The first Marian schema submitted at Vatican II made reference to errors concerning the nature of Mary's knowledge. In 1949, on the occasion of the sixtieth anniversary of *The American Ecclesiastical Review* ("Our Lady in the American Ecclesiastical Review," October 1949, 286–300), Lawrence P. Everett, C.Ss.R., wrote (286) that "every phase" of Mariology has been covered in the pages of that journal under the following six headings: "The Immaculate Conception," "The Assumption," "The Divine Maternity," "The Virgin Birth," "Mary's Grace," and "Mary's Knowledge."

35. O'Carroll, *Theotokos*, 334.

36. Francisco Suarez, *Misterios de la Vida de Cristo*, I, Disp. 19, 1, 4. Cf. Graef, *Mary: A History*, 293–95. Suarez did treat the subject of Mary's faith in *De Mysteriis Vitae Christi, Disputatio* XIX, sec. 2–5.

37. Peter Canisius, *De Maria Virgine incomparabili*, vol. 4 (Ingolstadii: Excudebat David Sartorius, 1577), chap. 2. Cf. René Laurentin, *Jesus au Temple* (Paris: Gabalda, 1966), 22–24.

38. *Testi mariani del secondo millennio*, 8 vols., ed. Luigi Gambero (Rome: Città Nuovo Editrice, 1996–), vol. 5, 600.

39. Stefano De Fiores, "Nigido, Placido," in *Maria: Nuovissimo Dizionario*, 3 vols. (Bologna: EDB, 2006–8), vol. 3, 704–9.

40. "*Gaude Maria Virgo, cunctas haereses interemisti quae Gabrielis Archangeli dictis credidisti*" (from *Tractus: Missae de sancta Maria in sabato II & III*).

41. O'Carroll, *Theotokos*, 14; Graef, *Mary: A History*, 301–10. Some references to Mary's faith in this period are found in St. Louis de Montfort (*Love of Eternal Wisdom*, 107, *Secret of Mary*, 68, and *True Devotion to Mary*, 214). Although he does not treat Mary's faith systematically or in depth, St. Alphonsus Liguori touches on it in Part Four of *The Glories of Mary* in his consideration of her virtues.

42. Josef Neuner and Jacques Dupuis, *The Christian Faith in the Doctrinal Documents of the Catholic Church* (New York: Alba House, 1982), no. 121.

43. Piet F. Fransen, *The Hermeneutics of the Councils and Other Studies* (Leuven: Leuven University Press, 1985), 271.

44. Alois Müller, "Contemporary Mariology," in *Theology Today*, vol. 1: *Renewal in Dogma*, ed. J. Feiner et al. (Milwaukee: Bruce, 1965), 109.

45. René Laurentin, "Grandeur et misère de la méthode déductive," in his *Court traité de theologie mariale*, 4th ed. (Paris: Lethielloux, 1959), 85–88. Gustave Weigel spoke of how ecclesiologists of 1960 differed from those of 1910: "The men of 1910 were more abstract; they looked for a tight, local, skeletal blueprint of the Church considered as an organization. . . . Scripture as the living Word of God was shelved in favor of a catena of text proofs serving as majors and minors

of syllogisms. History was not lovingly pursued in order to see what the Church actually was in time." Gustave Weigel, "Foreword," in Hugo Rahner et al., *The Church: Readings in Theology* (New York: P. J. Kenedy and Sons, 1963), x.

46. Juniper B. Carol, *Fundamentals of Mariology* (New York: Benziger, 1956), 7–9, here 7.

47. Eric May, "Mariological Societies," in *Mariology*, ed. J. B. Carol, vol. 3, 272–75.

48. *Alma Socia Christi: Acta Congressus Mariologici-Mariani Romae anno sancto MCML* (Rome: Academia Mariana, 1951–58), vol. 1, 298.

49. Pius XII, Apostolic Constitution Defining the Dogma of the Assumption, *Munificentissimus Deus* (November 1, 1950), 14.

50. Pius XII, Encyclical Letter *Proclaiming a Marian Year to Commemorate the Centenary of the Definition of the Dogma of the Immaculate Conception Fulgens Corona* (September 8, 1953).

51. Pius XII, Encyclical Letter *Proclaiming the Queenship of Mary Ad Coeli Reginam* (October 11, 1954), 51.

52. Hugo Rahner, *Maria und die Kirche* (Innsbruck: Marianischer, 1951), 2, trans. as *Our Lady and the Church* (New York: Pantheon, 1961).

53. Müller, *Ecclesia–Maria*, 19–26. Müller spoke of the Mary–Church comparison as a "comet in the Mariological sky," an observation also cited by Gerard Philips in "Marie et l'Église: Un thème théologique renouvelé," in *Maria: Études sur la Saint Vierge*, ed. Hubert du Manoir (Paris: Beauchesne, 1949–71), vol. 7, 365.

54. Heinrich Maria Köster, *Die Magd des Herrn, theologische Versuche und Überlegungen* (Limburg: Lahn, 1946), 25. Cf. Stefan Hartmann, *Die Magd des Herrn: Zur heilsgeschichtlichen Mariologie Heinrich M. Kösters* (Regensburg: Pustet, 2009).

55. Heinrich Köster, "Quid iuxta investigations . . . minimum tribuendum sit B.M. Virgini in cooperatione eius ad opus redemptionis," in *Maria et Ecclesia*, vol. 2, 21–49.

56. René Laurentin, *Court traité de théologie mariale* (Paris: Lethielleux, 1968), 119. The original 1953 work underwent five revisions, the last in 1968, with the title changed to *Court traité sur la Vierge Marie*. After Vatican Council II, Laurentin would avoid theological neologisms: "The spirit of the Vatican II is that we do not become prisoners of a late vocabulary which created 'mariology' and '*culte marial*' separate from the Christian worship" (1968 ed., 11f).

57. René Laurentin, *Structure et Théologie de Luc I–II* (Paris: Gabalda, 1957), and *Jésus au Temple: Mystère de Paques et foi de Marie, en Luc 2, 48–50* (Paris: Gabalda et Cie, 1966).

58. Otto Semmelroth, *Urbild der Kirche, Organischer Aufbau des Mariengeheimnisses* (Würzburg: Echter, 1950), trans. as *Mary, Archetype of the Church* (New York: Sheed and Ward, 1963), 30.

59. Albert Gelin, *The Poor of Yahweh* (Collegeville, MN: Liturgical Press, 1964) 94.

60. Max Thurian, *Marie, mère du Seigneur, figure de l'Église* (Taizé, France: Presses de Taizé, 1962), trans. as *Mary, Mother of All Christians* (New York: Herder and Herder, 1964), with chapters titled "Mary, Daughter of Sion," "Full of Grace," "Poor Virgin," "Dwelling of God," "Handmaid in the Faith," "Mother of the Messiah King," and "Mother of the Suffering Servant." Lucien Deiss, *Marie, fille de Sion* (Paris: Desclée de Brouwer, 1959), with a chapter "The Faith of Abraham and the Faith of Mary," trans. as *Mary, Daughter of Sion* (Collegeville, MN: Liturgical Press, 1972).

61. The studies on the Assumption were related to the Divine Maternity and the Virginity; they were in honor of the papal definition. The transition to the programs on Mary and the Church was announced in the following terms: the Assumption of Mary indicates the destiny of the Church, as the Cistercian Serlon de Savigny noted: *"Illa praecedit, haec sequitur"* (in "Marie et l'Église," *Études Mariales*, 1951).

62. On the society, see Carl Feckes, *Die heilsgeschichtliche Stellvertretung der Menschheit durch Maria* (Paderborn, Germany: F. Schöningh, 1954).

63. *Acta Synodalia Sacrosancti Concilii Oecumenici Vaticani II, Periodus secunda*, II (Vatican City: Typis Polyglottis Vaticanis, 1970), 6, 567.

64. *Acta Synodalia, Periodus prima*, I/4, 92–97 ("Schema Constitutionis Dogmaticae de Beata Maria Virgine, Matre Dei et Matre Hominum").

65. *Acta Synodalia, Periodus secunda*, II/1, 366–67.

66. Thomas A. Thompson, S.M., "Vatican II and Beyond," in Graef, *Mary: A History*, 410–12.

67. Since the Christotypical Mariology influenced both the Marian devotion of the period and the theological formation of most of the participants of Vatican II, Joseph Ratzinger wrote, "The immediate outcome of the victory of ecclesiocentric Mariology was the collapse of Mariology." Joseph Ratzinger, "The Place of Marian Devotion and Piety," in Benedict XVI and Hans Urs von Balthasar, *Mary: The Church at the Source* (San Francisco: Ignatius, 2005), 22.

68. *Catechism of the Catholic Church* (CCC), 2619.

69. Benedict XVI and Balthasar, *Mary: The Church at the Source*, 66.

70. "The Covenant begins with a woman, the 'woman' of the Annunciation at Nazareth." John Paul II, Apostolic Letter on the Dignity and Vocation of Women on the Occasion of the Marian Year, *Mulieris Dignitatem* (August 15, 1988), 11.

71. John Paul II, Encyclical Letter on the Blessed Virgin Mary in the Life of the Pilgrim Church, *Redemptoris Mater* (March 25, 1987), 14.

72. CCC, 144.

73. See John Paul II, *Redemptoris Mater*, 19.

CHAPTER 3

From Epinal to Plateau d'Assy

Religious Art in the Marian Century

JOHANN G. ROTEN, S.M.

There are many inspiring and challenging ways of approaching Marian art up to Vatican II and on its eve. There is, for the University of Notre Dame, the witness of Ivan Meštrović, who died on January 16, 1962, in South Bend, Indiana, and whose monumental art dots and consecrates the architectural profile of the campus. Ivan Meštrović's art would have been a highly illustrative case in point to highlight religious and Marian art during the first half of the twentieth century. A song and a prayer at the same time, Meštrović's art represents a glorious attempt to leave behind the narrow clichés of cultural and political nationalisms of his century in order to embrace the God-given human reality in its essence and visible grandeur.[1] A second approach for the taking would have been to relive the history of the Catholic Art Association (CAA) from 1937 to 1970 to study the founding and formative years of this association before the war—its restoration, growth, conflicts, and challenges, as well as the downward spiral to the end of the association in 1970. In other words, to document "The Search for Right Reason in an Unreasonable World," as Maureen Murphy calls the effort in her 1975 dissertation submitted to the University of Notre Dame.[2] The history of the CAA is a combination of lofty philosophical principles and down-to-earth educational endeavors that never blended and merged. According to Murphy, "It was a distillation of neo-Thomistic and Pre-Raphaelite teachings on art, one which considered all good work done 'with reason,' i.e. in accordance with the four causes, as art."[3] According to the author, the association was marked from the beginning by a dualism, not least because of the discrepancy between the willingness of the majority of its members— many of them teaching sisters—to contribute to the revival of Catholic art and the philosophical concerns of people like Graham Carey, one of the association's promoters and *maîtres à penser.* "When the philosophical ultimatum was issued in 1958," writes Murphy, "it sowed the seeds of the organization's destruction."[4] We will retain from this experiment a new awareness of Catholic art and the practical endeavor in Catholic schools across the country to liberate art education from the staid canons of nineteenth-century devotional art. May it be added that the Neo-Thomistic nomenclature of grounding principles at this stage was no longer able to sustain and direct the effort of artistic renewal.

Both Meštrović and the CAA reflect a lively commitment to Catholic religious art. Both of these representatives of religious and Catholic art stand for a new artistic sensitivity and a new artistic impulse on the eve of Vatican II. Thus the period before the Council is not synonymous with the "dark age" of Catholic art, although there may be some truth in the popular wisdom that it is the *déjà vu* that is the beautiful. For this presentation I have opted for a broader historical and motivational context that includes both devotional and artistic Marian art.[5] I would like to situate these two types of Marian imagery within the context of the Marian century (ca. 1830–1950), highlighting important developments and typical features. The title chosen for this chapter points in this direction: from Epinal to Plateau d'Assy.[6] If Epinal is associated with popular imagery frequently identified with the so-called art of St.-Sulpice, Plateau d'Assy evokes a radical change in artistic ambition, purpose, and style. Epinal points roughly to the middle of the nineteenth century and so to the beginning of the Marian century; Plateau d'Assy, in turn, points to the conclusion of that period and coincides with the eve of Vatican II. Epinal stands for a long tradition frequently returned to and revived, Plateau d'Assy for a short-lived and, for some, a controversial experiment in breaking tradition and reinventing art. I have chosen this geographical parameter to bring into focus the great variety and riches of the Marian image in the Marian century. Speaking of riches, it will become obvious that these riches are not, in the first place, the fruit of Church-inspired promotion. Rich and varied, Marian art is a tributary to Catholic revival movements and inspired artists but not only that. It gained impetus from Protestant artists of the late nineteenth century,[7] from secular art in the twentieth century, from the impact of photography[8] and especially filmography, and, not least, from a growing cultural pluralism in the first half of the twentieth century.

ART AND THE CHALLENGE OF INCARNATION

Catholic Christianity prides itself on being visual not least because of its doggedly incarnational commitment.[9] The incarnate God is a visual God, but he is also a mediating and a mediated God. According to theological grammar there is no visible form without divine revelation, no "splendor of form" without the primacy of the form-giving causality.[10] Now God is mediated also in what we call *ascending* theology. It points to the importance of the visible form, without which there would be no focal point for divine radiance in time and space. Jesus Christ is the only and ultimate visible form of both God *and* the world. He is the mediated mediator. Christian art will always have to be measured against the God–human reality of Jesus Christ, and thus against the archetypal criterion of what we might call the *rectitudo imaginis*.

In fact and historical reality, Christian art tends to oscillate between the two poles—between splendor and form, between divine and human, between categories of descending and ascending theology. Eastern iconography will forever be the witness of divine incursion into, and timeless presence in, the world. Western religious art takes a different stand. It is a priceless report card on how changing cultures grappled with the Incarnation and its artistic representations. Gothic art opened wide its windows to the light from above. The Renaissance artist found solace and praise in the beauty of creation. If the baroque period lent credence to a new synthesis between heaven and earth, its Romantic counterpart would be drawn to subjective religious experience and its artistic render-ing with symbolic and intimist imagery.

Similarly, Marian art has never been immune to the paradoxical character of the Incarnation and its theological and cultural conse-quences. Marian art evolves with the ebb and flow of this- and other-worldly movements and periods. The enthroned image of the Byzantine empress, widely publicized in Romanesque art, lost its hieratic stance in the S-lined Madonna of fair love. In contrast, the largely secularized image of the Renaissance recovered its otherworldly destiny in the image of the Queen of Heaven, ornate with scepter and crown and typical of the Counter-Reformation.

THE MARIOLOGICAL DISCOURSE ON THE EVE OF VATICAN II

Since the presentations at the conference that inspired this volume paid special attention to the eve of Vatican II, it would seem important to narrow the scope of this presentation. Fine-tuning my approach, I would like to develop a tableau of major trends in Marian studies on the eve of Vatican II in order to determine if these theological trends can be verified in art. Does art imitate life? Is there a correspondence be-tween the theological discourse about Mary and the way in which this particular period translates in categories of artistic imagination? Ab-sorbed and assimilated by the Vatican II document on Mary, some-times called the Church's first comprehensive memory of the Blessed Virgin, the erroneous impression persists that Mariology before Vati-can II ought to be considered *quantité négligeable*.[11] Nothing could be more misleading. Three of the major articulations of *Lumen Gentium* chapter 8, namely those regarding (1) Mary's active involvement in the salvific events, (2) her faith journey toward the accomplished religious personality, and (3) her role as model and exemplar of the Church,[12] are the fruit of important individual and collective contributions to Mar-ian studies prior to Vatican II.[13] I would like to highlight six major trends in Marian studies that characterize the development and significant articulations of Mariology prior to the Second Vatican Council. Crest-ing on the eve of Vatican II, these movements or trends either marked the culmination and the end of a historically significant development or initiated a new era in Marian discourse building on past insights and conclusions.[14] Some of these conclusions were left behind as unfinished business; others would dictate a sea change and open new perspectives in Mariology.

The Search for and Intense Discussion Regarding a Fundamental Principle in Mariology

The discussion of a fundamental principle in Mariology was triggered by M.J. Scheeben in the late nineteenth century (1882–1902) and continued—with interruptions—until the eve of Vatican II.[15] Centering in a first period on Mary's Divine Motherhood, new explorations of the issue (e.g., by Terrien, Feckes, Roschini, Dillenschneider, and de Broglie) would bring about a change in perspective after the first third of the twentieth century by recentering Mary in the Church, making of her the Archetype of the Church (as did, e.g., Semmelroth, Congar, de Lubac, and Laurentin). However, already in the 1940s attempts were made (e.g., by R. Guardini, K. Rahner, A. Müller, E. Schillebeeckx, and H. Volk) to give the fundamental principle a resolutely anthropological profile highlighting Mary's personal journey within the larger context of salvation history.[16] The search for a fundamental principle in Mariology would remain a largely open and undecided issue on the eve of Vatican II and beyond. It consecrated the laudable effort to give Mariology the status of science and concentrated the discourse on essentials, generating other essentials that enriched the overall scope of Mariology.

From a Christotypical Perspective to the New-Old Vision of Ecclesiotypical Marian Discourse

A consequence, in part, of the rediscovery of patristic theology by movements such as *nouvelle théologie*, the ecclesiotypical shift was indirectly related to the search for a fundamental principle, on the one hand, and the growing suspicion and rejection of Neo-Scholastic reasoning and method, on the other.[17] In general, Christotypical Mariology tended to show a lack of historical sensitivity. It easily overlooked

Mary's individuality and relegated her role to that of member of the Church. The result of this shift would be the retrieval of Mary as Archetype and supereminent member of the Church. Discussion and research on the relation between Mary and the Church are summarily dated about the middle of the twentieth century. From 1951 to 1953, the French Mariological Society (SFEM) devoted its annual meeting to the study of Mary and the Church.[18] Key to the comparison Mary–Church was the notion and historical reality of the *divine plan* of salvation. Mary's place in salvation history was perceived as analogous to that of the Church. The role of both was explicated in reference to the Incarnation and the redemptive work of Christ. The overall conclusion to these colloquies would establish Mary's primacy with regard to the Church, but it simultaneously reinforced the Augustinian idea of Mary's integration into the Church.[19] The two distinctive traits of primacy and integration would broaden the historical and cultural impact of the theological figure of Mary thanks to the ecclesiotypical tradition.

The Culmination of the So-Called Privilege Mariology

This ecclesiotypical tradition would find its most tangible expression in the dogmatization of the Assumption and the declaration of Mary's Queenship, the former unfortunately without any major theological and pastoral consequences.[20] The period preceding Vatican II was marked by the hotly debated doctrinal questions of Mary's mediation and co-redemption. The origin of this movement can be found in the Christotypical analogy of Mariology. A high degree of relationality between mother and son led necessarily to frequent comparison between their persons and roles. The movement was further prompted by analogical reasoning that made room for the principle of convenience. Therefore, it was convenient, albeit to a lesser degree, that Mary be called Co-redemptrix and Mediatrix of all graces.[21] But in spite of the highly abstract character of its theological method and conclusions, the Mariology of the time had a strong and motivating *Sitz im Leben*. There was a terrible need for redemption from the tragedies and consequences of two world wars, and thus an urgent call for trustworthy mediation between heaven and earth.

The Rediscovery of the Historical Dimension in Mariology

Neo-Scholasticism imploded under the onslaught of a newly discovered ethos of history.[22] This led to the rediscovery of Scripture and the questioning of its historical credibility. The newly discovered ethos spawned interest in cultural anthropology and the comparative study of race and civilizations. The liturgical awakening operated a long-awaited change in perspective by bringing God to the people in the vernacular. Ecumenism was still another newly discovered option in dealing with denominational fixism. Catholic theology itself rediscovered history in patristics and its importance for the archetypal theological formulation of the Christian message. All of these developments would teach Mariology to open and widen its thematic perspective and methodological outlook. On the eve of Vatican II Mariology took stock of its history and identity through associations, conferences, and publications. More important, it reshaped its methodological perspective by situating Mary in the famous "plan of God,"[23] which would become the paradigm of salvation history in chapter 8 of *Lumen Gentium* and open the way to a pronounced anthropological orientation of Mariology after the Council.[24]

An Intense and Multifaceted Devotional Atmosphere

Devotion thrived on major Marian apparitions—those of Lourdes, Fatima, and La Salette and also Beauraing and Banneux—but was deeply influenced by the abiding effect and impact of the dogmatization of the Immaculate Conception and related spiritualities. A host of Marian devotions and spiritualities promoted by religious congregations and movements were offered to the faithful, among them the rosary, the Miraculous Medal, and devotions to the Heart of Mary, Our Lady of Perpetual Help, Our Lady of Mt. Carmel, and the Sorrowful Mother, to mention only some of them.[25] A heritage mostly of the nineteenth-century devotional tradition, these prayers, novenas, processions, medals, and scapulars satisfied a somewhat personal and affective spiritual need but at the same time fostered religious culture and cohesiveness.

The Strong Social Definition of the Marian Movement

The first half of the twentieth century enjoyed the juxtaposition of a variety of Marian movements.[26] Aside from the classical formations of congregations and confraternities, the early decades saw the emergence not only of Catholic action and its strong Marian commitment[27] but also the foundation of new Marian associations such as the Schönstatt Movement (1914), the Miles Immaculatae (1917), and the Legion of Mary (1921). Of a different order, but important as a measure of the social expression of the Marian movement were the regular national and international Marian conferences and the rapid multiplication of Mariological societies. The strong social definition of old and new movements finds a special expression in the apostolic and even militant orientation of their foundational charters. Some of this dynamic acumen of Marian devotion and spirituality, its apostolic dimension, was lost after Vatican II. Mary became, for a time, a largely therapeutic Madonna, no longer *sender* but primarily *gatherer.*

THE ARTISTIC EQUIVALENT

Examining the relationship between Marian theology and Marian art leading up to Vatican II, we seem to be able to discover a certain degree of correspondence—similarity and even reciprocity—between the two domains. Art reflects theology, and theology seems to gel with what can be described as a theological image. Following are some characteristics of Marian art that illustrate the parallelism between the six theological features presented and our observations regarding Marian art. A necessary caveat applies. We would like these comparisons and characteristics to be understood not as conclusions hewn in stone but as reading hypotheses for what follows.

1. We discover in Marian art, especially toward the middle of the twentieth century, a tendency toward what we would like to call the foundationalist or essentialist image. This tendency characterizes the attempt to picture what artists considered essential in their rep-

resentation of Our Lady. By the same token, artists eliminated what appears to have been purely anecdotal or superfluous. We find similar developments in devotional and more artistic imagery. As mentioned, the theological parallelism to the essentialist image consists in the search for a fundamental principle.

2. Marian imagery replicating the ecclesiotypical shift in Mariology appeared to be more relational and integrated. It found identity in representations of the Pentecost scene. At the same time, a more creation-centered image discovered additional incentive to explore the riches of new cultural interpretations. In spite of this expansionist tendency, the ecclesiotypical image remained integrated in a Church-related situation.

3. On the eve of Vatican II there was an evident *mediating* quality in Marian art relating ideal and real but powerful, a Marian image oscillating between this- and other-worldliness. We attributed the theological discourse about mediation and co-redemption to the so-called privilege Mariology. The artistic equivalent gradually softened the remote character of its Marian representations. The images adopted a more anthropomorphic and democratic identity, without abandoning compassion and mercy.

4. The explosion of historical interest in theology found its equivalent in Marian art. There was a growing tendency to represent Mary in domestic situations and cultural settings, marking her return to space and time, to gentle ordinariness but also to high drama in the present. Styles and costumes catered to the needs of the time and the emerging dictate of cultural pluralism.

5. The devotional atmosphere found artistic expression in many of the pronounced subjective and affectively tinted Marian representations. However, as the twentieth century progressed, the devotional image in particular mutated to greater sobriety and realism. The historical situation and its growing pessimism regarding human nature would provoke the need for a greater proximity with Mary. Simultaneously, the figure of Mary gradually adopted features of marked humanness as we find it in the expressionist movement of this period.

6. The lively and multifaceted social character of Marian devotion and apostolic endeavor was reflected in Marian art during the whole

Marian century. Its major recipient and vehicle was the devotional image and its very widespread dissemination in households and prayer books. Frequently a tool of catechetical endeavor, holy cards and related artifacts marked the stations of Christian life from baptism to the grave, suggesting and promoting a childlike relationship with Mary, more and more devoid of apostolic impetus, as we approached the eve of Vatican II.

The attempt to show that there is an evident correspondence and parallelism between the theological discourse about Mary and its visualization in the arts leads to the obvious conclusion that the religious image, whatever its exact definition,[28] plays an important role in mediating religion, popular religion in particular.

In the following pages I focus on two types of religious images,[29] as I announced earlier with the two geographical metaphors of Epinal and Plateau d'Assy. Epinal symbolizes the strong devotional image as it evolved during the Marian century. Plateau d'Assy will lead to a better understanding of the artistic image and its somewhat erratic and multilayered development during the same time.

THE POPULAR IMAGE BETWEEN CONTINUITY AND TRANSFORMATION

Popular imagery developed in the fifteenth century and reached a temporary apex in the middle of the nineteenth century.[30] It was generically known as images of Epinal, named after a modest town in northeast France known for its mass production of popular images.[31] Epinal had reached the zenith of its commercial success at about the beginning of the Marian century and was instrumental in widely disseminating the visually inspirational Marian literature of the time.

Popular images were first printed as wood engravings. The Pellerin Company of Epinal used this process until 1865, when popular taste shifted to metal engravings, which allowed for finer print and increased production. The introduction of lithography in the first half of the nineteenth century again revolutionized the printing process, leading eventually to chromolithography, which enabled color printing.[32] Color was an important part of popular imagery. Applied by the stencil method before moving to chromolithography, the traditional colors of blue, red, and yellow were enriched with shades of indigo, brown, greenish blue, and orange red. Developing a wide range of colors was important not only to make holy cards more attractive but also to heighten the decorative impact of the ever more popular large-sized images on the walls of homes and schools. They were frequently presented, Marian images in particular, in heavy, brightly colored floral frames.

This is not the place to pursue the very interesting and culturally as well as religiously informative history of popular religious art.[33] But it should be mentioned, as obvious as this may be, that the production of religious imagery was never limited to Epinal. Other famous centers in and outside of France could be mentioned. There were especially three centers that had a major impact on the history and production of popular imagery. Germany was one of these centers, made famous by the engravings of Dürer, Holbein, and Lucas Cranach. However, the production of popular images declined rapidly in the seventeenth century. The Netherlands and Belgium were known for a long and rich tradition of popular imagery; the Catholic southern regions provided devotional images, and the Protestant northern regions focused on biblical scenes. The town of Antwerp became famous for its artists who found inspiration in old and contemporary masters, a success in part due to the distribution of devotional art by Jesuits in mission countries all over the world. After the eighteenth century, Turnhout and the Brepols Company took the place of Antwerp. Places famous in France for the production of religious and popular imagery include Toulouse, Chartres, Orléans, Lille, Metz, and Paris. In the case of Paris, the move of the imagery industry to St.-Sulpice and its environs in the middle of the nineteenth century eventually coined a devotional style identified as intimist and sentimental.

Marian images made during the Marian century participated in the general characteristics of popular imagery. In particular, they share the two objectives of religious art: They tend to be both informative and inspirational. They show and tell, with subscriptions frequently placed on holy cards, how to sustain and enrich the life of faith and prayer.

Missionaries adopted devotional images to help the faithful understand and remember the Church's teachings. The weight attributed to these two objectives was not always the same. Expression and style are subject to transformation, and so is fashion. What was rejected at one time due to new artistic insight and endeavors is periodically reclaimed by popular demand. Continuity and transformation in popular Marian art seem to have been oscillating during the Marian century between a pronounced figurative, narrative, and inspirational style and the more detached, abstract, and informative expression of the image of Our Lady.

THE EPINAL PARAMETER

The colorful Epinal images of the Marian Library Collection at the University of Dayton are typical of the middle and second half of the nineteenth century.[34] They not only reflect the coloring and style of the Epinal images; they also convey the intended meaning of this art form. Epinal stands for a down-to-earth and childlike religious sensitivity. The representation of the sleeping Christ Child (*Sommeil de Jésus*) is a familiar image. Its popular appeal comes with a simple moral lesson of silence and attention—silence and attention that can easily be extended to school and family life. Not only does the rather nondescript representation of the Mother of God (*Mater Dei*) lend this title a familiar and nonthreatening look; at the same time, a catechetical statement is made that highlights one of the most widely promoted and celebrated titles of Mary in the nineteenth century: Mother of God. The prayer at the bottom of the image reinforces the unity between doctrine about and devotion to the Mother of God. The image of Our Lady of Prompt Succor (*N.-D. de Bon-Secours*) illustrates the great variety of Marian devotions present and originating in the nineteenth century. The figure of Mary itself is of a composite nature and pinpoints its devotional diversity by combining mantle, heart, and crescent. The overall message is one of mercy and power, typical of Marian devotion in the Marian century. Similarly powerful but more ethereal is the representation of the Immaculate Conception of the Glorious Virgin Mary (*L'Immaculée Conception de la Glorieuse Vierge Marie*). As mentioned, the Immaculate Conception would be, all

Figure 1 *Sommeil de Jésus.* Large-sized polychrome print, 1850–55, Pellerin, Epinal.

Figure 2 *Mater Dei.* Large-sized polychrome print, 1850–55, Pellerin, Epinal.

Figure 3 *N.-D. de Bon-Secours.* Large-sized polychrome print, 1850–55, Pellerin, Epinal.

Figure 4 *L'Immaculée Conception de la Glorieuse Vierge Marie.* Large-sized polychrome print, 1850–55, Pellerin, Epinal.

the way to the eve of Vatican II, one of the signature images of both Marian doctrine and devotion. The four images represent what may be called the Epinal parameter of Marian popular art. Inspirational and informative, the Epinal parameter captures past and present actuality (i.e., the Immaculate Conception), catechetical and moral endeavor, and unifies doctrinal and devotional concerns.

THE PRESENCE OF THE APPARITION IMAGE

Apparition images have a preeminent place in Marian devotional art of the whole period under scrutiny. "In many ways," according to N. Glisson, "images of apparitions are similar to 'sacramentals' which continue and make an event present in response to the faith of the individual. They do not lock the event into a past contextual scene, as do paintings of the lives of Mary and the saints. Rather, they present an image of Mary never bound by the restraints of an earthly life."[35] The "sacramental" character of the apparition image conveys immediacy and proximity. At the same time, it puts an insurmountable distance between apparition and seer and reinforces the spiritual origin and powerful character of the apparition image. Thus the images of the Miraculous Medal, La Salette, Lourdes, Fatima, and other apparition images deeply marked the religious and Marian imaginations of countless faithful during the Marian century. The most prominent apparition images of the time—the Miraculous Medal, Lourdes, and Fatima—are typical representations of the *Orante*: the autonomous figure of Mary, hands folded in a prayer of adoration and supplication, for Lourdes and Fatima, or hands outspread in a gesture of mediating divine light and grace in the image of the Miraculous Medal. The image of Mary without the child Jesus but regal and remote, close to God and present to the world, was overwhelmingly present during the latter part of the nineteenth century and the early decades of the twentieth. We observe here a remote consequence of what I called privilege Mariology but also a more immediate influence of the image of the Immaculate Conception in the representations of the Miraculous Medal, Lourdes, and Fatima.

AN IMAGE OF ABSTRACT SENSUALITY

The late nineteenth-century and early twentieth-century image reflects the merger of two tendencies. The autonomous image remains prominent, a softened and somewhat less militant version of the post-Reformation image of the Queen of Heaven. It adopts some of the characteristics of the German *Jugendstil*, the French style of St.-Sulpice, and the English *pre-Raphaelite* tradition[36] and achieves a quality of abstract sensuality that is suggested by the predominantly pink and blue pastel colors, the sweet shallowness of its design, and the quasi-ethereal femininity of Our Lady. This idealized but slightly ambiguous rendering of Mary's figure has a strong emotional appeal, not least because of the impression of her simultaneous presence (colorful and subdued sensuousness) and absence (the remote, abstract, untouchable quality). There is a suggestion in this image of the eternal feminine as hailed by Goethe and reformulated in metaphysical categories by Gertrud von le Fort.[37] At the same time, this multifaceted depiction of Mary resembles a copy of the symbolist ideal of the "femme rêvée," mysterious and fragile, a creature destined to inhabit a world of spirits. It should not come as a surprise that this devotional image of Mary can be divisive in the impression it makes on people: for some it pictures the ideal of the eternal woman, for others an ideal impossible to reach.[38]

HOLLYWOOD REALISM AND THE MARIAN IMAGE

Due in part to the influence of photography and religious film in the 1930s and 1940s,[39] but also inspired by the growing rejection of the art of St.-Sulpice by intellectuals and artists,[40] a new devotional type emerged. It was largely a product of what we like to call "Hollywood realism." The representation of Our Lady is cast in a historical or modern-day setting and posture. She is more frequently reunited with her child, but only rarely does she venture into more elaborate motifs, as in the heydays of Epinal representations of Mary. The facial expressions are those typical of an actress and correspond to the aesthetic canons of the times, especially those of the movie industry. Hollywood realism seemingly succeeded in bringing Mary down to earth. However, by making her into

Figure 5 Hollywood Madonna. Mother and Child,
anon. ca. 1950, postcard.

an object of our leisure culture, Hollywood realism transformed her
from the exalted ideal of the past to a glamorous and sometimes artificial
idol of the prewar present and beyond.[41]

THE ELEMENTARY MADONNA

The elementary Madonna image marked a further step in the development of the Marian image. Was it still identified as a popular image, or
did it belong to the category of artistic images? There is no doubt that it
bore the stamp of some of the new creeds of contemporary art. In the

late 1950s and early 1960s, the artistic influence of expressionism and abstract art caught up with devotional art and provoked a rupture. The actual result of this rupture may have been, in the end, more ideological than artistic. Disavowed as kitsch,[42] that is, artificial, hollow, and affected, the devotional image fell victim to incipient religious reform in various domains from Bible to liturgy and to its call for new authenticity, honesty, and truth.[43] Not unlike the artistic and, in part, the liturgical images, the new devotional art developed a strong reactionary opinion and attitude against some of its own past expressions. Personal traits of physiognomy, sweet and colorful elements of the image, were eliminated, with only stark and elementary lines and contours of the figure of Mary retained. The iconoclastic character of this new devotional image, along with its harsh geometricism, was part of a plan to rediscover and radically redesign the essential elements of Marian representations.[44] The new approach, on top of attempting to rediscover the elementary Madonna, was intended to grant creative freedom to the artist, and to any individual, to paint or draw the Mary picture of their choice. Rather signified than represented, the empty-faced Madonna did not prevail. Soon after the Council, the harsh geometric rendering of Mary's image would soften again with the so-called Pop Madonna, retrieving, in part, its figurative or natural characteristics. Toward the end of the century still another transition would be made with the advent of the so-called "image of unanimity."[45] Indeed, during the last decade of the twentieth century, religious and Marian art had come a step closer to a certain convergence of artistic, devotional, and liturgical images. The image of unanimity attempted to hold a middle ground between plainly abstract and exaggeratedly figurative qualities with the intention of appealing to both the individual and the liturgical community.

Conclusions drawn from the various types of the popular Marian image point in two directions. For some authors, theologians but not artists, the primary attributes of the popular Mary are power and mercy, both of which are bridges between God and the world and thus between theology and culture. Other authors describe the popular image with more detail, as a living presence—maternal, mediating, and sharing in human concerns and suffering. In short, as mother Mary connotes communion, and as woman she serves as a model of Christian existence.[46]

Figure 6 The Elementary Madonna. Joseph
Barrish, 1966, clip art.

THE ARTISTIC IMAGE: AN EXERCISE IN CONTRAST
AND COMPLEMENTARITY

Contrasting Epinal with Plateau d'Assy, I would like to highlight the
difference between the devotional and the artistic image of Mary.
Chronologically speaking, the experiment of Plateau d'Assy corresponds
to the period almost immediately preceding Vatican II. The name Plateau d'Assy stands for a church and a small town in southeastern France
looking down on Chamonix and up to the Mont Blanc, the highest
mountain in Europe. Notre-Dame-de-Toute-Grâce, the parish church,
was a model of honest, sincere, and functional architecture and was well

integrated into the landscape.[47] The construction achieved in 1946, the church was ready to become a laboratory of contemporary religious art thanks to the contributions of renowned artists such as Léger, Rouault, Chagall, Lipchitz, Matisse, Bonnard, Lurçat, and Richier. However, the sources of inspiration and *spiritus rectors* were two Dominicans, Fr. Marie-Alain Couturier and Fr. Pie-Raymond Régamey.[48] Their experiment would be much discussed and abundantly commented on, but in the end it would remain isolated, and the Church of Assy would be stranded as a museum as well as a mausoleum of a daring project to reunite Church and contemporary art.[49] The experiment would nonetheless contribute to create a new consciousness and understanding of sacred art in the period after the Council.

Plateau d'Assy may be isolated as a concrete experiment, but it translated a strong desire during the period from 1920 to 1950 to bridge the gap between Church and artists. Religious art inspired by the human tragedies of the Great War, such as Rouault's *Miserere* (1916); the conversion and religious vocation of known artists like Alfred Manessier and Willibrord Verkade; and the foundation of schools and periodicals dealing with sacred art[50] were among the indicators of rapprochement. Eager to penetrate what was considered layers of nonauthenticity in contemporary art, expressionism and religion frequently joined forces to discover the core of human reality, as can be observed, for instance, in some of the Marian art by Emil Nolde.[51]

In fact, the common denominator of art in the first half of the twentieth century, art identified with the names of great artistry, was expressionism. Notwithstanding the confusing multiplicity of currents and schools like those of fauvism, cubism, Dadaism, surrealism, and abstract expressionism, the overriding thrust goes by the name of expressionism, with its radical program of deconstructing and reassembling the representation of the human person. Profoundly marked by two world wars and by cultural transformations without precedent, expressionism has been obsessed with the artistic rendering of a human condition maimed and broken, and thus with the discovery of the deeper identity of the human person. Some of these attempts have roots in the nineteenth century and in the broad currents of realism, symbolism, and impressionism. Marian art of the Marian century was marked, directly or indirectly, by most of these currents and schools.[52]

A TWOFOLD CHANGE OF PARADIGM

The images and illustrations presented lead to two important conclusions. First, religious and Marian art, in particular the latter, underwent important transformations that can easily be evidenced by contrasting Johann Friedrich Overbeck's *The Triumph of Religion in the Arts* (1840) and Max Ernst's *The Virgin Spanks the Son of Man before Three Witnesses* (1926). Overbeck's monumental painting hails the vocation of artists to be the Meistersingers and troubadours of religion. In this painting the world of art is gathered in front of Mother and Child proclaiming the triumph of religion in the arts. The parallelism with Raphael's *Disputa* is plainly palpable. Overbeck's artistic creed projects three ways or possibilities to fulfill the mission of the artist. The artist can walk the way of nature with Dürer, the way of the sublime with Michelangelo, or the way of beauty with Raphael. Overbeck opted for the third possibility and made Raphael's Madonna the central figure and reference of many of his paintings.[53]

The transformation occurred in the first decades of the twentieth century. *The Virgin Spanking* by Max Ernst signaled a change in paradigm. Religion no longer triumphed in the arts. It was then art that triumphed over religion. Demystified and spoiled of its halo, religion became the object of smug and complacent observation through the little window on the left of Ernst's painting by the three founders of the surrealist movement, André Breton, Paul Eluard, and Max Ernst himself. According to Breton's *Surrealist Manifesto* (1924), any type of expression is a pure psychic automatism exempt from aesthetic or moral concerns.[54] The new paradigm in art centered on the person of the artist and his psychic automatisms. Religion, in turn, was transformed into a laboratory of experimentation. Degraded by some to food for art, it would nonetheless be an important source of inspiration in dealing with the tragedies of contemporary history. What has been pointed out so far does not amount to a comprehensive statistical evaluation of the paradigm shift mentioned. It pinpoints a critical threshold dividing two different mentalities and their impact on the arts.

The second shift highlighted the transformation of art between Romanticism and expressionism, two movements presenting us with a rich Marian heritage. Philipp Runge's *Rest on the Flight into Egypt* (1805–6) is centered on the Child Jesus. Awakening to the first light of day while his parents, especially St. Joseph, and their donkey are still plunged in the semiobscurity of the fading night, he appears to be in playful conversation with the little angel in the nearby blooming tulip tree. The face of the mother, whose veil envelops the child, seems pensive, even preoccupied. It is the face of the Madonna, anticipating from the beginning the future passion and death of her child. The idyllic setting, the metaphorical character of the tree as a tree of life, and the immense and already sun-swept landscape in the background are some of the typical ingredients of romantic genius: the peaceful and inspiring combination of nature and symbol, the realism of the dying embers in the foreground, and the grandiose panorama that fills the horizon.

Transformation occurred with Jacques Lipchitz's *Notre-Dame-de-Liesse* (1947–50) at the Church of Plateau d'Assy. This massive bronze sculpture was Couturier's idea of a large-scale image of Our Lady. Mary stands in a heart-shaped canopy with outstretched arms welcoming the dove of the Holy Spirit into her mind, heart, and body. The quasi-identification of person and heart suggests both her welcoming joy and her total dedication to the presence of the Spirit. Angels uphold the canopy, and between them the sacrificial lamb, a symbol of the Eucharist, is looking up to the Virgin. At the back of the heart-shaped form, Lipchitz, a Jewish artist faithful to the religion of his ancestors, inscribed the deeper meaning of this artwork. Its intention is "to foster understanding between men on earth that the life of the spirit may prevail."[55] Romanticism gives way to expressionism. The narrative and symbolic style is reduced to essentials couched in quasi-abstract form. The whole is highly expressive, the message supplanting the medium, the idea replacing the story. The heart of the matter is called abstraction. Expressionism tends to transcend the form in order to liberate a maximum of meaning. Lipchitz's *Notre-Dame-de-Liesse* reflects Couturier's conviction "that abstraction— pure form with no decoration or adornment to diffuse the essence of truth—had the capacity for being the most spiritual of all art."[56]

Expressionism and the use of abstract forms allow for an exercise in personal freedom by the artist, but not only the artist. The same freedom is granted to the spectators and their interpretation of the artist's work. It is at this point that a possible conflict with religion arises. Will the personal reading of religious content by the artist be compatible with what religion considers its own sacred space? Many of the samples shown indicate that there is no hiatus between expressionist art and truly authentic Christianity.

In the end, three conclusions or perspectives may be offered to read the Marian art of the period covered by the Marian century. First, Marian art can be understood as a laboratory in which art increasingly takes advantage of and uses religion without necessarily emptying it of its sacred content. Second, Marian art safeguards its many-splendored message despite changing forms of expression, oscillating between naturalism and expressionism, between the senses and the spirit, between the proverbial *sacrum* and *profanum*. And third, the development of Marian art between Epinal and Plateau d'Assy invites a constant return to and a reminder of the ever-present foundational image of Mother and Child and its abridged synthesis of the Christian message.

SYNTHESIS EVER PRESENT

Periods are part of the constant flow of time and its historical interpretation. Styles come and go: the reflection of a passing artistic sensitivity and cultural identity. The message of religious art will forever fluctuate between culture and religion, prompted by the dialectical movement that seems a given in their relationship. Whatever the result of these observations on Marian art—whether sacred or secular, kitsch and popular, or of genuine artistic quality but seemingly non-Christian, whether of pious inspiration or for aesthetic enjoyment only—there remains the abiding and irreversible reality of Mother and Child. Marian art finds its typical, and therefore foundational, expression in the representation of Mary and the Christ Child. From the fresco of the Priscilla catacombs to Raphael's *Madonna Tempi* and Chagall's rendering of Mother and Child (1911), Marian art, in its simplest and both liveliest and loveliest expression, is a synthesis ever present of what Christianity stands for. A veritable *verbum abbreviatum illustratum*, as I have written elsewhere, "it brings together in a single and most attractive image the many facets of God's self-revelation to the world. It stresses in particular the unbreakable unity and complementarity between God and humankind. Symbol of the Incarnation, the icon of Mother and Child suggests and anticipates in subtle ways the semantics of redemption."[57] Indeed, God gives himself away and assumes fragile human reality, the beginning of redemption in divine kenosis. Jesus Christ's ontological and practical identification with the little ones coincides with a new self-understanding and new stature of the human person as illustrated in the figure of the mother representing the whole human race.

Marian art on the eve of Vatican II was a striking confirmation of this foundational Christian reality. Contested and at times vilified, popular and devotional art continued to inspire personal piety and contributed to illustrating the beliefs and habits of Christian life at the time. Its ever-growing variety and adaptation to mutating religious sensitivity amplified and diversified its expression. By the same token, it became a welcome quarry of artistic inspiration for future generations to prospect and explore. The more artistic form of Marian art described as laboratory, at least as regards Plateau d'Assy, and in spite of the largely secular inspiration and provenance of its Marian works, prepared the way to a new relationship between Church and art. This development found a friendly and staunch supporter in Paul VI—the initiator of the collection of modern religious art at the Vatican Museum in 1973[58]—and thus vindicated some of Fr. Couturier's ideas about the relationship between Church and art that he wrote about in 1941: "La pensée Catholique, parce que catholique, ne peut accepter que certains domaines de l'esprit lui soient des mondes fermés, car il est justement dans sa mission de vivre en symbiose, en Communion avec toute la vie du monde" [Catholic thought, precisely because it is catholic (i.e., universal), cannot accept that certain areas of the spirit would be worlds closed off to it, for it is rightly part of its mission to live in symbiosis, in Communion with the whole life of the world].[59] Part of this universal truth applicable to Marian art is contained in the three characterizations of Mary as God's masterpiece, God's dwelling place, and Seat of Wisdom.[60] The beauty of God's masterpiece, Mary, is a beauty of promise and fulfillment, essentially the work of the Holy Spirit; she is the overflowing presence of God's goodness in an earthen vessel. However, Mary does not allow for aesthetic fixation on herself. As God's dwelling place she points to *Deus semper major* and to the Church *semper reformanda*, for which she stands. As Seat of Wisdom, Mary represents and exemplifies both divine origin and finality for each of us.

NOTES

1. See, e.g., I. Meštrović, *About My Art* (New York: Kolo, 1924).

2. Maureen Murphy, "The Search for Right Reason in an Unreasonable World: A History of the Catholic Art Association, 1937–1970" (Ph.D. dissertation, University of Notre Dame, 1975).

3. Ibid., 200.

4. Ibid., 201.

5. The artistic image as understood here is identified with the names of prominent artists, some of them the inspirers or major representatives of schools or movements of the time.

6. Important events and developments in the history of ideas are not infrequently identified with names of persons or locations. "Epinal" stands for a small town in eastern France known for its mass production of religious images in the nineteenth century. "Plateau d'Assy" refers to a church and a village in the French Alps. The name stands for a courageous attempt to marry twentieth-century art with Church architecture. Both locations highlight the importance of the Marian century and of France as the place of art in and for Mariology.

7. Michael Morris, "Some Protestant and Catholic Images of Mary in Nineteenth- and Twentieth-Century Art," *Marian Studies* 49 (1998): 41–67.

8. Joy Sperling, "Multiples and Reproductions: Prints and Photographs in Nineteenth-Century England—Visual Communities, Cultures, and Class," in *A History of Visual Culture: Western Civilization from the 18th to the 21st Century*, ed. Jane Kromm and Susan Benforado Bakewell (Oxford: Berg, 2010), 298–303.

9. Balthasar, in *Theo-Drama: Theological Dramatic Theory*, vol. 3: *The Dramatis Personae: The Person in Christ*, trans. Graham Harrison (San Francisco: Ignatius, 1992), 447, speaks of the pathos of Christian individuals, relating it to the fact that incarnation was "brought about uniquely by them, by individuals; it continues to rest upon them." At the root of ongoing incarnation there is Jesus Christ, "the unique individual in world history who becomes universally present and universally necessary." He receives the particular feminine response to God in Mary, "an answer initially given by a single woman."

10. Thomas Aquinas, 3 *Sent.*, d. 23, q3, a1, sol.1, ad2; *ST* Ia5, 4, ad1.

11. A critical bibliography of nineteenth- and early twentieth-century Mariology would surface precious gems of early insights and initiatives on behalf of the Mary–Church relationship. To mention only two little-known but important examples: Johannes-Theodor Laurent's *Die Heiligen Geheimnisse Mariä* (Mainz: Kirchheim, 1856), one of the first great systematic presentations on Mary and the Church and a source of inspiration for M.J. Scheeben, and Lodovico di Castelplanio's *Maria nel Consiglio dell'Eterno* (Naples, 1872–73), a four-volume work and still another influence on Scheeben.

12. Johann Roten, "Memory and Mission: A Theological Reflection on Mary in the Paschal Mysteries," *Marian Studies* 42 (1991): 85.

13. Edward Schillebeeckx and Catharina Halkes, *Mary: Yesterday, Today, Tomorrow* (New York: Crossroad, 1993), 17–19.

14. René Laurentin, *Court Traité sur la Vierge Marie*, 5th éd., revised following the Council (Paris: Lethielleux, 1967), n.p.

15. Jan Radkiewicz's *Auf der Suche nach einem mariologischen Grundprinzip: Eine historisch-systematische Untersuchung über die letzten hundert Jahre* (Konstanz: Hartung-Gorre Verlag, 1988) seems to be even now the most thorough and comprehensive study on the question of the fundamental principle.

16. This presentation follows the author's developments on Mary's memory in patterns of recent theological reflection. See Johann Roten, "Memory and Mission: A Theological Reflection on Mary in the Paschal Mysteries," *Marian Studies* 42 (1991): 93–98.

17. For a concise presentation of this phenomenon, see Johann Roten, "Mary–'Personal Concretization of the Church': Elements of Benedict XVI's Marian Thought," *Marian Studies* 57 (2006): 265–76.

18. SFEM, "Marie et l'Église," I, II, III, *Bulletin de la Société Française d'Études Mariales* 9–11 (1951–53).

19. These two traits will favor a personalized and concrete reading of the Church as we find it in Ratzinger's perception of Mary as the "personal concretization of the Church." As he was writing in the wake of authors like de Lubac, Semmelroth, Balthasar, and Laurentin—and their mainly preconciliar works—there is no doubt that these scholars marked Ratzinger's Marian thinking. It may not come as a surprise that both Ratzinger and Laurentin use practically identical terms to characterize Mary. Ratzinger's personal concretization of 1978 echoes Laurentin's "suprême réalisation personnelle" of 1952—the eve of Vatican II notwithstanding. See Roten, "Mary–'Personal Concretization of the Church,'" 274.

20. Classical Mariology distinguishes four methodological principles: (1) the principle of transcendent singularity; (2) the principle of fittingness or convenience; (3) the principle of eminence, and (4) the principle of analogy or resemblance to Christ. See G. Roschini, *Mariologia*, vol. 1 (Rome: A. Belardetti, 1947), 351–69. Combined, these principles constitute what is termed privilege Mariology. According to E. Neubert, the rules of fittingness and privileges "have never helped the theologians to discover a new truth, but only to confirm truths arrived at by the Christian consciousness of the faithful. On the contrary, the rule of analogies between the privileges of Christ and those of Mary is precise and fruitful." E. Neubert, *Mary in Doctrine* (Milwaukee: Bruce, 1954), 7. René Laurentin wrote in 1973: "Both the Immaculate Conception and the Assumption are subsidiary doctrines, and these pronouncements, whose significance was considerably exaggerated in the writing of the time, which implied that they would be vital sources for a new era in the Church, appear in retrospect as of minor importance. Nothing indicates that they have prompted any re-

newal, even where devotion to Mary is concerned. On the contrary, the defini-tion of the Assumption was followed by a kind of distaste, both for the dogma and for the feast." See Eamon R. Carroll, "A Survey of Recent Mariology," *Marian Studies* 37 (1986), 180; Paul E. Duggan, *The Assumption Dogma: Some Reactions and Ecumenical Implications in the Thought of English-Speaking Theologians* (Cleveland, OH: Emerson, 1989), 160.

21. For a history of the movement between 1926 and 1946, see Gloria Fal-cão Dodd, *The Virgin Mary, Mediatrix of All Grace: History and Theology of the Movement for a Dogmatic Definition from 1896 to 1964* (New Bedford, MA: Academy of the Immaculate, 2012), 185–235.

22. The impact on Mariology can be shown in the proceedings of the many national and international congresses and in some of the more prominent encyclopedic works on Mary. A striking example of this shift in method can be observed in the work of Emilio Campana (1874–1939). A disciple of Cardinal A. H. M. Lépicier, O.S.M., Campana wrote a much-publicized and -used manual of Mariology in 1909. See *Maria nel Dogma Cattolico*, 6th ed. (Turin: Marietti, 1945). Campana's second work of importance—*Maria nel Culto Cattolico*, 2 vols. (Turin: Marietti, 1933)—shows an evident change in method insofar as it delib-erately combines the history and theory of Marian devotion.

23. Marie-Joseph Nicolas, "Marie et l'Église dans le plan divin," *Études Mariales* 11 (1953): 163.

24. An early pre-conciliar example of this development can be seen in Thomas J. M. Burke, S.J., (ed.), *Mary and Modern Man* (New York: The America Press, 1954), a collection of essays attempting "to explore the relevance of Mary as a cultural ideal for modern man" (vii).

25. Vol. 5 of *De Cultu Mariano Saeculis XIX et XX usque ad Concilium Vaticanum II apud varias nationes* (Rome: Pontificia Academia Mariana Internationalis, 1991) witnesses the vast and varied expressions of Marian devotions of the time.

26. See, e.g., Hilda Graef, *Mary: A History of Doctrine and Devotion*, with a new chapter covering Vatican II and beyond by Thomas A. Thompson, S.M. (Notre Dame, IN: Ave Maria Press, 2009), 398.

27. May it suffice to mention the names of two individuals: Eduard Poppe (1890–1924) and Joseph Cardinal Cardijn (1882–1967). Prominent figures of the Belgian church, they both believed in the importance of the unity between social action and spirituality and in the prominent role of Mary in this endeavor. See Th. Koehler, "Maria nella vita della chiesa nel sec. XX dal 1914 fino al 1974," in *Storia della mariología*, vol. 5 (Pallanza: Centro Mariano Chaminade, 1976), 49–55.

28. This definition is frequently a matter of school, style, and even ideol-ogy. See the controversy regarding the meaning of sacred art in Violette-Anne Onfroy-Curley, "The 'Querelle de l'Art Sacré' and the Church of Assy: Renewal or Denial of the Sacred in Art?" (M.A. thesis, Department of Theology, University of Dayton, 2009), 2–6.

29. To accommodate the limitations of space for text and visuals, the main focus of this chapter is on the devotional Marian image. For the second type of religious image, the artistic expression of this devotion, I limit myself to a general introduction and conclusion.

30. See Alan Shestack, *Fifteenth-Century Engravings of Northern Europe from the National Gallery of Art*, catalogue (Washington, DC: National Gallery of Art, 1967).

31. The history of Epinal, its printing companies, and its meaning for religious and Marian popular art is well documented. See M.-B. Bouvet, *Le grand livre des images d'Epinal* (Paris: Solar, 1996), and J. Mistler, *Epinal et l'imagerie populaire* (Paris: Hachette, 1961).

32. The historical context is sketched in Helena W. Lepovitz, *Images of Faith: Expressionism, Catholic Folk Art, and the Industrial Revolution* (Athens: University of Georgia Press, 1991).

33. *Imagiers de paradis: Images de piété populaire du XVe au XXe siècle* (Brussels: Crédit Communal, 1990).

34. This collection comprises thirty-four large-sized reproductions that can be grouped according to the following themes: Jesus Christ and the Holy Family (4); the Life of Mary (7); the Saints and Mary (2); Marian titles (10); and places dedicated to Mary (11). See Violette-Anne Onfroy-Curley, *Images of Epinal: A Modern Bible of the Poor*, exhibit brochure (Dayton, OH: Marian Library/International Marian Research Institute, University of Dayton, 2000).

35. N. Glisson, "Images of Visions: Marian Devotional Images from the Nineteenth and Twentieth Centuries in North America," *Marian Studies* 49 (1998): 103.

36. A reaction against academic art of the time, which sought abstraction, codification, and universalization, the art of popular taste turned to a softened and somewhat sentimentalized style close to the hearts of the people, which was available and affordable. Regarding the appeal of Saint-Sulpician art, see Onfroy-Curley, "The 'Querelle de l'Art Sacré' and the Church of Assy," 14.

37. *Die ewige Frau: Die Frau in der Zeit; Die zeitlose Frau* (Munich: Kösel and Pustet, 1934).

38. See Stéphane Michaud, *Muse et madone: Visages de la femme de la Révolution française aux apparitions de Lourdes* (Paris: Seuil, 1985).

39. M. Morris, "Some Protestant and Catholic Images of Mary in Nineteenth- and Twentieth-Century Art," *Marian Studies* 49 (1998): 58–59.

40. The success of Saint-Sulpice art, described as a "saccharine religious experience," was perceived as residing in the thrust to promote laziness of the mind, meditation, and heart. See Onfroy-Curley, "The 'Querelle de l'Art Sacré' and the Church of Assy," 17–18.

41. In the words of a contemporary witness: "Questi films testimoniano l'importanza della Vergine nella vita della Chiesa. Spesso, però, si manifesta una

curiosità troppo umana che stenta a rendere le dimensioni religiose della vita di Gesù e di Maria." [These films testify to the importance of the Virgin in the life of the Church. Often, however, an overly human curiosity is manifested, which struggles to render the religious dimension of the life of Jesus and Mary.] See Koehler, *Maria nella vita della Chiesa*, 32.

42. T. Corringe, "Theological Table Talk: Kitsch and the Task of Theology," *Theology Today* 56 (July 1999): 231.

43. See, e.g., Marie-Alain Couturier, *Art et liberté spirituelle*, with a preface by Kim En Joong (Paris: Cerf, 2008, 1958), 16.

44. It should be noted that the development of abstract painting happened early in the twentieth century. Not only did Picasso and Braque mount a severe critique against representation in their Cubist period (1908–9), but, most famously, Vassily Kandinsky, in his 1912 essay *On the Spiritual in Art*, related abstraction to spiritual revival. Sarah Warren, "The Reality of the Abstract Image: Rethinking Spirituality in Abstraction," in *A History of Visual Culture*, ed. Kromm and Bakewell, 319.

45. Frédéric Debuyst, *L'art chrétien contemporain de 1962 à nos jours* (Paris: Mame, 1988), 56–63.

46. See Johann Roten, "Popular Religion and Marian Images," *Marian Studies* 45 (1994): 68.

47. Onfroy-Curley, "The 'Querelle de l'Art Sacré' and the Church of Assy," 41.

48. The ideas of Couturier and Régamey are inspired by their preoccupation with a growing and widening hiatus between the Catholic Church and artists of the twentieth century who were creating religious art. According to these authors, genuine art is religious in nature. It is of a deeply personal inspiration and has universal significance. See, e.g., M.-A. Couturier, *Sacred Art* (Austin: University of Texas Press, 1989), and P.-R. Régamey, *Religious Art in the Twentieth Century* (New York: Herder and Herder, 1963).

49. For the history of the controversy about Plateau d'Assy, see Onfroy-Curley, "The 'Querelle de l'Art Sacré' and the Church of Assy," 54–79.

50. Other than Couturier and Régamey, Maurice Denis (1870–1943) was one of the major reformers of Catholic religious art in the first half of the twentieth century. His call to sanctify nature led to a new perception of Marian art. Denis published his ideas on art in *Nouvelles Théories sur l'art moderne, sur l'art sacré, 1914–1921* (Paris: Rouart and Watelin, 1922). In Germany, the Beuron School promoted the revival of Catholic art with linear sobriety and quasi-geometric simplicity in form and expression. See Hubert Krins, *Die Kunst der Beuroner Schule: Wie ein Lichtblick vom Himmel* (Beuron, Germany: Beuroner, 1998).

51. See W. Haftmann, *Emil Nolde* (New York: Harry N. Abrams, 1959).

52. For the broader historical context, see W. Haftmann, *Painting in the Twentieth Century*, 2 vols. (New York: F. A. Praeger, 1956), and H. H. Arnason,

History of Modern Art (New York: Harry N. Abrams, 1968); for the present context, see Johann Roten, "Popular Religion and Marian Images," *Marian Studies* 45 (1994): 75–76.

53. K. Gallwitz, ed., *Die Nazarener in Rom: Ein deutscher Künstlerbund der Romantik* (Munich: Prestel, 1981), 155.

54. A. Breton, *Manifestoes of Surrealism*, trans. Richard Seaver and Helen R. Lane (Ann Arbor, MI: Ann Arbor Paperbacks, 1971).

55. W. S. Rubin, *Modern Sacred Art and the Church of Assy* (New York: Columbia University Press, 1961), 126–27.

56. Lai-Kent Chew Orenduff, *The Transformation of Catholic Religious Art in the Twentieth Century: Father Marie-Alain Couturier and the Church at Assy, France* (Lewiston, NY: Edwin Mellen, 2000), 161.

57. Johann Roten, "Mary and the Way of Beauty," *Marian Studies* 49 (1998): 114.

58. See "Paul VI et l'art," *Journée d'études* (Paris), January 27, 1988 (Brescia, Italy: Pubblicazioni dell 'Istituto Paolo VI,' 1989).

59. M.-A. Couturier, O.P., *Art et Catholicisme* (Montreal: Editions de l'Arbre, 1941), 80–81.

60. See *Catechism of the Catholic Church* (Liguori, MO: Liguori Publications, 1994), 191–92, 721–26.

RESSOURCEMENT
THEOLOGIANS
AND RESPONSE

CHAPTER 4

"A Very Considerable Place in the Mystery of Christ and the Church"?

Yves Congar on Mary

CHRISTOPHER RUDDY

It must be admitted from the outset: Mary plays a marginal role in Yves Congar's theology, one more corrective than constructive (or, at most, constructive by way of correction). Of his nearly one thousand publications from 1924 to 1967, for instance, Mary figures prominently in fewer than twenty—the most significant of which were a short book and a handful of articles published largely between 1950 and 1955.[1] Such massive, influential works as *True and False Reform in the Church* or *Lay People in the Church* make virtually no substantial reference to Mary, to the point that it is nearly impossible to imagine someone writing a book on the "Marian profile" of Congar's ecclesiology, as has been done regarding that of Hans Urs von Balthasar.[2] And when one considers his sustained, even violent, polemic against the "galloping Mariology" that he held to have afflicted much of the Catholic life and thought of his era,[3] one might reasonably wonder what good might come from a closer examination of his thought on Mary. Where does one go after reading passages from his personal journals such as the following, written after a discussion in September 1963 with the Belgian Cardinal Leo Suenens, one of the Second Vatican Council's four moderators: "The mariological *zelanti* would like 'to add new flowers' to Mary's crown. This maximizing theology is not healthy. IT WOULD BE MUCH BETTER TO DO NOTHING."[4] Or this comment, in response to a Spanish bishop's conciliar intervention on Mary: "IDIOCIES: a combination of verbalism, abstract dialectic and sentimentalism."[5]

And yet Congar's writings on Mary, secondary as they may be, merit exploration because they help to shed light on the mystery of Christ and the Church, offer a window into Congar's own life and thought, and help us understand the historical and theological movements that shaped twentieth-century Catholicism, especially in relation to Vatican II. Congar identified three different Marian "periods" in his life: (1) the period of the "simple" devotion of his youth and early religious life, which saw him writing "Ave" at the top of his papers, as did Aquinas, he notes with perhaps some defensiveness; (2) the period of his struggle against a "galloping Mariology," a period that overlapped with Pius XII's pontificate; and (3) a "third stage" from the 1960s onward, marked by his standing in the "mainstream" of Catholic and ecumenical theology.[6] This chapter, befitting a book about a conference on Mary on the eve of the Second Vatican Council, focuses on the second of these periods, wherein Congar labored against an untethered Mariology, even a Mariolatry, and for an integrated, ecumenical Mariology situated firmly in the twinned saving mysteries of Christ and his Church. One can only smile, in this context, when one reads the full title of the eighth and concluding chapter of *Lumen Gentium*: "The Blessed Virgin Mary, Mother of God, in the Mystery of Christ and the Church."

I proceed in three steps. First I look at Congar's critique of a maximalist Mariology and his counterpointed effort to develop a more balanced, soteriological theology of Mary. Second I examine his correction of the Marian "minimalism" that he saw as characteristic of Protestantism, particularly in its Barthian, neoorthodox strains. Finally I consider the achievements and legacy of Congar's Mariology, taking into account our sometimes markedly different contemporary ecclesial and theological context.

CONGAR'S CRITIQUE OF A MAXIMALIST MARIOLOGY

Congar wrote: "I saw [during a September 1961 meeting of the Council's Preparatory Theological Commission] the drama which I have experienced all my life. The need to fight, in the name of the Gospel and of the apostolic faith, against a development, a Mediterranean and Irish proliferation, of a Mariology which does not come from Revelation, but is backed up by pontifical texts."[7] Congar's Mariology unfolded largely in the clash between two theological approaches: an isolated maximalism and an economic-soteriological integration. This conflict took place on the level of both method and doctrine. Methodologically, Congar's thought was marked by a sustained polemic and argument against what he called a "separated Mariology"[8] in which theologians considered Mary apart from economic or soteriological concerns and considered Mariology as a separate branch of theology. He held that such separation was inseparable from a broader "movement which isolated mediations and magnified them to excess." The pope was isolated from the college of bishops; religious from other believers on account of their purportedly greater call to holiness; and priests from their people, both liturgically and culturally.[9]

In Congar's view, this isolation had medieval roots, stretching back to the eighth century. Most broadly, it dovetailed with the rise of Scholasticism and dialectic. Dialectical Scholasticism studied things "not so much in a total synthesis, according to their meaning and relationships, as in themselves, in their nature and their own contours; then [it sought] to analyze the nature and the properties of each thing thus considered in itself and for itself."[10] Scholasticism, Congar writes, was an intellectual advance, prioritizing "analytical knowledge, explicit and precise, according to a somewhat Cartesian ideal."[11] But he also notes its flaws. First it gave rise to separated theological treatises on Mary and on the Church especially, which formerly had been integrated, as with Aquinas, into the treatise on Christ.[12] Mariologically, Congar locates the source of this shift from an economic, integrated approach to a separated, self-contained one in two monks: the eighth-century Ambrosius Autpertus and the ninth-century Paschasius Radbertus. The former was the first in Latin literature to give sermons whose subject was Mary herself, while the latter placed Mary above the Church and began to apply themes to

Mary as an individual that had previously been applied to the Church as a whole.[13] Congar sees a similar evolution at work in iconography, whereby in the West, from the twelfth century onward, Mary was increasingly depicted by herself or even as being at the center, crowned by Christ. He notes the then-Protestant Max Thurian's comment that the Miraculous Medal depicts Mary "with open arms, without Jesus."[14] In contrast to what was seen in a more patristic mode of theology and iconography, Mary "began to be considered *in herself* and no longer in the economy of salvation. The doctrine of her personal privileges was developed."[15]

One consequence of this isolated method was a methodological maximalism in which theologians and church leaders sought to "obtain the maximum 'development' of certain mariological theses."[16] Such development was a farce, in his view, given its ahistorical, decontextualized proof texting of Scripture and tradition. This thoroughly "non-resourced" Catholicism stood in contrast to a genuinely "re-sourced Catholicism," centered in Christ and equally "biblical, liturgical, paschal, communitarian, ecumenical, and missionary."[17] Writing in his journal a year before the Council began, he noted the parallels between the incremental yet seemingly inexorable growth of papal authority and that of Mariology:

> It is the same way of behaving, the same process. In both cases, an enormous outgrowth resting on two or three texts, with no certainty that these texts meant originally what they are now being taken to mean, and in which the ancient tradition had not seen all that is now seen in them, even if, sometimes, it had not understood the opposite. They go on repeating, here *"Tu es Petrus,"* there *"gratia plena," "stabat," "conteret caput tuum,"* etc. In each case, tirelessly, patiently, across the centuries little steps forward are constantly being taken which, at the time, seem of little account. One is not too happy, perhaps, indeed, one does not agree; but one will not create a schism over that, one will not even maintain simple resistance over such a trifle. In each case, there is ONE idea only: to increase, to take as far as possible either a power or a glory. In each case, there is only one aim, and advantage is taken of everything for the sake of that. EVERYTHING IS MADE USE OF. In each case you are told, it is pointed out to you that, having granted such and such, you cannot refuse such

other; that having gone as far as three, you cannot not agree to go as far as ten. . . . In each case, a point gained is never let go of, they just go on adding to it.[18]

The end result was a degeneration into an amateurish "spiritual theology"[19] originating from a particular spiritual experience or devotion; lacking a perspective on the whole Christian mystery; cut off from the sources of Christian tradition; wanting in scholarly rigor and submission to objective, revealed truth; cheapened by sentimentality; and propounded by "fourth-rate theologians" unknown in other fields of theology and not distinguished "by the balance of [their] thought."[20] These are the very "idiocies" derided by Congar in his conciliar journal.

By contrast, Congar proposes an economic, resourced, and holistic approach to Mariology. He situates Mary in the divine plan of salvation and within the Church as a whole.[21] She must always be located within and not above the Church, not even as the "neck" connecting Christ and the Church, an image of St. Bernard that Congar rejects.[22] Second, Congar's approach undertakes the work of *ressourcement*. While an isolated maximalism tends to work by deduction from atemporal principles, Congar returns to the sources of Christian tradition, especially scriptural and patristic ones. He is mindful that tradition is not simply a collection of texts but the "living deposit, the living principles of the economy of salvation."[23] Finally, his method evinces a "healthy respect for the whole of things."[24] It takes seriously the analogy of faith and sees both Christian life and thought as suffused by mediation in every relationship and activity.[25]

Alongside these theological grounds, Congar's rejection of an isolated maximalism likely has a deep personal source: his relationship with Daniel Lallement, the priest and philosopher who helped him as an adolescent to discover his priestly and religious vocation and to develop a scholastic rigor of thought. Congar remained grateful for that formation, but the two men grew apart over time due to intellectual and political differences. Congar saw in Lallement's "Mariolatry" the "substitution for Christianity of a Mariano-Christianity"[26] and recalled him saying, "It is no longer I who live, but Mary who lives in me,"[27] an obvious allusion to Galatians 2:20. Allied to Lallement's intense Marian devotion was what Congar described as a supernaturalism that rejected the world and the historical dimensions of human existence.[28] Given the almost primal desire for contact with the world that is manifested in Congar's diaries,[29] it seems likely that he associated intense Marian devotion with a reactionary, cramped political, spiritual, and ecclesial worldview.

In terms of doctrine, Congar's constructive Mariology emerges most clearly in his 1954 article "Marie et l'Église dans la pensée patristique," which offers a careful reading of patristic thought as a corrective to what he regards as the distorted reception of that thought across succeeding centuries, particularly in Matthias Scheeben and his heirs. Congar begins by noting that the first four centuries of the Christian era offered "three main affirmations" concerning Mary: that (1) Mary is the "Type" of the Church, precisely in her virginal maternity; (2) Mary is the recapitulation of Eve; and (3) there is a continuity between Mary and the Church that parallels that between Christ and the members of his body.[30] I focus on this first affirmation, both because Congar considers it the central patristic insight into Mary and because it exemplifies the heart of his mariological thought.

Congar's point of departure is that the Church Fathers rarely considered Mary in herself; they considered her only in relation to Christ and the Church. In contrast to some postpatristic theologians, they did not speak of her "privileges," her redemptive causality, or her causality or spiritual maternity vis-à-vis the Church.[31] "The mystery of Mary," he writes, must instead be placed "within the framework of the mystery of the Church, and this mystery within the framework of the economy [of salvation]."[32] This tethering or integration of Mary to ecclesiology and soteriology is the foundation of Congar's Mariology.

Congar holds that much modern or even "post-Bedian" Mariology has gone astray by limiting its analysis to the two terms "Mary" and the "Church" while forgetting the broader, more fundamental third reality of the divine economy.[33] The "two-term" approach, which Congar associates with modern-day heirs of Scheeben's Mariology, results in seeing the Church as dependent on Mary, as a stream depends on a source or spring. Congar admits that some patristic texts, taken in isolation and then used to support Neo-Scholastic "theses" as supposedly *probatur ex traditione*,[34] can be interpreted in this manner. This approach, though, reads the Fathers through a lens foreign to them, a lens more Aristotelian than Platonic. According to Congar, where the former approach seeks truth in things themselves or through precise philological and historical studies, the Fathers followed a Platonic approach. They thus "sought truth in an idea above time, of which events were only successive expressions and progressive realizations, and of which texts were but a manifestation or a witness. They contemplated a heavenly reality descending to the earth, unfolding and revealing itself there."[35] Salvation history is thus read as a series of words, deeds, and persons that prefigure or prepare for the definitive reality of Jesus Christ by Mary's virginal maternity. "Typological" interpretation flows directly from such a view of reality.[36]

Congar argues that for the Fathers the "most decisive trait" of this economy of salvation was that "we are born from above," spiritually, not carnally,[37] and its end or culmination is the Church, "the first creature of God" and "the very reality of salvation and of communion with God."[38] He notes further that "the earliest Christian thought" moved in the framework of St. Paul's affirmation in Galatians 4:26 that our mother is the heavenly Jerusalem from above, and not carnally, from below.[39]

Mary and the Church are linked through this wholly spiritual birth from above. Virginal motherhood means, most deeply, that this birth comes entirely from God alone and has nothing of the earthly.[40] Mary's own virginal motherhood bears witness to this birth from above, for her fiat in faith is "not the energy by which she conceived and bore Jesus, but more the disposition by which the unique energy of the Holy Spirit was able to work in her."[41] Mary is thus not the source, in herself, of what is realized in the Church, but rather the first-typical appearance and realization of the mystery of the Church, which preexists believers.[42] She is in the Church, not above it or before it. The Fathers, most clearly the Alexandrians and other Africans but also Irenaeus, thought first of the Church, which is the goal or end of the economy, and then saw Mary as the one in whom this mystery is realized "first and decisively."[43] "There is continuity, but not communication," Congar writes, "because, for the Fathers, the principle of this continuity is found in the plan of God, not in the power [vertu] of Mary's maternity itself. This is what, in particular, the patristic idea of 'type' expresses."[44] One thus cannot derive the Church from Mary as an effect from a cause.[45] Mary and the Church are rather "one and the same mystery in two moments."[46] For Congar, Mary is thus the one whose virginal motherhood is a type or instantiation of the Church's virginal motherhood. She must always be understood as existing within the Church and in relationship to Christ, the Church, and the divine plan of salvation:

> Except in what touches on Christology and the economy of salvation, [the Church Fathers] do not seek to put forth affirmations of a Marian theology, that is to say, to develop and systematize statements on the personal privileges of the Virgin Mary, a "Lehre von Maria" [doctrine or teaching on Mary]. They are concerned with a doctrine of the economy of salvation, which is realized in the Church and begun in Mary. In this perspective, we repeat, the continuity between Mary and the Church is not direct, as by an extension of the maternity of Mary which would engender members [of the Church] just as she conceived and bore the Head. This continuity is established [*faite*], not by the spiritual energies of the Virgin Mary, but by the mystery that God unfolds and realizes, both in Mary and in the Church.[47]

CORRECTION OF MARIAN "MINIMALISM"

Congar writes: "In Christology as well as in ecclesiology and Mariology the crux of the argument [between Protestants and Catholics] is the part played by mankind, the scope and extent of creaturely co-operation with the Creator."[48] A second Marian deformation that Congar seeks to redress was the converse problem of minimalism in neoorthodox Protestant thought. Whereas Congar's critique of Catholic maximalism centered on its methodological and doctrinal isolation of Mary as well as its distorted reading of the Church's tradition, his fundamental difference with a Protestant minimalism concerned its diminishment, even denial, of creaturely cooperation in the economy of salvation. Two works are particularly relevant here: *Christ, Our Lady, and the Church* and "Marie et l'Église chez les Protestants"; both were published in 1952, just two years after Pope Pius XII's dogmatic definition of Mary's Assumption.

Writing on the fifteen hundredth anniversary of Chalcedon, Congar argues in *Christ, Our Lady, and the Church* that ecclesiological and mariological differences between Catholics and Protestants flow from a Christological difference over the salvific role of Christ's humanity.[49] His interlocutors are Protestant theologians, especially Martin Luther and Karl Barth. Congar sees in Barth a conception of God's action as touching "our world without entering it," for it is "free, unpredictable and discontinuous,"[50] as well as an ecclesiology that envisions the Church's task as that of John the Baptist in Grünewald's "Crucifixion," that is, pointing to Christ without actually touching him. Congar likewise sees in Luther the conviction that *"everything* in the work of God must proceed from God alone and be solely God's doing. . . . The humanity of Christ plays no part in the causality of Redemption in Luther's thought."[51] Congar holds that the Reformers generally envisioned the Incarnation not as an elevation of human nature so that it becomes an instrument of salvation but rather as the "burying of God in a human nature."[52] The result is, in the case of Luther, at once a Nestorian gulf between Christ's two natures and a monophysite-monoenergetic denial of a full human nature. Motivated by a rightful desire to affirm God's transcendent otherness, such approaches nonetheless fail to account for the reality of divine self-communication and also exclude any salvific role for Christ's humanity. Congar holds instead that "the sacred Humanity united to the Divinity without confusion or division is the instrument of our salvation, and the means by which all grace is communicated to us."[53] The mariological and ecclesiological consequences of human mediation-agency are evident:

> But in setting up this union of heaven and earth accomplished in person by Jesus Christ, a share is also to be attributed to our Lady through her cooperation in the mystery of the Incarnation, and to the Church because it communicates to us the effects which flow from the Incarnation. This is no doubt why the story of Jacob's ladder is often applied to our Lady by ancient writers, and why the Liturgy uses it in the Office of the Dedication of a Church with profound ecclesiological application. Here then, it may be reiterated, is a meeting point upon which our Lady and the Church conclusively

and positively converge; each, that is, represents the part that human instrumentality is given in the work of salvation through the Incarnation; the one brings it about, the other communicates it to men and permeates the world with its effects.[54]

Congar thus concludes the first part of *Christ, Our Lady, and the Church* by stating, "Our [Catholic] belief about our Lady and the Church derives from the wholeness of the traditional testimony of the undivided Church concerning Christ."[55]

A year later, in 1952, Congar published an essay, "Marie et l'Église chez les Protestants," which applied this Christological argument more closely to recent neoorthodox Protestant studies of Mary and her relationship to the Church.[56] He begins by noting that Protestant thought on Mary has grown out of a broader reaction against Catholic devotional excesses and doctrinal positions (e.g., merit, human satisfaction, human mediation), a reaction that excludes any soteriological role for Mary.[57] Protestantism instead commonly makes a twofold affirmation: (1) Mary is within (and not above or beyond) the bounds of the Church, and (2) her particular role in the Church is in the realm of faith in the Word and as a type of the Church but without exercising any kind of redemptive mediation.[58] She offers an exemplary witness but not any communication of grace or salvation. Moreover, she is on the same level as other witnesses (e.g., Abraham, John the Baptist, Peter),[59] and is unique only in that her faith and obedience are exercised directly and immediately to Jesus through her motherhood.[60]

Mary is therefore affirmed as the virginal mother of Jesus according to the flesh but not the spirit.[61] From her physical maternity flows neither a soteriological role proper to Mary nor a spiritual maternity.[62] Congar notes that Protestants accordingly criticize the Catholic "suture point" between Mary as Mother of God and Mary as mother of the mystical body that is the Church.[63] She is acceptable as a figure or type of the Church only insofar as she is an exemplary witness of an obedient faith in the Word of God;[64] though the first and most perfect of the faithful, she remains a member of the Church.[65] Protestant thought thereby recognizes a certain ecclesial maternity in preaching and faith but not a Marian maternity.[66]

Having completed his survey of modern neoorthodox Protestant thought on Mary, Congar turns to examine four roots of the Marian disagreement between Catholics and Protestants: Christology, the place of human cooperation in God's saving work, conceptions of grace, and theological method. First Congar argues, as I mentioned earlier in this chapter, that Christologically a certain type of dialectical scholasticism gave rise to a separated Mariology that began to examine Mary in herself, sometimes apart from a constant reference to Christ. He holds that the two Marian dogmas concern Mary's dignity in herself ("even if they always have a clear Christological reference"[67]) and that some Catholic theologians' uses of "Mediatrix" and especially "Co-redemptrix" do not always appear to be "felicitous [heureux]."[68] In contrast, he notes that the Orthodox, in their theology and iconography, do not practice such separatism and admits that Protestant thought raises a legitimate question as to how well Catholic theology has always upheld the biblical affirmation of the "unity and absolute sufficiency" of Christ's mediation.[69]

Second, Congar returns to the role of human cooperation in God's gracious saving work. He notes again that Protestantism excludes human cooperation: "God is always subject and never object; in contrast, the human person, in matters of salvation, is always object and never subject."[70] Jesus's conception and birth, in this view, are not something that Mary does but something that she receives; she has no active role save that of her fiat, which "receives and recognizes that God is at work in her."[71] Congar likewise notes that, on these grounds, several Protestants are able to see, perhaps surprisingly, in Mary's Immaculate Conception an affirmation that Mary's cooperation is "founded on pure grace, on a restoration through the anticipated grace of the Cross and Easter of a [human] nature we hold to be spoiled by sin."[72] Congar comments that one might view these Catholic–Protestant differences concerning human cooperation through the lens of the *analogia entis*, as does Karl Barth, but he suggests that the perspective of the *imago Dei* is more helpful, for it permits and calls for partnership and response between God and God's rational creatures; if the *analogia entis* is the "distant" or "remote" ground of human cooperation, the *imago Dei*, disfigured but not erased by sin, is that cooperation's "immediate" and "proper" foundation.[73]

Related to the role of human cooperation is a third area of difference: grace. Congar refers here again to Max Thurian, who argues that Protestants see grace less as the "incarnation of divine power in humanity" and more as the "elevation of the Christian with Christ to the right hand of the Father, not stopping on earthly things but pushing ahead for heavenly treasure."[74] Thurian adds that Protestants likewise view God's graceful action more as the "merciful attitude" of the Father than as the "physical transformation" worked by the Holy Spirit.[75] One sees grace as an act or decision of God, while the other sees it ontically and physically, communicated to man and changing his nature.[76] Congar holds that, at root, Catholicism conceives of grace as an "economy of communication" and as a "theology of Incarnation," whereas Protestantism sees grace through "a logic of announcement and anticipation [attente], of promise received in faith";[77] its ideal is "less Mary than John the Baptist,"[78] in Congar's incisive phrase.

Connected directly to these different conceptions of human cooperation and grace is a final difference of theological method: Catholic thought works within a sapiential-ontological framework that seeks to know the ontic reality of things, while Protestantism adopts a soteriological-dialectical method in which God is revealed only in what he is and does for humanity. Whereas Catholics are "interested in the reality of the gifts of God in us, Protestants want to see only God giving or, better, God deciding to give and regard all interest in the gift itself as a betrayal of the one who gives it."[79] One may say that, for Congar, Catholic theology is participatory, while Protestant theology is oppositional. He concludes this section by noting once again that for (neoorthodox) Protestant thought, "God is always the subject, humanity never."[80] The Marian ramifications are evident.

Toward the end of his article, Congar notes several promising Protestant theological efforts to articulate a more appreciative theology of Mary, the foremost of which is the Lutheran theologian Hans Asmussen's 1950 book *Maria, die Mutter Gottes*. He sees in Asmussen's work the possibility of a more fruitful Protestant response to the question "Salvifically, is Mary on the side of God or of humanity?" Asmussen holds that Mary is on the side of humanity, as she does not exercise any salvific mediation alongside God. He notes, though, that Ephesians 1–4 speaks of a "visible salvation" (Eph. 1–2) that has been entrusted to human ministers (Eph. 3–4) in such a way that these ministers can be considered to be on the side of God. One may indeed say that we are all on the side of God in a real way. He then proposes that one see Mary as exercising a salvific mediation not next to Christ (*Mittlerschaft neben*) but in Christ (*in Christus*).[81] She can thus be, salvifically, on the side of both God and humanity, all the while respecting Christ's unique salvific mediation and humanity's utter dependence on his mediation. The ecumenical promise of Asmussen's position is clear.

Congar concludes "Marie et l'Église chez les Protestants" by acknowledging the twofold situation that existed as he wrote in 1952: (1) an emergent Protestant rediscovery of Mary and (2) Pope Pius XII's dogmatic definition of the Assumption, which, Congar holds, arrested that rediscovery and caused a "year of struggle" for ecumenism.[82] Encouraging this Protestant rediscovery of the mystery of Mary through reflection on the mystery of Church, he returns at the end of his article to the hope that he had expressed in *Christ, Our Lady, and the Church*: that this renewal of interest in the mysteries of the Church and Mary will lead to a renewed consideration of the mystery of the redemptive incarnation, which alone gives the former mysteries their proper scope and meaning.

One senses Congar's confidence that such a *ressourcement* will lead to a more accurate, ample appraisal of Mary's role in the economy of salvation and to the healing of ecumenical divisions. The theological and ecumenical advances of the past sixty years have vindicated that hope: a more integrated and resourced theology has contributed to the surmounting of much Protestant minimalism and Catholic maximalism, at least on the theological level.

THE ACHIEVEMENTS AND LEGACY OF CONGAR'S MARIOLOGY

In *Fifty Years of Catholic Theology*, an extended interview published in 1987, Congar said, "I am completely in agreement with ch. VIII of *Lumen Gentium*: Mary has a very considerable place in the mystery of Christ and the Church."[83] I want in this conclusion to offer an evaluation of the place of Mary in Congar's thought. My judgment is threefold: positive, negative, and mixed.

Positively, one can commend the weighty, enduring aspects of Congar's theological method and doctrine. Methodologically, his integrative and historically resourced approach was enormously helpful in advancing Catholic ecclesiology. He was, as the country song goes, *nexus mysteriorum* before *nexus mysteriorum* was cool or safe! His studies on Mary in patristic and medieval thought are tours de force of *ressourcement* scholarship. Doctrinally, his emphases on human agency and the integrity of human nature in the Christian life and work of redemption, as well as on the Church's communal-interpersonal (and not merely suprapersonal) nature,[84] are valuable in their own right and for their contributions to Marian thought. Likewise, the sobriety born of such rigorous scholarship led to his recovery of the patristic insight, on the eve of the Council, that Mary plays an essential, distinctive role within the Church.

One must also consider Congar's achievement in the light of its conciliar and ecumenical reception. As "the" theologian of Vatican II, according to Avery Dulles and Étienne Fouilloux,[85] Congar was involved in the drafting of what would become chapter 8 of *Lumen Gentium*.[86] His overall ecclesiological vision, and likely his preconciliar Marian scholarship, made a significant contribution to that chapter's integration of Mariology, Christology, soteriology, and ecclesiology. One sees also a more contemporary legacy in the various ecumenical dialogues that began after Vatican II. *Mary: Grace and Hope in Christ*, the 2004 agreed statement by the Anglican–Roman Catholic International Commission, and *Mary in the Plan of God and in the Communion of Saints*, the 1999 statement by the French Reformed–Catholic Groupe des Dombes, are documents that achieved a remarkable degree of consensus on the basis of their patient, learned *ressourcement* of scripture and tradition. Both their method and their substance owe much to the path opened up by Congar through his scholarship and his ecumenical labors. The order of the four sections of *Mary: Grace and Hope in Christ*, for example, is thoroughly Congarian: "Scripture," "Tradition," "Economy-Plan of God," and "Mary in the Life of the Church."

And yet, for all of these achievements, we must also consider the drawbacks to Congar's mariological thought. His overriding aim was less to open up or explore a theology of Mary than to correct theological and devotional excesses. It is therefore more reactive than constructive, more concerned with corralling than cultivating. Congar dismisses the Scheebenian trajectory too easily and flatly, as well as what he calls the "metaphysics of femininity."[87] More deeply, he perhaps does not emphasize sufficiently Mary's unique dignity among all creatures, including the angels, and the consequences that flow from that uniqueness and elevation. Congar's sobriety was and is necessary, especially in the face of a "galloping Mariology," but one may be forgiven for thinking that it leaves important matters undeveloped and undervalued.

There is, moreover, a decided coolness in Congar's Marian thought. Perhaps Mariology was too fraught with theological and spiritual struggles for Congar to give it any warmth or enthusiasm. It is clear that his distaste for Marian maximalism was tied to his broader frustrations with what he called "Baroque theology,"[88] that is, the devotional and ecclesiological excesses of French Catholicism in the post-Revolution era, as well as with his own early spiritual and theological formation. His critique of Mariolatry, as we have seen, is bound up with a broader polemic against a distorted supernaturalism that denigrated the natural and cut believers off from the world and from "life." I suspect that Congar never really shook the influence of his early spiritual father, Daniel Lallement. Congar freely and generously acknowledged his debt to his early mentor, but it is also tenable that he was limited by his reaction against that worldview for most of his adult life.

Finally, there is the mixed, even inadvert, legacy of Congar's Mariology. Borrowing a phrase from *Gaudium et Spes*, one might say that the "signs of the times" are somewhat different in 2014 than they were in 1920, 1950, or 1964. I close by highlighting two of those signs. First, the Marian maximalism of Congar's time has been succeeded largely by a minimalism. The dominant trend in much Marian theology today is to affirm that Mary is "truly our sister." That emphasis on sorority and solidarity is essential, but what happens when Mary becomes "only our sister" and her maternity, uniqueness, and preeminence among all creatures are obscured or passed over?[89] There is little danger today in most Catholic theology of a fixation on "personal privileges."

Second, given Congar's status as the greatest Catholic ecclesiologist of the twentieth century and likely of all time, one might wonder about his contribution, however unintended, to postconciliar Catholic ecclesiology's relative neglect of Mary. Gilles Routhier has written of his "regret" that postconciliar "ecclesiologists have not contributed in a significant way to Mariology,"[90] while Cesare Antonelli has suggested that Catholic ecclesiology as a whole has struggled in recent decades to make Mary a "constitutive dimension" of its work.[91] Massimo Faggioli has likewise noted that contemporary discussions of Vatican II's ecclesiology focus mostly on episcopal collegiality and ecumenism.[92] That simultaneous neglect of Mary in ecclesiology and focus on ecclesial structures is perhaps not coincidental. Joseph Ratzinger has written, "A purely structural ecclesiology is bound to degrade Church to the level of a program of action."[93] An ecclesiology without Mary, he suggests, is fated to become impersonal and functionalistic.

Accordingly, a problem today for much of Catholic ecclesiology is not a galloping Mariology but an anemic, even largely absent, one (apart from some Balthasarian and Latino/a theologians).[94] Numerous histories and theologies of Vatican II present chapter 8 of *Lumen Gentium* less as the "crowning" of the Council's ecclesiology than as a clipping of an excessive Mariology. One may legitimately ask how much of that neglect is due to the reception, in less capacious hands, of the emphases and the trajectory of Congar's thought.

Congar was certainly right when he concluded his response to his interviewer's question about Mary by saying, "Mary must have her place in the Church."[95] He, more than anyone else, helped prepare the way theologically for Vatican II.[96] It is no slight to his unparalleled legacy to suggest that a new work of integration, *ressourcement*, and discernment is needed today if Mary is to reclaim her rightful place in the mysteries of Christ and his Church.

NOTES

1. See Pietro Quattrocchi's bibliography in Jean-Pierre Jossua, *Yves Congar: La théologie au service du peuple de Dieu* (Paris: Cerf, 1967), 219–72.

2. Brendan Leahy, *The Marian Profile in the Ecclesiology of Hans Urs von Balthasar* (New York: New City Press, 2000).

3. Yves Congar, *Fifty Years of Catholic Theology: Conversations with Yves Congar*, trans. John Bowden (Philadelphia: Fortress, 1988), 62, 64.

4. Yves Congar, *My Journal of the Council*, trans. Mary John Ronanye and Mary Cecily Boulding (Collegeville, MN: Liturgical Press, 2012), 315.

5. Ibid., 580.

6. Congar, *Fifty Years of Catholic Theology*, 62.

7. Congar, *My Journal of the Council*, 54.

8. Yves Congar, *Le concile au jour le jour: Deuxième session* (Paris: Cerf, 1964), 110. This phrase echoes Henri de Lubac's criticism of a "separated theology" marked by divisions between nature and the supernatural, the Church and the world, and so on. See Joseph A. Komonchak, "Theology and Culture at Mid-Century: The Example of Henri de Lubac," *Theological Studies* 51 (1990): 579–602.

9. Congar, *Fifty Years of Catholic Theology*, 63. See also Congar, "Mother Church," in *The Church To-day*, trans. Sr. M. Ignatius (Cork, Ireland: Mercier, 1967), 40–42.

10. Yves Congar, "Marie et l'Église chez les Protestants," *Sainte Église: Études et approches ecclésiologiques* (Paris: Cerf, 1964), 491–518, quote on 504. This article was first published in 1952.

11. Ibid., 505.

12. Ibid. See Congar's report on a lunch in Rome during Vatican II with the Orthodox theologians Alexander Schmemann and Nikos Nissiotis: "In their view, a *De Beata* [a separate conciliar schema on Mary] is a fairly doubtful step. In the East, Mary is a DIMENSION of everything: of christology, the history of salvation (continuity with Israel), ecclesiology, and prayer. That is why the Orthodox mix her up with everything without ever producing a treatise *De Beata*." Congar, *My Journal of the Council*, 383.

13. Yves Congar, "Marie et l'Église: Perspective médiévale," *Revue des Sciences philosophiques et théologiques* 39 (1955): 409. See also Congar, "Mother Church," 41.

14. Congar, "Marie et l'Église chez les Protestants," 505.

15. Congar, "Mother Church," 41.

16. Congar, *Le concile au jour le jour*, 111.

17. Ibid.

18. Congar, *My Journal of the Council*, 58. See also 442, 475.

19. See Yves Congar, *Christ, Our Lady, and the Church: A Study in Eirenic Theology*, trans. Henry St. John (Westminster, MD: Newman, 1957), 77–82.

20. Yves Congar, "Chronique: Année 1953," appendix to *Sainte Église*, 618–58, quote on 626. All translations are mine unless otherwise noted.

21. Yves Congar, "Marie et l'Église dans la pensée patristique," *Revue des Sciences philosophiques et théologiques* 38 (1954): 8, 10, 22, 38. See also, Congar, "Notes théologiques à propos de l'assomption," in *Les voies du Dieu vivant: Théologie et vie spirituelle* (Paris: Cerf, 1962), 223–26.

22. Congar, *Fifty Years of Catholic Theology*, 63; see also Congar, "Marie et l'Église: Perspective medieval," 409–11.

23. Congar, "Notes théologiques à propos de l'assomption," 221–23. See also his *Le concile au jour le jour,* 111. In *My Journal of the Council,* p. 475, he writes: "I think that, when the return to the sources, the Christological and paschal recentering, ecumenical dialogue and real concern for the world will have at last reached the hearts of the bishops and of the Pope, these mariological developments [deformations, in Congar's judgment] will experience a reversal, and that health and sobriety will again be found in these areas, too."

24. Congar, "Mother Church," 40.

25. On the analogy of faith, see Congar, "Notes théologiques à propos de l'assomption," 220.

26. Yves Congar, *Journal d'un théologien: 1946–1956* (Paris: Cerf, 2001), 43.

27. Ibid., 39.

28. Congar notes that Lallement forbade him to join the Boy Scouts as he thought them too naturalistic: "The simple fact of bare knees horrified him"! (*Journal d'un théologien,* 32).

29. One example among many: "Dinner, to which Mgr Prignon invited us ([Gérard] Philips, [Charles] Moeller, [Gustave] Thils) at a restaurant in the Piazza Navona, in the open air. We saw normal people again, to whom our Byzantine intrigues would have absolutely NOTHING to say!" (*My Journal of the Council,* 558). See also 26.

30. Congar, "Marie et l'Église dans la pensée patristique," 5.

31. Ibid., 8–9, 28.

32. Ibid., 38.

33. Ibid., 13, 27.

34. Ibid., 10.

35. Ibid.

36. Ibid., 12.

37. Ibid., 13.

38. Ibid., 10.

39. Ibid., 13.

40. Ibid., 6, 13, 18–19, 32.

41. Ibid., 33.

42. Ibid., 13. See also ibid., 28. On the Church's preexistence, see ibid., 10, n. 16.

43. Ibid., 14.

44. Ibid.

45. Ibid.

46. Ibid., 16.

47. Ibid., 22.

48. Congar, *Christ, Our Lady, and the Church,* 25.

49. For an overview and commentary on this book, see Joseph Famerée, *L'Écclésiologie d'Yves Congar avant Vatican II: Histoire et Église* (Leuven: Leuven/Peeters, 1992), 129–38.

50. Congar, *Christ, Our Lady, and the Church*, 10.
51. Ibid., 28–29.
52. Ibid., 29.
53. Ibid., 31.
54. Ibid., 15.
55. Ibid., 40.
56. Congar excluded what he termed the "liberal" Protestant theology of that time from his article, judging it to be insufficiently orthodox. See Congar, "Marie et l'Église chez les Protestants," 493, n. 6.
57. Ibid., 492.
58. Ibid., 494.
59. Ibid., 497–98.
60. Ibid., 497.
61. See ibid., 499, 493. Congar notes that Protestant thought here bases itself heavily on Paul's letter to the Galatians, especially 4:4–5, with its contrasting of flesh and spirit.
62. Ibid., 499.
63. Ibid.
64. Ibid., 501.
65. Ibid., 502.
66. Ibid.
67. Ibid., 505.
68. Ibid., 506.
69. Ibid.
70. Ibid., 507.
71. Ibid. Congar quotes here Pierre Maury, a French Reformed theologian and disciple-friend of Karl Barth.
72. Ibid., 509. Congar notes that it is "superfluous to add" that Protestantism nonetheless rejects the dogma of the Immaculate Conception as "unacceptable" scripturally and even "formally anti-biblical."
73. Ibid., 508.
74. Ibid., 509. Congar takes these quotes from Thurian's contribution on Reformed Mariology in *Ways of Worship: The Report of a Theological Commission of Faith and Order* (London: World Council of Churches, 1951), 307.
75. Congar, "Marie et l'Église chez les Protestants," 509.
76. Ibid., 510. Congar adds here a criticism of the emphasis in some of the Catholic theology of his day on an overly materialistic or quantitative understanding of grace rather than the more "biblical and traditional" conception of uncreated grace.
77. Ibid., 511.
78. Ibid.
79. Ibid., 512.
80. Ibid.

81. Ibid., 516.

82. Ibid., 515.

83. Congar, *Fifty Years of Catholic Theology*, 63.

84. Congar, "Mother Church," 38, 42–44. In Congar's view, an interpersonal approach emphasizes that the Church is formed by the faithful, while a "suprapersonal" one stresses that the faithful are formed by the Church, a church understood largely as "the institution in which we obtain the means of salvation existing somehow outside ourselves" (42). In such a view, "men are nothing more than her 'products'; she is set up over them as a storehouse" (38). Congar proposes, instead, that both views be held together dialectically.

85. Avery Dulles, "Preface," in *Yves Congar: Theologian of the Church*, ed. Gabriel Flynn (Grand Rapids, MI: Eerdmans, 2005), 27; Étienne Fouilloux, "Frère Yves, Cardinal Congar, Dominicain: Itinéraire d'un théologien," *Revue des Sciences philosophiques et théologiques* 79 (1995): 400.

86. See Cesare Antonelli, *Il dibatto su Maria nel concilio Vaticano II: Percorso redazionale sulla base di nuovi documenti di archivio* (Padua: Messaggero, 2009).

87. Congar, "Marie et l'Église dans la pensée patristique," 23.

88. Congar, *Journal d'un théologien: 1946–1956*, 24.

89. See, for instance, Robert Imbelli's review of Elizabeth Johnson's *Truly Our Sister: A Theology of Mary in the Communion of Saints* in *Worship* 78 (November 2004): 568–70. *Lumen Gentium* (LG) affirms in several places both Mary's uniqueness and her relatedness vis-à-vis humanity; for example, see LG 53.

90. Gilles Routhier, "Quarante ans après Vatican II, qu'est devenu le Mouvement marial?," *Istina* 50 (2005): 326.

91. Antonelli, *Il dibatto su Maria nel concilio Vaticano II*, 592.

92. Massimo Faggioli, "Council Vatican II: Bibliographical Overview 2005–2007," *Cristianesimo nella Storia* 29 (2008): 602.

93. Joseph Ratzinger, *Mary: The Church at the Source*, trans. Adrian Walker (San Francisco: Ignatius, 2005), 27.

94. For example, Richard Gaillardetz and Catherine Clifford's otherwise helpful *Keys to the Council: Unlocking the Teaching of Vatican II* (Collegeville, MN: Liturgical Press, 2012) does not address Mary's role in the Council's ecclesiology.

95. Congar, *Fifty Years of Catholic Theology*, 65.

96. See Dulles, "Preface," and Fouilloux, "Frère Yves, Cardinal Congar, Dominicain."

CHAPTER 5

Mary and the Holy Spirit in the 1950s

Presaging Lumen Gentium

MATTHEW LEVERING

In what way is the Virgin Mary relevant to Christians? How should we think about her without either minimizing or exaggerating her place? In the first volume of his magisterial *I Believe in the Holy Spirit*, Yves Congar observes that "it is very important to remain conscious of the deep bond that exists between the Virgin Mary and the Spirit, and consequently of a certain common function [between Mary and the Spirit] despite the absolute disparity of the conditions."[1] Yet Congar also thought that some influential streams of Catholic theology prior to the Second Vatican Council had functionally replaced the Holy Spirit with Mary. Congar provides a quotation from St. Bernardino of Siena to the effect that "Mary has at her disposal 'a certain jurisdiction or authority over the temporal procession of the Holy Spirit, to such an extent that no creature has ever received the grace of any virtue from God except through a dispensation of the Virgin herself.'" Congar adds, "This is clearly unacceptable."[2] Similarly, in his noteworthy discussion of Mary in the third volume of his *Theo-Drama*, Hans Urs von Balthasar critically surveys some examples of exaggerated Marian piety, beginning with the twelfth century.[3] Among twentieth-century saints, Maximilian Kolbe stands out for his strongly worded Mariology (but he did not thereby neglect Trinitarian theology). In his letters he frequently makes statements such as the following: "So close is the bond between the Holy Spirit and the Immaculate Virgin, that the Holy Spirit, who has so fully permeated the Immaculate's soul, exercises his influence on every human being, only through her."[4] For Kolbe, writing in the 1920s and 1930s, even "the definition of *Spouse of the Holy Spirit* is too vague an image to express the life of the Holy Spirit acting within her and through her."[5]

The cutting-edge Mariology of the 1950s was much more tempered with regard to Mary and the Spirit. In what follows I survey three Marian treatises authored in the 1950s by theologians who helped to shape the Second Vatican Council, René Laurentin, Otto Semmelroth, and Karl Rahner. In different ways, these theologians attempted to speak about Mary in a manner that is grounded in Scripture and connects Mary with the Church and with ourselves.[6] The main task of my chapter is simply to display their approaches so as to acquaint readers with a representative sampling of Mariology on the eve of the Council, particularly with respect to Mary and the Spirit. But I also have a constructive purpose in mind. Namely, I consider that Laurentin's biblical approach does the best job of drawing out the implications of Mary's relationship with the Holy Spirit, and thereby of showing the reasons for an appreciation of Mary's privileges. Semmelroth and Rahner, too, offer valuable insights, but their focus on broader realities, respectively the Church and God's gracious self-communication, paradoxically renders them less able to portray the broader implications of Mary's unique and particular relationship with the Holy Spirit. By examining these mariological works from the 1950s, I therefore hope to aid in the contemporary articulation of the teaching in *Lumen Gentium* (LG) that Mary is "the beloved daughter of the Father and the temple of the Holy Spirit," as befits her reception of "the high office and dignity of the Mother of the Son of God" (LG 53).[7]

RENÉ LAURENTIN: MARY'S CONSECRATION BY THE HOLY SPIRIT

Laurentin's *A Short Treatise on Marian Theology* was translated into English in 1956 on the basis of what was shortly thereafter published as the second French edition of the book (the first edition having appeared in 1953).[8] Laurentin begins with a relatively lengthy section on Mary in Scripture. He discusses her virginity, Jesus's insistence that her dignity does not consist simply in a kinship relationship (see Mark 3:31–35 and Luke 11:27–28), Mary's Magnificat and its Old Testament parallels, Mary as the fulfillment of the "Daughter of Sion," the association of Mary with the Cross, Mary as the "woman" or new Eve (mother of all the living in the order of grace), and the Marian symbolism present in Revelation 11–12 in light of Genesis 3:14–15. In this section, however, the Holy Spirit is rarely mentioned explicitly, although Laurentin does confirm that in Luke 1–2 "the operation of the Holy Spirit" is at work.[9]

Laurentin's second section treats the years AD 90–431, ending with the Council of Ephesus's proclamation of Mary as *Theotokos*, the Mother of God. Justin Martyr and Irenaeus of Lyons developed the Eve–Mary parallel. Various Fathers debated Mary's perpetual (and integral) virginity and whether Mary was sinless. Laurentin's third section very briefly treats the period 431–1050, noting the emergence of the Marian liturgical feasts. In the West, Mary's sinlessness and her bodily Assumption were resisted more than in the East. Laurentin's fourth section, on the years 1050–1563, notes the increased attention to Mary's cooperation in the work of her Son, as well as the significance of John Duns Scotus for resolving problems associated with Mary's sinlessness (her Immaculate Conception). In this period, too, there was a growth of exaggerated Marian piety, including among theologians. Laurentin's final two sections treat the period 1600–1950, with discussion of the development of systematic Mariology, the two dogmatic definitions, exaggerations in Marian piety, and the helpful work of John Henry Newman and Matthias Scheeben. Laurentin concludes that "an entirely new question is coming to the fore to-day: that of Mary and the Church."[10] In these historical sections, Laurentin is solely surveying the development of Marian doctrine; he mentions the Holy Spirit simply in connection with the Spirit's guidance of the Church's Magisterium.

The second part of Laurentin's book is where we should expect to find reflection on Mary and the Holy Spirit. Laurentin is first concerned to show that Mary's privileges were fitting but not necessary; otherwise they would not be works of God's free grace, nor would the perfect freedom with which Mary acted be adequately respected. Laurentin goes on to focus on Mary's growth in grace, with attention to her role in the transition from Israel to Christ's earthly ministry to the (eschatological) Church. He presents the movement from Abraham to Mary to be one of a less than fully holy person to a holy person. Here he does not mention the Holy Spirit explicitly, but he does say that Mary, as Israel/bride, was "crowned with the fullness of grace" that "bore Mary towards God with a soaring impulse of all her being, an impulse of faith and love."[11] She was enabled to be *the* means by which the incarnate Son of God entered the world, not a mere means, but a means fully enlivened by grace. There was no necessity that this should happen, Laurentin insists: "God's *proposal* and the *action* he performed surpassed anything that knowledge of Mary's perfection would have permitted even the most intelligent of the angels to foresee."[12]

At this stage Laurentin brings in the Holy Spirit. He notes that in Luke 1:35 and Matthew 1:20 we learn that the Holy Spirit acted so as to accomplish the virginal conception of the Christ child in Mary. Laurentin comments in this regard that "we know from the Bible that the action of the Holy Spirit has sanctification for its object."[13] We should not imagine, then, that the Spirit did not sanctify Mary as God's temple; rather, the Spirit, in enabling her to conceive the incarnate Son, made Mary, in the most complete way possible for a mere human, "wholly God's."[14] In this light, Laurentin interprets the phrase "divine motherhood" in terms of its formal, efficient, and final cause. The temporal generation of the Son is "an image of his divine sonship," and Mary's "motherhood resembles the heavenly fatherhood in that it was the fruit of faith: that is, a spiritual, a holy act."[15] Laurentin refers to the Holy Spirit in this regard because the Spirit caused Mary's conception, a fact that Laurentin connects with the Church Fathers' idea that "Mary conceived the Word by faith."[16] Since Mary was to be Mother of God, not merely mother of Jesus's human flesh, because his humanity and divinity are hypostatically united, God freely sanctified her uniquely among mere humans.

Laurentin goes on to compare Mary's divine motherhood with the baptismal character that we receive. He emphasizes the significance of Mary's faith and of the grace that flows to Mary as a result of her embrace of divine motherhood, and he directs our attention to the awe-inspiring character of Mary's motherhood of such a Son. He observes

that "just as the consecration of the [baptismal] character directs and
specifies our vocation and our grace as the vocation and grace of *children* of
God, so Mary's motherhood specifies her vocation and grace as the vocation and grace of Mother of God."[17] Here he again identifies Mary's vocation as flowing from the work of the Holy Spirit. Just as in Exodus
40:34, after Moses had finished building the tabernacle, "the cloud covered the tent of meeting, and the glory of the Lord filled the tabernacle,"
so now, says Laurentin, "the same operation of the Holy Spirit gives reality to the incarnate presence of God in his mother and to the consecration of that divine mother herself."[18] Laurentin grants that this analogy
between Mary and the tabernacle/temple is imperfect, but the imperfec-
tion of the analogy only amplifies the significance of the Spirit's interior
work in Mary: "Mary is no material temple and her act of receiving was
free and perfect. The action of the Holy Spirit aimed at assimilating
her—co-naturalizing her, in so far as that was possible—to the divine
Person to whom she was to be mother."[19] Thus the Holy Spirit accomplishes the conception of Jesus in Mary's womb, not as though Mary
were an extrinsic observer or only physically present, but by at the same
time interiorly consecrating Mary's soul, as becomes clear in her free
consent "to God's fructifying action and to the coming of God."[20]

Laurentin develops further his comparison between what happens
to us at baptism (the reception of the baptismal character and sanctifying
grace) and what happened to Mary through her consent to be the mother
of the Christ. When Mary said, "Let it be to me according to your word"
(Luke 1:38), she "received a gift which was the created basis of the relationship she contracted to the person of her Son: her quality of Mother
of God, along with a correlative gift—of the order of sanctifying grace—
the grace thanks to which she could live conformably to her quality of
Mother of God."[21] It makes sense that the Holy Spirit gave her, then and
there, the grace to accomplish her mission, a mission that consists in a
unique and extraordinary relationship to the Son of God. But surely
Mary, immaculately conceived, already possessed this grace? Laurentin
argues that although Mary had the fullness of sanctifying grace, she
could still receive something like a "character" that configured her to
Christ (and to the Church), and her fullness of grace could also always be
deepened.

Laurentin proceeds to discuss Mary's virginity, her motherhood of the members of Christ's mystical body, and her cooperation with her Son's work of salvation, a work whose sacrificial character Simeon prophesied to her. Laurentin also notes that during most of Jesus's ministry, Jesus was parted from Mary. This changed at the Cross, where Mary was present. Laurentin argues that by her presence, her status as a redeemed creature, a woman, and a person of faith were incorporated into the mystery of redemption. Because she possessed true charity, she was able to suffer with Jesus, to cooperate with him in his sufferings. Grace configured her most perfectly to the superabundant salvation that Christ accomplished for us on the Cross. In her presence at Pentecost, Laurentin sees a parallel with the Annunciation: the Holy Spirit, having previously formed Christ's body, at Pentecost formed his mystical body. Laurentin draws the connection: "Her prayer, which had prepared for the birth of the Church, continued to be the crowning prayer of the Church."[22]

Does Laurentin link the Holy Spirit with Mary's Assumption? He emphasizes that as the immaculate one, Mary possesses all the graces that the Church possesses; since the Church will never die, so it might have been fitting for Mary not to die. In Laurentin's view, the question of her death—as distinct from her Assumption—will remain a mystery until the eschaton. Assumed to the side of the glorified Christ, Mary intercedes consciously on behalf of all humankind, whereas in her earthly life, as a wayfarer, she did not know all those for whom Christ died. It is fitting, Laurentin thinks, that God willed to bring about a full communion of male and female in this intercession for the human race rather than leaving Christ in his humanity as the sole glorified human body prior to the general resurrection. Mary's intercession in love is efficacious because her will is entirely united, interiorly, with her Son's. But Laurentin does not mention the Spirit explicitly in this discussion.

Laurentin concludes that although Mary's holiness enabled her free consent and thereby "mediated" the Incarnation of the Son, her Son is indeed the one Mediator, and her mediation does not add to, but rather participates in, the mediation of her Son. In the eschatological consummation of all things, furthermore, no longer will Mary represent the Church's future, but instead she will be seen as fully like all members of the Church, even if preeminent among the members of the Church due to her degree of glory. With respect to the interior dimension of the Church, "the life of faith and charity, the spiritual regeneration of mankind by grace, the interiorizing and shedding abroad of the gifts of the Holy Spirit," Laurentin considers that Mary's relationship to Christ perfectly actualizes the Church and is continued in the Church.[23] As an important final note, he adds that we should not only link Mary with Christ and the Church but also be sure to carefully distinguish Mary from Christ and the Church, since Mary, as the unique *Theotokos*, is distinct from both.

OTTO SEMMELROTH: MARY AND THE CHURCH

Otto Semmelroth first published his *Urbild der Kirche* in 1954, and it appeared in English as *Mary, Archetype of the Church* in 1963.[24] He begins with a short summary of the new Marian movement, in which the emphasis is on Mary's free personhood rather than solely her role in the plan of redemption. The same thing, he observes, holds for the theology of the Church, which now emphasizes the mystical body rather than a juridical congregation. He then seeks an "overall illuminating vision" or "basic Marian principle," which he finds not in her divine motherhood or her bridal motherhood or her status as the new Eve but rather in her role as the type of the Church.[25]

Does Semmelroth give the Holy Spirit an explicitly central position in his exposition of this "basic Marian principle?" Not surprisingly, he insists that "the life of grace was the supernatural life-principle abounding with special perfection in the Archetype [i.e., Mary] of the Church."[26] He does not mention the Spirit, but we can take the Spirit as being implied by the life of grace. In conversation with historical-critical and patristic exegesis, Semmelroth devotes significant attention to the Eve–Mary–Church typology in Revelation 11–12, in light of Genesis 3:15, and to the Mary–Church typology in John 19:26–27. Emphasizing the *bridal* motherhood of Mary, indebted to Scheeben, he urges that this bridal aspect points to Mary as the type of the Church. As he says, "Because Mary was to be the Type of the Church, she was given existence as the virginal Mother of God."[27] Although Mary's and the Church's "*pleroma* of grace" receives mention at this juncture, the Holy Spirit is generally absent from Semmelroth's quest for the "basic Marian principle," even if one assumes—as I do—that grace, for Semmelroth, is appropriated to the Holy Spirit.[28]

Semmelroth's next chapter examines Mary as "co-redeemer," a title that in his view applies to the Church and indeed to all Christians without jeopardizing Christ's status as the unique Redeemer: "Man co-redeems because he is redeemed."[29] Again, Mary's association with grace appears forcefully. Semmelroth holds that like the Church, "Mary is the mediator of all redemptive graces imparted to men."[30] The goal is an increasingly profound union with Christ, or divinization. In this regard, but without specific reference to Mary, Semmelroth gives the Holy Spirit a leading role. Since the Holy Spirit is the Love of the Father and the Son, "like the kiss of sacred love exchanged by lovers," the Holy Spirit draws us into this communion of love.[31] Semmelroth states, "The Holy Spirit, whom the Father breathes out to the Son, also touches us who have our being in the Son. . . . Having our being in the Son, we breathe with Him when the Son breathes out the Holy Spirit as an expression of divine love for the Father."[32] Taken up by faith in the Son into the Trinitarian communion, we share—in some sense—in the spiration of the Spirit.

Having established our sharing in the Trinitarian communion, Semmelroth next emphasizes that our "divinization" comes about by a free, divinely caused process of "grace," and he adds, more explicitly, that "the newness of Christian existence is a participation in the life of the Holy Spirit," without of course overcoming the Creator–creature ontological divide.[33] As Christ's bride, the Church receives "the grace of His work," but each member does so as having personally encountered Christ and taken up the Cross.[34] Grace, Semmelroth emphasizes, does not do away with personal free will but rather works through "our free power of decision," our free surrender of self to the beloved.[35] While we cannot save ourselves in a semi-Pelagian way, we can say no to God's grace. This is why we can speak of "co-redemption," and why Mary's "Let it be to me according to your word" (Luke 1:38) is so significant. As Semmelroth says, "Mary, the Type of the Church, standing on its pinnacle representing it, pronounces the *fiat* of receptivity and willingness."[36]

Although Pope Benedict XV, in his 1918 encyclical *Inter Sodalicias*, affirmed that one "may truly declare that Mary has redeemed the human race together with Christ," Semmelroth, like Pope Benedict XV, is well aware that the notion of co-redemption can be gravely misunderstood.[37] Indeed, Scheeben had cautioned against its use. For his part, arguing against a number of scholars, Semmelroth rejects the notion that Mary, at the Cross, co-merited within Christ's saving work. Christ's merits are for everyone—including Mary—the sole cause of redemption. Christ alone is the Redeemer and the Mediator.

What, then, is Mary's cooperative role? Semmelroth highlights the Eve–Mary typology, along with patristic and modern papal teachings, to argue that Mary "is the Type of the truly co-redeeming Church which gives salvation."[38] In this regard he invokes Pius XII's 1943 encyclical *Mystici Corporis* 12, "Through the Church every man performs a work of collaboration with Christ in dispensing the graces of Redemption, thus acting as 'co-redeemer.'"[39] Christ's saving work must be accepted by humans; by accepting it, humans participate in it and can be said to accomplish co-redemptive works. The Church consists in those who have freely entered into this relationship with Christ as his mystical body or bride. Semmelroth states, "By co-operating with the Redemption in taking Christ's work and fruits upon itself, humanity becomes the Church filled with Christ's *pleroma*."[40] Mary's fiat accomplishes this in a manner that makes her the type of the whole Church. Her co-operation or co-redemption consists simply in her reception of Christ's redemption; indeed, the whole Church co-redeems in this sense. Semmelroth credits "the influence of grace" in Mary's bridal "receptive, active appropriation of Christ's work."[41]

Semmelroth next addresses the topic of mediation. He argues that if Mary is the type of the Church in actively receiving the redemption won by Christ, "Mary's position as the Mediator of all graces—stemming particularly from her role as Archetype of the Church—should not offer any difficulties either to the mind or to any resulting religious observance."[42] In other words, if we first understand how the Church is "Mediator," we will be able to understand how Mary, as type of the Church, is Mediator. The Church's mediatory role can be understood only in terms of the mystical body, against all individualism. Quoting Thomas Aquinas, Semmelroth notes that the Holy Spirit fills and unifies the Church. Individuals receive the graces of redemption in Christ, therefore, not as mere individuals but within the mediation of the Church. The Church does not thereby mediate between Christ and the individual; rather, the individual, precisely as a member of the Church, receives these graces.

Connecting this portrait of the Church to Mary, Semmelroth observes that Mary's fiat gives her "the fullness of graces that flow into the Church."[43] He cites various popes along with Bernard of Clairvaux and Cyril of Alexandria to show that the notion of receiving the grace of Christ in some sense "through Mary" is nothing new. Everything that Mary does, Semmelroth argues, she does as the type of the Church; her receptivity opens not only herself but also the Church to the fullness of the graces that flow from Christ. In Semmelroth's words, "Mary, as Type and pinnacle of the Church, affirmed Christ's work and thereby disposed both herself and the Church within her for the *pleroma* of salvation."[44] Mary "disposed" herself and the Church for the fullness of salvation. In this sense she and the Church mediate salvation, but the fullness of salvation comes from Christ alone. At the Cross, then, Mary represents the whole mystical body and actively "receives the plenitude of redemptive grace for the entire Church."[45] She does so as the type of the Church, and therefore her reception of the fullness of grace was never for herself alone. She is always sharing her fullness of graces, the graces of the redemption won by Christ, with the whole Church. Semmelroth underscores that "the Church's grace was first received by Mary and continues to flow from her into the Church and its members."[46] This grace manifests itself when the whole Church, and each believer, imitates Mary's co-operative receptivity to the graces of Christ's redemption.

The chapter on Mary's mediation, then, contains numerous references to grace but none to the Holy Spirit, although we should again assume that grace here is appropriated to the Holy Spirit. Semmelroth next turns to Mary's bridal motherhood. He observes, "In the divine motherhood, Mary was given the most perfect opportunity to prefigure the Church in a co-redemptive way. In the eyes of her fellow creatures who venerate her, no one is as exalted as she to whom such intimate relationship with her Creator was given in the divine motherhood."[47] Again Semmelroth focuses on Mary's link with the Church, the mystical body and bride of Christ. Mary's divine motherhood is linked intimately with the whole Church's motherhood; the Son requires a personal response that receptively co-operates with and completes his redemptive work. As the type of the Church, Mary "goes forth as Bride of the *Logos* and utters her *fiat* to Him as He comes to redeem mankind."[48] Throughout her life, including at the Cross, Mary "typifies the Church in her bridal and receptive co-operation with the work of the God-man."[49] In this chapter Semmelroth mentions the Holy Spirit when reflecting upon the virginal conception: the Holy Spirit's role in the conception of Christ ensures that the accomplishment of redemption can be seen to come from God, not from human resources. The human role, actualized in Mary or the Church, is a co-operative and (actively) receptive one characterized by receiving and participating in Christ's redemptive work, his self-sacrificial love. Mary's virginity, Semmelroth argues, signifies her bridal receptivity and fidelity to the redeeming God, her charitable fruitfulness through "the Breath of the Holy Ghost."[50] Mary's motherhood is virginal, therefore, primarily because she is the type of the Church.

In closing, Semmelroth discusses Mary's sinlessness and bodily assumption under the rubrics of "Redemption of the Soul" and "Redemption of the Body." He defines being redeemed as "a sharing of life with the Triune God."[51] Mary's sinlessness allows her in this way, too, to be the type of the Church, since she thereby fully shares in the Trinitarian life insofar as possible here on earth. Again, Semmelroth's point is that "in Mary the Church has said her *fiat* to the work of the Bridegroom. In Mary the Church has received her holiness and plenitude of graces."[52] Semmelroth considers this important in accounting for the holiness of the Church as a communion in the Trinity. Since Mary was assumed body and soul into heavenly glory, Mary also exhibits the reality that "the more grace reigns in the Church and in her members, the closer the body will participate in the Redemption."[53] As the type of the Church, Mary fully possesses the grace of redemption, is fully redeemed, and is fully "the temple of the Holy Spirit."[54]

KARL RAHNER: MARY AND HUMANITY

In 1956, Karl Rahner published his *Maria, Mutter des Herrn*, a short collection of eight sermon-conferences or lectures given at the University

Church of the Holy Trinity in Innsbruck, Austria, prefaced by a short essay titled "A Short Outline of the Teaching of Faith about Mary" and published in English in 1963 as *Mary, Mother of the Lord*.[55] This book pales in comparison to the influence of some of his other writings on Mary,[56] but it provides a window into at least some of his thinking about Mary during the 1950s.

In Rahner's view, the statement "Mary is the virgin Mother of Jesus Christ" tells us "everything" about Mary so long as "one considers whose mother she is, and in what way she is his mother."[57] In developing this statement, Rahner first describes the Creator-creation relation and observes that God creates the world "in order to communicate himself to it, with his own intrinsic reality, freely," so that in fact "God himself comes forth from himself, and the world is drawn up into God's own life, in a process that will only be concluded when the world reaches its fulfillment."[58] Since humans know and love, humans "are capable of receiving directly God's communication of himself, in the proper sense of the term, if God gives himself freely and gratuitously."[59] God offers this grace to every single human being. God also "bears witness to his salvific will" in the concrete history of salvation, in Israel and in Jesus Christ and his Church. Humans are free to accept God's gracious "self-communication," a self-communication that God addresses "to the community of human persons" and that attains its "ultimate peak" and "irrevocable final phase" in the incarnation of the Word, who is truly man and truly God.[60] When humans accept this self-communication, this acceptance "is produced by the efficacious grace of God who is giving himself."[61]

On this basis, Rahner introduces the person of Mary. Her relationship to her Son, he argues, is not merely physical; she conceived in faith, having freely consented to the angel's words. She is the Mother of God because her Son's humanity is united hypostatically with his divinity. At this stage, Rahner does not mention the Holy Spirit's action; instead he focuses on Mary as the new Eve and Co-redemptrix, citing the connection between John 2:4 and John 19:25–27. He also briefly highlights the connection between her "divine motherhood" and "personal holiness," which he links to the title "blessed" given to her by her cousin Elizabeth (Luke 1:45). He notes that Mary is fully redeemed and is thereby the type of the Church. He briefly reviews her Immaculate Conception through the foreseen merits of her Son, her perpetual virginity, her Assumption, and her intercessory role, subordinate to her Son, as "mediatrix of all graces."[62] Even more briefly, he summarizes the scriptural data about Mary's life, and he surveys the historical development of Marian piety.

After this prelude, which mentions the Holy Spirit directly only with respect to the guidance of the Church in the development of doctrine, Rahner's first lecture, "Mary in Theology," emphasizes theological anthropology. All theology is about God because God is all in all; and yet God has communicated himself in the man Jesus Christ. "Consequently," Rahner says, "no doctrine of God is possible any more without a doctrine of man, no theology without anthropology."[63] Since God was born of Mary, there must be Mariology. Furthermore, humans are a community or family; none of us is a mere individual, unaffected by other humans. God wills that in his plan of salvation we depend on each other. We cannot look at Jesus as an isolated individual; God gave Mary an integral role with respect to Jesus, a role to which we must pay attention. Mary acquaints us with a central aspect of "the Christian idea of man" and calls us "away from the loneliness and isolation of the individual."[64]

The next lecture is titled "The Fundamental Idea of Mariology." After surveying the traditional contenders—divine motherhood, new Eve, bridal motherhood—Rahner offers his own way of approaching the issue, namely by asking what Christianity is, and what perfect Christianity is. He defines Christianity as "the eternal God himself, coming himself to a man, and himself by his grace influencing this man, so that he freely opens his heart for the whole glorious infinite life of the triune God to enter the poor heart of this tiny creature."[65] Perfect Christianity, then, is perfect reception of God's self-communication, a reception that manifests itself in unconditional service to others patterned on God's own self-communication. Mary does this: in faith she perfectly receives God's self-communication in Jesus Christ, and she perfectly acts it out in unselfish service. Rahner concludes, therefore, that "she is the noblest of human beings in the community of the redeemed, representative of all who are perfect, and the type or figure that manifests completely the meaning of the Church, and grace, and redemption, and God's salvation."[66] Unlike her Son, Mary is solely a human. Having been perfectly redeemed, her receptive participation in God's self-communication is what we must all aspire to attain.

The third lecture treats Mary's Immaculate Conception. After defining sanctifying grace as "God himself, his communications to created spirits, the gift which is God himself," Rahner observes that such grace "means freedom, strength, a pledge of eternal life, the predominant influence of the Holy Spirit in the depths of the soul, adoptive sonship and an eternal inheritance."[67] This is the second reference to the Holy Spirit in the lecture; the first describes God's summons to Mary and thus, in a sense, to all humanity, as suffused not by judgment but by "tender, holy joy, the gentleness of the Holy Spirit, light and life and kindness, mercy, consolation, and beauty unalloyed."[68] Rahner focuses on the point that "the Immaculate Conception means that God surrounds the life of man with redemptive love" and "God surrounds this life of humanity with loving fidelity" so as to reveal that "God loves humanity as such" and that "eternal mercy from the beginning has enveloped man." Moreover, we "are enveloped from beginning to end by God's power, his love and his fidelity to us even in what is most individual and our own."[69] In the last paragraph of this lecture Rahner comments: "May the blessed Virgin forgive us for having spoken more about man in general than about her alone."[70]

The fourth lecture is titled "Mary the Mother of God." When describing the events of the annunciation (Luke 1), Rahner makes no mention of the Holy Spirit. Instead he turns to a reflection on the relationship of God and the world of rational creatures: "There actually does arise in the history of this world a tremendous dialogue between the free God and free man."[71] The infinite freedom of God could have interacted with finite human freedom in any number of ways. The key existential question for humans is whether God will abandon us to the nothingness from which he brought us forth "or whether it is his will to take his creature to his heart and share with him his innermost life."[72] In Jesus Christ, God revealed mercy, presence, and love as God's ultimate response to humanity. As Rahner says, "The eternal God has himself determined that the world itself shall definitively be drawn into his eternal mercy, and it now has a goal which infinitely transcends it and yet is its own: God's own self."[73] By grace, God enabled Mary freely and unconditionally to accept the coming Christ child. The "sovereignty" of God's grace means that his mercy is the source of everything good, even our freedom: "When God gives, when he gives his gifts, when he freely disposes of his gifts, these things become precisely what is most our own, precisely because it is he, the infinite and omnipotent, who gives them."[74] Although Rahner goes on to extol Mary's divine motherhood as both a sheer grace and Mary's free act, going beyond simple physical motherhood and "placing her whole self, body and soul, at the service of God and his redemptive mercy to mankind," he does not connect the gift of God with the Holy Spirit.[75] Instead the gift of God is the solution to the existential crisis in which humans find themselves, and Mary's role is exalted because of her unique relationship to the Word of God, and thus to us, in the history of redemption.

The fifth lecture examines Mary's perpetual virginity. Rahner pays particular attention to Mary's virginity in childbirth, arguing that this doctrine means to say simply that "the process of her motherhood could not take place in exactly the same way as in a human being subject to concupiscence as a consequence of original sin."[76] Regarding her choice to remain a virgin, Rahner suggests that it was "a consequence of her vocation to divine motherhood, a factor intrinsic to this principal function and dignity of hers."[77] She remained a virgin in conceiving her Son because God willed that his entrance into history should be seen as sheer grace rather than as arising from human resources, even though Jesus took his human nature from Mary. Mary remained a virgin because her uniquely fruitful vocation flowed from and was receptive to "divine grace alone, not only in her mind and heart, though that was the most important, but also in her visible and tangible earthly existence."[78] All Christians, not only consecrated virgins, must imitate Mary in renouncing certain earthly goods in order to remain focused on God's sheer gift, a gift that this world cannot provide.

The sixth lecture, on Mary's sinlessness, begins with the observation that "beyond what is contained in Scripture, the Church knows nothing of the life of the blessed Virgin or the external events of which it was made up."[79] Yet the Church knows that Mary was completely and utterly preserved from sin. How can this be? Rahner argues that Mary is most redeemed, and to be most redeemed means to be preserved entirely from sin. He adds that for the Church to be "holy," the Church must have at least one member in whom "redemption by the grace of God produced its complete effect, and in such a way that this perfect victory becomes plainly manifest for us pilgrims."[80] Mary's sinlessness, then, is not an achievement of her own but the victory of God's grace and mercy. As Rahner shows from Scripture, Mary's life, viewed from the outside, appears "unexceptional and ordinary."[81] It therefore took the Church some time to recognize fully the work of grace in her; her splendor was hidden in humility. The fact that her life involved difficulties, misunderstanding, and sacrifice, that her life was in many ways a normal life, should remind us, Rahner says, that God's grace is powerfully at work even in our very ordinary lives. In this lecture Rahner mentions the Spirit once in connection with the Church's doctrinal development; God's "grace" does not appear to be implicitly associated with the Holy Spirit since Rahner has in view God's determination to be merciful to all human beings, a determination that was then applied in a unique way to Mary.

Rahner's seventh lecture is devoted to Mary's Assumption. Rahner remarks, "About this the Church really does not need to know anything from history, except that Mary, as the mother of the Lord, is the most perfect fruit and work of his redemption."[82] The task of understanding Mary's status as perfectly redeemed required that the Church contemplate Mary over centuries, guided by the Holy Spirit "into the depths of the one, ever identical and yet never ossified revelation of our Lord."[83] The outcome of Mary's life, Rahner argues, cannot be other than the affirmation of the whole reality of her life, body and soul. Since we are body-soul unities, our perfect consummation must glorify us in our entirety. Christ's Resurrection unto glory shows us that this is indeed our goal. No less an end could be fitting for Mary, given that she "was the highest, unmatched realization of redemption in a human being endowed with grace, as Mother of God and consequently as the perfect type or representative of redemption in its very essence."[84] Rahner also suggests that in Mary we find that merely human "flesh is already saved forever"; we do not have to reject our bodies or idolize our bodies.[85] Mary, assumed to the side of her Son, is thus fully the type and model of the Church.

The final lecture takes up Mary as "Mediatrix of Graces." She is so as one who intercedes on behalf of all believers by her active prayer. Certainly Jesus alone is the only Mediator of our salvation. Jesus alone is the bond between God and humankind. How, then, can Mary be "Mediatrix"? Rahner answers that to understand how this can be, we need to recall that all members of the community or family of the human race depend on each other. In a certain way, then, we all "mediate" grace to each other insofar as we serve, love, teach, minister to, and pray for each other. We mediate the grace that Jesus Christ alone brings to the human race. On earth we do this in a way that is generally limited by our knowing only a few people. By contrast, the blessed in heaven serve and pray for all of us; they do so not as impediments to our contact with the one Mediator but as members of the one community of love that the Mediator has established. God loves us not strictly as individuals but as members of this communion of love, of which it is true that "all are intermediaries. We are for all, and all are for us."[86]

Not all of us mediate Christ's grace and love to the same degree and in the same way; our mediation depends in part on the service that, by grace, we accomplish in our earthly lives, since God wills to give each of us a different place in the communion of saints. Among mere humans, "none has had a profounder, more comprehensive function, or one more decisive for the whole divine plan," than Mary.[87] Mary's function, her free and loving consent "which co-operated in determining the whole history of the world," has an eternal place in the communion of saints.[88] God has willed that our salvation eternally depend on her "Yes" without denying that her fiat flows from his sheer grace and "continues inalienably to belong to God and to Christ."[89] All the grace that we receive from God, therefore, bears a relation to Mary's free, active love for Christ and his entire mystical body; Mary uniquely serves, loves, and prays for each of us.

MARY AND THE HOLY SPIRIT ON THE EVE OF THE COUNCIL

This chapter has traced three ways, from the eve of the Second Vatican Council, of showing the significance of Mary in Christian life. In addition to acquainting readers with the Mariology of the 1950s, I hope to have made clear that Mary's relationship to the Holy Spirit is best understood when one follows the biblical portraiture, as Laurentin does.

Laurentin discusses Mary's privileges in light of her role as Israel or the bride who received in faith the extraordinary grace of "divine motherhood" through the overshadowing of the Holy Spirit. Her motherhood, in this sense, was a spiritual act rooted in the graced faith that she exhibited in her fiat. The overshadowing Holy Spirit did not simply make the infant Christ present in her womb; rather the Holy Spirit also consecrated her and assimilated her to her Son so that she could fulfill her unique vocation as Mother of her Son. In Mary we see most fully how a relationship to the incarnate Son requires a relationship to his Spirit. At the Cross, Mary cooperated in Christ's suffering through her faith and charity. At Pentecost she was present when the Spirit, having overshadowed her in the conception of her Son's body, overshadowed the Apostles in bringing forth her Son's mystical body. In her mediation Mary actualizes and typifies the Church. In short, Laurentin's approach takes us through Mary's life and shows us how deeply her unique relationship with the Holy Spirit marks her vocation.

For his part, Semmelroth underscores at every opportunity that Mary is the type of the Church. She is filled with the "*pleroma* of grace" just as the Church is; she is co-redeeming because the Church is co-redeeming; she has a mediatorial role because the Church does. The Church, Semmelroth suggests, shares even in Christ's breathing forth of the Spirit, as his mystical body. Mary is the "Type and Pinnacle" of the Church. At the Cross she received redemptive grace for the whole Church; her fruitfulness comes always from her "bridal and receptive co-operation" with her Son. She is filled with the "Breath" of the Holy Spirit and shares, in her sinless earthly life and her glorified life in heaven, as fully as possible in the life of the triune God. She is the "temple of the Holy Spirit," which is another way of saying that she must be understood always as the type of the Church.

When compared with Semmelroth's approach, Laurentin's gives more attention to the actual individual person of Mary, to her distinctive and unique experience of the Spirit. Semmelroth attends to her fiat and her receptivity at the Cross, but he generally studies the mysteries of Mary in order to show something about the Church. I think that the result is that he gives a less rich portrait of the particular ways in which Mary and thus the Church is Spirit-filled, and he is unable to illumine fully the uniqueness of Mary and her transcendence of the type through her personal distinctiveness and particularity. Mary has experienced things that no other member of the Church has experienced, and this must count for something, as Laurentin makes clear.

Rahner's approach is rooted in his theology of grace as God's self-communication, God's assurance to the world of his enveloping and all-embracing mercy and love. Theology and anthropology are inextricably linked. Mary's faith is important for Rahner because it shows her complete acceptance of God's self-communication (which attained its peak in the Incarnation). Mary shows us what the human being is and what Christianity is. In the dialogue between divine and human freedom, we see God's love for us in the sheer grace of his loving entrance into the world for us and in the sheer grace of Mary's free and fruitful reception of his self-communication. In Mary, God's grace shows itself to be at work with extraordinary power in an ordinary human life. Indeed, all of us mediate God's love to each other, but Mary does so most perfectly because our salvation depends on her fiat, which itself was the fruit of sheer grace.

In Rahner the particular mysteries of Mary's life and her experience of the Spirit matter less than does the fact that she exemplifies what grace is and what humans are. Mary shows us why God created the world, namely, so as to freely communicate himself to it. She acquaints us with "the Christian idea of man." In what God does for her, we see God's mercy, love, and powerful embrace; we see what God wills for us. God's gracious self-communication is everything. The particular details of Mary's life and the specific person of the Holy Spirit do not have much of a role in Rahner's book, although he assumes the presence of both. His goal is to show us the meaning of grace, but in so doing, his approach all too often leaves out or neglects the actual unique movement of the Holy Spirit in Mary's life as portrayed in Scripture. Unlike Laurentin and (somewhat less) Semmelroth, Rahner hardly mentions the Holy Spirit.

My suggestion is that the more we wish to show how Mary's privileges, such as her unique experience of the Holy Spirit, apply broadly to the Church and to all of us, the more we should attend, as Laurentin especially did, to the concrete and specific details of the biblical portraits of Mary. Oddly enough, the more that Semmelroth and Rahner attempted to show that everything about Mary applies to something broader, namely, to the Church and to all of us, the less firm was their hold on the very thing that makes Mary worth considering, that is to say, her unique consecration by the Holy Spirit for her vocation as Mother and "handmaid" of the Lord. The Spirit made Christ present in her womb, and the Spirit configured her to her Son so that she could live out her motherhood, not least at the Cross and at Pentecost. By attending carefully to the particular events of Mary's life, Laurentin managed to display the universal significance of Mary's motherhood, and hence her unique actualization of the Church. In so doing, Laurentin, even more than Semmelroth or Rahner, anticipated the achievements of *Lumen Gentium*. He also showed the path for interpreting and appreciating the insistence of such saints as Maximilian Kolbe that even a formulation like "Spouse of the Holy Spirit" can hardly acquaint us with the unique and extraordinary fruitfulness of Mary's relationship with her Son through the Holy Spirit working within her, which we glimpse at moments such as the Annunciation and the Cross.

NOTES

1. Yves Congar, O.P., *I Believe in the Holy Spirit*, trans. David Smith (New York: Crossroad, 1997), vol. 1, 163. See also Cardinal Léon Josef Suenens, "The Relation That Exists between the Holy Spirit and Mary," in *Mary's Place in Christian Dialogue: Occasional Papers of the Ecumenical Society of the Blessed Virgin Mary, 1970–1980*, ed. Alberic Stacpoole, O.S.B. (Middlegreen, England: St Paul, 1982), 69–78; Alan Clark, "The Holy Spirit and Mary," in *Mary's Place in Christian Dialogue*, 79–88; Jarislaw Jasianek, "La Presencia del Espíritu Santo en la Maternidad de María," *Scripta Theologica* 38 (2006): 671–700.

2. Congar, *I Believe in the Holy Spirit*, vol. 1, 164. Congar, only a little earlier, notes that Leo XIII quoted Bernardino approvingly in his encyclical *Iucunda semper* (1894), in *Acta Sanctae Sedis*, vol. 27 (Rome: Typographia Polyglotta, 1894–95), 177–84. Congar goes on to quote further from another sermon of Bernardino in order to show the problematic tendency of his mariological language. For the relevant text of Bernardino, see *S. Bernardini Senensis Opera Omnia*, vol. 2 (Florence: Quaracchi, 1950), 157, as quoted in Heribert Mühlen, *L'Esprit dans l'Église*, vol. 2 (Paris: Cerf, 1969), 151–52.

3. Hans Urs von Balthasar, *Theo-Drama: Theological Dramatic Theory*, vol. 3: *The Dramatis Personae: The Person in Christ*, trans. Graham Harrison (San Francisco: Ignatius, 1992), 312–15.

4. Maximilian Kolbe, O.F.M. Conv., *Stronger Than Hatred: A Collection of Spiritual Writings*, trans. Edward Flood (Brooklyn, NY: New City Press, 1988), 45.

5. Ibid., 46–47.

6. For further background, see especially the chapters by Brian E. Daley, S.J., and Peter J. Fritz in this volume.

7. For further discussion, see Juan Luis Bastero, "El Espíritu Sancto y María en *Lumen Gentium* y en el Magisterio de Pablo VI," *Scripta Theologica* 38 (2006): 701–35. Similarly, Pope Paul VI observes in his Apostolic Exhortation *Marialis Cultus* (February 2, 1994), p. 26, that "the sanctifying intervention of the Spirit in the Virgin of Nazareth was a culminating moment of the Spirit's action in the history of salvation."

8. See René Laurentin, *Court traité de théologie mariale* (Paris: P. Lethielleux, 1956). For a lengthier edition of this book, published after the Second Vatican Council, see Laurentin, *Court traité sur la Vierge Marie* (Paris: P. Lethielleux, 1968). This edition also appears as *A Short Treatise on the Virgin Mary*, trans. Charles Neumann, S.M. (Washington, NJ: AMI, 1991).

9. René Laurentin, *Queen of Heaven: A Short Treatise on Marian Theology*, trans. Gordon Smith (London: Burns and Oates, 1956), 19.

10. Ibid., 70.

11. Ibid., 84.

12. Ibid., 91.

13. Ibid.

14. Ibid., 92.

15. Ibid.

16. Ibid., 93.

17. Ibid., 97, emphasis in original.

18. Ibid., 99.

19. Ibid.

20. Ibid., 101.

21. Ibid., 102.

22. Ibid., 113.

23. Ibid., 130.

24. See Otto Semmelroth, S.J., *Urbild der Kirche* (Würzburg: Echter, 1954).

25. Otto Semmelroth, S.J., *Mary, Archetype of the Church*, trans. Maria von Eroes and John Devlin (New York: Sheed and Ward, 1963), 11; cf. 23–24.

26. Ibid., 32.

27. Ibid., 52.

28. Ibid., 54–55.

29. Ibid., 63.

30. Ibid., 62.

31. Ibid., 65.

32. Ibid.

33. Ibid.

34. Ibid., 68.

35. Ibid.

36. Ibid., 71.

37. Ibid.

38. Ibid., 79. Semmelroth later observes, "If—in spite of the inherent inadequacies of the terms—what we have developed here were to be ordered according to the traditional terminology of *redemptio objectiva* and *redemptio subjectiva*, we would say the following: Mary co-operated directly, not with *redemptio objectiva*, if by this term we mean the work of Christ alone; and not with *redemptio subjectiva*, as long as this term is taken to mean only the application of the fruits of redemption to individual men. Rather, Mary co-operated with her own *redemptio objectiva*, which redemption, however, *simultaneously signifies* the reception of the fruits of salvation for the entire Church and which is therefore objective with regard to the individual" (ibid., 88–89).

39. Quoted in Semmelroth, *Mary, Archetype of the Church*, 82. Semmelroth goes on to say that his interpretation of Mary's collaboration "can be the only meaning Pius X had in mind when he says that Mary merited '*de congruo*' what Christ merited '*de condigno*.' The pertinent pronouncements of the more recent Popes (Leo XIII, Pius X, Benedict XV, and Pius XI) can be interpreted only according to the ecclesiological concept of co-redemption as we have demonstrated it. They cannot be understood according to the pattern of cooperation with either objective or subjective redemption, if these concepts are understood in the way we have outlined them. . . . The papal pronouncements can be interpreted clearly and with no difficulty from the ecclesiological point of view" (ibid., 85–86).

40. Ibid., 84.

41. Ibid., 88.

42. Ibid., 93.

43. Ibid., 101.

44. Ibid., 103.

45. Ibid., 104.

46. Ibid., 109.

47. Ibid., 117.

48. Ibid., 123.

49. Ibid., 128.

50. Ibid., 136.

51. Ibid., 146.

52. Ibid., 149.

53. Ibid., 165.

54. Ibid., 169.

55. See Karl Rahner, S.J., *Maria, Mutter des Herrn: Mariologische Studien*, ed. Regina Pacis Meyer, in Rahner, *Sämtliche Werke*, vol. 9: *Maria, Mutter des Herrn* (Freiburg: Herder, 2004), 515–68.

56. Probably his most influential Mariological work is his "The Interpretation of the Dogma of the Assumption," *Theological Investigations*, vol. 1: *God, Christ, Mary and Grace*, trans. Cornelius Ernst, O.P. (Baltimore, MD: Helicon, 1961), 215–27.

57. Karl Rahner, S.J., *Mary, Mother of the Lord: Theological Meditations*, trans. W.J. O'Hara (New York: Herder and Herder, 1963), 9.

58. Ibid., 10.

59. Ibid.

60. Ibid., 11.

61. Ibid.

62. Ibid., 16.

63. Ibid., 26.

64. Ibid., 30–31.

65. Ibid., 35.

66. Ibid., 37.

67. Ibid., 48.

68. Ibid., 46.

69. Ibid., 44, 47, 50, 52.

70. Ibid., 52.

71. Ibid., 57.

72. Ibid., 58.

73. Ibid., 58–59.

74. Ibid., 60.

75. Ibid., 61.

76. Ibid., 64–65.

77. Ibid., 66.

78. Ibid., 70.

79. Ibid., 73.

80. Ibid., 77.

81. Ibid., 79.

82. Ibid., 83.

83. Ibid., 84.

84. Ibid., 89.

85. Ibid., 91.

86. Ibid., 99.

87. Ibid., 100.

88. Ibid., 101.

89. Ibid.

CHAPTER 6

Karl Rahner's Marian "Minimalism"

PETER JOSEPH FRITZ

Near the end of his life, Karl Rahner lamented the Catholic faithful's loss of Marian devotion. The marginalization of Marian devotion in postconciliar Catholicism, Rahner wrote, resulted from human weakness, even narrow-mindedness.[1] To countervail this tendency, in his final year (1984) Rahner contributed to a volume by Marianne Dirks titled *Für eine neue Liebe zu Maria* (For a New Love of Mary).[2]

I begin my chapter this way because I suspect that a treatment of Rahner's relationship to Mariology and to the Second Vatican Council must include an apologetic dimension. Rahner is, of course, most often associated with the "progressive" or "liberal" wing of post–Vatican II theology and Church life. This wing tended to drift away from Marian devotions. They did this in keeping with a "minimalism" with respect to Mary that they believed prevailed at the Council. It may seem to be an obvious inference, if Rahner is rightly associated with the progressives, that he advocated their distraction from the Marian path. He was, after all, a self-described Marian "minimalist."[3] But something else was afoot with Rahner's Marian minimalism than his demotion of Mary. This "something else" is what I explore here.

The bulk of this chapter defines Rahner's Marian minimalism through a historical and systematic treatment of his Mariology from the mid-1940s through 1964. I begin with Rahner's discussion of the mariological problematic in a review essay from 1948. Then I examine the chief example of Rahner's Mariology, which went unpublished during his lifetime, the *Assumptio-Arbeit*. Two sections follow regarding Rahner's participation in Vatican II: one on his fit with the "inclusion" party that advocated a place for Mary within the schema on the Church and one on Rahner's 1964 essay on the Council's Mariology. A fifth section extends the timeline a bit by articulating how Mary remained of interest to Rahner up to his death.[4] I argue that Rahner's distinctive Marian minimalism grounded itself in his heartfelt, lifelong Marian devotion, which approached yet never fully embraced maximalism, thus avoiding excesses of theological prose and devotional poetry and effecting a polyvalent fullness consonant with Catholicism's constitutive ethos.

PROBLEMS OF CONTEMPORARY MARIOLOGY

Rahner's theological interest in Mary, which hitherto had been comparatively understated,[5] came to the fore in the mid-1940s. This increase in interest coincided with Pope Pius XII's 1946 letter to all Catholic bishops asking whether they wished him to pronounce the bodily Assumption of Mary into heavenly glory as a divinely revealed dogma. This letter, entitled *Deiparae Virginis Mariae*,[6] seems to have spurred Rahner's engagement with mariological questions.[7] But more immediately of concern to him was a book published the following year by Heinrich Maria Köster called *Die Magd des Herrn: Theologische Versuche und Überlegungen* (The Handmaid of the Lord: Theological Essays and Observations).[8] This book prompted Rahner to compose a substantial review essay titled "Probleme heutiger Mariologie" (Problems of Contemporary Mariology).[9] Why did Köster's text so interest Rahner? Karl Neufeld proposes that Rahner concerned himself with Mariology not because of university and teaching obligations but because of the ramifications of Marian teachings in the lives of everyday Catholics.[10]

One can add that Rahner regarded Mariology as a crucial measure of the wellness or the pathology of European Catholic theology and life in the 1940s. By this time, German Mariology had reached an impasse; minimalists conducted "Mariology only as an enumeration of previously defined propositions," while others praised Mary so highly that Rahner feared they forsook "the healthy soil of the Church."[11] These extremes in Mariology reflected wider trends in midcentury European Catholicism: theology was dominated by arid propositionalism, and life perpetually wavered on the verge of fideism.

Köster's book is, Rahner believes, a refreshing change of pace from this state of affairs. Rahner praises Köster for his balance, writing that Köster clearly commits himself "to avoiding unclear and sentimental exuberance in Mariology just as much as a rationalistic minimalism that tries to throttle the urge of a faithful person's consciousness toward deeper knowledge of the essence and the salvation-historical status of Mary."[12] Thus Köster positions himself well to address the lively mariological controversies of the 1940s.

This all said, though, Rahner detects in Köster's book similar instabilities to those of other Mariologies and of contemporary Catholicism more generally. Köster attempts to determine about Mary what cannot be determined;[13] he specifies her station too precisely, thus sharing the propositionalism of Neo-Scholastic theologians. And he unduly elevates Mary above the rest of the human race; he estimates her too highly as the "personal apex of the world,"[14] thus reflecting the fideist trend of enthusiastic Marian piety. Rahner relentlessly critiques Köster's text, using this book as a proxy for other Mariologies. The shortfalls of Köster's book, which to Rahner's mind ranks among the best 1940s-era Mariologies, indicate the failures of the rest of this theological trajectory. Rahner's critique is not merely negative, though. He begins laying the ground for a way forward.

It is worth pursuing a few details of Rahner's critique.[15] Rahner's central target is Köster's attempt at a "higher synthesis" of contemporary positive and negative answers to the question of whether Mary participates in "objective redemption."[16] The "positive" party implicates a long tradition, including Albert the Great and Bonaventure. It holds that Mary contributes to salvation, if in a manner subordinate to Christ. The "negative" position predicates itself upon the fact that Mary, as a nondivine person, is one of the redeemed. She cannot be a co-redeemer. Köster achieves his synthesis by agreeing with the negative perspective that Mary cannot grant redemption since she stands firmly on the human, not the divine, side. But in keeping with the positive view, since Mary exists within the order established by Christ, she can participate in the objective redemption of other human persons from the human side. Mary does this by accepting on behalf of all humanity the salvation that Christ alone effects.[17] Köster takes this idea even further, maintaining that Christ and Mary partake in a polarity that structures the act of salvation. God's active saving work in Christ meets its counterpoint in humanity's passive acceptance of salvation in Mary.[18]

Rahner deems this "higher synthesis" inadmissible on two main counts: (1) it attributes to Mary a role in objective redemption by illicitly curtailing the meaning of Christ's humanity in the event of salvation, and (2) it misdirects the relationship between the individual (Mary) and the whole of humanity.[19] Rahner's Chalcedonian Christological commitments make him nervous with respect to Köster's diminishment of Christ's human nature so that Mary can play the human role in redemption. Though Rahner never directly accuses Köster of heterodoxy—he deems any flirting with Christological heresies to be inadvertent—he nevertheless points to the danger of maintaining a Kösterian Christological position.[20] This is all the more unfortunate because Köster does not need to put himself in such peril. Mary's cooperation in the mystery of salvation does not entail a downgrading of Christ's humanity. Köster's desire for a clear-cut answer to the question of Mary's role in redemption leads him astray.

The same goes for Köster's elevation of Mary above the rest of humanity. Presenting Mary as "the pinnacle of created personality" strikes Rahner as understandable, since he too esteems Mary highly. But it remains problematic. Köster's wish for Mary to represent all of humanity clashes with his distancing of her from the rest of humanity. Rahner draws a sophisticated yet illustrative distinction with respect to the phrase *"im Namen,"* which Köster uses to describe Mary's representation of humanity. *"Im Namen"* can mean "on behalf of another" in two senses: (1) "on the authority" of another, with competence and responsibility and (2) "in the name of another," yet without any moral accountability for the damage or usefulness of one's action.[21] It is not clear that Mary represents humanity in either of these cases: nothing in particular qualifies Mary as a "competent representative," nor can one detect in Scripture or tradition warrant for Mary's unregulated standing-in for everyone else as the chief recipient of salvation. If Köster's account should hold, the privileges Mary possesses and enacts would appear unattainable by her fellow humans—even by Christ's human nature! For Rahner, were Köster to relinquish his requirement that Mary be the "supraindividual epitome of humanity," the meaning of her role in salvation history would become much clearer.[22] Almost immediately after writing this essay, Rahner set out to improve upon Köster's project.

THE *ASSUMPTIO-ARBEIT*

Despite its troubles, Köster's text proved generative for Rahner's own Mariology in the *Assumptio-Arbeit*, a monograph on Mary's Assumption that Rahner began writing in the late 1940s, as soon as he perceived the definition of a new Marian dogma looming on the horizon.[23] Reading and critiquing Köster prodded Rahner to seek a better way of situating Mary within salvation history; of relating Mary to her Son, the Redeemer; of speaking about her privileges;[24] and, conversely, of ensuring that Mary's connection to other human persons remains clear and unbroken. Along the way he adopted the strategy he appreciated in Köster: avoiding both rationalistic minimalism and enthusiastic fideism. Though he believed he succeeded in evading pathological minimalism, a Jesuit censor would disagree.[25] The charge of "minimalism" would damn the publication of the *Assumptio-Arbeit*.

I focus on the center of this text, which is the point that the censor found most questionable. It appears in the crucial fourth chapter, "*Die Glaubenslehre von der Eschatologie der seligsten Jungfrau*" (The Doctrine of the Faith on the Eschatology of the Blessed Virgin).[26] There Rahner formulates a "*Grundprinzip*," or "basic principle," for Mariology: "Mary is redeemed in the most perfect way."[27] Rahner reaches this succinct expression of his focus after more than 250 pages of rather "maximal" reflection on mariological sources from the patristic, medieval, modern, and contemporary eras, including magisterial teachings through Pope Pius XII.[28] He treks through these historical thickets to guide his reader in properly raising key questions about Mary's Assumption. Rahner's concern in centering his text on the principle of Mary as *die vollkommenste Erlöste*, the most perfectly redeemed one, lies in countering what he took to be a centrifugal, as opposed to centripetal, force operating in midcentury Mariology.

Comments from two other Rahnerian essays that derived from the *Assumptio-Arbeit* can illuminate my point. Rahner critically remarks that, with regard to the dogma of the Assumption, contemporary Mariologies fail "to enter more deeply into the inner meaning of the new dogma."[29]And elsewhere he declares, "All honor to the countless number of Mariological works being written today. . . . But how many themes, important in themselves, remain unexamined! Over how many questions does there reign the graveyard calm of weariness and boredom!"[30] I say "centrifugal force," then, to render Rahner's objection that Mariologians tend to flee from the theological center—the mystery of redemption in Christ's death and resurrection—to peripheral matters. These matters leave behind deeper questions of meaning, thus risking a disorientation of the faithful, who must contend with the difficult-to-understand new dogma. A basic principle for Mariology can help to orient not just people's inquiry into the dogma of the Assumption but also people's living out of its significance.

The fact that Rahner proposed a basic principle for Mariology was hardly novel. Stating such a principle was customary in Mariologies from the early seventeenth century forward. But he diverges from the modern mariological tradition, and thus from Pope Pius XII and his promulgation of the dogma of the Assumption in *Munificentissimus Deus* (1950), when he channels the basic principle away from Mary's private privilege and toward her full integration into salvation history.[31] The elevated eschatological index of Rahner's Mariology facilitates this shift. Whereas the conventional basic mariological principle, Mary's motherhood, connotes privatization, Rahner's principle avoids it. He emphasizes—and herein lies his minimalism—that one must not lose sight of the fact that Mary is one human person among many. She is blessed *among* women (cf. Luke 1:42). She shares in the same pilgrim journey as all human persons. Indeed she is distinct from other pilgrims in that she has already arrived at a destination toward which others still travel.[32] But the fact that "the redemption of the world came through her redemption to its goal" does not separate Mary from the rest of humanity; in fact, it is precisely why "her redemption is not a merely 'private matter' ['*Privatangelegenheit*'] . . . but something that belongs to the conditions of our own redemption."[33] Rahner's stress on Mary's belonging to the human race ends up underscoring her constitutive place in the salvific economy. Minimizing her personal privilege maximizes her salvation-historical significance.

In the summer of 1950, Rahner submitted a complete draft of the *Assumptio-Arbeit* to Jesuit reviewers in Innsbruck. He hoped that the book might appear by the time the pope promulgated the new dogma. This did not happen. The following year Rahner submitted a new draft for further review. Two censors approved the book, but provincial leadership sought a third opinion. This third censor did not concur with his predecessors. Rome sided with the third censor, officially blocking the publication of the book in a notice dated April 12, 1952.[34]

Regina Pacis Meyer reports on the main lines of the official censure. Notable is the document's judgment on Rahner's basic mariological principle: "What K. Rahner developed regarding the fundamental principle of Mariology, what one could express with the phrase: '*Maria fuit perfectissimo modo passive et active salvata*' [Mary was saved in the most perfect way, passively and actively], wholly displeases the censor."[35] The principle did not correspond to the scriptural evidence regarding Mary, nor was there any discernible way that it contributed to the definition of Mary's motherhood or her "office (*Amt*)."[36] The censor brought forth other objections to Rahner's text, especially with respect to the theology of death developed in the text and in an appendix.[37] But the most devastating aspect of the censor's critique lay in his rejection of Rahner's fundamental principle. As Meyer summarizes the censor's conclusion regarding this issue, "Rahner could hardly modify his fundamental principle in such a way that he could adequately respond to [the] difficulties" raised by the censor.[38] Rahner's approach was too "negative" or "minimalistic" to produce a positive result.

Rahner attempted to appeal the censor's blocking of the *Assumptio-Arbeit*'s publication, but to no avail. Letter exchanges between his older brother Hugo and the Jesuit leadership also failed to change the situation.[39] Disappointed and not much consoled by Hugo's encouragement,[40] Rahner moved on to other things. But Pius's dedication of 1954 as a Marian year revived Rahner's interest in the *Assumptio-Arbeit*. He made some alterations to it then. Neither these nor a new letter exchange with the provincial would end in the book's publication. Over the next few years, up to 1959, Rahner would add periodically to the book, but more pressing matters, like editing the *Lexikon für Theologie und Kirche* and, eventually, attending the Vatican Council, ensured that the *Assumptio-Arbeit* would not be published during his lifetime.[41] Though manuscripts of the book were known to a small group of Rahner's students and colleagues, it would not be made public until its 2004 release in volume 9 of his *Sämtliche Werke*.

The effort Rahner put into researching and writing the *Assumptio-Arbeit* would not be fruitless. Out of these labors came what are now familiar essays on the Immaculate Conception, Mary's Virginity, and the Assumption.[42] Also related are Rahner's May 1953 spiritual conferences on Mary, which he published in 1956 as a slim book, *Maria, Mutter des Herrn*.[43] Rahner made somewhat of a mariological impression on Catholic theology and life, but not the impact he would have, had the *Assumptio-Arbeit* been printed. Later in life Rahner facetiously mused that the censor may have inadvertently spared him some embarrassment because of the outdated, deficient biblical theology Rahner used in the book.[44] But this scarcely outweighed the disservice of fostering the impression that Rahner was a reckless Marian minimalist.

AT VATICAN II: "INCLUSION" AND RAHNER'S MARIOLOGY

Eleven years before the opening of the Second Vatican Council and the same year that Karl Rahner's travails with the *Assumptio-Arbeit* began, Hugo Rahner published a book called *Maria und die Kirche* (Mary and the Church).[45] This brilliant *ressourcement* Mariology went a long way toward setting the stage for the conciliar debates on Mary. Its basic purpose was

"to show from the warm-hearted theology of the great fathers and doctors that the whole mystery of the Church is inseparably bound up with
the mystery of Mary."[46] Hugo contends that for the Church Fathers and
the medieval Schoolmen, Mary was essentially a symbol for the Church.
Modern theologians forgot this ecclesiological function of Mary and
constructed theologies that unhelpfully set Mary apart from the Church
by unduly emphasizing her privileges. So Karl was not the first Rahner
to assume such a stance. And he was not the only theologian seriously
influenced by Hugo.[47] The very fact that a majority, if a slight one, of the
bishops at Vatican II supported the inclusion of Mary in the schema on
the Church shows that Hugo's ecclesiotypical way of thinking about her
had gained great currency.

Hugo's ideas manifest themselves most clearly in Karl's essay "Mary
and the Apostolate" (1955), which appears in the collection of pastoral
essays *Sendung und Gnade* (1959).[48] Karl forcefully argues for Mary as the
"type of the Church," *Maria typus Ecclesiae*, a phrase he attributes to St.
Ambrose but which, as he would have known from reading Hugo's book,
dates back at least as far as Hippolytus at the end of the second century.[49]
He also calls Mary a "living pattern for the apostolate"—by which he
means the different apostolic missions of all the faithful, against any
one-sided clericalism or laicism.[50] In this way, Karl follows cues from
Hugo's chapter "Growth in Holiness," which discusses the patristic and
medieval notion that all the baptized ought to pattern their striving toward virtue on Mary, to the point that each of the faithful will bear and
give birth to Christ through holy living.[51]

But Karl distinctively reshapes Hugo's ecclesiotypical view of Mary.
Beyond Hugo's Marian *ressourcement*, he reflects on how Mary as the
type of the Church aligns with Mary as the most perfectly redeemed
person. He comments, "Considered as a redeemed human being, a fruit
of the redemption . . . there is no one who could more clearly represent
what Christian existence is than the most blessed Virgin Mother of
God."[52] He continues, "What the Church is, in her functioning, is shown
at its clearest and in its pure, full completeness in the Mary-event."[53]
Mary as *typus ecclesiae* and as *die vollkommenste Erlöste* coincide,[54] revealing the proper orientation of apostolic life. Mary reveals this orientation
because she concretely enfleshes apostolicity. Rahner deems this crucial

because "the true spirit of a true Christian apostolate is not the spirit of anarchy, not the spirit of the 'enthusiasts,' but a spirit which has the courage to submit to flesh, to concrete precisions."[55] He recommends a bounded ecclesiology patterned on Mary's giving of the Spirit through the enfleshed Word and her suffering beneath the Cross of her Son.[56]

Given what I have said so far, it makes good sense that Karl Rahner would be appointed Cardinal Franz König's adviser at Vatican II on Marian and ecclesiological matters. And when König delivered a speech at the Council on October 24, 1963, advocating Mary's inclusion in the schema on the Church, Rahner's fingerprints appeared quite patently on the text. We have in König's own words that he asked Rahner to make an outline on which he based this speech.[57] But it is worth examining König's speech itself to detect Rahner's influence.

König's remarks followed those of Cardinal Rufino Santos, who promoted a separate schema on Mary based on her heightened dignity, which places her above the rest of the people of God and outside the concerns of the Church's pilgrim situation on earth.[58] König opens by indicating his intention not to speak against the Marian doctrine and piety expressed by the previous speaker. Nor, König states, does he wish to ignore the Marian and mariological movement of the past century,[59] or even the petitions from six hundred Council fathers appealing for a conciliar definition of a new Marian dogma. But since a majority of the members of the Theological Commission, including Rahner, believed that the conciliar statement on Mary would best be integrated within the schema on the Church, König presents reasons supporting this case.

The reasons take four forms: theological, historical, pastoral, and ecumenical.[60] König spends the most time with five theological reasons, so I shall focus on these, in particular the third, fourth, and fifth. The third reason is that, although the eschatological end of the Church, to which Mary pertains, ought to and will be exposed by the schema on the Church, the "*terrestrial* life and soteriological function of the Virgin should not be passed over in silence."[61] Mariology would profit from reintegrating Mary into this earthly aspect of the Church. Reintegration "shows [Mary's] genuine significance and proportion, so that the value of the doctrine about the Blessed Virgin in relation to Christ as the unique Mediator and to the Church [would be] better and more clearly perceived."[62] Fourth,

Mary's place and office in the Church is founded on her being the type of the Church. Like the Church, she receives everything she has from Christ and passes this on to others. Like the Church, she is both the fruit and the medium of redemption.[63] Fifth, although Santos and others feared that a decision for inclusion would unduly privilege a certain theological school (ecclesiotypical) over another (Christotypical), inclusion would not mean a one-sided victory of the former over the latter.[64] The Church cooperates actively with Christ in salvation, and so does Mary, in a heightened way, as "the most sublime cooperatrix with Christ through his grace in both the completion and the propagation of the work of salvation."[65]

In König's speech we discover an approach to Mariology similar to that we have found in Rahner. The opening statements on not contradicting Marian piety and doctrine echo Rahner's appreciation of Köster's refusal to countenance a rationalistic Marian minimalism and Rahner's similar rejection of such minimalism in the *Assumptio-Arbeit*. König's plea to the Council fathers to reintegrate Mary into salvation history reflects Rahner's same request to Köster. So, too, are there echoes of Rahner's revised version of ecclesiotypical Mariology, which, again, by no means marginalizes Mary's special relationship to Christ, nor does it rob her of her specific, sublime station in the salvific economy. While these points may not have allayed the concerns of Santos and the "separate schema" party, König and Rahner certainly took these concerns into account.

As is well known, König's speech came to represent the majority conciliar opinion. Mary was included in the Constitution on the Church and was not granted her own document. Karl Rahner went, then, from a younger brother admiringly appropriating Hugo's *ressourcement* Mariology to fusing this work with his own theology of Mary as *die vollkommenste Erlöste* to momentously contributing to the conciliar debate over "inclusion."

THE CONCILIAR MARIOLOGY AND "MINIMALISM"

Slightly in advance of the promulgation of *Lumen Gentium*, Rahner published an article in *Stimmen der Zeit* that promised to explicate the Council's Mariology. It became clear, though, that Rahner's primary purpose was to name and to mediate the conciliar contest between Marian "maximalists" and Marian "minimalists." In this article he develops a taxonomy of maximalists and minimalists. He devotes more space to this issue than to any other, including the ecumenical significance of the conciliar Mariology, which indubitably bears great import for him.

Maximalists advocate open theological speculation on and fervent devotion to Mary, while minimalists promote temperance. The latter group accuses the former of being cavalier, even heterodox. The former charges the latter with disrespect for the Virgin Mother of God. Rahner tries to mitigate the opposition. He argues that, "soberly speaking, the substantive differences of opinion among Catholics on these issues probably are not as great as an affectively charged judgment on both sides might first think."[66] I shall restate this thesis: though the conciliar Mariology may look like an undue concession to minimalistic abstemiousness or a clear victory for it, it is not; it expresses the vast area of theological and devotional agreement that appears when emotionally driven vitriol stops.

The central pages of the article articulate a vision for pluralism in Mariology and Marian piety. Rahner contends that "the representatives of both sides must, first of all, genuinely and actively realize . . . that there are many dwelling places in the house of the one Father and the one Mother Church, that it is thus unnecessary, that it would indeed be a lack of true Catholic fullness, if Catholic Mariology or Marian piety were the same everywhere."[67] Rahner alludes to Jesus's words from John 14:2 to underscore the contrast between disputes over Mary and Christ's desire for unity among his followers. Both sides fail to acknowledge the possibility of "many dwelling places" in the Father's house. They also seem unable even to recognize how the other side could want to reside in a different "dwelling." Latin–southern European maximalists cannot even imagine how their piety and speculation on Mary (including whether she possessed, even in the womb, knowledge of the mystery of the Trinity) could grate on the nerves of central European Catholics. They also cannot believe how little devotion to the Madonna they find in their neighbors to the north. Central European minimalists cannot comprehend how the southerners can be so un-self-consciously exuberant with respect to Mary. Mutual mistrust and misunderstanding abound, militating against catholicity.

Rahner urges both sides not to attack one another on theological grounds, nor to accuse one another of heresy. He tenders allowances to both sides: to central European minimalists he grants that theologians can and should pronounce a "No" to unbridled theological speculation, even if some Catholics will suspect them of being less pious, and to the southern maximalists he admits that minimalists could be less cool toward piety.[68] Lest these statements entrench differences, though, Rahner maintains that unity must prevail through open communication. And this conversation between the sides must be tolerant and respectful, given that a greater love must supervene over "brotherly antagonism and struggle."[69]

Rahner summarizes his position: "There are different theological schools that cannot in any way, in their pluralism, be 'raised' ['aufgehoben'] to higher unity; there are various orders and spiritualities that strive on various paths toward one goal, without each individual being able to tread all ways himself."[70] Rahner asserts that both sides of the maximalist–minimalist debate must remain. Neither may be eliminated. When Rahner exhorts his readers to a Catholic pluralism, he really means it. He is not proposing a simple, unfettered "letting be,"[71] which would be unproductive insofar as it would encourage the insularism that led to the maximalist–minimalist tensions in the first place. Instead he implores both maximalists and minimalists to sensitize themselves to the dynamics of their particular positions and in the process to become mindful of how these positions square with the "one truth and love of Christ."[72]

It is true that Rahner identifies with the minimalists. But he says something notable to his fellow minimalists. He exhorts them to realize that "we" do not need to hide that "we can be quiet, shy, and sorrowful people devoted to the Blessed Virgin. But we 'minimalists' should admit to ourselves that our theology and our devotion to the Blessed Virgin and Mother of God, who is also the mother of our faith, can and should still grow."[73] Rahner's exhortation is provocative. It suggests that Marian minimalism is really a variant of Marian maximalism. Rahner's high-minded theology never strays from the simple devotional life of the everyday person devoted to the Blessed Mother. In fact, his Marian minimalism would have no critical teeth without its bearer's intimate familiarity with Marian theology and devotion. The Marian minimalist who loses sight of this ineluctable connection to the devotional matrix of Marian maximalism will lose all orientation and, perhaps, any genuine Catholicism.

Rahner's statement on the conciliar Mariology antedated the closing of the Council by over a year. Already, though, it defended the continuing significance of Marian theology and devotion for the postconciliar Church. Far from being a triumphalist, minimalistic progressive, Rahner showed himself to be an ardent Catholic committed to the pluriform honor due to Christ's Blessed Mother. Stefan Hartmann is right, then, to chastise Cardinal Leo Scheffczyk for illegitimately accusing Rahner of "reductionism."[74] Contrary to Scheffczyk's fears, Rahner's filing of Marian minimalism under the larger category of Marian maximalism did not have a parallel with the "general diminution of the Christian in a 'worldly' world."[75] Instead, Rahner's measured presentation of the conciliar Mariology aimed to maintain authentic Catholic openness and to stop Catholics' tacit imitation of a modern world based in closure.

THE END OF RAHNERIAN MARIOLOGY?

Dominik Matuschek notes that after the Council Rahner made a definite turn away from direct involvement with Mariology. He concerned himself more with "atheism, interreligious encounter, or ecumenical dialogue."[76] Neufeld observes that Rahner sometimes gives the impression that the mariological and Marian-devotional projects of the preconciliar period were rendered obsolete in the postconciliar period by other themes more focally pertinent to spreading the Christian message. But even so, Neufeld contends that Rahner never fully gave up Mariology; in fact, he "ordered it anew."[77] In this way, Rahner heeded his own advice from "Zur konziliaren Mariologie."

Rahner's 1966 lecture "The Second Vatican Council's Challenge to Theology," which was originally delivered at the University of Notre Dame, occasions some of Rahner's most negative, even dismissive, comments regarding the preconciliar mariological boom. He suggests that midcentury mariological efforts exacerbated the "monolithism" of Neo-Scholastic manual theology.[78] Instead of contributing to Christian theological reflection, such Mariologies left theology proper largely untouched. Rahner declares, "For it seems to me that, however praiseworthy it may have been on the whole, the quantity and extent of technical study in the field of Mariology in the last few decades is *also* (although not *only*) a sign of the tacit assumption that, apart from the field of history of dogma which works retrospectively, progress is only possible in peripheral areas of theology."[79] Preconciliar Mariology, then, served mainly to aggravate the pathologies of preconciliar theology more generally, the main one being preconciliar theology's unwillingness to confront itself with the center of the Christian message. Mariology became an escape hatch from the theological center through which theologians could flee to the periphery. This theological escapism likewise avoided pressing problems of the modern world, such as atheism. Rahner points to the irony at play in theology's misplacement of its focus: "We do not have the 1,000 volumes on 'atheism' which would be needed if we were to justify the innumerable books of Mariology which we do have."[80]

The dour tone of this lecture with respect to Mariology contrasts sharply, though, with Rahner's high estimation of the Marian devotion of the rosary in another address delivered in the same year. Rahner ruminates on an odd trend in contemporary European (and, one could add, American) culture: "It is strange. The most complex techniques of Yoga are considered reasonable, yet the old Christian methods of prayer and meditation, for example the rosary, are regarded as unmodern. But why precisely? Is this the result of experience or is it merely that the practitioners are all too eager to know better?"[81] Rahner continues with more rhetorical questions, gradually hammering home the point that Christian life in the future must retain continuity with the past, not just formally but materially. Marian devotions like the rosary will be central to this material continuity. Rahner adds apposite thoughts in an essay from 1968. The experiential dimension of his thoughts is worth serious consideration. He inquires,

> Why should we replace a two thousand year old Christian practice of meditation and asceticism by what we have read somewhere about Zen Buddhism and Yoga? It is certainly a rewarding task to synthesize Eastern and Christian piety and asceticism. But it is surely naïve to esteem *a priori* psychotherapy and the practices of Yoga more highly than the traditional Christian devotions. If a person does not understand or like the rosary, for example, he is perfectly free, as a Christian, not to say it; yet for me it is a very wonderful thing, and it

is my own private experience that it is said also by people of whom one would not believe it.[82]

Presumably the "people" to whom Rahner refers at the end of this quote would include his fellow Marian minimalists, who are inaccurately perceived as too progressive to say the rosary. I rehearse these comments in order to show that the acerbity with which Rahner speaks of Mariology on some occasions should not be read in isolation from his heartfelt commitment to Marian devotion. Furthermore, his plea for a more ecumenical theology, which likely would preclude the Marian enthusiasm of the 1940s and 1950s and would include sensitivity to the objections of atheists, must never be elided with the vapid New Age spiritualities that proliferated after Vatican II.

In short, Rahner's postconciliar comments on Mariology and Marian devotion have a double-edged quality. This quality results from his theological-spiritual consistency. Rahner consistently insists that Catholic theology and life must maintain material continuity with the preceding process of tradition. Preconciliar Neo-Scholastic theology risked breaking this material link by formalizing the content of faith out of existence. Preconciliar Mariology became suspect because it aided and abetted Neo-Scholastic theology's mistakes. On the other side, and ultimately more importantly, Rahner was vexed by postconciliar spirituality's willingness to relinquish traditional Marian devotions in favor of the novel flavors of the East. In his last decade and a half of life, Rahner became increasingly worried that the material continuity of tradition upon which the ethos of Catholicism depends risks being broken by people who think they "know better" than their forbears.

Rahner expressed this perspective in the 1983 essay "Courage for Devotion to Mary." I began my chapter with words from this piece, which to my mind ranks among the most significant Rahner ever wrote. It explicitly sets itself against what elsewhere Rahner calls the "prosaic scantiness of today's piety."[83] He does not swerve from his prior efforts to balance Marian minimalism and maximalism, but he does inflect this balance differently in light of two decades of negative developments vis-à-vis Mary. He offers a twofold warning against hanging on to Marian devotions simply for the sake of nostalgia but also against ridding oneself of Marian devotions in the name of progress. The title of the article—invoking the courage needed in the postconciliar Church to continue Marian devotion—shows that Rahner casts the bulk of his suspicion toward minimalistic "progressives," as does the following passage:

> Undoubtedly we have the right to reject certain forms of the veneration of Mary, as the Second Vatican Council emphasizes, when such forms turn into superstitions or employ practices that contradict the uniqueness of the mediation of Jesus Christ or the free sovereignty of divine grace, or when they hold the absurd opinion that it is easier to be certain of Mary's love than of the infinite mercy and love of the eternal God. So it is quite legitimate to keep our own religious practice away from a legitimate devotion to Mary. Yet even though this aloofness is allowed, we should not hold it up as a principle. It is better to remain open to a further development in our religious life, in which a more intense and explicit veneration of Mary can also have a place.[84]

One can distance oneself a bit from Marian devotion, but *never* on principle. Catholic principles demand a constant connection to Mary.

Marian minimalism was, at the time of the Council, a critical tactic to keep Marian theology and devotion from becoming unhinged. But to Rahner's mind, given the "prosaic scantiness" of postconciliar piety, a true Catholic must be courageous enough to recognize the Marian maximalism that attends and subtends the Catholic ethos. And the true Catholic must be courageous enough to reclaim something like Marian maximalism.

Rahner delivered a lecture in Munster in 1968 on the Virgin Birth that he would return to again and again over the next decade and a half, most notably in his final theological colloquiums at Innsbruck in the early 1980s.[85] I shall close this final section with words Rahner spoke at one of these colloquiums in May 1983. He remarks, "When each of us prays a 'Hail Mary,' and really from our innermost heart, then this is without question much more meaningful than all of our learned talk."[86] These words must be heeded as we venture forward into the sixth postconciliar decade. Rahner teaches us that if we ever feel inclined to minimize our words about Mary, the resulting minimalism should manifest itself as the simplicity of traditional Marian prayer.

RAHNER AND THE RENEWAL OF MARIAN THOUGHT

This chapter has provided an overview of Rahner's multifaceted occupation with Mariology and Marian devotion, which was most direct and intensive on the eve of Vatican Council II but which, I have argued, endured in various forms until the end of his life. In English-language scholarship, we tend not to acknowledge this area of Rahner's interest. There are honest reasons for this, but so, too, are there less reputable ones.

On the honest side, the many pieces Rahner wrote and published on Mary are scattered among numerous books, and several of these have never been translated into English. Also, as I have repeatedly noted, Rahner's main text on Mary was never published. On the less honest side, the stock reading of Rahner as a progressive, modernizing theologian has led to myopia amid his supporters and critics alike, rendering them incapable of even noticing Rahner's Marian writings, let alone digging through German texts to locate them. In addition to contributing to the wider discussion about Mary on the eve of the Council, then, I hope that this chapter can help to flesh out the English-language academy's picture of Rahner.[87]

Karl Neufeld is the best guide for discovering the truth about Rahner's Marian minimalism. After discussing Rahner's early-1980s Innsbruck colloquiums on Mary, Neufeld reflects on the censoring of the *Assumptio-Arbeit*. He reframes as advantageous what could easily be deemed a liability. He suggests that the denial of the great Rahnerian mariological monograph was precisely what allowed Rahner to be a lifelong Mariologian. The sublimation of the grand statement on Mary became the condition for Rahner's many minor statements on her, including his work behind the scenes of Vatican II.[88] I propose that we can draw a lesson from the itinerary of Rahner's fragmented scholarship on Mary. In a time when the Marian aspect of the Catholic ethos seems to have collapsed in large sectors of the world, we can labor to revive this aspect through small yet pointed efforts, always in the hope that these minimal efforts will foster a maximal Marian fullness that befits Catholic theology and life.

NOTES

1. See Karl Rahner, "Courage for Devotion to Mary," in *Final Writings: Theological Investigations*, vol. 23, trans. Hugh M. Riley and Joseph Donceel, ed. Paul Imhof (New York: Crossroad, 1992), 129–31.

2. Rahner's main contribution was a reprint of the "Courage for Devotion to Mary" essay. The original German essay appears in Karl Rahner, *Geistliche Schriften: Späte Beiträge zur Praxis des Glaubens, Sämtliche Werke*, vol. 29, ed. Herbert Vorgrimler (Freiburg: Herder, 2007), 280–90. For the foreword to Dirks's volume, see ibid., 480. For the volume itself, see Marianne Dirks and Karl Rahner, *Für eine neue Liebe zu Maria* (Freiburg: Herder, 1984).

3. Karl Rahner, "Zur konziliaren Mariologie," *Stimmen der Zeit* 174 (1964): 87–101. It is notable that in this article Rahner always places "minimalist" and its partner "maximalist" in quotation marks. For this insight, see Stefan Hartmann, "Die 'offene' Mariologie Karl Rahners," *Zeitschrift für katholische Theologie* 132 (2010): 293–311, esp. 308, n. 73. Translations of material from Rahner's "Zur konziliaren Mariologie" are mine.

4. Dominik Matuschek insists that Mariology is the key to Rahner's thinking and that after Vatican II there has been "only an apparent marginalization of Mary." Instead the "Rahnerian interest in Mary is unbroken." He argues further that Rahner's postconciliar theology borrows heavily from his preconciliar Mariological work, though he never explicates these borrowings. Matuschek, *Konkrete Dogmatik: Die Mariologie Karl Rahners* (Innsbruck: Tyrolia, 2012), 15–16, 398, 454–55. All translations from this book are mine.

5. The exceptions come in Rahner's theological dissertation *E latere Christi* (1936) and the latter parts of the monograph *Aszese und Mystik* (1939). For both of these works, see Karl Rahner, *Spiritualität und Theologie der Kirchenväter: Sämtliche Werke*, vol. 3, ed. Andreas Batlogg, Eduard Farrugia, and Karl-Heinz Neufeld, index by Jeanne Schlösser (Freiburg: Herder, 1999).

6. Pius XII, Encyclical Letter, *Deiparae Virginis Mariae* (May 1, 1946), on the possibility of defining the Assumption of the Blessed Virgin Mary as a dogma of faith.

7. See Regina Pacis Meyer, "Editionsbericht," in *Maria, Mutter des Herrn: Mariologische Studien, Sämtliche Werke*, vol. 9, ed. Regina Pacis Meyer (Freiburg: Herder, 2004), xxiii–xxiv.

8. Heinrich Maria Köster, *Die Magd des Herrn: Theologische Versuche und Überlegungen* (Limburg, Germany: Lahn, 1947).

9. Karl Rahner, "Probleme heutiger Mariologie," in *Sämtliche Werke*, vol. 9, 681–703, first published in Gottlieb Söhngen, ed., *Aus der Theologie der Zeit* (Regensburg: Gregorius, 1948), 85–113.

10. Karl Neufeld, "Mariologie in der Sicht Karl Rahners," *Ephemerides Mariologicae* 50 (2000): 291.

11. Matuschek, *Konkrete Dogmatik*, 35.

12. Rahner, "Probleme heutiger Mariologie," 681. All translations of this text are mine.

13. See ibid., 694.

14. See ibid., 695.

15. A more extensive treatment is given in Matuschek, *Konkrete Dogmatik*, 252–58.

16. Rahner, "Probleme heutiger Mariologie," 682–83.

17. Ibid., 684.

18. Ibid.

19. Ibid., 703.

20. For the details of this argument, see ibid., 685–94.

21. Ibid., 695–96.

22. Ibid., 699–700.

23. See Meyer, "Editionsbericht," xxiv.

24. This phrase evokes the title of a brief yet helpful essay on Rahner's Mariology by Philip Endean. See Endean, "How to Think about Mary's Privileges," in *Mary: The Complete Resource*, ed. Sarah Jane Boss (New York: Continuum, 2007), 284–91.

25. See Meyer, "Editionsbericht," xxxv–xxxvi.

26. Rahner, "Assumptio Beatae Maria Virginis," in *Sämtliche Werke*, vol. 9, 3–392, esp. 125–308. All translations from this text are mine.

27. See ibid., 268, 271, 273, 275, and 284 to see how Rahner gradually arrived at this formulation. On the articulation of the foundational principle, see Matuschek, *Konkrete Dogmatik*, 131–35, 239–41.

28. Dazzlingly impressive is Rahner's meticulous historical scholarship in the third chapter, "Die Geschichte der Lehre von der Assumptio der heiligen Jungfrau" [The History of the Doctrine of the Assumption of the Holy Virgin]. See Rahner, "Assumptio," 50–125.

29. Karl Rahner, "The Interpretation of the Dogma of the Assumption," in *God, Christ, Mary, and Grace: Theological Investigations*, vol. 1, trans. Cornelius Ernst (Baltimore: Helicon, 1961), 215.

30. Karl Rahner, "The Prospects for Dogmatic Theology," in *Theological Investigations*, vol. 1, 11.

31. For more on Rahner's divergence from Pius XII, see my "Between Center and Periphery: Mary and the Saints in Rahner," *Philosophy and Theology* 24 (2012): 301–5.

32. See Rahner, "Assumptio," 284.

33. Ibid., 308.

34. Meyer, "Editionsbericht," xxxi.

35. Ibid., xxxv.

36. Ibid.

37. See Rahner, "Assumptio," 133–82, on Mary's death and 348–92 for the appended excursus on the theology of death. A later form of this excursus is translated by W. J. O'Hara as *On the Theology of Death* (New York: Herder and Herder, 1965).

38. Meyer, "Editionsbericht," xxxvi.

39. Ibid., xxxix–xlii.

40. See the rather poignant letter of February 18, 1955, from Hugo to Karl in *Encounters with Karl Rahner: Remembrances of Rahner by Those Who Knew Him*, ed. and trans. Andreas Batlogg and Melvin Michalski, trans. edited by Barbara Turner (Milwaukee: Marquette University Press, 2009), 359–62.

41. Neufeld, "Zur Mariologie Karl Rahners," 433.

42. Karl Rahner, "The Immaculate Conception," in *Theological Investigations*, vol. 1, 201–13; Rahner, "The Dogma of the Immaculate Conception in Our Spiritual Life," in *The Theology of the Spiritual Life: Theological Investigations*, vol. 3, trans. Karl-Heinz and Boniface Kruger (New York: Crossroad, 1982), 129–40; Rahner, "*Virginitas in Partu*: A Contribution to the Problem of the Development of Dogma and of Tradition," in *More Recent Writings: Theological Investigations*, vol. 4, trans. Kevin Smyth (Baltimore: Helicon, 1966), 134–62; Rahner, "The Interpretation of the Dogma of the Assumption" (cited earlier). For the original German of these articles, see Rahner, *Sämtliche Werke*, vol. 9, 597–607, 580–89, 653–78, and 502–11, respectively.

43. Karl Rahner, *Maria, Mutter des Herrn: Theologische Betrachtungen*, in *Sämtliche Werke*, vol. 9, 515–68; translated into English as *Mary, Mother of the Lord: Theological Meditations*, trans. W. J. O'Hara (New York: Herder and Herder, 1963).

44. See Meyer, "Editionsbericht," xiii, n. 11, and Hartmann, "Die 'offene' Mariologie Karl Rahners," 294.

45. The book is available in English translation as Hugo Rahner, *Our Lady and the Church*, trans. Sebastian Bullough (New York: Pantheon Books, 1961).

46. Ibid., 3.

47. Neufeld, for one, underscores the parallels between the brothers' viewpoints on Mary. See Karl Neufeld, "Zur Mariologie Karl Rahners: Materialien und Grundlinien," *Zeitschrift für katholische Theologie* 109 (1987): 437, n. 15. Translations from this article are mine.

48. Karl Rahner, "Mary and the Apostolate," in *The Christian Commitment: Essays in Pastoral Theology, Mission and Grace*, vol. 1, trans. Cecily Hastings (New York: Sheed and Ward, 1963), 114–35.

49. Ibid., 116–17, 119. See H. Rahner, *Our Lady and the Church*, 7–8.

50. K. Rahner, "Mary and the Apostolate," 120, 122–23.

51. H. Rahner, *Our Lady and the Church*, 69–79.

52. K. Rahner, "Mary and the Apostolate," 117.

53. Ibid., 119.

54. Cf. Karl Rahner, *Einübung Priesterlicher Existenz* (Freiburg: Herder, 1970), 285–87.

55. K. Rahner, "Mary and the Apostolate," 128.

56. Ibid., 130–31. See reflections akin to those in "Mary and the Apostolate" in Karl Rahner, "The Priestly Office and Personal Holiness," in *Servants of the Lord*, trans. Richard Strachan (New York: Herder and Herder, 1968), 95–106.

57. Franz Cardinal König, "My Conciliar Theologian," in *Encounters with Karl Rahner*, 51.

58. See *Acta Synodalia Sacrosancti Concilii Oecumenici Vaticani II (AS)*, session 2, part 3 (Vatican City: Typis Polyglottis Vaticanis, 1972), 338–42. Translations from this text are mine.

59. Ibid., 342.

60. Ibid.

61. Ibid., emphasis in original.

62. Ibid.

63. Ibid.

64. For a careful parsing of König's points, see Frederick M. Jelly, "The Theological Context and Introduction to Chapter 8 of *Lumen Gentium*," *Marian Studies* 37 (1986): 57. Thank you to an anonymous referee for alerting me to this article.

65. *AS*, session 2, part 3, 344.

66. Rahner, "Zur konziliaren Mariologie," 92.

67. Ibid., 98.

68. Ibid., 99.

69. Ibid.

70. Ibid.

71. Ibid.

72. Ibid.

73. Ibid., 101.

74. See Leo Cardinal Scheffczyk, "Mariologie und Anthropologie: Zur Marienlehre Karl Rahners," in *Karl Rahner: Kritische Annäherungen*, ed. David Berger (Siegburg, Germany: Franz Schmitt, 2004), 308–13, and Hartmann, "Die 'offene' Mariologie Karl Rahners," 310.

75. Scheffczyk, "Mariologie und Anthropologie," 313, my translation.

76. Matuschek, *Konkrete Dogmatik*, 440.

77. Karl Neufeld, "Mariologie in der Sicht Karl Rahners," 296.

78. Karl Rahner, "The Second Vatican Council's Challenge to Theology," in *Writings of 1965–67*, vol. 1: *Theological Investigations*, vol. 9, trans. Graham Harrison (New York: Herder and Herder, 1972), 6.

79. Ibid., 5, emphasis in original.

80. Ibid., 23.

81. Karl Rahner, "Christian Living Formerly and Today," *Further Theology of the Spiritual Life*, vol. 1: *Theological Investigations*, vol. 7, trans. David Bourke (New York: Seabury, 1971), 9–10.

82. Karl Rahner, "Institutional Spirituality of the Church and Personal Piety," in *Grace in Freedom*, trans. Hilda Graef (New York: Herder and Herder, 1969), 130.

83. Karl Rahner, "Against the Witch Hysteria," in *Theological Investigations*, vol. 23, 169–77, quote on 172.

84. Rahner, "Courage for Devotion to Mary," 138.

85. Neufeld, "Zur Mariologie Karl Rahners," 434. For the text from this lecture, see Karl Rahner, "Dogmatische Bemerkungen zur Jungfrauengeburt," *Dogmatik nach dem Konzil: Grundlegung der Theologie, Gotteslehre, und Christologie: Sämtliche Werke*, vol. 22/1b, ed. Albert Raffelt (Freiburg: Herder, 2008), 734–64.

86. Karl Rahner, "Marienverehrung heute," *Geistliche Schriften: Späte Beiträge zur Praxis des Glaubens: Sämtliche Werke*, vol. 29, ed. Herbert Vorgrimler (Freiburg: Herder, 2007), 452–58, quote on 458, my translation.

87. This chapter is by no means the first English-language venture toward this end. The treatment of Rahner in Elizabeth Johnson's *Truly Our Sister* is fair and illuminating. See Johnson, *Truly Our Sister: A Theology of Mary in the Communion of the Saints* (New York: Continuum, 2003), 108–9, 124–25. Also helpful are Brian Daley, "Woman of Many Names: Mary in Orthodox and Catholic Theology," *Theological Studies* 71 (2010): 846–69, and Leo O'Donovan, "In All Seasons: Karl Rahner on All the Saints," *Philosophy and Theology* 24 (2012): 313–30. I have modestly contributed to the discussion in the following: Fritz, "Between Center and Periphery" (cited earlier), and Fritz, *Karl Rahner's Theological Aesthetics* (Washington, DC: The Catholic University of America Press, 2014), 184–93. And not to be ignored are related reflections in Mary E. Hines, *The Transformation of Dogma: An Introduction to Karl Rahner on Doctrine* (New York: Paulist Press, 1989, and Nancy A. Dallavalle, "Feminist Theologies," in *The Cambridge Companion to Karl Rahner*, ed. Declan Marmion and Mary E. Hines (New York: Cambridge University Press, 2005), 272–73.

88. Neufeld, "Zur Mariologie Karl Rahners," 434.

CHAPTER 7

Catholica Mater

The Marian Insights of Henri de Lubac

TROY A. STEFANO

The great Marian moment of rediscovery arrived in the nineteenth century with Matthias Joseph Scheeben (1835–88), who, unlike his contemporaries or the majority of the Mariology of the previous millennia, saw
in Mary's motherhood the highest expression of her spousal relation to
God. Among modern theologians, Scheeben was the first to realize that
the category of spouse, unlike that of mother (when taken in isolation),
preserves Mary's constitutive embeddedness in the economy of salvation. This insight opened a new pathway for rediscovery that culminated
in the Second Vatican Council's *Lumen Gentium.*

The full implications of this insight, especially in its relation to
ecclesiology, were not realized by Scheeben. It was at the hands of the
theologians who wrote between his time and that of the Council that it
was brought to fruition. Among these figures stood Henri de Lubac
(1896–1991). His contributions not only were indisputable and influential at the Second Vatican Council, where he served as a theological
peritus, but also, more importantly, they still serve as a source of renewal and inspiration for many theologians and believers. For those
familiar with de Lubac's oeuvre, the choice to present his Mariology

may seem initially surprising.[1] For de Lubac did not write any particular book or treatise on Mary per se. De Lubac's explicit treatments of Mary are dispersed and integrated into his engagement with other themes, mostly the Church.[2] If I were to remain at the level of textual references and quantity, this chapter would be very short indeed. But to read de Lubac in such a fashion would be to remain at the surface and to do him a disservice.

The challenge for the reader of de Lubac lies in the fact that he makes the following four interpretive claims regarding Mary. First, that all he has said about the Church not only can be applied to Mary specifically but also derives from Mary as a person.[3] Second, that Mary is the embodiment not only of the Church, "in person and as person," but also of creation, and, as such, she concretizes the relationship between nature and grace.[4] Third, that if all of Scripture refers to Christ and the Church, and in the Church to the individual soul, the entirety of Scripture refers especially to our Lady, in whom is contained the singular and full perfection of the Church and the faithful soul. Thus all exegesis is related to Mary.[5] Fourth, that Mary is the indispensable guarantee that we will not turn the Incarnation into an abstraction and thus turn Christianity into an ideology.[6] Given these four claims, it is only fair to say that if de Lubac did not write a treatise on Mary it is because his entire corpus is thoroughly Marian. This dynamic points to de Lubac's presupposition that the Christian mysteries interpenetrate; they all mutually converge in the Incarnate One, and we never receive the Incarnate One apart from his mother's mediation.

It is my task to synthesize the scope of de Lubac's claims with the breadth of his corpus and to articulate his mariological insights in their full magnitude. My method is to show the way in which de Lubac's corpus sheds light on his claims about Mary. In the first section I begin by asking where, for Henri de Lubac, Mary's place is within the mystery of faith. In the second section I turn to consider what de Lubac sees as the main challenges to Mary. In the third section I articulate de Lubac's response to those challenges. I show in three points of "incarnational logic" how for de Lubac the economy of salvation extends into the economy of the Church. In the fourth section I point to how Mary is the point of convergence for and the indispensable guarantee of these three points of "incarnational logic."

THE PLACE OF MARY WITHIN THE MYSTERY OF FAITH

De Lubac describes Christian theology not as a straight syllogistic line but as a circle around which the theologian moves to consider the different aspects of a single mystery.[7] This means that Marian dogmas are not ends in themselves but are anagogic: they "point" toward a mystery, a reality that far exceeds but is nevertheless expressed in the dogmatic formulation. For this reason, the Church invokes Mary in symbols more than in definitions, in images more than in concepts, and in devotion more than in theorization.[8] For de Lubac, the mystery of the Cross is the ultimate point of reference. And if we are not to efface the truth of the Incarnation, dialectic must always give way to anagogy and symbol. Otherwise we would turn it into an abstract reality, and, in essence, we would make Christianity an ideology. This holds true for Mary and the Church. To say, "Mary is 'nothing other than . . .'" is a methodological red flag.[9] In such a case, we are fully identifying her with one of the aspects of her reality, expressed dialectically. Such is the case when she is reduced to a mere instrument for the Incarnation, for such a rationalist approach always simultaneously desacralizes and transforms the object of the mystery into an ideological parody, hollowing out the depth dimension of mystery.[10]

For de Lubac, the unity of the Christian mysteries has deep implications for theological considerations of Mary. Mariology, more than any other area of inquiry, emphasizes the interconnections of the Christian mysteries; thus it is the most defining property of Mariology that it can never be exclusively, or even predominately, mariological.[11] Mary must be understood within the context of salvation history or, more broadly, the economy of salvation. And it is for this reason that the category of Mary as spouse is so important for the proper interpretation of her divine motherhood.[12] De Lubac offers us the insight that our regard for Mary, whether operating intuitively or expressed self-consciously, forms our principal stance toward the entire Christian mystery. The reason for this is that Mary is the principle of embodiment and concreteness. Mary encapsulates, and—as a Jewish woman—recapitulates the historical and qualitative point at which God ceased to be merely the transcendent and impersonal God of philosophers and became the tripersonal God of history.

CHALLENGES TO THE CHURCH AND TO MARY: HUMAN COOPERATION AND EMBODIED PERSONAL MEDIATION

Mary has been the site of much contention since the Reformation. She has embodied, in many a Protestant's eyes, the twofold usurpation of Christ's mediation and God's absolute sovereignty.[13] But de Lubac tells us that "a demand of this kind is 'more Christian' in appearance only" since "neither the gratuitousness of the divine initiative nor the transcendence of the divine action has anything to suffer from an economy of salvation that was set up by God himself."[14] For, de Lubac posits, if we could see the internal logic of such an approach, we would realize that it effaces the true depths and importance of the Incarnation.[15] What is immediately at stake in Mary are the two intertwined mysteries of human cooperation in redemption and the economy of embodied mediation, by which he means the continued mediation of the Incarnation in the Church. Thus I expound on de Lubac's presentation of the Protestant understanding of human cooperation, ecclesiology, and Mariology as a specific way of reading the Incarnation.

Human Cooperation. In Luther's theology, the human being remains a sinner regardless of grace's work (*Simul justus et peccator*), since God imputes to the believer the merits of Christ.[16] And, in the view of Calvin, a person's salvation or damnation was predestined by the immutable will of God from all of eternity. For Barth, grace "remains grace," and human beings have "not the least control over it" because it is a one-way relationship "without reciprocity."[17] In the eyes of these theologians, they are preserving the unique, exclusive mediation of Christ and the absolute sovereignty of God, not only in initiating salvation but, more importantly, in effecting it.[18]

Ecclesiology. For Barth, "a Catholic understanding of soteriology is synergistic, a cooperation between divine grace and human effort. God in Christ does not save; God in Christ graciously enables and helps us to save ourselves."[19] Such a view regarding cooperation, in turn, affects one's view of the Church. In this view, for a "bodily" Church to propose to be an organ of grace would be the same as for a human being to claim to have "control" over God: it would entail the idolatrous attempt at "laying hands on God."[20] For Luther, there is the "bodily" church, which is nothing but a "human creation," and the heavenly church, which is divine; in Calvin the Church is defined (abstractly) as "the company of the faithful whom God has ordained and elected to eternal life."[21] And in Barth, it is his (famous) doctrine of election that takes the place of the Church. Thus for Barth all that is distinctly Catholic is precisely the human being "laying hands on God."[22]

Mariology. According to de Lubac's observation, not only does such a view regarding human cooperation affect the previously stated views regarding the Church but the regard for the Church of those who hold those views becomes concentrated (or concretized) in their regard for Mary. In fact, it is remarkable that here we see the inverse reflection of the Catholic belief that Mary is the *"typus Ecclesiae."* What is said of the Church at large is applied concretely to Mary. Despite the undeniable beauty of Luther's commentary on the *Magnificat*, one must note the remarkable lack of agency or freedom he allots to Mary. Luther stresses repeatedly that Mary has nothing of herself; indeed, she is but "nothingness."[23] It was largely Calvin who set the standard for the subsequent Protestant tradition in a threefold way: he absolutely rejected all forms of Marian piety; he insisted on the clear Christological boundaries within which Mary might be discussed; and he emphatically saw any concession to Mary's causal or personal role as an unforgivable betrayal of God's honor. This tradition culminated in Schleiermacher's abrupt and straightforward dismissal of Mary from dogmatic theology altogether.[24] Karl Barth most explicitly captures not only the dependence of Mariology and ecclesiology on one's stance regarding human cooperation but also the interrelationship between Mary and the Church. Barth is able to say, with his usual degree of vituperation: "Where Mary is 'venerated,' where this whole doctrine with its corresponding devotion is current, there the Church of Christ is not."[25]

HUMAN COOPERATION AND EMBODIED PERSONAL MEDIATION AS PRESERVING THE INCARNATION

De Lubac saw in the internal logic of the Reformers' tradition a specific reading of the Incarnation. In turn, his own fundamental conviction could be expressed in three points of "incarnational logic" that govern one's entire approach to Christianity and converge in what we say about Mary:

1. The Incarnation, from the vantage point of the divine intention to condescend to our sensible nature, sin, and weakness, entails "the divine mystery of the 'economy' according to man."[26] The Incarnation is as indispensable as our human nature. God, thus bodily mediated, is never consequently received unmediated apart from Christ's body. De Lubac reminds us, quoting John 14:7–9: "'If you had known me, you would without doubt have known my Father also. . . . Philip, he that seeth me seeth the Father also.' Nobody, even at the highest peak of the spiritual life, will attain a knowledge of the Father that will dispense him, from that point onward, from going through him who will, always and for all, be 'the Way' and 'the Image of the invisible God.'"[27] The Incarnate form—in all of its concreteness and uniqueness—is precisely the divine condescension apart from which there is no salvation or knowledge of the Father.

2. If the Incarnate One is unsurpassable, this poses the question of how to make the Incarnation universal. For de Lubac, this is the true point of divergence with the Reformers. He sees their internal logic as grounded in the mechanism by which they make Christ universal. That is, the method that underlies their approach to human cooperation, ecclesiology, and Mariology is one of abstraction. Then the Incarnation is seen only as a prelude to Redemption; in fact, the concreteness and uniqueness of the Incarnation itself becomes vaporized into soteriology. De Lubac claims that this effectively rejects the Incarnation.[28] It violates the concrete form of the Incarnate One, which itself is the concretization of the divine mercy in the form of condescending adaptation. Furthermore, it bypasses procedurally the divine intention (point 1) insofar as the divine intention makes the adaptation to our human weakness.[29] Soteriology must be rooted in the person of Christ rather than abstracting the concrete person into his work. The person of Christ can never be reduced to a function[30]—not even the function of saving us. It is always the *person* who acts.[31] Therefore, only a form of universalization from which Christ cannot be abstracted is acceptable. And for de Lubac this is none other than the "the economy of the Church," including the Marian mysteries, that flow out of Christ's side.[32] For this mode of mediation maintains the concrete, historical, and embodied form of the Incarnation itself, and thus entails its fulfillment and guarantee, not its usurpation.[33]

3. The third point to follow from this logic is that if the economy of the Church is the only guarantee and fulfillment of the Incarnation, and if the economy of the Church presupposes the cooperation of human freedom with grace and the preservation of nature as its conditions, the cooperation of human freedom with grace and the preservation of nature are themselves facets of the work and scope of the Incarnation.

If one can universalize the Incarnation via abstraction, one can dispense with the entire economy of the Church and Mary. But if one preserves the concrete, historical, and embodied form of the Incarnate One, Mary and the Church are the Incarnation's indispensable guarantee and fulfillment. At the heart of this matter is the way in which one interprets *"Christus descendit et ascendit ut impleret omnia"* (Eph. 4:10). How is the unique and particular life, death, and resurrection of Jesus Christ universalized? Or what is the relationship between Christology and soteriology, the concrete, unique person of Christ and the universal work of Christ? According to de Lubac, this is the crux of the second incarnational point and the source of divergences in understandings of human cooperation, ecclesiology, and Mariology; however one answers this question will determine the rest of one's understanding of the matter.[34]

For de Lubac, the first answer—which is that of the Reformation tradition considered earlier—attempts to make of the Incarnation a one-time historic event of insurmountable importance, but one that has now been procedurally surpassed and made accessible through nonhistoric and nonembodied means: a process of universalizing abstraction. The emphasis in this reading is on the accomplishment of the historic Christ, on the one hand, and on the unmediated reception of that accomplishment by the believer, on the other. And anything that comes between Christ's accomplishment and the believer's unmediated reception is deemed an idolatrous intrusion on Christ's unique mediation and God's absolute sovereignty. The result, as mentioned earlier, is that the theologian's abstracting movement goes from the historic Christ (*concretissimum*; Barth) to a "divine church" (Luther), "the faithful whom God has ordained and elected to eternal life" (Calvin), "the spotless bride of Jesus Christ governed and refreshed by the Spirit of God" (Zwingli), and "the invisible Church," which is "an undivided unity" and "infallible" (Schleiermacher).[35] But this vertical movement from the historic Christ to a supratemporal, supramundane entity bypasses history and embodied personal mediation. It establishes a direct relationship with the historic Christ and *that* Church. This gives the believer who is historically strad- dling the Christ of history and *that* Church with little to no role except that of pure receptivity. The Church, thus conceived, is extrinsic to the mediation of grace. And if the Church claimed to have any mediating power—or, more boldly, as the Catholic Church claims, if it believed it- self to be the "sacrament" of Christ, that is, the sign and instrument that both bears witness to *and* effects (mediates) Christ's revealing and sal- vific work in the world—such a claim would be idolatrous since it would detract from Christ's unique and exclusive mediation and God's absolute sovereignty. Furthermore, as is typical of de Lubac, he does not limit his critique to the Reformation but includes constrictions within the Catho- lic tradition. Thus any Catholic thinker who makes of the Incarnation an abstraction in order to pursue a more "intellectual faith" or to form an abstract utopia is subject to the same critique.[36]

This brings us to the second reading of how to universalize the In- carnation event. For de Lubac, to believe in the Incarnation is to hold that Christ is uniquely personal, free, concrete, historical, and embod- ied. In fact, the only form of mediation proper to Christ's uniqueness is one that itself emerges from him. De Lubac makes use of Nyssa's de- scription of "the divine mystery of the economy according to man," which, he says, expands into "the economy of the Church."[37] The sacra- mental economy of the Church or the role allotted to Mary is neither, therefore, a replacement of the Incarnation nor a distraction but is pre- cisely its fulfillment and extension in time. It is in this sense that de Lubac, like Johann Adam Möhler, considers the Church as the "Incarna- tion continued."[38] It is what Augustine called the *totus Christus*.

MARIAN CONVERGENCES

It is de Lubac's most significant mariological claim that the incarnational logic stands or falls with Mary. Mary's place is the promise and guarantee of the Incarnation, not its replacement or its distraction. There are three key terms that de Lubac uses to refer to Mary's significance: Immaculate

Spouse, Virgin Mother, and Mother of the Church.[39] There is a specific order and structure to these three terms that preserves the integrity of his incarnational logic. These terms represent a specific reading of the entire Christian mystery, and thus, if we understand the significance that de Lubac allots to each of these terms, we capture—at once—how he understands Mary, the Church, and the Incarnation. For the sake of clarity, I describe de Lubac's Mariology under the headings of those three terms (Immaculate Spouse, Virgin Mother, and Mother of the Church). For the categories of both Immaculate Spouse and Virgin Mother, I describe three aspects corresponding to the three incarnational points that they preserve, respectively. However, according to de Lubac, the category of Mother of the Church alone contains the entire mystery and thus all three points simultaneously. It is for this reason, above all else, that de Lubac bids us to call on Mary as our Mother; he believes that in that invocation rests the true purification, reform, and healing of the Church.

Mary as Immaculate Spouse

From the perspective of rediscovery, de Lubac synthesizes the Marian realizations of Scheeben with the ecclesiological discoveries of Möhler and of John Henry Newman: Mary as Immaculate Spouse is the key to understanding her within the scope of salvation history. It irrevocably situates her within the narrative of the Triune God's work of fusing the creature with its Lord in spousal love, which spanned the period from creation through Israel to Christ and is fulfilled eschatologically in divinization.

Point 1 of Incarnational Logic. Mary as Immaculate Spouse discloses God's intention of condescending to our weakness. The category of spouse at once discloses Mary's unique relation to the Word and her embeddedness in salvation history. Hence, to refer to Mary as Spouse of the Word we emphasize the narrative of God's condescension to human weakness in the economy of salvation. For God's spousal relation with Israel in particular and with creation in general becomes concretized in Mary as Spouse of the Word.[40] It is her "Yes" that begins the *matrimonium divinum*, the fruit of which is the Word made flesh.[41] De Lubac relies heavily on the Latin tradition of commentary on the Song of Songs and writes that the beloved Spouse who is awaiting the "kisses of his mouth" (1:2) is first and foremost the Virgin in whose womb, as in a bridal chamber, the Word was united with human nature—"the first kiss of the Word, which is the pledge of the final union."[42] As such, Mary as spouse at once invokes both the historical form of God's engagement with humanity and the intimacy that underlies such a form.

Point 2 of Incarnational Logic. Mary as Immaculate Spouse preserves the uniqueness and concreteness of Christ's form. When the Church professes the dogma of the Immaculate Conception it means, among other things, that Mary, by a special and unique act of God, is the first Spouse to flow out of Christ's side on the Cross.[43] Before Mary could be Mother to the Incarnate One, she had to share in his Cross.[44] The logic of the Immaculate Conception is something like this: the condition for Christ's pierced heart is Christ's Incarnation in Mary's womb; the condition for Christ's Incarnation in her womb is her total "Yes" to God; the condition for her absolute and total "Yes" to God is her freedom from sin; the condition for her freedom from sin is a unique act of grace by which God applied to her the merits of Christ in anticipation; and the condition for this unique application of Christ's merits is Christ's pierced heart. Here we arrive at a point of circularity at which one could say that Mary, as Immaculate Spouse, flows out of Christ's side in order that Christ, being born of her as Virgin Mother, may be pierced for us and for her.[45] This has two consequences. First, Mary does not condition the Incarnation of the Word, but, by the anticipatory sharing of his Cross, the Word establishes his own unique and concrete conditions, from which one cannot abstract anything. And second, in this God took the narrow path. He entrusted himself to human freedom, albeit one that was already achieved by his Cross; the triumph of the Word was not *despite* human freedom but precisely *in* it—corresponding to de Lubac's third point of incarnational logic. The dogma of the Immaculate Conception, therefore, is a doctrine of God's intimacy and vulnerability.

Point 3 of Incarnational Logic. Mary as Immaculate Spouse entails personhood and free cooperation with grace. God's spousal love is not mechanical, nor is it impersonal. God's love gives birth to persons, and persons are the recipients of God's love. Only persons can be free, and only persons can be called to a spousal relation with the eternal person of the Word. Mary's "Yes" to God initiates, from the human side, a history of receiving and living God's freedom.[46] Mary's "Yes" shows how, as God reveals himself in the *person* of the Word, he gives birth to persons as the correlative effect of his self-revelation. In the logic of the Incarnation, God did not "forcefully" initiate a history of freedom. De Lubac cites Newman in noting that the early Fathers "do not speak of the Blessed Virgin merely as the physical instrument of our Lord's taking flesh, but as an intelligent, responsible cause of it."[47] For this reason, de Lubac writes, "Catholic faith regarding our Lady sums up symbolically, in its special case, the doctrine of human cooperation in the Redemption and thus provides the synthesis, or matrix concept, of the dogma of the Church."[48]

Mary as Virgin Mother

De Lubac recounts a momentous shift in human thought patterns around the eleventh century, which took place deep "down, in the dark basements of the mind, in that mysterious zone where everything becomes entangled in advance, before seeing the light of day."[49] It was the emergence of dialectic as the exclusive modality of human reason itself and of doing theology. Among the many consequences there was within the Catholic tradition an increasing dissociation of Mary's spousal role from her maternal role. Thus, for example, Thomas Aquinas treats of Mary in the section of his *Summa Theologica* (*ST*) on the entry of the Son of God into the world (*ST* III, qq. 27–30). In this mode, Mary's spousal relation to the Word, so prominent in the early Church, is largely, if not entirely, subordinated to Mary's role in the Incarnation as the Mother of God. Her primary function, then, is as the guarantor of the Word's true humanity. De Lubac, following Scheeben, prioritizes Mary's spousal role, within which alone her divine motherhood can be understood. For to emphasize Mary as Immaculate Spouse is to ensure that Mary as Virgin Mother cannot be turned into an abstraction by seeing her as solely an instrument for the Incarnation. De Lubac maintains both aspects of Mary in tension, as is proper to the nature of a Christian mystery.

Point 1 of Incarnational Logic. Mary as Virgin Mother is within the scope of Mary as Immaculate Spouse. The spousal narrative in which Mary has her unique place began with God's love for his creation. This means that in Mary's womb, the Word was wed not to a particular man (as Nestorius would have it) but to human nature (as a whole) and all of creation. De Lubac writes, "Christ from the very first moment of his existence virtually bears all men within himself. . . . Whole and entire he will bear [human nature] then to Calvary, whole and entire he will raise it from the dead, whole and entire he will save it."[50] What this means is that Mary is the quintessence of creatureliness, of the world.[51] If in her the Word was wed to all of creation, she must stand for all of creation;[52] if in her the Word was wed to all of humanity, she must stand for all of humanity. As such, Mary is the principle of bodiliness, historicity, and createdness, with which the Word unites himself in his condescending adaption to our weakness. De Lubac comments extensively on this aspect of Mary's role. When, in the mystery of the Incarnation, "the heavenly King celebrated the wedding of his Son, giving him the Holy Church as his companion, Mary's womb was the bridal bed for this royal Spouse."[53] Her immaculate and luring beauty is an inverse reflection of God's self-emptying, spousal love. And her freedom to say "Yes" to God not only makes her the pinnacle of creation's receptivity to God but also makes her able to truly love, and thus to personally become the Bride of the Word. For that freedom is the touch of God's love: it is the first "kiss" of the Bridegroom.

Point 2 of Incarnational Logic. Christ is truly historical, unique, and embodied only if Mary is the "Sacrament of Christ." Mary, sanctified and freed to offer a total "Yes" to God as Immaculate Spouse, became the Mother of God when God emptied himself into her womb. The structure of Christ's own historicity is the "form" of his mediation; if Christ's condescension to adapt to our weakness came through Mary, Christ's form remains as the Incarnate One through Mary. Christ is *forever* from Mary's womb.[54] To speak to the contrary or to dispose of Mary is to turn him into an abstraction. The dispensability of Mary rests with the presupposition that Christ can be abstracted from his concreteness and thus from Mary, through whom he was made concrete in body and in history. To retain Mary as the one through whom we receive Christ is not only to invoke "an economy of salvation that was set up by God himself" but to ensure that the form of the Incarnate One is the form of divine mercy in history.[55] And this takes us to Mary's most essential role: to confess the full meaning of Mary as Immaculate Spouse and Virgin Mother is to say that she is the "Sacrament of Christ," the one whose significance resides in pointing to and making present the Word made flesh.[56] As Immaculate Spouse, she signifies the Bridegroom; as Virgin Mother, she effects what she signifies.

Point 3 of Incarnational Logic. Mary as Virgin Mother embodies the part of creation that is willingly fertilized by the Holy Spirit. Catholic talk of cooperation, merit, freedom, nature, and so forth is, in the final analysis, talk about God's free use of human beings and human realities in Christ.[57] In this God certainly took the narrow path: salvation was not achieved despite human freedom and at the expense of nature; rather the Word's triumph was precisely *in* human freedom and *while* preserving nature.[58] Mary embodies the fundamental characteristic of creation, awaiting fertilization by God, awaiting what de Lubac calls the *donum perfectum*, or "the second gift," the first gift being that of creation itself. Mary embodies God's love for his creation. And, as a specific woman, willingly fertilized under the shadow of the Holy Spirit, Mary embodies the part of creation that has been willingly fertilized by the Holy Spirit, namely, the Church.[59] In the economy of salvation, Mary is the Mother of God only because she is beloved Spouse; *mutatis mutandis*, in the economy of creation, she is the source of the race only because she is the answering person. Her "Yes" to God was not only the fulfillment of Israel's longing for God but also the long-awaited answer to creation's "groaning" (Rom. 8:22). It is here that we see de Lubac's contribution regarding the divisions and orders of nature and grace bear Marian fruit: creation's *desiderium naturale* is now personified and made concrete in Mary, who stands for all of creation. Mary—and therefore also the Church—is not only the sacrament of Christ, that is, the instrument and sign that makes him present and becomes truly herself as she points to Him, but truly the "sacrament of the world" or, more felicitously, "the sacrament of Christ for the world," in the sense of embodying both the heights of a theophanic universe that always "proclaims the work of the Lord" and the sign of God's salvific work for all of creation.[60] To pray with Mary is to pray *"ut (Ecclesia) fiat mundo salutis sacramentum,"* since Mary is—in person and as a person—*"mundus reconciliatus Ecclesia."*[61]

Mary and the Church

De Lubac makes the claim that to call Mary the *typus ecclesiae* is, in a sense, to see the full scope of her as Immaculate Spouse and Virgin Mother.[62]

Mary as Immaculate Spouse and the Church as Immaculate Spouse. De
Lubac makes clear that the relationship between Mary as Immaculate
Spouse and the Church as Spouse to Christ is not a matter of "transfer-
ring," as if as an afterthought, parallels from Mary to the Church or vice
versa.[63] When we consider Mary as the first Immaculate Spouse that
flowed out of Christ's side, we find embodied, in its entirety, the Church
in one person.[64] The only point in all of history in which the entire
Church was unified and gathered as one and its essence corresponded
fully to its existence was in the person of Our Lady. De Lubac sees in this
four important insights.

1. De Lubac argues that it is for this reason that the Church is a "she."[65]
   The Church is wholly personal because Mary is a person, and she is
   a person in her relation to the person of the Word, her Spouse and
   Son. Thus Mary's life offers the Church her "form," her intrinsic
   mode of existence.[66] As de Lubac writes, "We might say that they are
   'one single and unique mystery.'"[67]
2. If Mary is the "form" and "pleroma" of the Church, her life is the
   prehistory of the Church.[68] "Mary is the first-beloved; but in her all
   saintly souls, and primarily the Church, whose 'form' she is, are also
   loved."[69] This means that Mary's life is already an embodiment of
   what the Church will be. The Church is not an organization but an
   organism that has at its very heart a Marian experience.[70] And for
   that reason, Mary defines the essence of the Church.
3. The Church is not an extrinsic parallel or analogy. The relationships between Mary and the Church are "not only numerous and
   close; they are essential and woven within."[71] Hence Mary and the
   Church are not two species under the genus of Spouse to Christ,
   which would result in an extrinsic understanding of their relation.[72]
   Rather Mary embodied concretely and fully the genus of Spouse up
   to the foot of the Cross.[73] And when the Church, as such, was poured
   forth from Christ's pierced side, the spousal "form" and experience
   of Mary became universalized and extended to the Church. For this
   reason, de Lubac believed, the universalization of Christ entails, to
   some extent, the universalization of his spousal and filial relation to
   Mary.[74] "In her the whole Church is outlined, and at the same time

already completed; she is simultaneously the 'seed' and the 'pleroma' of it."[75] In order to understand the relationship between Mary as a specific person and the Church as such, one must consider the moment of universalization, that is, the Cross. Mary, as Spouse of the Word up to the point of the Cross, embodied the spousal relation in three senses: *in genere, specialiter,* and *singulariter.* They all converged in the one concrete person of Mary. But at the Cross, where the Church flowed out of the rib of the New Adam, the entire economy of embodied personal mediation that was in Mary alone was extended to the whole Church: now, the Church is Spouse *in genere,* the Christian soul is Spouse *singulariter,* and Mary is Spouse *specialiter.*[76] Therefore, if Mary is the "Sacrament of Christ," in which she signifies and brings forth the Word, then so also is the Church and every individual Christian. This universalization of Mary's spousal relation into the Church, and with it into every Christian, is the guarantee that we will not turn Christ into an abstraction but that we must maintain Christ's own concrete, historical form. It is the fulfillment of the economy established by God himself.

4. The universalization of Mary's spousal relation to Christ to that of the Church as such and to every single Christian has implications for the Church's essence. De Lubac calls Mary the "genuine universal concrete, which includes to an eminent degree and in a pure state the sum of perfection of all other members."[77] He calls her "the universal creature" in which God has placed "the fullness of all good." God has "filled her 'to an eminent degree with the substance of which the Church is formed'; he conferred on her 'in wonderful preeminence all the majestic qualities' with which he endows 'his Bride the Holy Church.'"[78] The Church's essence and existence fully coincided only in Mary. Her universalization entails inserting, as it were, a space between essence and existence in which the Church is journeying toward fulfilling her eschatological identity. And if the Church's essence is the eschatological chorus of faithful souls, that eschatological finality is defined by the one in whom it has already been realized *specialiter,* Mary.[79] In this we find the meaning of Mary's Assumption. De Lubac writes: "In the mystery of the Assumption—which marks, in our Lady, the complete and definitive

triumph of the divine action upon her, right up to its consequences in the bodily order—[the Church] sees no mere wonderful exception to the common destiny, which has nothing to do with us; rather, she hails in it the pledge and anticipation of her own triumph."[80] The Church's irresolvable tension between essence and existence is the very mystery of our transformation into a destiny already realized in Our Lady. And thus we can see the two sides of the Church in this tension: "The Church is of God (*ex Trinitate*) and she is of men (*ex hominibus*); she is visible and invisible; she is of this earth and this time, and she is eschatological and eternal."[81]

Mary as Virgin Mother and the Church as Virgin Mother. As Christ's Immaculate Spouse, Mary represents the whole Church as Spouse; likewise, by being the Virgin Mother of God she has, within her, the entirety of the collective Christ.[82] As de Lubac writes, "She bore One according to flesh, but spiritually she bore the whole human race."[83] We have already seen how Mary's spousal and maternal role can be summed up in calling her the "Sacrament of Christ," the one who signifies the Word as Spouse and who, as Mother, makes him present. As the Church flows out of Christ's side on Calvary, Mary's sacramental dimension becomes universalized: the very Christ whom Mary signified by her spousal relation is now signified by the whole Church as Spouse, and the earthly Christ whom Mary brought forth by her maternal relation is now brought forth by the whole Church. De Lubac sees in this three implications.

1. The condition for the universalization of Christ while maintaining his historical, embodied, and concrete form (point 2 of incarnational logic) is the universalization of the one who made him historical, embodied, and concrete. Therefore, by universalizing Mary as the Sacrament of Christ, the Church and every specific Christian became both Immaculate Spouse and Virgin Mother, bringing forth Christ's body in the world and for the world. De Lubac writes: "His word is born in each one of the faithful, as in the Church as a whole; but this is in the likeness of his birth in the soul of our Lady, and in addition, if faith is to bear its fruit, there must be in each of us the soul of our Lady, who magnified the Lord, and the Spirit of our

Lady, who rejoiced in God."[84] De Lubac makes clear that "in our eyes neither our Lady nor the Church in any way whatsoever replaces the humanity of Christ, as is feared even among those who make the most sincere of efforts to understand the matter." Rather the mystery "misunderstood by the Reformation is, *on the contrary, the indispensable guarantee of the importance of the Incarnation.*"[85] For de Lubac this means extending to the Church *in genere* what was applied to Mary *specialiter*: "the Sacrament of Christ." In fact, the very Spirit of Christ was at work not only in Mary but also in the Church, as her very soul and animating principle.[86]

2. If Mary as the Sacrament of Christ is universalized in such a way that the Church is the Sacrament of Christ, the Church and Mary have two aspects as regards their sacramentality. The first aspect is that of Spouse, and as such they are both *sanctified*. The second aspect is that of Virgin Mother, and as such they are both *sanctifying*. The first is the signifier; the second makes present what it signifies. The first ensures that Mary and the Church are means to an end— that is, Christ; the second ensures that they are never a dispensable means but that, until the end of the world, Christ is made present through his Mother. In order to understand why Mary and the Church are unsurpassable and indispensable signs, we need to see how they relate to the divine intention in the economy (point 1 of incarnational logic). The purpose of God's condescension is to adapt to our human weakness. Christ's concreteness is as unsurpassable as our bodiliness. This was made possible through Mary, who as sacrament is the preservation of the divine intention and work in Christ. Mary as sacrament is the preservation of the uniqueness of the historical form of God's condescension, from which nothing can be abstracted. And so the Church, as the extension and universalization of Mary as sacrament, "is essentially related to our present condition,"[87] as de Lubac writes. To dispense with the Church (or Mary), therefore, is to dispense with the concreteness of the Incarnation, whose form is correlated with our human weakness. The moment that Mary or the Church become ends-in-themselves, they lose their significance. But the moment we lose Mary or the Church, we lose the concreteness and uniqueness of the Incarnate One, whose

form is preserved and universalized *only* in them. Therefore de Lubac writes of Mary and the Church: "Her whole end is to show us Christ, lead us to him, and communicate his grace to us; to put it in a nutshell, she exists solely to put us into relation with him. She alone can do that, and it is a task she never completes; there will never come a moment, either in the life of the individual or in the life of the race, in which her role ought to come to an end or even could come to an end." In short, for this reason, de Lubac writes, "If the world lost the Church, it would lose Redemption too."[88]

3. If the Church and Mary are both the "sacrament of Christ," it is the Eucharist that is the point of continuity and preservation of the concrete and unique form of Christ (point 2 of incarnational logic), as well as the divine intention in condescending to human weakness (point 1 of incarnational logic). The Eucharist is the underlying bond between Mary and the Church, for the Eucharist is the very universalization of the Incarnate without abstraction. "Just as the maternal function of Mary is to give the God-Man to the world," writes de Lubac, "so the maternal function of the Church, which culminates . . . in the celebration of the Eucharist, is to give us Christ, 'the Head, Sacrifice, and Food of the members of his mystical body.'"[89] In short, "As Mary bore the earthly Christ, so the Church bears the Eucharistic Christ."[90] And just as Mary as sacrament preserves the earthly Christ from being turned into an abstraction, so does the Church as sacrament preserve the Eucharistic Christ from being turned into an abstraction.

The moment of the Cross, in which the earthly Christ becomes universalized into the Eucharistic Christ, is the ground and reason for the universalization of Mary as Spouse and Virgin Mother in the Church and every faithful soul.

Mary as Mother of the Church

When Mary stood at the foot of the Cross, her identity was revealed to her. The "hour" of Our Lord is also the "hour" of Our Lady. She arrived at that place from which her special grace derived, but now the ultimate reason for that initial "prevenient" grace was to be fulfilled and revealed: what flowed from Christ's side was the Church, in its fullness, the very purpose of the Incarnation, and at that very moment Mary became not only the mother of the earthly Christ but the mother of his ecclesial and Eucharistic body, the Church.[91] This means that her motherhood is not fully comprehensible until she is able to be invoked as Mother by all of us beloved disciples. The very body of the earthly Christ that she bore in her womb already contained his whole mystical body by anticipation.[92] But when Christ on the Cross gave her to John as Mother, he revealed to her and to us the true depths of "the economy according to man," becoming "the economy of the Church" and, correspondingly, Mary, the Immaculate Spouse and Virgin Mother of God becoming the Mother of the Church. The Church, therefore, has at its foundation a maternal memory of paschal birth. The moment when Christ was pierced on the Cross marked a special *transitus*. His self-offering—that is, his unique, concrete form, which is nothing other than the form of the divine mercy in history—was extended in the Eucharist. De Lubac calls the Eucharist the "heart of the Church,"[93] the center around which everything circumambulates.

We have seen how, for de Lubac, Mary took her origin from the side of Christ as Immaculate Spouse and, consequently, brought him forth as Mother. Thus the same applies to the Church's two aspects, except with regard to the Eucharistic body. The Eucharist realizes the Church as Spouse, but the Church as Mother produces the Eucharist.[94] For Henri de Lubac, the "mystery of our being brought to birth by the Church is the conclusion of the historical birth of Christ through Mary—its continuation, as it were, under the influence of the same Spirit."[95] Now we see the special status that de Lubac gives to the term "Mother of the Church."[96] Mary as Immaculate Spouse and Virgin Mother became universalized at the moment of the Cross, wherein the earthly Christ was universalized into the Eucharistic Christ. And if the very gesture of non-abstracting universalization shows the full depths of God's *kenosis*, Mary, as Mother of the Church, is precisely the invocation of those incarnate depths. To invoke Mary as our Mother is to say that the Christ made present in body, soul, and divinity under the appearance of bread and wine and into whom we are incorporated is from Mary's womb. It is to

say that the spousal and maternal mediations of the Church are themselves derivative of the concrete relation between Christ and Mary. And
that the bond between Christ and Mary remains the concrete archetype
of the self-emptying relation that God has formed between himself and
his creature, as between a Bridegroom and a Bride, a Virgin Mother and
her Son. In fact, to invoke Mary as our Mother, far from expressing a
merely pious sentiment that refers to a notion of tenderness, captures in
one appellation the concrete and unique work of the Incarnate One. It
captures that moment under the midday sun—in all of its truth, uniqueness, and concreteness—when the full depths of the Incarnation became manifest: the *transitus* of "the divine economy according to man"
into "the economy of the Church." As de Lubac bids us, "The motherhood of the Church no longer means anything to our systems—but we,
in order to free ourselves from their abstraction, need to return to our
mother."[97]

NOTES

1. There is very little written on this topic. In terms of monographs, for
example, one can profit greatly from Denis Dupont-Fauville's *L'Église Mère chez
Henri de Lubac* (Paris: Parole et Silence, 2009).

2. Thus, for example, *Méditation sur l'Église* (Paris: Aubier, 1953), whose
concluding chapter, "Our Lady and the Church," is the richest mariological
treatment in his entire corpus; *Paradoxe et Mystère de l'Église* (Paris: Aubier,
1967), in which he reflects in the third chapter on the significance of treating
Mary within *Lumen Gentium*; *L'Éternel Féminin* (Paris: Aubier, 1968), where he
reflects on Teilhard de Chardin's insights on Mary as embodying not only the
Church but creation; and *La maternité de l'Église* (Paris: Aubier, 1971), in which
he expounds in more detail the development of the mystical identity between
Mary and the Church in the Church Fathers. In this chapter I use the following
examples and references: *Splendor of the Church*, trans. Michael Mason (San
Francisco: Ignatius, 1999); *The Church: Paradox and Mystery*, trans. James R.
Dunne (Staten Island, NY: Ecclesia, 1969); *The Eternal Feminine: A Study on the
Text of Teilhard de Chardin*, trans. René Hague (London: William Collins Sons,
1970); and *Motherhood of the Church*, trans. Sr. Sergia Englund, O.C.D. (San
Francisco: Ignatius, 1982). I also make frequent use of these: *Catholicism: Christ
and the Common Destiny of Man*, trans. Lancelot Sheppard and Sr. Elizabeth Englund, O.C.D. (San Francisco: Ignatius, 1988); *Corpus Mysticum: The Eucharist
and the Church in the Middle Ages*, trans. Gemma Simmonds, C.J., Richard Price,

and Christopher Stephens (Notre Dame, IN: University of Notre Dame Press, 2006); and *Christian Faith: The Structure of the Apostles' Creed*, trans. Illtyd Trethowan and John Saward (London: Geoffrey Chapman, 1986).

3. This is the key claim of his Mariology in *Splendor of the Church*, 314–77.

4. This is precisely the connection he makes throughout *Eternal Feminine*.

5. De Lubac makes this claim in bits and pieces throughout his massive *Medieval Exegesis*, but he articulates it most concretely in *Splendor of the Church*, 352–65.

6. De Lubac, *Motherhood of the Church*, 163–64.

7. De Lubac, *Christian Faith*, 129–30 and 135–37.

8. De Lubac, *Paradox and Mystery*, 21, and *Splendor of the Church*, 15.

9. We find something similar in Hans Urs von Balthasar's *Theo-Logic*, vol. 1: *The Truth of the World*, trans. Adrian J. Walker (San Francisco: Ignatius, 2000), 16.

10. De Lubac identifies the turn to dialectic in the eleventh century as the origin of the tradition of Christian rationalism at the root of the modern period. See his *Corpus Mysticum*, 226–27.

11. This de Lubacian insight is captured especially keenly in Cardinal Joseph Ratzinger's *Mary: The Church at the Source*, trans. Adrian J. Walker (San Francisco: Ignatius, 2005), 30.

12. It is Scheeben's rediscovery of the centrality of Mary as spouse that opened up the pathway for de Lubac's (and *Lumen Gentium*'s) entire approach. See de Lubac, *Splendor of the Church*, 314–77, and *Motherhood of the Church*, 17.

13. De Lubac, *Splendor of the Church*, 314.

14. Ibid., 314–15.

15. De Lubac rightly sees arguments that Mary's dignity and prerogatives stem from what is "fitting" (*convenientia*) for the Mother of God, common among Neo-Scholastics, as inept. Not only do such arguments themselves give in to the dialectical impulse of prioritizing her divine motherhood to the exclusion of her spousal role, but they also do not reach to the real base of the problem.

16. Cf. Philipp Melanchthon, *Apology of the Augsburg Confession* (1531), Article IV (On Justification).

17. Karl Barth, *Die Theologie und die Kirche* (Munich: Chr. Kaiser, 1938), 295–96. See Hans Urs von Balthasar's description of Barth in *The Theology of Karl Barth*, trans. Edward T. Oakes, S.J. (San Francisco: Ignatius, 1992), 51.

18. De Lubac, *Splendor of the Church*, 314–16.

19. Tim Perry, "'What Is Little Mary Here For?': Barth, Mary, and Election," in *Pro Ecclesia* 19, no. 1 (2010): 53.

20. Cf. Karl Barth, *Die Kirchliche Dogmatik II/1: Die Lehre von Gott*, Part 1 (Zurich: Theol. Verlag, 1940), 656–57.

21. De Lubac, *Splendor of the Church*, 84–85.

22. For a powerful presentation of this aspect of Barth's writings, see Hans Urs von Balthasar, *The Theology of Karl Barth* (New York: Holt, Rinehart and Winston, 1971), 52. One can see this tradition's view of the Catholic belief about

the Church acutely expressed by none other than Friedrich Schleiermacher in *The Christian Faith*, ed. H. R. Mackintosh and J. S. Stewart (Berkeley, CA: Apocryphile Press, 2011), 103, §24.

23. Martin Luther, *Werke*, Weimar edition, ed. J. C. F. Knaake et al., vol. 7 (1883), 568. See also Hilda C. Graef, *Mary: A History of Doctrine and Devotion* (New York: Sheed and Ward, 1965), 6.

24. Cf. Friedrich Schleiermacher, H. R. Mackintosh, and J. S. Stewart, *The Christian Faith*, translation of the 2nd German edition (Edinburgh, 1928), 403–7.

25. Karl Barth, *Church Dogmatics* I.2, ed. T. F. Torrance and G. W. Bromiley (New York: T. and T. Clark, 1963), 143. Against that claim, one can point to the keen insight of John Henry Newman: "If we take a survey at least of Europe, we shall find that it is not those religious communions which are characterized by devotion towards the Blessed Virgin that have ceased to adore her Eternal Son, but those very bodies, (when allowed by the law,) [punctuation *sic*] which have renounced devotion to her. The regard for His glory, which was professed in that keen jealousy of her exaltation, has not been supported by the event. They who were accused of worshipping a creature in His stead, still worship Him; their accusers, who hoped to worship Him so purely, they, wherever obstacles to the development of their principles have been removed, have ceased to worship Him altogether." *The Development of Christian Doctrine* (Notre Dame, IN: University of Notre Dame Press, 1989), 426.

26. De Lubac, *Christian Faith*, 90, quoting Gregory of Nyssa, *The Life of Moses*, 159. Cf. de Lubac, *Christian Faith*, 38–62.

27. De Lubac, *Splendor of the Church*, 203.

28. De Lubac, *Christian Faith*, 46–47.

29. De Lubac, *Splendor of the Church*, 85.

30. De Lubac, *Christian Faith*, 48.

31. De Lubac, *Paradox and Mystery*, 14.

32. Cf. de Lubac, *Motherhood of the Church*, 19.

33. De Lubac, *Splendor of the Church*, 315.

34. De Lubac approvingly notes that the notion of the "concrete universal" was "applied to Christ and to the Virgin Mary by Blondel, Teilhard de Chardin [and] von Balthasar" to explain this idea. In "Mystique et Mystère," in *Théologies d'occasion* (Paris: Desclée de Brouwer, 1984), 73.

35. Huldreich Zwingli, *Sämtliche Werke*, vol. 1 (Berlin: Schwetschke, 1905), 538. Friedrich Schleiermacher, *The Christian Faith* (Edinburgh: T. and T. Clark, 1986), 678, §149.

36. De Lubac describes these intra-Catholic temptations at length in *Splendor of the Church*, 279–313.

37. De Lubac, *Christian Faith*, 40–41.

38. De Lubac, *Paradox and Mystery*, 24.

39. De Lubac, *Splendor of the Church*, 321–53.

40. Ibid., 342. See also de Lubac, *Eternal Feminine*, 9–16 and 109–32.

41. It is here that we can see Scheeben's rediscovery bearing the most fruit in de Lubac's thought. Scheeben wrote: "The factor that really forms the *personal character* in the divine motherhood and . . . represents the *grace of the divine motherhood* is a *supernatural, spiritual union of the person of Mary with the divine Person of her Son, which is effected by the will and power of God.* . . . The simplest, most precise and most natural description of this union with the divine Person is the term *matrimonium divinum* or *conubium Verbi* in the strictest sense of the word." Joseph Scheeben, *Handbuch der katholischen Dogmatik* (Freiburg: Herder, 1882), nn. 1588f.

42. De Lubac, *Splendor of the Church*, 366; cf. Rupert of Deutz's commentary *In Cantica canticorum de Incarnatione Domini*, and the opening of Book I, *Patrologia Latina* (PL) 168, cols. 839–40.

43. De Lubac, *Splendor of the Church*, 334–35.

44. See de Lubac, *Corpus Mysticum*, 368–69.

45. This circularity is the basis and the condition for Mary to be the Church as person and in person up until that point on the Cross. It also means that Mary's Immaculate Conception, as the basis for her spousal relation, is the concrete "type" of our baptism.

46. De Lubac, *Splendor of the Church*, 171–72.

47. Ibid., 314.

48. Ibid., 316.

49. See de Lubac, *Corpus Mysticum*, 220–47.

50. Ibid., 37–39.

51. See de Lubac, *Eternal Feminine*, 9–40.

52. De Lubac calls her "the universal creature" in *Splendor of the Church*, 351.

53. Ibid., 335. De Lubac quotes Gregory the Great, *Hom.* 38, *In evangelia*, no. 3 (PL 76, col. 1283).

54. De Lubac, *Eternal Feminine*, 128.

55. De Lubac, *Splendor of the Church*, 315.

56. Cf. ibid., 340.

57. In his *Mystery of the Supernatural*, 54–96, de Lubac makes clear that his approach to nature and grace has four main convictions underlying it: (1) The task is to see grace as gratuitous from the historical and existential concreteness of *now*, thereby preserving God's freedom and the gratuity of grace both speculatively *and, most importantly, existentially.* This is his main point. (2) God's call is constitutive, not *accidental*; thus the human desire for God as beatifying end is constitutive of what it means to be human. (3) This means that humans all have the same teleological options, which makes the human drama of infinite value (especially since heaven and hell are therefore the only two options, without a mitigating natural correlative). (4) This view is more "personalist" and "existential"—though not existentialist—and corresponds much better to de Lubac's reading of the tradition.

58. De Lubac, *Corpus Mysticum*, 368.

59. Paul McPartlan, "Mary for Teilhard and de Lubac" (paper delivered to the Oxford branch of the Ecumenical Society of the Blessed Virgin Mary, November 18, 1987), 2–3.

60. Henri de Lubac, *A Brief Catechesis on Nature and Grace* (San Francisco: Ignatius, 1984), 191–234.

61. Ibid., 211, and de Lubac, *Splendor of the Church*, 184.

62. See de Lubac, *Paradox and Mystery*, 55–58.

63. See de Lubac, *Splendor of the Church*, 320.

64. Ibid., 320–21 and 341–47.

65. Aidan Nichols, O.P., treats this aspect of de Lubac's writings in *Figuring Out the Church: Her Marks, and Her Masters* (San Francisco: Ignatius, 2013), 97–98.

66. De Lubac, *Splendor of the Church*, 320.

67. Ibid., 317.

68. Ibid., 342.

69. Ibid., 371.

70. De Lubac, *Motherhood of the Church*, 15, and *Paradox and Mystery*, 62ff.

71. De Lubac, *Splendor of the Church*, 316.

72. Ibid., 348.

73. De Lubac, *Eternal Feminine*, 123.

74. Cf. ibid. The idea behind this can be found even in Thomas Aquinas, who writes, "The closer something gets to a principle, the more it participates in that principle's effects," *ST* III, q. 27, a. 5, corpus.

75. De Lubac, *Splendor of the Church*, 342.

76. Ibid., 348–52.

77. Ibid., 351.

78. Ibid.

79. Ibid., 346–47.

80. Ibid., 345–46.

81. De Lubac, *Paradox and Mystery*, 23.

82. De Lubac, *Splendor of the Church*, 330.

83. Ibid., 330.

84. Ibid., 351.

85. Ibid., 315, emphasis mine.

86. Ibid., 377.

87. Ibid., 203.

88. Ibid., 203. See de Lubac, *Paradox and Mystery*, 7.

89. De Lubac, *Splendor of the Church*, 329.

90. Ibid.

91. Cf. ibid., 331.

92. Ibid., 330.

93. Ibid., chapter 4, "The Heart of the Church," 126–60.

94. Cf. ibid., 151–52.
95. Ibid., 337.
96. De Lubac, *Motherhood of the Church*, 159.
97. Ibid., 164. De Lubac wrote this as a meditation that he read at a Bible vigil at the Notre Dame Theological Congress in March 1966: "The Church is my mother because she brought me forth to a new life. . . . I am not deaf to the reproaches directed against my mother (truth to tell there are times when I am deafened by them), nor do I fail to see the justice of some of them. But I assert that [these reproaches] . . . are without force and will always remain so. . . . Happy are those who from childhood have learnt to look on the Church as a mother! . . . In a word, the Church is our mother because she gives us Christ. She brings about the birth of Christ in us." In *Paradox and Mystery*, 4–5.

CHAPTER 8

Mariology as Theological Anthropology

Louis Bouyer on Mary, Seat of Wisdom

Michael Heintz

In teaching theology to undergraduates, when encountering the text from the twelfth chapter of the Apocalypse about the woman clothed in the sun and adorned with a star-emblazoned crown, with the moon beneath her feet, I pose this question to the students: "Is this is a figure of Mary or of the Church?" The answer I am looking for, the only answer that the living tradition of the Church fully accepts is "Yes." As the beautiful preface for the Solemnity of the Assumption affirms, Mary is "the beginning and the pattern of the Church in its perfection and a sign of hope and comfort for your people on their pilgrim way" ("*ecclesiae tuae consummandae initium et imago, ac populo peregrinanti certae spei et solacii documentum*").[1] There is an intrinsic relation between Mary and the Church. Mary is both the starting point and the image of the Church in its perfection, and she is living proof, offering encouragement and affording sure hope to the Church on pilgrimage in this age.

This, of course, is the very language employed and, in a sense, canonized in the eighth chapter of the Dogmatic Constitution on the Church, *Lumen Gentium*, of the Second Vatican Council, a chapter that, despite the vagaries of its redaction history, follows quite seamlessly from the previous chapter, on the innately eschatological character of the Church on pilgrimage in this age in its communion with the Church in heaven, and flowers into an ecclesiology that is intrinsically Marian.[2] One could make the claim that a healthy and integral ecclesiology necessarily demands a vibrant and rich Mariology.[3]

BEGINNINGS OF A TRILOGY

In the decades preceding the Council, one of the most industrious—and, to my mind, underappreciated—theologians of what is often called the biblical and patristic *ressourcement* of the mid-twentieth century was the French Oratorian Louis Bouyer (1913–2004).[4] Bouyer, a student of Oscar Cullmann and a convert from Lutheranism, produced, in the roughly two decades preceding the Council, a flurry of remarkable and important works ranging from his profound meditation on the Holy Week liturgies, *Le Mystère Pascal*, to a study of Anthony of Egypt and early asceticism, a lengthy intellectual biography of John Henry Newman, and volumes on the meaning of the monastic life, the priesthood, a plea for an authentically Christian humanism, and a superb introduction to the spiritual life.[5] And it was also during this remarkably productive time that he undertook the first volume of a theological trilogy, one whose basic schema he outlined as follows:

> We hope to develop a theology of creation and of the whole economy of grace as designed by God for its benefit. It [the first volume] forms a kind of sketch of a *supernatural anthropology*, that is, the theology of man and of his destiny in the eyes of God. It is to be followed by a work on the Church and the people of God, in other words, an essay on *supernatural sociology*. A third essay, devoted to the world, both material and spiritual, from the physical universe to the world of angels, will set forth, as it were, a *supernatural cosmology*, the theology of the whole creation, considered as single whole.[6]

These words are found in the introduction to Bouyer's *Le Trône de la Sagesse*, which appeared in French in 1958 and in English in 1960, whose subtitle is "Essai sur la signification du culte Marial" (An Essay on the Meaning of Marian Devotion).[7] This sustained reflection on the human person, the Church, and all created reality, viewed under the aspect of grace and as the subject of the divine economy, was no doubt a rather ambitious undertaking. What Bouyer refers to as "supernatural anthropology" would be called, in the language of contemporary systematic theology, theological anthropology, the disciplined reflection on the human person, from created origin to supernatural destiny, in light of the grace of divine revelation. Bouyer, however, chooses as the subject of his reflection on "supernatural anthropology" not Jesus, but Mary. This is, in some ways, a surprising move. As beneficiaries of the legacy of Pope John Paul II, whose opening theological salvo, *Redemptor Hominis* (1979), was as much a catechesis on the human person as it was on the person of Christ, we are quite naturally to suspect that the ideal place to begin a reflection on the human person in the light of divine grace is the person of Jesus Christ. The Polish pontiff, in an implicitly and instinctively anti-Nestorian move, affirmed that, in encountering the one *prosopon* of Christ, we see the man who is God and the God who is man; in lovingly contemplating the face of Jesus we not only see God revealed, but we also discover ourselves. We are shown not only who God is, but what it means to be authentically and fully human. A very recent introduction to Catholic theological anthropology, for example, follows precisely this tack.[8] Bouyer, however, resists this and, we will see, not without reason.

Bouyer makes clear, as he undertakes his reflections on Our Lady, why she, not her Son, is to be the subject of his "supernatural anthropology." Anticipating an easy Protestant critique of his approach, we might ask: Is bypassing Christ in favor of his Mother an implicit rejection of his authentic and full humanity? Bouyer argues as follows: "We . . . believe that Christ was perfectly man, yet so perfectly, in so divine a way, that he was not, strictly speaking, *a* man, a human person, but God made man. That is why we hold it to be so important to reflect upon that wholly human person who was placed, by the Incarnation, in an absolutely unique relation with the Son of God himself."[9]

Here Bouyer is being completely faithful to the hypostatic union dogmatically affirmed at Chalcedon, namely, the subject of the act of the

Incarnation was the divine person of the Word, who, without loss of his divinity, assumed a complete human nature. The eternal Son is a divine person who has taken upon himself and united to himself a human nature. However, as Bouyer then asserts, "A human person, in fact, and no more than human, became the Mother of God, the Mother of the very Son of the eternal Father. We are, therefore, entitled to see in her and in her alone, all that grace was able to make of a creature, of a human nature, while still leaving it in its order as a created being."[10]

In support of this distinction, Bouyer cites the seventeenth-century cardinal and theologian Pierre de Bérulle (1575–1629) and the research of Bouyer's own contemporary, Charles Flachaire (d. 1914), on the Mariology of the founder of the French Oratory and confessor to St. Vincent de Paul: "The God-man (*l'Homme-Dieu*) is the exaltation of human *nature*; the Virgin Mother is the exaltation of the human *person*."[11] The human person of Mary offers a particular font for theological reflection on just what it means to be a human living in accord with the redemptive grace effected through and by her only Son. As Bouyer continues, "Our Lady shows forth what is, *par excellence*, the Gospel teaching, namely, how our human nature is raised by grace to a degree corresponding to the closeness of the bond that unites us to Christ. She was made the living throne of the eternal Wisdom, so in her we are able to discern, realized in time, all that the divine Wisdom held in store for us."[12] Mary, as first among the redeemed, reveals in its fullness the salvation effected by her son, Christ the Redeemer.[13]

What is more, not only is a redeemed humanity manifest personally in the Virgin Mother but she also reveals, in the order of grace, the spousal relation that the Church shares with her Redeemer:

Here we touch upon what the Gospel reveals as the great Mystery. The union of our nature with God himself took place in the womb of Mary, in the formation of Christ; and so we may apply to God and his work what had been said, in the first days of grace, of man and woman: "they shall be two in one flesh" [Gen. 2.24; cf. Mark 10.8]. No doubt the dignity of Spouse of Christ pertains to the Church as a whole, though each soul that has been redeemed shares in it, by virtue of Catholic unity. This spousal grace, however, if it is given to the whole body, yet has its supreme flowering, and indeed its beginning in the grace of motherhood; and this is peculiar to Mary, though the Church, of which she is the most exalted member, is, in its entirety, associated therewith. So it is that in her alone is to be found the fullness of Christ's gifts to the mystical Body in which is incorporated the humanity he united to himself in the womb of the Virgin.[14]

We will see that Bouyer has more to say about the characteristics Mary shares quite naturally and organically with the Church, in particular maternity and holiness.

AN "ESCHATOLOGICAL" HUMANISM

One of Bouyer's less-known works is titled *The Meaning of the Monastic Life*. Published in France in 1950—and unfortunately its English translation is long out of print—it begins rather cheekily by suggesting to monastics that theirs is not a special vocation in the Church; rather, Bouyer tells them, it is simply the vocation of every Christian, albeit lived with a particular energy and focus by monastics.[15] In effect, the volume functions as a treatise on the vocation of the baptized viewed through the lens of its most intense and devoted practitioners, so to speak. Bouyer dedicated the book to the Benedictine Dom Clément Lialine (1901–58), a convert from Orthodoxy and at the time director of Irénikon at the monastery at Chevetogne. In his dedication Bouyer acknowledged Lialine as inspiring the book, in particular thanking him for introducing Bouyer to the notion of an "eschatological humanism."[16] Aware and, given his temperament, probably hopeful that his proposal might "shock many modern Christians," Bouyer nonetheless pleads his case that "there is no integral humanism other than a radically eschatological humanism."[17] Fearful that some contemporary readings of St. Francis de Sales, for example, were leading to a deconstruction of the spiritual tradition, reducing or ignoring its necessarily ascetical elements, he was wary that as a result, "side by side with the negative, crucifying asceticism of the past centuries, there was room for a constructive, positive asceticism which would reject nothing in this world but would consecrate every-thing in it to the glory of God."[18] But such a humanism, in Bouyer's view, is necessarily inadequate and lacks at its heart the mystery of the Cross: "That the Christian effort must aim at an all-embracing consecration of self and of the world with all its glory and untarnished joy is beyond question. But the cross is precisely the Way which leads to this end, and there is no other."[19]

Bouyer recognizes the tension that seems inherent between a hu-manistic enthusiasm about the prospects for human flourishing and the Cross of Christ, which stands at the center of the Christian faith as an indictment of unredeemed human aspirations to autonomy. He seeks to navigate this by a delicate balancing of what he calls elsewhere a "meta-physical optimism" and a "historical pessimism"[20]—optimism in regard to the fundamental goodness of the created order but realistic pessimism about the obvious fact of human sinfulness and the prospects of unaided human efforts to overcome this; as he puts it concisely, "It is by losing love that we were lost"—by closing in on oneself (*incurvatus in se*, as Au-gustine would say), one shuts out the possibility of being genuinely loved by Another.[21] Bouyer unmasks the false opposition between asceticism and humanism, between the way of the Cross and human fulfillment. For it is precisely the created order, fashioned through the agency of God's *Logos*, that is the object of God's redemptive love, revealed in the *Logos* made flesh, Jesus Christ. In a properly and integrally Christian vi-sion, it is creation itself that is healed, elevated, and restored by the re-deeming work of Christ crucified; creation is not overcome or undone by the grace communicated through Christ's self-denying *agape* but rather restored and glorified by its full participation in its glorified Lord's self-giving and thus life-giving love. This is *the* mystery that Bouyer later was to delineate so thoroughly in one of his last books.[22] This *agape* is experi-enced, indeed even tasted, within the sacred liturgy, which offers to par-ticipants even here and now a share in the *eschaton*. An eschatological humanism is a life of proleptic anticipation, an anticipation actualized through participation in Christ and engendered through the sacraments, when the "then" is experienced and enacted "now," always under the as-pect of grace and within the realistic limitations imposed by a cosmos that still reels from the effects of sin.[23]

MARY AND THE MONASTIC LIFE

For Bouyer this life of proleptic anticipation is found most fully in the monastic life, in which the baptismal vocation is lived with a particular vigor and intensity, when, as he was so fond of recalling the words of the Apostle Paul, "Christ in us, the hope of glory,"[24] continues and extends his salvific work not through an apostolate of active charity or preaching but simply by the witness offered to the age to come through an embrace of the evangelical counsels. Thus, too, Mary becomes such a witness; in fact, she is the preeminent witness. Of course she is not recorded in the Gospels as having preached or participated in the apostolic ministry. However, it is she who bridges, as it were, the two covenants, consummating the old and introducing the new, and in so doing serves simultaneously as an icon of redeemed humanity in its fullness. For, as Bouyer would also write, "who does not see, finally, to what extent the Virgin Mary and her entirely unique existence, before and for the sake of the birth of Jesus, remain enigmatic to us if we do not see her as living in the heart of those mysterious currents of eschatological asceticism" that, he noted, the discoveries in the Judean desert were opening up to scholars in the latter half of the twentieth century.[25]

Later, in fact, Bouyer related the development of monasticism in the fourth century directly to the simultaneous development of mariological reflection: "For it is clear that Mary, then and there [in the fourth century], was seen as embodying in advance the essentials of the monastic ideal."[26] Bouyer examined, in liturgical witness to this theological development, the texts of the Byzantine liturgy for the feast of the Presentation of the Virgin in the Temple, celebrated on November 21 in the Western calendar. The Byzantine *troparia* for the feast had drawn, it would seem, upon the apocryphal *Protoevangelium of James*'s account of the child Mary's seclusion in the Holy of Holies, the recipient of angelic ministrations. Questions of canonicity and historicity aside, Bouyer argues that it is the theological significance of the account that inspired the hymnographers: "What caught all their attention is the idea that Mary, in order to be prepared for the role of Mother of God-made-man which was to be hers, had to lead a life of separation from the world, of absorption into the realities of faith, as they were accessible, already to the purest souls fed by the cult of the Old Testament."[27] We see Mary here as the consummation, as it were, of the faith of the Old Testament, precisely in anticipation of her pivotal role in the New. Thus "what the Presentation of Mary evokes for them [the hymnographers], is exactly that silent solitude with God which had been from the first the very soul of Christian monasticism. . . . Mary, according to them, is to be seen as the first and perfect achievement, in a human being, of the Spousal union of the creature with its Creator."[28]

In Mary is found "the perfect self-surrender, the perfect self-oblation of the creature, as involved for (and in) the self-offering of Christ Himself."[29] If the monk is the ideal type of eschatological humanism, Mary is herself the exemplar of the monastic: one who abandons "everything, according to the Gospel itself, just in order to find, or rather to be found by, God" and, as a result, to be a living anticipation of what St. Paul was later to preach: "It is no longer I who live, but Christ who lives in me" (Gal. 2:20).[30]

In the course of his magisterial *Introduction to the Spiritual Life*, published but a few years after he began his trilogy, Bouyer defends, in the face of a culture increasingly marked by individualism, pragmatism, and social activism, the integral importance of the monastic vocation for the very vitality of the Church, and he does so by invoking the vocation of the Virgin: "Without the monastic vocation, without the monastic life under their eyes, Christians who live in the world would infallibly be absorbed therein. If the Church did not have the monastery within her, it would be as though the apostolic community of Pentecost had not had Mary in its midst; the Church would be seized by the spirit of the world . . . would forget that the life of the Spirit can and should be a reality for us here and now, the life in which the eschatological life of the Kingdom is as it were anticipated."[31]

Mary personally instantiates Bouyer's eschatological humanism in that she manifests, from her Immaculate Conception to her glorious Assumption, all the possibilities of a redeemed humanity, of just what it might look like for a human person to be configured fully to Christ, her Son. As Bouyer concludes succinctly in the first volume of his trilogy, "She is, as it were, the living image, present within time, of what will be brought about in us all only at the end of time. Though unique and pre-eminent, she is yet the image of what we have to become."[32] In this way, Mariology *is* theological anthropology.

GRACE AND FREEDOM

In *The Spirit and Forms of Protestantism* Bouyer offers an autobiographical account of his own intellectual and spiritual journey from Protestantism to the Church and situates his only discussion of Marian devotion within the controversies over grace.[33] His argument might be said to work backward, as it were; or, more correctly, his tack may be simply a reflection of the oft-quoted dictum of Prosper of Aquitaine, *legem credendi lex statuat supplicandi*. Regardless, if one contemplates the various Marian feasts and solemnities that punctuate the annual cycle of the Church's worship, the constellation of mysteries forms a mosaic that appears as something of a comprehensive and integral catechesis on grace, and not grace as a reified abstraction but grace in action, if you will. As Bouyer puts it, "To say that Mary is holy, with a super-eminent holiness, in virtue of a divine intervention previous to the first instant of her existence, is to affirm in her case as absolutely as possible that salvation is a grace, and purely a grace, of God."[34] He is here referring to the Immaculate Conception, a doctrine that, more than any other, he suggests, "shows how much the Church believes in the sovereignty of grace in its most gratuitous form."[35] The vexing problem of divine grace and human freedom, which was one of the principal theological issues brought to the fore during the Reformation debates and subsequently, for Catholics, in the internecine battles over Jansenism, is, Bouyer contends, resolved by a meditation on the mysteries of Mary's life, beginning with her Immaculate Conception: "Our Lady, immaculate from her conception, is, so to speak, the symbol of the true solution to the problem, and shows it in its proper setting. She shows us, in her own person, how the coming into the world of the Son of God presupposed the presence of what we may call a preparatory holiness, one entirely focused on him who was to come, and actuated by his coming, though his coming was still in the stage of preparation."[36]

With "its proper setting" Bouyer refers to the issue of predestination, God's foreknowledge and the integrity of human freedom. In Bouyer's view it had, since the sixteenth century at least, been misconstrued because it was situated within what he refers to as "the individualistic standpoint" rather than what he prefers to call its "traditional" (i.e., Pauline) context.[37] It is the letter to the Ephesians that establishes the "proper setting." "We see," he notes, "that the object of predestination is not each individual in isolation, but, first of all, Christ, then the Church, as associated with him in the mind of God, and each person only 'in Christ and in the Church' (Eph. 5:32)."[38] On the basis of this perspective, then, "the whole of history is, thus, seen as the projection of the un-changing thought of God, an eternal thought, of which Christ is the focal point in time, as he is, in eternity, the essential object."[39] Further, as Bouyer indicates, Mary serves as an important and essential link, both between the Old and New Covenants and between Christ and the Church. Bouyer sees the Immaculate Conception as the culminating grace of the Old Testament, the "preparatory holiness" to which he had referred, brought to its denouement, as it were, and thus making way for a new dispensation of grace.[40] She is also the pivotal link between Christ and his Church, and this, too, is rooted in her graced response of faith. "Our Lady, then, is seen as pre-eminently the exemplar of predestina-tion, as being the link between Christ and the Church"; what, from the perspective of the Old Covenant is seen as a culmination of preparatory holiness is, from the perspective of the New, embodied by an hitherto unparalleled act of faith.[41] As Bouyer contends:

> Till the time of our Lady, the Word had gradually raised man from his state of sin, but it could not dwell and act unreservedly in man-kind, because it always met with a certain allegiance to Adam's sin. In Mary, however, it found a total faith [*la foi complète*], in her abso-lute abandonment of herself to the plan proclaimed. As a conse-quence, this plan was now possible of realization by the Word of God which, at last, came to identify itself with mankind's future, inasmuch as already present in germ, in the Virgin without sin. The Word, Son of the eternal Father, became Son, in time, of Mary.[42]

This faith, however, was not something unheard of. Rather it was seen throughout the Old Testament in figures who, to different degrees, abandoned themselves to God and who came to depend more and more on him, always, however, incompletely. In this sense Mary, whose Mag-nificat still echoes every eventide in the Body of her Son, the Church, is the last among the *anawim* of the Hebrew Scriptures and thus also the first among the *pauperes spiritu* in the order of grace, whom Bouyer describes elsewhere as "the voluntary poor . . . the ascetics who deliberately leave everything in the present age in order to live entirely in the expectation of the world to come."[43] And, in his lectures given at the University of Notre Dame in the summer of 1956 on the theological and narrative unity of the Scriptures, Bouyer asserts that, just as it was the *anawim* who assisted in establishing the Ark at Keriath-jearim and later in Jerusalem (cf. 1 Sam. 7:1), ensuring a fitting dwelling place for God's *Shekinah*, or presence, so is it Mary, by the humble faith born of such poverty, who herself becomes the very dwelling place for that divine presence at the Annunciation.[44] Here, in the mystery of the Annunciation, Bouyer discovers the final resolution to the problem of predestination, of the interplay of human freedom and God's grace: "From the standpoint of God's initiative, of predestination, we may say that it was because the moment had come when the Word had decided to take flesh that faith flowered in Mary. But from the standpoint of saving human freedom, it is equally true to say that the Word became incarnate at that moment rather than at any other because he had at last found a soul of entire faith, wholly disposed to receive him."[45]

This "entire faith" of Mary is the link between Christ and the Church, for her complete abandonment of self, her total act of faith, prefigured only inchoately in the Old Covenant, opens the way for the New, and thus she becomes a living icon of the vocation of the Church. She who came to bear in and from her own humanity the eternal Son becomes, by grace, the preeminent Christian disciple and is the image and type of all discipleship. She thus links Christ, her Son, to his followers, that is, all those who, like her, have, by grace, abandoned themselves, no doubt yet incompletely, to the Word made flesh from her own flesh. This "entire faith" of Mary is also why Bouyer looks to her, rather than to her Son, as the principal font for theological reflection on the human person: "Strictly speaking, it is in Mary, rather than in Christ, that the two mysteries of human freedom and predestination come together, since she receives the advances of grace in accord with a correspondent faith. Christ is above faith, for, in him, human nature being taken up into personal union with the divine Word, was, from the outset, established in the beatific vision, in direct consciousness of complete union with

God."[46] Bouyer is careful, however, to make it clear that this does not in any way distance Christ from us: "Christ's humanity, though possessed by a divine person, yet remains ours, because it first belonged to the person of Mary. It was given over to God, to his Word, in Mary's self-surrender by faith."[47] Mary serves, as it were, as the link between Christ and his spiritual posterity, the Church, that is, our humanity united to Christ's humanity through her humanity. Yet as such a link she is to be proclaimed, Bouyer says, in reference to preaching the Marian mysteries, "not so much as an un-heard of exception, but as the masterpiece of grace, which is the central and unvarying theme of Catholic preaching about her."[48] As already mentioned, to preach about Mary is to proclaim the theology of grace, refracted in the mysteries of her life, a grace that comes solely and supremely from her Son and is intended for all who share in her act of faith, her fiat to God's Word.

This is yet another way in which Mariology is, for Bouyer, theological anthropology, since Mary reveals what a graced and free response to the living Word of God can and should be. The faith she embodies is the truest expression of human freedom and, simultaneously, in the Incarnation of the Word, the supreme instance of grace. In an economy of sin, grace and freedom can be seen only as rival autonomies, divine and human, at odds with one another. In the new order established by the Incarnation, Mary's fiat, far from being an abdication of her freedom, reveals the genuine harmony between grace and freedom. In the history of the fallen cosmos, that particular moment, Mary's "let it be done to me in accord with your word," is arguably the freest choice ever made by a human person.[49]

VIRGIN AND MOTHER

Mary's unique status as one who experienced both motherhood and perpetual virginity provides Bouyer with a lens through which to examine both states of life, marriage and consecrated virginity, and, further, to reflect on the significance of both maternity and virginity particular to Mary's vocation. Bouyer argues that both marriage and virginity reflect, albeit in different ways, the same mystery: "The mystery of consecrated virginity is no other than the mystery of marriage; the mystery, in each, is identically the same. The reality may seem to have done away with the sign, which marriage is, but it has simply taken over the sign into itself, and so fulfilled it."[50] Of the two states of life, Bouyer sees marriage as the more fundamental, since it "indeed, keeps ever present before us the end to be attained, not as a kind of fantasy, but as a possibility already, in some way, realized."[51] And he puts it even more directly, "If the mystery of Christian marriage did not exist, were not proclaimed in this world, proclaimed, indeed, and realized in the fullest sense possible, the renunciation of the ascetic or the martyr, the renunciation of the virgin, would be purposeless self-destruction."[52] The "end" to which he refers has been, from the beginning, adumbrated by the natural institution of marriage, whose sacramental character comes properly to the fore in the new dispensation of grace: "From the very first, the union of man and woman had been, as it were, the image designed to make known to man his supernatural destiny . . . the sign of that state God had, at all times, willed ultimately for men, and which effects what it signifies, in spite of sin, in the union of Christ and the Church."[53]

Marital love was to reveal that radical intimacy to which God invites humanity, in his creative and redemptive wisdom. However, marred in the created order by sin and self-absorption, the sign will, as it were, limp in its complete realization of that reality. Thus the renunciation of marriage, in the state of consecrated virginity, itself becomes a sign also of that end, the intimacy with God that will be achieved fully only in the age to come; in this sense, both are eschatological signs—one signifying the end but unable ultimately to effect it fully, the other an anticipatory share in that same end accomplished through an act of renunciation and self-abandonment. As Bouyer puts it, "The nuptials which are alone eternal, those of the Lamb, are the appanage of those who have made themselves eunuchs for the Kingdom of God."[54] But, as Bouyer makes clear, it is nonetheless marriage that in fact gives consecrated virginity any real meaning or value, for it is still capable of signifying efficaciously, even if imperfectly so in this age, the shared end (what he calls the mystery) of both states of life. In his later *Dictionary of Theology* (less well known than the classic Rahner-Vorgrimler volume of similar title, with both appearing in English the same year), Bouyer had argued that "it is essential that

Christian virginity be viewed not as a negative condemnation or depre-
ciation of marriage, but as a means of hastening, through generosity of a
voluntary sacrifice, the full realization of this union between Christ and
the Church of which marriage itself is an efficacious sign."[55]

As he reflects on the significance of Mary's virginity, Bouyer turns
to one of his favorite patristic sources, Maximus Confessor (c. 580–662).
Integral to marriage in both the natural and supernatural orders is
human generation; yet the fruit of marriage is, as Bouyer puts it, "unable
to surmount the barrier of death." However, he says "virginity . . . embraced in view of the Kingdom of God, forestalls death by its renunciation of the natural process of generation."[56] It is precisely through Mary's
"entire faith" in God's Word, in his promise, that her virginity becomes
particularly fruitful. "In the case of Our Lady, we see it [her virginity] as
an expression of her faith in the power of the Creator to create anew, and
so it raises her, by her surrender to it, to the plane of the resurrection.
She derives from it the power to bring to a new birth, for eternal life, the
sons of Adam who lie under sentence of death."[57]

Spousal love, according to St. Paul's advice to the Ephesians, must
always be what Bouyer calls *amour crucifié*, a "crucified love." Consistent
with his lifelong aversion to what might be called "soft" (or, as one colleague of mine has characterized it, "invertebrate") spirituality and with
his conviction that there can be no authentic Christian life without the
Cross, Bouyer makes clear that Christian love must be a crucified love.
This is the meaning of *agape*, which tutors, purifies, and heals *eros*, which,
left to its own devices, will always veer off course, always miss its true
mark, and always settle for less.[58] This crucified love is what marks the
reciprocal and spousal relation of the Church in this age for Christ, as
witnessed in its preeminent member, the Virgin of Nazareth. And this is
what makes her virginity most fruitful. Her "entire faith," her complete
renunciation and abandonment of self, her "crucified love" makes her
virginity simultaneously maternally fruitful. As Bouyer puts it, this is
"the supreme truth revealed to us by Mary's virginal motherhood . . .
[that] by her renunciation in a spirit of perfect faith [*foi parfaite*], of the
very possibility of generation on the earthly plane, that of the first creation, she offered herself for the very generation of the human body of
the Son of God. And since he is in himself, not only the origin, but the

whole of the new creation, she also brought this new creation to birth in bearing him."[59] For Bouyer this results in a number of important correspondences relative to the entire economy of salvation:

> God himself shows he is Father precisely in the Cross of Christ, since it is there that he is revealed as triumphantly creative love, because he is seen as love that knows no bounds. Likewise, our human nature is shown in Mary as sharing in the definitive creation of *Agape*, because in her is seen the Mother of the new creation through virginity in perfect faith. So then, there is a correspondence between Mary's virginity and the Cross of Christ, as there is between the divine Motherhood of a creature and the Fatherhood of God who made himself Father of mankind, and as the faith of Mary corresponds to the gift of the Word.[60]

Here, Bouyer says, in the virginal maternity of Mary, "the supreme potentialities of human nature under the influence of grace are exhibited" as the capacity to participate in the very redemptive work of the Triune God.[61] Finally there is a further correspondence that Bouyer addresses, this one between the Holy Spirit, who eternally recapitulates the Son in the Father, and Mary, who, in the economy, makes possible our recapitulation in her Son. Bouyer puts it quite neatly: "We defined Mary's motherhood as a relation which brought the Son into our humanity, a relation containing in itself the possibility of our ultimate inclusion in the Son. Mary, then, is the person in and through whom was effected, within human history, the recapitulation proper to the Spirit, within the life of the Trinity."[62]

This maternity is shared with—or, more precisely, extended to—the Church; what is her "exclusive privilege" will be shared by all the members of her Son's Body, the Church. And the Church will share with her in the age to come, as its final dignity and glory, all that she already embodies. And such glory, for all members of the Church, "derives wholly from their union with Christ, their intimate association with the font and fullness of holiness."[63] Ecclesial maternity, however, is first and foremost Marian, and the Church, Bouyer asserts, can be called "Mother" only by being a "continuation" of Mary's own maternity.[64] Similarly, as to its holiness, only in the age to come will the Church possess "without spot or wrinkle" (Eph. 5:27) that very holiness which Mary already enjoys for, according to Bouyer, "in her it flowered before any other saint in the new covenant." Moreover, "the virginal state of being directly and permanently consecrated to God will, finally, pertain to the entire Church as a single community; but, as an individual, Mary will always possess it as her singular privilege."[65] The Church's relation to Christ is spousal, while the precise relation of Mary to Christ is, according to Bouyer, "still more mysterious . . . for by it Christ chose to make himself dependent on her; the Church will, ultimately, come to be the Spouse of Christ, in the full sense of the word. Mary is already the Mother of Christ, the Mother of God made man."[66]

"IT IS FIRST IN MARY THAT THE CHURCH IS SEEN"

Since, as Origen suggested, the end is like the beginning, let me conclude by returning to the *Roman Missal*. There we find another preface composed in the wake of the Council in dependence on *Lumen Gentium*, chapter 8, for the votive mass *De Beata Maria, Ecclesiae Matre*, Our Lady, Mother of the Church. This preface captures in beautiful language the intrinsic relation between Mary and the Church and reflects many of Bouyer's emphases, which, he would no doubt be quick to point out, are nothing more than what is to be found in the living tradition of the Church as it has reflected on the significance of the Word of God entrusted to it. The text reads:

It is truly right and just, our duty and our salvation, always and everywhere to give you thanks, Lord, holy Father, almighty and eternal God, and to proclaim your greatness with due praise, as we honor the Blessed Virgin Mary. Receiving your Word in her Immaculate Heart, she was found worthy to conceive him in her virgin's womb, and, giving birth to the Creator, she nurtured the beginnings of the Church. Standing beside the Cross, she received the testament of divine love and took to herself as sons and daughters all those who by the Death of Christ are born to heavenly life. As the

Apostles awaited the Spirit you had promised, she joined her supplication to the prayers of the disciples and so became the pattern of
the Church at prayer. Raised to the glory of heaven, she accompanies your pilgrim Church with a mother's love and watches in kindness over the Church's homeward steps, until the Lord's Day shall
come in glorious splendor. And so, with the Angels and Saints, we
praise you, as without end we acclaim . . . .

As for the identity of the woman described in the twelfth chapter of
the Apocalypse, Bouyer offers his own answer, found in his *Dictionary of
Theology*: "It would indeed seem that if the woman who appears in the
sun, her head crowned with stars and the moon beneath her feet, is not
purely and simply the Virgin, but rather the Church, it would in any
case be the Church as represented by the Mother of a unique male
Child, the victor over the serpent, who is obviously the Messiah. That
amounts to saying that if the woman represents the Church, it is first in
Mary that the Church is seen."[67] This last line in many respects captures the core of Bouyer's Mariology. For if the Church—not as a reified
abstraction but as a living and organic reality, including you and me—is
best seen in Mary, we can also see ourselves somehow in her, both *in via*,
through a life of "entire faith" and "crucified love," and *in patria*, with
her and like her, sharing in the glory of her only Son, the Eternal Wisdom of God Incarnate.

As the first installment of a trilogy, Bouyer's reflections on Mary, his
"supernatural anthropology," can also be recast in light of his "supernatural cosmology," adumbrated in one of his earlier works and expressed
with an evocative beauty worth quoting:

Across this continuous chain of creation, in which the triune fellowship of the divine persons has, as it were, extended and propagated
itself, moves the ebb and flow of the creating *Agape* and of the created *eucharistia*. Descending further and further toward the final
limits of the abyss of nothingness, the creating love of God reveals
its full power in the response it evokes, in the joy of gratitude in
which, from the very dawn of their existence creatures freely return
to him who has given them all . . . like an infinitely generous heart,
beating with an unceasing diastole and systole, first diffusing the

divine glory in paternal love, then continually gathering it up again to its immutable source in filial love.[68]

It is precisely the maternity of the Church, the implied third term, as it were, in this relationship between the paternal divine love and its filial response, that is the *locus in quo* this dynamic, organic, and graced *perichoresis* takes place. To Mary was entrusted the eternal Wisdom of God. It is the "mystery," as St. Paul would call it, of God's eternal plan made manifest finally and fully in Christ.[69] Through Mary, Seat of this Wisdom, God has united himself eternally to our humanity. It is Mary, Mother of God and the New Eve, the New Mother of all the living, whose virginal maternity is the condition of possibility for the Church's motherhood.[70] Moreover, it is she who is also the preeminent member and the living icon of that very Church in its fullness. She embodies, both personally and quite literally, the supernatural destiny of each and every believer who has been brought to life through the death of her only Son.

NOTES

1. A. Ward and C. Johnson, *The Prefaces of the Roman Missal: A Source Compendium with Concordance and Indices* (Rome: Tipografia Poliglotta Vaticana, 1989), Latin, 399, English, 401.

2. *Lumen Gentium* 68 employs precisely the same language used in the *Roman Missal*'s Preface for the Solemnity of the Assumption and clearly served as a basis for its composition.

3. In the decade preceding the Council, Louis Bouyer had consistently argued that Mariology is essential to Catholic faith and theology. See his *Le Culte de la Mère de Dieu dans l'Église catholique* (Chevetogne, Belgium: Éditions de Chevetogne, 1952), 9, and *Le Trône de la Sagesse: Essai sur la signification du culte Marial* (Paris: Cerf, 1957), 9.

4. Jürgen Mettepenningen, in *Nouvelle Théologie, New Theology: Inheritor of Modernism, Precursor of Vatican II* (London: T. and T. Clark, 2010), makes no mention of Bouyer; Gabriel Flynn and Paul Murray, in *Ressourcement: A Movement for Renewal in Twentieth-Century Catholic Theology* (Oxford: Oxford University Press, 2012), 289–302, include an essay on Bouyer by Jake Yap. Cf. the brief biography by Bouyer's literary executor, Jean Duchesne, *Louis Bouyer* (Perpignan, France: Éditions Artège, 2011); for a study of his thought, cf. Davide Ziordan, *Connaissance et mystère: L'itinéraire théologique de Louis Bouyer* (Paris: Cerf, 2008).

5. Louis Bouyer, *Méditation sur la liturgie des trois derniers jours de la Semaine Sainte* (Paris: Cerf, 1945); *La vie de saint Antoine: Essai sur la spiritualité du monachisme primitif* (Abbaye de Saint-Wandrille, Fontanelle, France: Éditions de Fontanelle, 1950); *Newman: Sa vie, sa spiritualité* (Paris: Cerf, 1952); *Le sens de la vie monastique* (Turnhout, Belgium: Brepols, 1952); *Le sens de la vie sacerdotale* (Tournai, Belgium: Desclée, 1960); *Humain ou chrétien?* (Paris: Desclée de Brouwer, 1958); *Introduction à la vie spirituelle: Précis de théologie ascétique et mystique* (Tournai-Paris: Desclée, 1960). A chronological bibliography of Bouyer's works up to 1988 was published in *Communio* 16 (1989): 277–82.

6. Louis Bouyer, *Woman and Man with God: An Essay on the Place of the Virgin Mary in Christian Theology and Its Significance for Humanity*, trans. A.V. Littledale (London: Darton, Longman and Todd, 1960), viii–ix, emphasis added. This is the rather unhelpfully titled English translation of the French *Le Trône de la Sagesse: Essai sur la signification du culte Marial* (Paris: Cerf, 1957); a subsequent release of the Littledale translation in the United States (New York: Pantheon, 1962) more correctly titled the work *The Seat of Wisdom: An Essay on the Place of the Virgin Mary in Christian Theology*. Bouyer's earlier essay published in Collection Irénikon, *Le Culte de la Mère de Dieu dans l'Église catholique* (Chevetogne, Belgium: Éditions de Chevetogne, 1952), offers a kind of *primitiae* of what would appear later in *Le Trône de la Sagesse*.

7. The second volume envisaged in his introduction, *L'Église de Dieu* (Paris: Cerf) (English edition, 1982), appeared in 1970; the third volume, *Cosmos: Le monde et la gloire de Dieu* (Paris: Cerf), was published in 1982. The English translation appeared in 1988 as *Cosmos: The World and the Glory of God* (Petersham, MA: St. Bede's, 1988). In a lengthy interview in the twilight of his career, Bouyer spoke of how his own trilogy was inspired by the work of the émigré Russian theologian Sergei Bulgakov (1871–1944); cf. *Le métier de théologien: Entretiens avec Georges Daix* (Geneva: Ad Solem, 2005), 210–11.

8. On "Jesus as Exemplar," see Susan A. Ross, *Anthropology: Seeking Light and Beauty, Engaging Theology: Catholic Perspectives* (Collegeville, MN: Liturgical Press, 2012), 9–11; as a point of contrast to Bouyer's "supernatural anthropology," Jesus's Mother is mentioned only three times in Ross's text.

9. Bouyer, *Woman and Man with God*, vii, emphasis in original.

10. Ibid., vii–viii; it is important to note that Bouyer clearly held that Jesus nonetheless was revelatory of our identity and destiny as children of God. Cf. his *Le sens de la vie sacerdotale* (Tournai: Desclée, 1960), 24. What Bouyer seems to be emphasizing, however, is that Christ's filiation is both eternal and natural; Mary reveals how this identity is, for a fully human person, entirely the work of grace.

11. Ibid., viii, n. 1, quoting Flachaire, *La Dévotion à la Viege dans la littérature catholique au commencement du XVII siècle* (Paris: Société Saint-Paul, 1957), 91, emphasis mine; cf. Pierre de Bérulle, *Elevation à la très sainte Vierge* (Paris: Migne, 1856), 526.

12. Ibid., viii.

13. A generation later, the Orthodox theologian Alexander Schmemann, commenting on the cycle of liturgical feasts devoted to Mary, said much the same: "They [the Marian feasts] remind us of the various moments in the life of Mary, but they are not mere reminiscences. Indeed, they reveal what human life is at its perfection, for Mary to us is the Mother of God and thus the best, the ultimate, the perfect fruit of mankind. She is the one in whom we know what God wanted when He created human beings. . . . When we think of her heavenly love, of the whole life, we know that *this* is real human life, and also we realize how far we are from it." From Schmemann, *Liturgy and Life: Christian Development through Liturgical Experience* (New York: Orthodox Church in America, 1974), 84. See also the text of a talk given at the University of Dayton and later reprinted as "Mary, the Archetype of Humanity," in *Celebration of Faith*, vol. 3: *The Virgin Mary* (Crestwood, NY: St. Vladimir's Seminary Press, 1995), 45–55.

14. Bouyer, *Introduction a la vie spirituelle*, viii, translation emended.

15. Louis Bouyer, *The Meaning of the Monastic Life* (New York: P. J. Kenedy and Sons, 1955), ix. This is the English translation of *Le sens de la vie monastique*. This work also contains a beautiful description of the economy of creation and salvation as Bouyer conceives it and offers a précis of the view that undergirds his trilogy; cf. 27–37.

16. It is worth noting that Bouyer anticipated by almost a decade the use of the language of "eschatological humanism" made famous by the American Jesuit John Courtney Murray (who used the term in contradistinction to "incarnational humanism"). J. Hooper and T. Whitmore, eds., *John Courtney Murray and the Growth of Tradition* (Kansas City, MO: Sheed and Ward, 1996), 120, n. 17. For a very recent call for a restored "incarnational humanism," which the author sees as rooted in the spirit of Ignatius of Loyola, cf. Glenn Olsen, *On the Road to Emmaus: The Catholic Dialogue with America and Modernity* (Washington, DC: Catholic University of America Press, 2012).

17. Bouyer, *The Meaning of the Monastic Life*, x.

18. Ibid.

19. Ibid. Bouyer addresses the relationship between humanism and asceticism at length in his *Christian Humanism* (Westminster, MD: Newman, 1958).

20. Cf. Louis Bouyer, *Introduction to the Spiritual Life* (Notre Dame, IN: Christian Classics, 2013), 183; this section draws from my own introduction to the new Christian Classics edition of Bouyer's *Introduction to the Spiritual Life*, 10–11.

21. Bouyer, *Introduction to the Spiritual Life*, 207.

22. Louis Bouyer, *The Christian Mystery: From Pagan Myth to Christian Mysticism* (London: T. and T. Clark, 1989).

23. Cf. the Preface for Virgins and Religious in the *Roman Missal*, where this is also made explicit. One should also consult the opening pages to one of

Bouyer's earliest works, *The Paschal Mystery* (Chicago: Regnery, 1950), which both outlines Bouyer's understanding of the sacramental nature of the Christian life and—in conjunction with his much later *The Christian Mystery*—reveals the deep coherence of his thought.

24. One could make the case that Colossians 1:27 is the scriptural leitmotif of Bouyer's theological vision; it is repeated no fewer than sixteen times in his *Introduction to the Spiritual Life*.

25. Louis Bouyer, *The Meaning of Sacred Scripture* (Notre Dame, IN: University of Notre Dame Press, 1958), 247.

26. Louis Bouyer, "The Blessed Virgin Mary and Christian Monasticism," in *Word and Spirit* 10 (1988): 35.

27. Ibid., 36; cf. also Bouyer, *Woman and Man with God*, 131–33.

28. Bouyer, "The Blessed Virgin Mary and Christian Monasticism," 36–37; of course, it is precisely in this way that Mary is also a figure and an anticipation of the Church.

29. Ibid., 37.

30. Ibid., 36.

31. Bouyer, *Introduction to the Spiritual Life*, 249–50. For more on this notion, cf. the instructive final chapter of David Fagerberg's *On Liturgical Asceticism* (Washington, DC: Catholic University of America Press, 2013), fittingly titled "The Face of Asceticism."

32. Bouyer, *The Meaning of the Monastic Life*, 129.

33. Louis Bouyer, *The Spirit and Forms of Protestantism* (Princeton, NJ: Scepter, 1956); the French original is titled *Du Protestantisme à l'Église* (Paris: Cerf, 1954).

34. Bouyer, *The Spirit and Forms of Protestantism*, 245.

35. Ibid.

36. Bouyer, *Woman and Man with God*, 106–7.

37. Ibid., 106.

38. Ibid.

39. Ibid., 108; cf. also 126.

40. Ibid., 103–5, 114, 119.

41. Ibid., 108.

42. Ibid., 114.

43. Bouyer, *The Meaning of Sacred Scripture*, 171; cf. also 67, 112.

44. Cf. ibid., 112; this book was based on Bouyer's twenty-four lectures given at Notre Dame.

45. For "a soul of entire faith" (*un coeur pleinement croyant*), see Bouyer, *Woman and Man with God*, 115.

46. Ibid., 123; for this he cites St. Thomas, *Summa Theologica* 3.7.3 and 3.34.4.

47. Ibid.

48. Bouyer, *The Spirit and Forms of Protestantism*, 245.

49. Cf. Bouyer, *Woman and Man with God*, 185, where, in speaking about the recapitulation to the Father by the Spirit of those who are united to the Son, he makes clear that grace in no way eradicates freedom.

50. Bouyer, *Woman and Man with God*, 92.

51. Ibid., 91.

52. Ibid.

53. Ibid., 92–93, translation slightly emended.

54. Ibid., 94.

55. Louis Bouyer, *Dictionary of Theology* (New York: Desclée, 1965), 456.

56. Bouyer, *Woman and Man with God*, 94.

57. Ibid.

58. Much of what is said in *Woman and Man with God*, 90–100, anticipates the teaching of Benedict XVI's first encyclical letter, *Deus Caritas Est* (December 25, 2005), 9–15.

59. Bouyer, *Woman and Man with God*, 98, translation emended.

60. Ibid., 99, translation emended.

61. Ibid.

62. Ibid., 186; Bouyer goes on to say that "this means that Mary herself has a very special likeness to the Spirit." Cf. the remark of Stratford Caldecott that "in the West, our theology of the Spirit has tended to take the form of Mariology." I owe this reference to David Fagerberg.

63. Bouyer, *Woman and Man with God*, 129, translation emended.

64. Ibid., 130.

65. Ibid.

66. Ibid., 129; perhaps one way of making this distinction clearer is to say that, in relation to us, the Church is Mother; in relation to Christ, the Church is spouse. Mary is Mother in relation to both Christ and the Church.

67. Bouyer, *Dictionary of Theology*, 299.

68. Bouyer, *The Meaning of the Monastic Life*, 29.

69. Cf. note 23.

70. Cf. Bouyer's commentary on the Johannine account of the crucifixion in his *The Fourth Gospel* (English, Westminster, MD: Newman, 1964; originally published in French, 1955): "'Behold thy mother . . . behold thy son,' [is] the epitome of the process we can now discern: the Christian entrusted by Christ to the Church and the Church put before the Christian, in such a way that all in each one and each in all finds the same Lord. Mary's maternity, extending beyond Jesus to all his followers in him, is seen therefore as the principle of the Church's maternity." Cf. also the later work of Bouyer's slightly older contemporary, Henri de Lubac, *The Motherhood of the Church* (San Francisco: Ignatius, 1983; originally published in French, 1971).

MARIAN MODALITIES
IN THE CHURCH

CHAPTER 9

A Pondering Heart

The Immaculate Conception and the Sorrowful Mother in the Theology of Basil Moreau

KEVIN GROVE, C.S.C.

In a significant portion of modern Marian scholarship, nineteenth-century French Mariology is looked upon with academic opprobrium. The oft-quoted Barbara Corrado Pope, in her essay "Immaculate and Powerful," exemplifies the common thrust of these arguments. That is, that the doctrine of the Immaculate Conception functioned as a papal reinforcement of conservative governmental ideals against postrevolution secular, or modern, values.[1] Catholic France was the "inspiration and recipient of much of this papal activity."[2] Marian apparitions then reinforced these ideals. What is found is not the Mary of the Bible, who, Pope explains, had doubts and hesitations, but rather a Mary who was a "pure and passive vessel" not the "first disciple" on account of discipleship being a male-only enterprise.[3] Pope suggests that in France the Mary of Scripture disappeared into doctrine and conservative politics in favor of "kings and the old social order."[4] One can find in the secondary literature of the past several decades arguments that Mary during this period—extending from the nineteenth century until the Second Vatican Council—was used by the Catholic Church in order to support everything from the economic growth of apparition towns to anti-Darwinian ideas stemming from Mary's identity as the new Eve.[5] Despite their vast variance in scope, many of these scholarly claims, I suggest, are united by a rather consistent methodology. Scholars examine apparition narratives and then papal pronouncements.[6] Neither apparition narratives nor papal documents are unimportant. But perhaps something in the middle— that space of a believer's life when not on Marian pilgrimage and not directly contemplating papal teaching—can round out the vision of this time in Western Europe, which is generally called the golden age of Mariology and lasted from the time of Pius IX's apostolic constitution *Ineffabilis Deus* (December 8, 1854) to that of Pius XII's *Munificentissimus Deus* (November 1, 1950). I suggest that ordinary preaching might provide just such an image of the church at prayer during this time.

Basil Moreau was a minor though well-trained theologian, professor, and religious founder who was writing both before and after the promulgation of *Ineffabilis Deus*, the 1854 apostolic constitution on the Immaculate Conception. What makes Moreau interesting is that he was not doing something all that new. In fact, he ticks a number of the boxes for which the aforementioned scholarship would categorize him as one likely to evacuate Mary's historical person and model discipleship. Moreau was an Ultramontanist—unwaveringly loyal to Pius IX—and there is ample evidence to make an argument that he was a monarchist. Yet, whether in spite of himself or not, Moreau managed to hold together not only the theological doctrine of the Immaculate Conception but also the historical person of Mary, who suffered a great deal and was a woman of many sorrows. Rather than conceptualizing this in Marian titles or abstraction, Moreau found a synthesis possible in a description of her pondering heart, the Mary of whom Luke speaks in the infancy narrative. That pondering heart of Mary was indeed immaculate but also sorrowful. Moreau was a preacher for over fifty years; the examples from his extant corpus of writings about Mary illustrate rather the opposite of the scholarly sketch I have just laid out. And for that reason, the rest of this study concerns the possibility that not all ought to be lost about this era of nineteenth-century Mariology.

My method is simply to investigate Moreau's writings in light of his time. Though many of his sermons have been lost, we have a complete

sermon on the Immaculate Heart of Mary as well as a complete meditation written for his religious, with an Ignatian structure, on the sorrows
of Mary. The sermon was written in 1841, three years after the founding
of the Congregation of Holy Cross and more than a decade before the
official dogma of the Immaculate Conception. We do not know the audience or name of the church where Moreau preached, but he preached in
French, likely in the Diocese of Le Mans, in the Department of La
Sarthe. External evidence suggests that Moreau was an avid preacher,
well known for his skill at the task, and we know that he was invited to
preach retreats and missions until the end of his life.[7] The second text,
the meditation, was designed for both novices and vowed religious for
the feast of the "Compassion of the Blessed Virgin," which was at that
time the Friday before Passion Sunday. Moreau's meditations were a
project of his ongoing effort in different forms for nearly twenty years.
Unlike the sermon, Moreau meant this meditation for individual contemplation and prayer. Before assessing the texts themselves, we can note
that their ecclesial and postrevolution context reveals Moreau's achievement concerning Mary.

L'ÉCOLE FRANÇAISE AND THE FRENCH REVOLUTION: CHARTING MARY'S RISE AND FALL IN FRANCE

Moreau was born into a French culture that had in recent history known
the best and worst of times of Mariology. Before the French Revolution,
seventeenth-century devotion to Mary in France had been dominated by
what later has been termed French School spirituality. Pierre de Bérulle
(1575–1629), father of this school, is credited with renewing Mariology in
France by asserting its dependence on Christ, the Incarnate Word.
Scholars, notably Hilda Graef, have considered this emphasis to be one
of the French School's real theological strengths concerning Mary.[8]
Generally, this theological school tended to stress the Incarnate Word
and the Trinity, and the sources for their images were largely patristic.
That said, Bérulle's Marian piety at times went afoul of the Church, suggesting, for instance, a vow of servitude to Mary. The vow and its corresponding corporal practices were denied approval by the Holy Office

in 1621, though individuals could practice servitude to Mary as a private devotion.[9] Bérulle's other significant Marian considerations focused on what he called the hidden life of Christ with Mary, which included the time Mary carried Christ in her womb as well as her maternal authority when he was a little boy. A second figure, and one perhaps as important for the French School's Mariology, was Jean-Jacques Olier (1608–57), the founder of the Sulpicians, the society of apostolic life that would provide the young Moreau's intellectual training in Paris. Olier is credited with popularizing the prayer, "*O Jesu vivens in Maria,*" literally, "Jesus living in Mary." But Olier also at times struggled in presenting a theologically co-herent picture of Mary and Jesus. For instance, Olier explained that from the moment of her Son's conception Mary was the mother not of a devel-oping child but of a perfect man who needed no growth in knowledge or wisdom.[10] Finally, John Eudes (1601–80) composed a late seventeenth-century treatise on the admirable heart of Mary, recommending medi-tation on Mary's states and mysteries, including those from her early life.[11] These and other French School preachers, like Louis de Montfort (1673–1716), prompted an increase of Marian devotion in the two hun-dred years leading up to Moreau and the nineteenth century. They were not beyond critique, either from within the Church or from thinkers of the time—famously, of course, Blaise Pascal (1623–62).[12] Yet they mark a time of the flourishing of thinking concerning Mary and the Incarnate Word. These were the thinkers who, through the Sulpicians in Paris, intellectually and spiritually formed the student Moreau.

In many ways this Marian thinking was reversed in the years of the French Revolution, just before Moreau was born (1799). The most radi-cal of Jansenist thinkers would challenge Marian doctrines not con-cretely evidenced in Scripture.[13] And the de-Christianization move-ments of the 1790s attempted to replace the figure of Mary in French religious culture. At Notre Dame in Paris, for instance, "a young actress was carried into the cathedral by four citizens to represent the Goddess of Reason."[14] She was clothed in white, with a blue cloak and red cap. The parody could not have been clearer: Notre Dame had been supplanted. The white- and blue-clad Blessed Virgin had been replaced by a white-and blue-clad, red-capped maiden representing deified reason.

Even after a later concordat between Napoleon and Pope Pius VII restored some rights to Catholicism in France, the Church in France itself remained a divided reality. Any scholarly discussion of the Church as such needs to take this into account. Moreau's own theological training, for instance, was influenced by the debates between Gallican and Ultramontane theology, and division on this point would delay for nearly two decades French episcopal support for his young congregation's papal approval. In short, both the theological environment of the French School and the social and religious upheaval of the revolution provided the context for Moreau's writing about Mary. Precisely on account of these realities, the Mary that emerges in Moreau's writing is a very striking figure.

CHRISTOLOGICAL HARMONY:
LINKING INCARNATION TO PASSION

Moreau began his sermon on the heart of Mary with concrete consideration, not abstraction. His opening concern indicates that the project was for him, first, a scriptural one.[15] Mary, according to Moreau, could be carefully studied only because the Holy Spirit had revealed some of her thoughts, allowing the believer to glimpse, beyond her actions, her interior disposition. For instance, Mary held and pondered matters in her heart upon the departure of the shepherds in the Lucan infancy narrative (2:19). What she pondered, why she held those things in her heart, and why such a practice might be beneficial to nineteenth-century French Catholics are the matters of Moreau's sermon. Moreau is able to unite all of these threads with any sort of coherence, however, only by showing how each of them relates to Jesus. Mary's maternal relationship to her son remains the matter of her pondering. Her heart was a place properly prepared for such contemplation on account of God's preparation of it and her carrying the infant in her womb. And, finally, Mary's interactions with Christ and John at the Cross provided a link to Mary's heart for the people immediately in front of Moreau hearing his sermon.

The reason for Moreau's focus on Mary's heart, and not some other aspect of Our Lady, was not primarily societal or pious, though the heart was an important part of nineteenth-century French devotion.[16] His reason for contemplating it was quite simply that the Gospels spoke of it. From that starting point, Moreau moved to speak of how this makes sense: "After the humanity of the Eternal Word, Mary's heart is the most beautiful masterpiece ever to leave the hands of the Creator."[17] This, for Christians, should be of no surprise since the Triune God decided that the mystery of the Incarnation would be accomplished in Mary's womb. And it was Mary who not only bore the child Jesus in her womb but during those months began to experience the profundity of her relationship to her son. Moreau exclaims, "Think of the impressions of grace" ("*Impressions de grâces*") that Mary must have encountered during the nine months the Incarnate Word spent in her womb.[18] If Christ is as a sun giving off light, Mary was the first unique recipient of that when his prenatal heart was beating in the same body as her own. Moreau then uses this image of the heart—seemingly a seat of emotion and meditation—for the rest of Jesus and Mary's interactions. It was Mary who held the infant Jesus in her arms. Mary experienced in her heart the emotions of "daily and mutual" ("*l'épanchements journaliers et mutuels*") sharing in the life of Jesus for the first thirty years of his life.[19] Mary considered in silent meditation the actions of Jesus not only when he was young but in his active ministry. She became for Moreau the exemplar of one who contemplated the traits of Christ and the words that came from his mouth.

There are ways in which, in this very image of Mary and Jesus, Moreau exhibits some of the traits for which his era is criticized. Describing Christ as a sun giving off light seemingly reveals the propensity of French School thinkers to concentrate on the overwhelming reality of Christ in Mary's life. Moreau, however, presents what he understands to be the fullness of divinity in the midst of quite normal human relations: Christ's prenatal heart was beating in the same body as her own—the knowledge of which even modern mothers still revel. Mary held Jesus, had authority over him, and knew him in the daily activities of life. What appears here is a Mary who—at the level of experience and perhaps without full comprehension—must have been working through the human aspect of raising a son who was the Word having assumed her flesh.

In striking distinction from the normative scholarly claims about Mary, Moreau's explication of the heart of Mary allowed him to explain for his congregants that Mary is the model of discipleship, more so than the Twelve.[20] Giving three examples of Christ's disciples, Moreau claims that Mary loved Christ more. That is, more than Thomas, the fearless disciple who encouraged following Jesus to Jerusalem; more than Peter, who defended Jesus in the garden, ultimately professed his love for him three times, and was left to feed the flock of the Savior; more even than the Beloved Disciple, who rested his head on his master's breast. More than all of these, Mary loved Christ. And because of this, Mary had to suffer more than anyone else at his death. Moreau, however, relates Mary not only to Christ but also to the other two persons of the Trinity. In this case, he relates God the Father to Mary and contrasts him with her.[21] The Father loved the world to the point that he might give his only Son up to death for the life of the world. Moreau, citing the Pauline image, describes this as the excess of divine love for human beings. And Moreau says that Mary's heart, too, was capable of a certain excess of love, since she made a sacrifice of her son. But here is the difference: God the Father, for Moreau, was by essence impassible. Mary was passible, and it is precisely that human ability to suffer that makes her so important. She gave up her innocent son. No grief can match what she felt then. She suffered and was martyred, in one sense, that day on Calvary. Moreau is not at all claiming Mary as the redeemer but is rather exploring the depths of sorrow as complete configuration to the redemption wrought in Jesus Christ.

This provides the link Moreau used to connect the contemplation of the Incarnation and the Cross in the heart of Mary. He reads back into the history of Mary's actions her cooperation in the Father's providence. Indeed, Moreau describes her not at all as a passive vessel of the divine plan but actively, as the "minister" (*"le ministre"*) of the Father's designs.[22] Moreau invites his congregants to consider what it was that Mary did: she presented Christ for his circumcision, when his blood first flowed; she presented him in the temple, when Simeon told her a sword of sorrow would pierce her soul; she met him on the way to Calvary and climbed the mountain with him to his sacrifice. Then Mary stood at the Cross of her dying son, and again, the details of his death escaped neither her notice nor her contemplation. No one could look on injustice from a posture of love in the same way as Mary. In short, for Moreau, because Mary was created by God to be immaculate and the source of life for the Incarnate Word, she became a cooperator in both the sufferings of her son and in the designs of salvation. These designs were for us, for humanity, and thus Moreau continues to explain how we are to relate to Mary.

The definitive scene of Moreau's sermon is the Passion from John's Gospel (19:25–29). The argument goes as follows. As he was dying on the Cross, Jesus had to have had love for humanity in his mind. As he looked at his mother and the Beloved Disciple, Christ said, "Woman, behold your son."[23] In this instance, John the Beloved stood in for the rest of us, also beloved. Moreau preaches that when Jesus said, "Woman, behold your son," "it was as if he were saying to her: New Eve, here is your family. You are, henceforth, alone the true Mother of the living. You have borne all these children in your sorrow, and I wish you to love them even as you have loved me.'"[24] Moreau continues, explaining to his French congregants how Jesus meant these words: "Most happy children of Adam, know your new mother; I yield thee all my rights over her, so have recourse to her in all your needs. If her womb did not bear you, her heart has given birth to you in this great hour, and if anything could equal my tenderness for you, it would be her own: 'Behold your Mother.'"[25] Mary bore and loved the Savior with the tenderness that divine excess had created in her heart. Because she bore Christ in this way, she loved him the most of anyone. And she was the most sorrowful. The Incarnation and the Cross represent complementary facets of the same heart, of the same created excess of love, which ultimately the Savior gave to the rest of humanity. Thus, the Immaculate Heart of Mary bears forth the mystery of the Incarnation. The same heart knew agonizing sorrow in being so intimately connected to Jesus Christ through his earthly life. But it would be the immaculate and sorrowful heart of Mary, capable of love in excess, that would—at the Savior's command—turn its love to all human hearts ready to contemplate the mysteries she held in hers.

This still leaves open the question of what comprises the "pondering" of Mary's heart in Moreau. And I wish to propose an answer. In the first and obvious sense, it involves a contemplation of Jesus Christ; in his sermon Moreau gets from conception to Cross. Yet there is a further quality of how this pondering might take place, and that, surprisingly, is in silence. The pondering of the heart is a contemplative activity that is undertaken as Mary did it, silently. In the more joyous moments of this pondering, Moreau describes the silence of astonishment at realizing the handiwork of the divine. But this silence further takes on the quality of suffering beyond the expression of words. Writing on the final two sorrows of Mary for the meditation of Holy Cross religious, Moreau explains that concerning the taking down of Christ's body from the Cross and Mary's being alone while Jesus was in the tomb, "silence seems more appropriate here when everything becomes silent and alone."[26] In other words, the contemplation of both the pinnacle of incarnational mystery and the abyss of Calvary's devastation were undertaken by the heart of Mary in the only expression that is beyond words: silence.

ECCLESIAL FIGURE: WRITING BEFORE
THE IMMACULATE CONCEPTION

Moreau's sermon further gives a glimpse of the decade before the promulgation of *Ineffabilis Deus*. Moreau treats the matter very frankly: "It is true that we question the gospels in vain to find whether the heart of the Blessed Virgin was conceived without the stain that dishonored our own souls."[27] Moreau explains that the Fathers of the Church did not teach the Immaculate Conception in the first centuries, and the Doctors of the Church were not in full agreement on announcing it to the people. Nevertheless, Moreau says to his people, "The prime devotion of our age" is to the "Immaculate Heart of the Mother of the Savior."[28] He argues it on the grounds that the traditions concerning Mary point to it. He figured that the Apostles must have left oral instruction with their disciples on the virtues and history of Mary. Conciliar history, especially at Ephesus, in condemning Nestorius, was one step in recognizing the immaculate dignity of Mary. Finally, Moreau appeals to the breadth of the devotion: theologians teach it, preachers preach it, Doctors of the Church support it, and universities are bound by oath to support it. Moreau's local bishop, Jean-Baptiste Bouvier, had allowed for the feast in his own diocese. Moreau writes of the fact that for eighteen centuries the Immaculate Conception had not become an article of faith: "Faith in it was left free to be prompted spontaneously in each of the faithful as the fruit of love for the Sacred Heart of Jesus."[29]

Devotion to the Virgin Mary, which publicly had shifted so radically during the French Revolution and following, could be seen to be promoted by this forty-two-year-old cleric, preaching over a decade before the papal promulgation of the doctrine. Socially, the doctrine of the Immaculate Conception could mean fidelity to tradition that emerged after a time when other traditions were overturned, for better or worse, in great social strife.

PAPAL THEOLOGY, PASTORAL PRAXIS

The ecclesial realities that Moreau's writings reveal, however, ought not to obscure his main purpose and audience. Both of these texts, the sermon and the meditation text, were meant to build up the faith of others. At the end of his sermon, Moreau details how it is that the people of God become the sons and daughters of Mary; Christ gave her to us and us to her through St. John at the foot of the Cross. Moreau's meditations are the clearest evidence of this. Mary's heart gives the praying individual an examen for contemplation. As Mary pondered Christ in her heart, so ought her loyal children in Holy Cross.

Moreau explains in his meditation that his purpose is to create a repulsion for sin but also to arouse compassion. To undertake this sort of endeavor in the spiritual life means to contemplate the heart of Mary and in particular the ways in which the sword of sorrow (Luke 2:35) pierced her soul. Before Moreau, Christian tradition had already developed seven instances of such sorrows to Mary. These were first spoken of by Bernard of Clairvaux (1090–1153), but contemplation of the sorrows only later came to be a devotional practice in the Servite spirituality of the thirteenth century. Moreau takes each of these sorrows as a way of discerning Mary's love for Christ and then cultivating it within the self. In order, the sorrows are the prophecy of Simeon, the flight into Egypt, the loss of Jesus in the temple, the encounter with Jesus carrying the Cross, the Crucifixion, his being taken down from the Cross and placed into the arms of Mary, and his burial.

The meditative quality appears when Moreau asks questions about each of the sorrows. For instance, concerning the image of Jesus being lost in the temple, Moreau, in Ignatian fashion, enters into the scene: "What a shock that must have been for Mary! She retraces her steps, questions all passers-by and searches at the homes of relatives and friends. In spite of all that, she finds her divine child only three days later."[30] Thus in short pieces of meditation Moreau invites his reader into the scene itself but then poses a question: "Do we seek out God with the same diligence when we have lost him?"[31] Thus reflection on the disposition of Mary as she must have gone from person to person inquiring about her son should prompt the same vigor in those who lose God in their own spiritual lives. A second example and equally compelling image of the Virgin is that of her flight into Egypt with Joseph and the infant Jesus. Moreau points out that the journey was a dangerous one: fleeing to a foreign land, the feeling of being searched for by henchmen, the difficulty of desert roads, hunger and thirst. And although Moreau says that Mary trusted in God in all these things, trust did not preclude the reality of suffering in her life.

The closing images of Moreau's meditation are those of Mary holding the body of Jesus and his being placed in the tomb. Mary, who bore the child Jesus in her womb before birth, held the adult Jesus in her arms after death. Both of these actions of Mary—the actions of a woman, a mother—are to be contemplated by Moreau's retreatant in the humble fullness of silence. In that silence Moreau saw in Mary the possibility of a unified contemplation of the entire life of Christ, from Incarnation to tomb. What is not present at this point in the meditation is a consideration of Mary and the resurrected Christ. The goal of the meditation, however, is to learn love and compassion of the kind that Mary exhibited for Christ. Contemplation of the Resurrection is considered elsewhere in Moreau's meditations. He instructs those praying this meditation to conclude by singing the *Stabat Mater.*

A PONDERING HEART FOR THE CONTEMPORARY WORLD

A century after Moreau, Cardinal Leo Joseph Suenens made famous a quip that he attributed to Karl Rahner, that there is a temptation to abstraction in matters of faith, and abstractions have no need of mothers.[32] Moreau wrote at a time when Marian theology was going through a transition at the level of the whole Church. There were papal pronouncements and, of course, the apparitions so frequently studied. In the midst of all of this, Moreau represented a regular preacher. And, at a time when he might have been prone to be drawn to the most marvelous of abstractions, his contemplations remained markedly concrete, markedly historical. Mary could meditate on the Incarnation and the Paschal Mystery precisely because she was there. Mary was the historical person whose fiat in response to the Spirit resulted in her carrying Jesus Christ. She knew that reality better than any other historical person. She loved Jesus more and, on account of it, suffered more from the time of the words of Simeon to the silent cry of the *pietà*. The image of the heart may itself be objected to as an abstraction, but such an objection is rather easily countered when its scriptural origin is articulated as fitting by someone as intellectual and pastoral as Moreau. Mary's immaculate and sorrowful heart is the heart of one person, a woman, Mary, whose own pondering, time and again, remains the model and example, revealed by God, of how to relate to and love God. Moreau's Mary may not emerge as "truly our sister," but she does emerge as one who could conceivably be truly our mother—from learning the heartbeat of her prenatal baby to raising her child to knowing the pain of not being able to take away the suffering of another.

Moreau was not doing twentieth-century theology, and it would be methodologically problematic to draw him into a conversation that he was not having. Yet twentieth- and twenty-first-century conceptions of Moreau's era may have been far too quick to pass off the nuance that might have been written into something like the heart of Mary, sorrowful and immaculate. These scholarly claims are often leveraged without any support when a twentieth-century theologian writes of the nineteenth, "Both in popular preaching and in theological discussion Mary had become a more and more autonomous figure. She was no longer seen in the Trinitarian, Christological, or ecclesiological contexts within which the early Christians had seen her."[33] At least in the singular example of Moreau we see the paradigmatic opposite—a Mary in relation to the life of the Trinity, the most human example of Christological access and contemplation, and a woman who draws together ecclesial reality, having become the mother to all at the foot of the Cross. Mary's interactions with those first doubters and believers, as the best disciple, were part and parcel of Moreau's imaginative consideration of Christ, the providence of the Father, and the Pentecost gifts of the Holy Spirit.

An architectural example illustrates the tension. In the international works of the Congregation of Holy Cross, the religious order that Moreau founded, Mary's name would grace institutions more frequently than any other patron. Mary, as the Immaculate Conception, would be enshrined by Fr. Edward Sorin, C.S.C., in gold atop the University of Notre Dame's main building, modeled after Giuseppe Obici's statue near the Spanish Steps in Rome. Such a gilded icon of doctrine might seem the ultimate evacuation of the historical Mary in favor of what has become "immaculate and powerful." But a more charitable and indeed more probable reading might be possible. For a thinker like Moreau it would have been impossible to enshrine a doctrine *qua* doctrine in gold, but so decorating a mother who teaches how to relate to Christ—and opens up the imagination to all points of Jesus's life—would be a worthwhile pondering.

As it turns out, this nineteenth-century Mary, sorrowful and immaculate, continues to translate from the rich origins of that time into contemporary restatements of what the heart of such a mother might look like. The current *Constitutions of the Congregation of Holy Cross*, written in the modern era for a religious order that does apostolic work in our time, suggest that believers might indeed be helped by just such a pondering heart. This is the restatement of a nineteenth-century image of the Mary about whom Moreau wrote: "There stood by the cross of Jesus his mother Mary, who knew grief and was a Lady of Sorrows. She is our special patroness, a woman who bore much she could not understand and who stood fast. To her many sons and daughters, whose devotions ought to bring them often to her side, she tells much of this daily cross and its daily hope."[34]

NOTES

I am grateful to the Gates Cambridge Trust for funding this research.

1. Barbara Corrado Pope, "Immaculate and Powerful: The Marian Revival in the Nineteenth Century," in *Immaculate and Powerful: The Female in Sacred Image and Social Reality*, ed. C. Atkinson, C. Buchanan, and M. Miles, (Wellingborough, England: Crucible, 1987), 181–84. John Shinners Jr. agrees, expanding the conclusion to suggest that both nineteenth- and twentieth-century apparitions reveal a "politically conservative" Mary helping European and North American religions in their tendencies "to be zealously concerned with guarding tradition." See Shinners, "Mary and the People: The Cult of Mary and Popular Belief," in *Mary: Woman of Nazareth*, ed. D. Donnelly (New York: Paulist Press, 1990), 174–75.

2. Pope, "Immaculate and Powerful," 183. There were, of course, a number of other apparition sites from 1830 to 1930. John Beevers identifies the European locations: five in France, one in Ireland, one in Portugal, and two in Belgium. See Beevers, *The Sun Her Mantle* (Dublin: Brown and Nolan, 1953), 10.

3. Pope, "Immaculate and Powerful," 195. Kathleen Coyle shares the same view about the nineteenth-century understanding of Mary and Christ. Though Coyle points to modern theologies identifying Mary as a disciple (e.g., Gustavo Gutierrez's *The God of Life*), she describes Mary from the nineteenth century to Vatican II as "autonomous" and as having little attention "paid to Mary's own dependence on Christ." See Coyle, *Mary in the Christian Tradition: From a Contemporary Perspective* (Mystic, CT: Twenty-Third Publications, 1996), 61.

4. Pope, "Immaculate and Powerful," 195.

5. Victor Turner and Edith Turner, "Postindustrial Marian Pilgrimage," in *Mother Worship* (Chapel Hill: University of North Carolina Press, 1982), 152–53.

6. This is the case with Turner and Turner, Pope, and more recent mariological texts. Sally Cuneen's *In Search for Mary: The Woman and the Symbol* (New York: Ballantine, 1996), proceeds from recounting the apparitions of Catherine Labouré, La Salette, and Lourdes to addressing Turner and Turner's anthropological analysis of Mary and economy, Mary and post-Napoleonic France, and Mary and the hidden, nonhierarchical domain of the Church (233–34). Sandra Zimdars-Swartz's *Encountering Mary: From La Salette to Medjugorje* (Princeton, NJ: Princeton University Press, 1991) similarly examines first the private aspect of devotion and then how it conflicts with various public aspects of it, including Church authorities. For her method, see 19–21.

7. Correspondence from his first years of priesthood (after he was ordained in 1821) with his spiritual director, Mollevaut, indicated that Moreau was a sought-after, busy, and avid preacher. At the end of his ministry, he spent the final six years of his life after resigning as superior general of the Congregation of Holy Cross as an active preacher of parish missions. Records indicate that from 1866 to 1872 he preached in more than fifty French parishes. Etienne Catta and Tony Catta, *Basil Anthony Mary Moreau*, trans. Edward L. Heston (Milwaukee: Bruce, 1955), vol. 1, 108, 129, 397–405; vol. 2, 970–74.

8. Hilda Graef, *Mary: A History of Doctrine and Devotion* (Notre Dame, IN: Ave Maria Press, 2009), 301–10.

9. Ibid., 303.

10. In ibid., 305, Graef points out that this is impossible to reconcile with Luke 2:52.

11. Eudes divides his treatment of Mary by means of meditating on the hearts of God the Father, God the Son, and God the Holy Ghost, thus giving a Trinitarian structure to his treatise. This is coupled with images of Mary as well as reflections on the Magnificat, phrase by phrase. Though Eudes does treat the sorrowful heart of Mary (especially in his explication of the Marian

title "Hill of Calvary"), Moreau is not simply reproducing Eudes but rather proposing his own synthesis.

12. Pascal's "Ninth Letter Written to a Provincial by One of His Friends" (July 3, 1656) is one example. Pascal writes of a Jesuit's book, *Paradise Opened to Philagie by Means of a Hundred Easily Performed Devotions to the Mother of God* and says that "devotions to the Virgin are a powerful means of winning salvation." But he protests against those who are encouraged to practice devotion without "changing their evil life." See Blaise Pascal, *The Provincial Letters*, trans. A.J. Krailsheimer (Middlesex, England: Penguin, 1967), 132–34.

13. Dale K. Van Kley, *The Religious Origins of the French Revolution* (London: Yale University Press, 1996), 108.

14. Christopher Hibbert, *The Days of the French Revolution* (Harmondsworth, England: Penguin, 1989), 232.

15. Basil Moreau, "The Immaculate Heart of Mary," in *Basil Moreau: Essential Writings*, ed. K. Grove and A. Gawrych (Notre Dame, IN: Ave Maria Press, 2014), 167.

16. See K. Grove and A. Gawrych, "Sulpician Spirituality and the French School," in *Basil Moreau: Essential Writings*, 17–20.

17. "Le cœur de Marie est le plus beau chef-d'œuvre qui soit sorti des mains du Créateur après l'humanité du Verbe éternel." Moreau, "The Immaculate Heart of Mary," 168. See T. Rév. Père Basile-Antoine Moreau, "Le cœur de Marie," in *Sermons: Publiés par ordre du chapitre général (1920) de la Congrégation de Sainte-Croix* (Montreal: Congrégation de Sainte-Croix, 1923), 570.

18. Moreau, "The Immaculate Heart of Mary," 171, and "Le cœur de Marie," 572.

19. Ibid.

20. Here Moreau could not be more different from Pope and the other secondary literature that suggests that the nineteenth century had no model of Mary as a disciple as post–Vatican II Mariologies do (see note 4). It is worth noting at this point, however, that not all post–Vatican II theologies of Mary find seeing her as a disciple to be helpful in every aspect. For a presentation of contemporary concerns about the symbolism of Mary as a disciple, see Elizabeth Johnson, *Truly Our Sister: A Theology of Mary in the Communion of Saints* (London: Continuum, 2003), 95–101.

21. There is an understandable reluctance in current feminist theological method to use Mary as a feminine face of God. It seems that what Moreau is doing here is quite distinct from that; he is, rather, positing the human face of Mary. Again Johnson is particularly helpful in *Truly Our Sister*, 71–92.

22. Moreau, "The Immaculate Heart of Mary," 173.

23. Ibid., 174. Moreau, "Le cœur de Marie," 575.

24. Moreau, "The Immaculate Heart of Mary," 174. In the original: "Mulier, ecce filius tuus; comme s'il lui disait: nouvelle Éve, voilà votre famille, vous êtes seule désormais la véritable mère des vivants, vous les enfantez tous

aujourd'hui dans la douleur et je veux que vous les aimiez comme vous m'avez aimé moi-même." Moreau, "Le cœur de Marie," 575.

25. Moreau, "The Immaculate Heart of Mary," 174. In the original: "Et vous, trop heureux enfants d'Adam, connaissez votre nouvelle mère; je vous cédé tous mes droits auprès d'elle, recourez à son amour dans tous vos besoins. Si ses entrailles ne vous ont pas portés, son cœur vous enfante en ce moment, et si quelque chose pouvait égaler ma tendresse pour vous, ce serait la sienne. Deinde dixit discipulo: Ecce mater tua." Moreau, "Le cœur de Marie," 575. The "deinde dixit discipulo" is missing from the English.

26. Basil Moreau, "Friday after Passion Sunday: Meditation on the Mystery of the Transfixion or Compassion of the Blessed Virgin," in *Basil Moreau: Essential Writings*, 290. In the original: "Mais le silence semble mieux convenir ici où tout devient silencieux et solitaire." Basile Moreau, "15 Septembre," in *Méditations Chrétiennes*, 3rd ed. (Notre Dame de Sainte-Croix: Chez L'Auteur, 1872), 423. The text quoted here was also used in the third edition of Moreau's meditations for Our Lady of Sorrows (September 15).

27. Moreau, "The Immaculate Heart of Mary," 168. In the original: "Il est vrai que ce serait en vain que nous interrogerions les Livres [S]acres, pour savoir si le cœur de cette vierge bienheureuse a été conçu sans la tache qui déshonore notre âme." Moreau, "Le cœur de Marie," 570.

28. Moreau, "The Immaculate Heart of Mary," 169. In the original: "Or la dévotion de notre époque, c'est le cœur immaculé de la mère du Saveur, et tel est l'objet principal de la louange que nous devons lui adresser en ce jour solennel." Moreau, "Le cœur de Marie," 571.

29. Moreau, "The Immaculate Heart of Mary," 170. In the original: "Foi reste libre, pour être en chaque fidèle plus spontanée, et comme le fruit de l'amour pour le cœur de Jésus." Moreau, "Le cœur de Marie," 572.

30. Moreau, "Friday after Passion Sunday," 289. In the original: "Quel coup de foudre pour Marie! Elle revient sur ses pas, elle interroge tous les passants, elle va dans les maisons de sa famille et de ses amis, et cependant elle ne retrouve son divin Enfant que trois jours après." Moreau, "15 Septembre," 422.

31. Moreau, "Friday after Passion Sunday," 290. In the original: "Est-ce ainsi que vous recherchez Dieu quand vous l'avez perdu?" Moreau, "15 Septembre," 422.

32. United States Conference of Catholic Bishops (USCCB), "Behold Your Mother: Woman of Faith," in *Mary in the Church: A Selection of Teaching Documents* (Washington, DC: USCCB Publishing, 2003), 30, par. 85.

33. Coyle, *Mary in the Christian Tradition*, 60.

34. *Constitutions of the Congregation of Holy Cross* (n.p.: Congregation of Holy Cross, 1988), 8.120.

CHAPTER 10

Remembering 1854 in 1958

O'Connor's Edited Collection on the Immaculate Conception as a "Sign of the Times"

ANN W. ASTELL

> *You know how to interpret the appearance of the sky, but you cannot interpret the signs of the times.*
>
> —Matthew 16:3

> *The use of this epithet "Marian" is a sign of the times.*
>
> —René Laurentin

> *The Church has always had the duty of scrutinizing the signs of the times and of interpreting them in the light of the Gospel.*
>
> —*Gaudium et Spes*

To commemorate the centenary of the apostolic constitution *Ineffabilis Deus*, promulgated by Pope Pius IX on December 8, 1854, an international symposium on the Immaculate Conception was held at the University of Notre Dame on June 30–July 2, 1954. Edward Dennis O'Connor, C.S.C., subsequently edited a collection of essays, *The Dogma of the Immaculate Conception: History and Significance*, which was published by the University of Notre Dame Press in 1958, the year that marked the one hundredth anniversary of the apparitions of the Blessed Virgin Mary in Lourdes, France. The volume thus conveniently honored Mary as the Immaculate Conception in a double sense—as the Magisterium had defined the mystery and as Mary had identified herself to the young visionary Bernadette Soubirous (1844–79), whom Pope Pius XI had canonized just twenty-five years earlier, on the Feast of the Immaculate Conception, December 8, 1933.

More than fifty years have passed since the publication of Fr. O'Connor's edited collection, and it remains the most cited, most comprehensive collection on the development of the doctrine in the English language.[1] *Habent sua fata libelli.* This ancient adage teaches us: "Books have their own fates." These fates accord, in part, with the intelligence and talent of their writers; with the multiple circumstances of their historical publication, distribution, translation, and reviews; and with the capacities of their readers, as Terentianus Maurus's proverb, when quoted in its entirety, specifies: "pro captu lectoris."[2] The fate of O'Connor's book, published on the eve of the second Vatican Council, gives us pause and commands our reflection: What are the factors, positive and negative, that explain its enduring authority and interest? What makes it, despite its now evident blind spots, one of the great mariological books of the twentieth century?

In the immediate aftermath of the divisive vote of October 29, 1963, taken during the Second Session of Vatican Council II,[3] René Laurentin published a critique of his fellow Mariologists in which he voiced two main complaints about (1) the "tendency in Mariology to close in on itself and cut itself off from the rest of theology," engaging in highly specialized and "esoteric" studies,[4] and (2) the "lack of coordination of the mass of studies" so that "isolated efforts are put side by side, but . . . not organized to be of service to some enterprise in scale with the [modern] age."[5] Neither of these criticisms justly applies to O'Connor's collection, which exhibits a systematic interdisciplinary organization, historical breadth and depth, and a conscious effort (as indicated in O'Connor's preface) to articulate how the Immaculate Conception of Mary stands "in relation to the other mysteries [of faith] with which it has been associated in the divine plan."[6] This desire for theological integration informs the Marian vision of its learned contributors, some of whom went on to play key roles in Vatican Council II, partly in creative tension with one another. Indeed, the international gathering of Mariologists represented within the pages of O'Connor's 1958 collection may be seen as a prelude to the Council (1962–65), for which Pope John XXIII would call on January 25, 1959.

FROM THE COLLECTION TO THE COUNCIL

Contributing to the edited collection were thirteen scholars, whose names I list here in the order of their published essays: Monsignor Charles Journet (1891–1975), professor of dogmatic theology at the Grand Séminaire, Fribourg, Switzerland, and editor of the review *Nova et Vetera*; Georges Jouassard (1895–1981), dean of the Faculty of Theology of the University of Lyons, France; Francis Dvornik (1893–1975), professor of Byzantine history, Dumbarton Oaks Research Library and Collection, Harvard University; the Dutch liturgical historian Cornelis Adrianus Bouman (1911–88); Carlo Balić, O.F.M. (1899–1977), president of the International Marian Pontifical Academy and of the Scotist Commission, in Rome, Italy; Wenceslaus Sebastian, O.F.M., professor of dogmatic theology, Regina Cleri Seminary, Regina, Saskatchewan, Canada; René Laurentin (b. 1917), professor of dogmatic theology, University of Angers, France; Marie-Joseph Nicolas, O.P. (1906–99), professor of dogmatic theology at the Institut Catholique de Toulouse; Urban Mullaney, O.P. (1915–89), professor of dogmatic theology, Dominican House of Studies, Washington, D.C., and co-editor of *The Thomist*; Charles De Koninck (1906–65), president of the Canadian Academy of St. Thomas and professor of philosophy and theology at Laval University, Quebec; Edward D. O'Connor, C.S.C. (b. 1922), professor of theology, University of Notre Dame; George C. Anawati, O.P. (1905–94), director of the Dominican Institute of Oriental Studies, Cairo, Egypt; and the noted French art historian Maurice Vloberg (1885–1967).

Four members of this distinguished cast were to play a direct part in the drama of the Second Vatican Council: Georges Jouassard, Charles Journet, Carlo Balić, and René Laurentin. Jouassard was a consultor to the preparatory commission, under the direction of Cardinal Alfredo Ottaviani (1890–1979).[7] Journet belonged to the theological subcommission, chaired by Marie-Rosaire Gagnebet, O.P. (1904–83), which prepared the schema *De Ecclesia* in advance of the Council.[8] A close friend of Jacques Maritain (1882–1973), Journet attended the Third Session of the Council in 1965, during which he lent his strong support to the conciliar documents *Dignitatis Humanae* and *Nostra Aetate*. (Pope Paul VI elevated Journet to the College of Cardinals on February 22, 1965.)

Balić had been instrumental in crafting *Munificentissimus Deus*, Pope Pius XII's Apostolic Constitution on the Assumption (1950). He participated in the work of the "prior subcommission" for the Council (1960–62) and assisted Pietro Parente (1891–1986) as one of "the Seven" who prepared the revised schema on the Church in 1963.[9] Balić was the principal redactor of the *De Beata* section on the Blessed Virgin Mary, initially prepared as the fifth chapter of the schema *De Ecclesia*,[10] then considered controversially for treatment as a separate document,[11] and finally, as a result of a close vote taken by the Council on October 29, 1963, revised again for inclusion as chapter 8 of *Lumen Gentium*.[12]

Laurentin played a variety of roles at the Council itself and in its preparation. Before the start of the Council, Laurentin responded critically to the preliminary schema on Christian marriage,[13] opposed Balić's proposed entitlement of Mary as "Mater Ecclesiae" in a draft from early July 1961 of the Marian section of the schema *De Ecclesia*,[14] and offered sharp criticism of an early draft of the schema on the social order (*De ordine sociali*).[15] Frequently in attendance at the Council, Laurentin published a chronicle of its proceedings.[16] In April and May of 1963, Laurentin belonged, along with Yves Congar, Karl Rahner, and others, to the so-called Belgian squad, which prepared the revised text of the document on the Church.[17] Together with Balić, Gerard Philips (1899–1972), and others, Laurentin worked on the redaction of the final, Marian, chapter in *Lumen Gentium*, "The Role of the Blessed Virgin Mary, Mother of God, in the Mystery of Christ and the Church."[18]

Cardinal Avery Dulles, S.J. (1918–2008), has called that chapter "a skillful and prudent compromise between two tendencies in modern Catholic theology, one of which would emphasize Mary's unique connection with Christ the Redeemer; the other, her close connection with the Church and all the redeemed."[19] Anticipating that "compromise" (if that indeed is the appropriate word), Edward O'Connor's edited collection of 1958 on the Immaculate Conception includes essays by Mariologists representing both trends. Indeed, O'Connor's preface to that volume consistently conjoins them, admitting no contradiction between them. The dogma of the Immaculate Conception, he writes, is "of the highest significance for Mariology, first of all, but also for Soteriology and Ecclesiology."[20] Our doctrine, he continues, "is . . . of the highest significance for the theology of Redemption and of the Church, in which it constitutes a special chapter."[21]

Despite the "both-and" perspective shared by O'Connor's collection and the conciliar document, however, they do have different emphases. Whereas chapter 8 of *Lumen Gentium* enfolds Mariology into ecclesiology, placing the mystery of Mary at the heart of the mystery of the Church as its revealed archetype, O'Connor's collection on the Immaculate Conception tends in the opposite direction: it begins with Mary and extends into ecclesiology a historical narrative of a mysterious, personal, Marian redemption effected in, with, and through Christ. In Laurentin's book *The Question of Mary*, he succinctly expresses this contrast: "from one side, the Church in Mary; from the other, Mary in the Church."[22]

Laurentin rightly rejects the labels "maximalist" and "minimalist" that emerged in the polemics of the Council, observing that "a much more complex multiplicity" can be observed in the thinking of the foremost Mariologists and, indeed, generally speaking, of the Council fathers.[23] This is so, he declares, because "in different degrees they [were] all trying to synthesize the two," namely, the "Christotypical" and the "ecclesiotypical" features in the Church's Marian doctrine. They affirm both Mary's unique closeness to Christ, her special conformity to her divine Son through grace and her cooperation with him in his saving work, and also her virtuous presence among the members of Christ's Church, his mystical body.[24] "It is the resultant combination," observes Laurentin, "which gives to each his particular outlook."[25]

HISTORY, MYSTERY, AND THE MEDIATION OF GRACE

O'Connor's 665-page book is an edited collection of essays. While it is not a monograph, O'Connor has structured, introduced, and personally contributed to the multiauthor volume in such a way that *The Dogma of the Immaculate Conception: History and Significance* may indeed be said to have a "particular outlook" that holds together the Christotypical and ecclesiotypical features in a single, specifically soteriological "point of balance"—a "point of balance" (to borrow Laurentin's term)[26] that suggestively links Mary's then anticipated new titles as Co-redemptrix and Mediatrix to the Church's own mystery as a sacrament, a source of Christ's grace for the world in each of its ages, *per saecula saeculorum*. O'Connor observes in his preface to the collection: "There are strong indications that the Church is on the way towards a definition of Mary's co-redemption and mediation of graces."[27] He clearly sees such a definition as the logical extension of the dogma of the Immaculate Conception—a dogma of "structural importance" (O'Connor argues) for the Church's self-understanding and for the entire "system" of the Church's faith.[28]

O'Connor and the other contributors do not explicitly use the Council's language of "mystery,"[29] "pilgrim people,"[30] and "sacrament"[31] to describe the Church per se. However, the collection's heavy emphasis on the long, rich, and complex history of doctrinal development, beginning with the biblical exegesis of the Church Fathers, is consonant with the call to *ressourcement* that animated the Council. It actually performs, through the sheer fullness of its historical account, a narrative theology of epic sweep within which the mysteries of Mary and the Church are inseparably intertwined. As Journet writes in the lead essay for the collection, "The Church needs time, trials, 'challenges,' the unfolding of history, its progress and catastrophes, that she may know, as it were by inclination and affective knowledge, what she was when, in the presence of Christ, she was found entirely recapitulated in Mary; and also that she may know all that she is now through Mary."[32]

The subtitle of O'Connor's edited collection, *History and Significance*, announces its structure. Unlike other collections of essays—for example, those published in 2004 to mark the one hundred fiftieth anniversary of the definition of the dogma of the Immaculate Conception[33]— O'Connor's is "not merely a collection of miscellaneous essays on the subject; they have been organized . . . in order to provide not just interesting reading but a useful tool."[34] Following Journet's introduction, which thematizes the evolution of the doctrine from its hidden origins in Scripture and in the deposit of faith, are six essays that give detailed accounts of different moments in that historical development, with Jouassard providing a patristic survey (inclusive of the early writings of the

Eastern and Latin Fathers); Dvornik focusing on Byzantine mariologists writing from the sixth to the fourteenth centuries; Bouman outlining the main trends within the liturgical tradition, from its first beginnings in the late seventh century in the Byzantine East to the Mass and Office of Pius IX (1863) in the West; Balić tracing the medieval controversies through the time of John Duns Scotus; Sebastian giving a two-part history of the controversies from the death of Scotus to the end of the eighteenth century; and Laurentin delineating the successive papal decisions concerning the feast, the title, and the doctrine of the Immaculate Conception, beginning with those of Pope Sixtus IV (1471–84) and ending with the bull of Pius IX, *Ineffabilis Deus* (1854).

Providing complementation to these historical surveys in part 1 are the supplementary studies and appendixes of part 3: George C. Anawati's essay, "Islam and the Immaculate Conception," Maurice Vloberg's copiously illustrated study of the evolution of the iconography of the Immaculate Conception, and translations of five important primary texts in the history of the dogma, starting with an excerpt from the *Proto-Gospel of James*.

These historical accounts—erudite, replete with extensive notes—are theological investigations. They highlight the theological content of the studied sources themselves and also the essayists' theological interpretations of those sources. The latter reveal the signs of their particular times (cf. Matt. 16:3) and witness to the operation of the Holy Spirit in the long historical life of the Church: in the East and the West, in the liturgy and devotion, among the clergy and the laity, in argumentation on both sides of an issue, in public and private revelation, in interreligious and ecumenical dialogue, and in the actions (and the waiting) of the Magisterium. "We are enveloped in mystery," writes Jouassard at the end of his patrology, "a mystery that God allows our dull minds to penetrate slowly. . . . Let us strive today to listen to all our brothers, including those of the Eastern Church, [as well as] the ancient Fathers."[35] Dvornik similarly concludes his essay with a call for Western "attention to the work of Byzantine theologians."[36] Anawati, for his part, calls for Christian-Muslim dialogue, citing Mary's role "in the mediation of graces" to humanity and "the reflections of the Christian faith in Mary so mysteriously preserved in Islamic texts and in the hearts of Moslem believers."[37]

Given this attitude of appreciative openness on the part of the book's editor and contributors, the absence of any chapter devoted to the complex role of Protestant theology in the history of the doctrine of the Immaculate Conception and to Jewish-Christian historical relations is striking.[38] The name of Martin Luther (1483–1546), who professed his personal faith in Mary's sinless conception, appears only once in the O'Connor collection,[39] Calvin's not at all.[40] More than anything else, this absence—a limiting "sign of the times"—marks O'Connor's 1958 collection as a preconciliar work. If one judges by the titles listed in O'Connor's bibliography (1830–1957) of books on the Immaculate Conception published in six different languages (English, French, German, Italian, Latin, and Spanish), one must conclude that no substantial ecumenical work by mariologists, apart from the study of Byzantine sources, had been accomplished before Vatican Council II.[41]

The historical account, then, for all its richness, remains incomplete, both in its chronological range (O'Connor had originally planned to include an additional chapter) and in its ecclesial perspective.[42] It is limited, too, *qua* history, because no history—even one theological in its narrative—can ever give a full account of its own significance in relation to what is, in the end, a divine mystery. "The importance of any doctrine," writes O'Connor, "does not lie chiefly in its history, but in its intrinsic significance as truth, and in its rank in the hierarchy of truths, which do not depend on historical contingencies."[43] Therefore, O'Connor turns, in the second and central part of the collection, to four studies of the Immaculate Conception by dogmatic (that is, systematic) theologians, with Nicolas showing the compatibility of the dogma with the teaching of St. Thomas Aquinas (1225–74), when that teaching is viewed in its "general framework";[44] Mullaney linking the foreseen privilege of the Immaculate Conception to God's works of creation, redemption, and sanctification;[45] De Koninck spelling out the connections between Mary's Immaculate Conception and her other privileges: her Divine Motherhood, Assumption, and Co-redemption;[46] and, finally, O'Connor himself addressing the Immaculate Conception as the key to Mary's personal spirituality, both in itself and in its influence on the spiritualities of others.[47]

What may we say about these four essays fifty-five years after their publication? De Koninck's is the most typical of the mariological writings of the 1950s in that its logic operates within the confines of Mariology itself. The elegant essays of Nicolas and Mullaney (both Dominicans) show the influence of a Neo-Thomist scholasticism, confident in its synthetic powers and eager to show the relevance of the Marian mystery to other mysteries of the faith. Mullaney, for example, concludes his chapter with a bold consideration of "each of the four [Aristotelian] causes of the Mystical Body of Christ in relation to the role . . . the Immaculate Conception has in regard to that cause," a Neo-Thomist theological investigation he hopes will yield "some picture of the place of Mary's Immaculate Conception in the Church and its life."[48] O'Connor's chapter on the personal spirituality of the Virgin is arguably the most proleptic of the set, reflecting the rising interest in mysticism, personal and communal, and anticipatory of the Council's charismatic description of the Church itself as *corpus mysticum* and mystery.

The difference in theological style between the seven historical essays and the two supplemental essays (found in parts 1 and 3), on the one hand, and the four speculative essays in part 2, on the other, is striking. What gives coherence to the book as a whole—apart from the contributors' shared devotion to Mary Immaculate—is the constantly reiterated witness to, and expectation of, doctrinal development as a proof of the Holy Spirit's presence in, and guidance of, the Church in its understanding of Mary and thus of itself as Christ's bride. The historical theologians, on the one hand, bear witness to the long process of doctrinal development leading up to the definition of 1854; the dogmatic theologians, on the other hand, anticipate, as a further development of the teaching on the Immaculate Conception, the declaration of Mary as Co-redemptrix.

"Since the definition," O'Connor observes, "the meaning of the Immaculate Conception has been explored with greater profundity than before, particularly as regards its relations with other Marian mysteries."[49] Alluding to "the teaching of Popes, Fathers of the Church, and theologians, that Mary is our co-redemptrix," Mullaney expresses "assurance that the holy Virgin herself is a true part of this mystery [of redemption]."[50] Nicolas asserts: "It is easy to see how Mary, who is herself one of the redeemed, can contribute to the redemption of the human race. . . . [Indeed,] the meaning of the grace of the Immaculate Conception would be incomplete, if she did not."[51] De Koninck devotes his entire essay to proving precisely this thesis.

For his own part, O'Connor attempts quite a different theological investigation, a study of the "spirituality of the Blessed Virgin" with reference both "to her personal life" and to the lives "of others insofar as they are influenced by her."[52] O'Connor conjoins these topics, in part because his argument about Mary's "inner life" draws on the witness of saints devoted to her, such as Saints John Eudes, C.J.M. (1601–80) and Louis-Marie Grignion de Montfort (1673–1716), and in part because any description of Mary's inner life (no matter how abstract) must take into account "the maternal relationship that obtains between her and the entire Mystical Body—Head and members."[53]

MARIAN SPIRITUALITY, THE "MARIAN PRINCIPLE," AND THE MODERN ECCLESIAL MOVEMENTS

The first pages of O'Connor's chapter on the spirituality of the Blessed Virgin may be described as Neo-Thomist in their description of the harmonies obtaining between Mary's soul and body, among the faculties of her soul, and, more broadly, between her nature and grace.[54] O'Connor then proceeds to supplement his Thomistic exposition with applications from "the doctrine of the classical mystical theologians—St. John of the Cross, in particular—on the development of the life of grace" and the effects of "transforming union."[55] Seeking to avoid the twin errors of portraying Mary as either "too ordinary" or too "astounding[ly]" miraculous, O'Connor insists: "Our Lady was, like us, subject to the trials and darkness intrinsic to faith and to the laws of spiritual progress through merit. . . . The divinization brought about by divine grace in Mary did not detract from her humanness."[56]

Pointing out that "Mary serves in the sanctification of others in two ways: as model and as helper," O'Connor concludes that the careful distinctions in his foregoing analysis fail to capture the dynamism of Mary's spiritual life as it affects the life of the Church. "Seldom does piety distinguish between imitating [Mary's] example and invoking her [maternal] help."[57] Rather the mystery of Mary's holiness is such that the members of the Church are "sanctified by contact with her holiness."[58] Moreover, "this influence is not a mere result of Mary's personal holiness," O'Connor writes, "but a kind of participation in it."[59]

If O'Connor's edited collection attempts to balance the *nouvelle théologie* of the historians with the Neo-Thomism of dogmatic theologians, joining "history" with "significance," its precise "point of balance" is perhaps best expressed in O'Connor's own essay, which combines (however falteringly) an abstract dogmatics with accounts of historical and mystical experience, virtuous action, and the witness of popular devotion. In O'Connor's portrait of "the spirituality of the Immaculate Virgin,"[60] Mary's inner life gives form to the Church's own.

Hans Urs von Balthasar (1905–88), whose writings exerted an influence on the Council fathers, would later refer to this form as the "Marian principle," which exists, in polarity with the "Petrine principle," as a vital principle of the Church's unity.[61] Voicing an insight later taken up by Popes John Paul II and Benedict XVI,[62] Balthasar saw the Marian principle especially alive in the modern ecclesial movements—both those whose foundation predated Vatican II (for example, the Legion of Mary; the various Fatima associations; the Focolare Movement, which is also known as the Work of Mary; and Schoenstatt) and those established in the wake of Vatican II's "universal call to holiness" (*Lumen Gentium*, chapter 5).[63] In 1998, Pope John Paul II hailed the rise of these movements as "one of the most significant fruits of that springtime in the Church which was foretold by the Second Vatican Council."[64]

When Edward Dennis O'Connor wrote in 1958 about the faithful's "participation" in the spirituality of the Blessed Virgin and thus in her holiness, he did not refer to any of the existing ecclesial movements of that time, although he was later to write extensively on the Catholic Charismatic Movement.[65] An important link exists, however, between O'Connor's chapter in *The Dogma of the Immaculate Conception* and one of the major movements, L'Arche, founded in Trosly-Breuil, France, in 1964 by the Canadian philosopher Jean Vanier (b. 1928). Among the French Dominicans whose writings O'Connor cites as providing a model for his own Marian investigation in 1958, he names Thomas Philippe, O.P. (1905–93), Jean Vanier's spiritual father, the man from whom the young Vanier first learned (as he testifies) "the silence of prayer and the prayer of silence."[66]

Vanier had met the Dominican priest in 1950 at L'Eau Vive, an international center of spiritual renewal, ecumenism, and interreligious dialogue that Père Thomas Philippe had founded in 1947 in close proximity to Saulchoir, the Dominican priory and House of Studies on the outskirts of Paris, where Edward Dennis O'Connor was studying.[67] Père Thomas had been sent from Rome in 1942 to Saulchoir by the Holy Office as a visitator, charged with the unhappy responsibility to remove Marie-Dominique Chenu, O.P. (a leader in the *nouvelle théologie* and, later, a *peritus* at the Council), from his post as master of studies. Contrary to its customary practice, the Holy Office then required Père Thomas, still a young priest, to assume in obedience (however awkwardly) Père Chenu's vacant position at Saulchoir.[68]

L'Eau Vive was frequented by such figures as Jacques Maritain; Charles Journet; Olivier Lacombe, renowned for his study of Hinduism; and the Canadian psychiatrist John W. Thompson, famous for his role at the Nuremberg trials.[69] Père Thomas Philippe was the soul of L'Eau Vive. As O'Connor writes elsewhere, the teaching of Père Thomas—itself "the fruit of profound personal mystical experience"—had "an extraordinary power to foster the spiritual lives of others."[70] While a professor of theology and philosophy at the Angelicum in Rome, Philippe had spent long hours of prayer at the "Mater Amabilis" chapel near the Piazza di Spagna, where, in 1937, he had had a mystical experience of "profound union with the Virgin Mary," a transforming experience that affected his personality, as well as his spiritual direction of others at L'Eau Vive.[71] Accused of "unorthodoxy and spiritual direction that was too mystical" (as Kathryn Spink phrases it), Philippe, whom the Holy Office had used to remove Chenu, was himself removed by that office from L'Eau Vive and Saulchoir in 1952. He was sent into isolation (first in a psychiatric hospital and then in a monastery) and subjected to a period of severe ecclesiastical discipline, during the first part of which he was "not permitted to celebrate Mass, hear confessions, or have any other form of ministry."[72] Finally, in 1963, after ten years of "exile," Philippe, long attracted to the special presence of God in the poor and interested in psychology, was allowed to accept the position of chaplain at Val Fleuri, a home for the mentally disabled in Trosly-Breuil, thus setting the stage for Jean Vanier's foundation of L'Arche there in 1964.[73]

The name "L'Arche" evokes both Noah's Ark and the "Ark of the Covenant," which Vanier, together with Pére Thomas, identifies explicitly with "Mary, Mater Misericordiae, who holds out her arms to embrace all the suffering of the world."[74] The daily prayer of L'Arche asks Mary to bless the home of the mentally handicapped and of the volunteers who live with them and to make it "a true home, a refuge for the poor, the little ones . . . a refuge for those who are sorely tried."[75] Pére Thomas served as a chaplain for L'Arche in Trosly-Breuil until his death in 1993. Today L'Arche and its affiliated organizations have familylike houses for the mentally disabled throughout the world and have made an important contribution to ecumenism.

In 1958, however, Père Thomas still lived under the shadow of ecclesiastical censure. Given this history, O'Connor's repeated citation of Père Thomas Philippe's *Les tresors du Coeur Immaculée de Maria* (retreat conferences transcribed, mimeographed, and distributed by the Couvent du Coeur Immaculée, Bouvines par Cysoing, Nord, France) is remarkable— all the more so, perhaps, because O'Connor cites Philippe for the first time in an early footnote, together with Réginald Garrigou-LaGrange, O.P. (1877–1964), Philippe's teacher and former colleague at the Angelicum, who also wrote about Mary's interior life.[76] O'Connor would later edit and revise Carmine Buonaiuto's English translation of one of Philippe's retreat courses.[77] In a foreword to that volume, Henri J. M. Nouwen (1932–96) mentions that O'Connor had met Père Thomas already in 1948—ten years before the publication of *The Dogma of the Immaculate Conception*. "Father O'Connor knows Père Thomas in ways few do," Nouwen observes. "For many years he has come to Trosly and listened to Père Thomas and let his heart be touched by him. This translation is thus the work of a true disciple."[78]

I would like to suggest that O'Connor's edited collection might also be described as "the work of a true disciple" of Père Thomas Philippe, whom O'Connor, in a 1995 essay, describes as "a very competent theologian formed in the Neo-Thomism of the French Dominicans between the two World Wars."[79] Neo-Thomist in his Mariology, Marian in his mysticism, Père Thomas had a heart that was drawn into the crucible of all the vital intellectual movements of his day, into the deep mysteries of human beauty and affliction and the charitable practices demanded by them. O'Connor has similarly given us, in the many pages of *The Dogma of the Immaculate Conception*, a striking combination of dogmatic theology and narrative (historical) theologies supplemented by interreligious and artistic expressions. The counterpose of these elements exhibits a creative polarity but also an organic coherence that is attractive to anyone who has the patience to discover it.

Perhaps this unity is itself an effect of a "Marian principle" (to echo, once again, Balthasar's phrase). "Marian spirituality," writes Pére Thomas Philippe, "is characterized by a close union of doctrine and practice. It is objective, because based directly on the dogmas of the Church, especially the two recently defined ones. At the same time it is a spirituality of littleness . . . of personal intimacy with Jesus and Mary [and of service to the poor]."[80] Judging by this standard, O'Connor's edited collection is "the work of a true disciple" of Mary, dedicated explicitly, as it is, "to her whose heart, because untouched by sin, is both Sanctuary of the Godhead and Refuge of Sinners."

Having observed that "Mary was enabled [by grace] to be *more human* than anyone else," O'Connor adds a thought-provoking footnote to his essay "The Spirituality of the Immaculate Virgin": "It follows that the development of Mariology presupposes not only a profound and rigorous theology of grace, as mentioned above, but likewise a rich and sure appreciation of *human* values."[81] This sentence alone attests to the importance of O'Connor's book as a sign, prophetic indeed, of the times of its composition (those Cold War years on the eve of the Council), but also of ours, when not only "human values" but even the value of the human per se—human life, human dignity—need the sort of affirmation that a more developed Mariology can give them.

NOTES

1. In *Gateway to Heaven: Marian Doctrine and Devotion, Image and Typology, in the Patristic and Medieval Periods*, vol. 1 (Hyde Park, NY: New City Press, 2012), Brian K. Reynolds cites O'Connor's work first in a long footnote, adding that it "remains one of the most comprehensive collections" (330, n. 1).

2. The proverb, often quoted by postmodern theorists, appears in a medieval grammatical treatise, *De literis, syllabis, et metris* (1286). It inspired Walter Benjamin's famous essay "Unpacking My Library: A Talk about Book Collecting," first published in German in 1931 in *Literarische Welt* and republished in *Illuminations: Walter Benjamin, Essays and Reflections*, ed. Hannah Arendt, trans. Harry Zohn (New York: Schocken, 1968), 59–67.

3. As the very close vote indicates, the Council fathers were almost evenly divided in their answer to the question of whether the topic of the Blessed Virgin Mary should be treated in a separate document or included within the document on the Church. Cardinal Rufino Jiao Santos (1908–73) of Manila presented the arguments in favor of a separate document; Cardinal Franz König (1905–2004) from Vienna urged the reasons for inclusion. See George H. Tavard, *The Thousand Faces of the Virgin Mary* (Collegeville, MN: Liturgical Press, 1996), 203; William G. Most, *Vatican II, Marian Council* (Athlone, Ireland: St. Paul Publications, 1972), 9–10.

4. René Laurentin, *The Question of Mary* [*La Question Mariale*, 1963], trans. I. G. Pidoux (Techny, IL: Divine Word Publications, 1967), 22, 24.

5. Ibid., 18.

6. Edward Dennis O'Connor, C.S.C., "Preface," in *The Dogma of the Immaculate Conception: History and Significance*, ed. Edward Dennis O'Connor, C.S.C. (Notre Dame, IN: University of Notre Dame Press, 1958), xiv.

7. See Joseph A. Komonchak, "The Preparatory Commission," http:/jako monchak.files.wordpress.com/2012/02/preparatory-theological-commission.pdf.

8. See Joseph A. Komonchak, ed., *History of Vatican II*, 2 vols. (Maryknoll, NY: Orbis, 1995), vol. 1, 286, 291.

9. See ibid., vol. 1, 227; vol. 2, 29, 396.

10. See ibid., vol. 1, 257–59.

11. See ibid., vol. 1, 259–60; vol. 2, 211–12, 212.

12. See ibid., vol. 2, 480–81.

13. See ibid., vol. 1, 253–54.

14. See ibid., vol. 1, 258. For the fifth chapter Balić had proposed the title "De Maria Matre Iesu et Matre Ecclesiae." Despite its rejection by the members of the Doctrinal Commission, Pope Paul VI would later give Mary the title *Mater Ecclesiae*, "Mother of the Church," on November 21, 1964. Ibid., vol. 2, 480–81, n. 313.

15. See Komonchak, *History of Vatican II*, vol. 1, 261. According to Joseph A. Komonchak, Laurentin objected to its defense of private property.

16. See ibid., vol. 2, 547. See also René Laurentin, *Bilan de la première session* (Paris: Seuil, 1963).

17. See Komonchak, *History of Vatican II*, vol. 2, 406.

18. See Walter M. Abbott, S.J., ed., *The Documents of Vatican II: All Sixteen Official Texts Promulgated by the Ecumenical Council 1963–1965*, trans. from the Latin by Joseph Gallagher et al. (New York: Corpus, 1966), 85–96.

19. Avery Dulles, note 256 in *Documents of Vatican II*, ed. Abbott, 85.

20. O'Connor, "Preface," x.

21. Ibid.

22. René Laurentin, *The Question of Mary* [*La Question Mariale*, 1963], trans. I. G. Pidoux (Techny, IL: Divine Word Publications, 1967), 73.

23. Ibid., 61–62.

24. Ibid., 64.

25. Ibid.

26. Ibid., 96.

27. O'Connor, "Preface," ix.

28. Ibid., ix–x.

29. The first chapter of *Lumen Gentium* is titled "The Mystery of the Church." As Avery Dulles explains, "The term 'mystery' indicates that the Church, as a divine reality inserted into history, cannot be fully captured by human thought or language." Dulles quotes the speech of Pope Paul VI, given at the opening of the second session of Vatican II (September 29, 1963): "The Church is mystery. It is a reality imbued with the hidden presence of God. It lies, therefore, within the very nature of the Church to be always open to new and greater exploration" (*Documents of Vatican II*, ed. Abbott, 15, n. 1).

30. Chapter 7 of *Lumen Gentium* is titled "The Eschatological Nature of the Pilgrim Church and Her Union with the Heavenly Church." The fifth section of chapter 8 is titled "Mary, a Sign of Sure Hope and of Solace for God's People in Pilgrimage" (*Documents of Vatican II*, ed. Abbot, 78, 95).

31. *Lumen Gentium* chapter 1, par. 1, calls the Church a "sacrament of intimate union with God and of the unity of all mankind" (*Documents of Vatican II*, ed. Abbot, 15).

32. Charles Journet, "Scripture and the Immaculate Conception: A Problem in the Evolution of Dogma," in *The Dogma of the Immaculate Conception*, ed. O'Connor, 3–48, quote on 47.

33. See, for example, the ten articles published in the 2004 issue of *Marian Studies* 55, "The Immaculate Conception—Calling and Destiny," which reflect the proceedings of the fifty-fifth Annual Meeting of the Mariological Society of America in Houston, Texas, May 19–22, 2004. See also Donald H. Calloway, M.I.C., ed., *The Immaculate Conception in the Life of the Church* (Stockbridge, MA: Marian, 2004), which contains six chapters based on papers given at the International Mariological Symposium held at the John Paul II Cultural Center in Washington, D.C., February 20–21, 2004.

34. O'Connor, "Preface," xi.

35. Georges Jouassard, "The Fathers of the Church and the Immaculate Conception," in *The Dogma of the Immaculate Conception*, ed. O'Connor, 51–85, quote on 84.

36. Francis Dvornik, "The Byzantine Church and the Immaculate Conception," in *The Dogma of the Immaculate Conception: History and Significance*, ed. O'Connor, 87–112, quote on 112.

37. George C. Anawati, O.P., "Islam and the Immaculate Conception," in *The Dogma of the Immaculate Conception*, ed. O'Connor, 447–61, quote on 461.

38. A promising new avenue for Jewish-Christian dialogue on the subject of the Immaculate Conception can be found in Peter Schäfer, *Mirror of His*

Beauty: Feminine Images of God from the Bible to the Early Kabbalah (Princeton, NJ: Princeton University Press, 2004). Schäfer argues that the developing cult of the Virgin Mary in the West stimulated related trends in medieval Jewish spirituality. More recently, Jewish historian Miri Rubin has published *Mother of God: A History of the Virgin Mary* (New Haven, CT: Yale University Press, 2010). For a study of the Jewish novelist Franz Werfel's Mariology, see Ann W. Astell, "Artful Dogma: The Immaculate Conception and Franz Werfel's *Song of Bernadette*," *Christianity and Literature* 62, no. 1 (2012): 5–28.

39. See Wenceslaus Sebastian, O.F.M., "The Controversy over the Immaculate Conception from after Scotus to the End of the Eighteenth Century," in *The Dogma of the Immaculate Conception*, ed. O'Connor, 213–70, esp. 250.

40. For important recent discussions of the Immaculate Conception in ecumenical dialogue, see Thomas A. Thompson, S.M., "The Immaculate Conception in the Catholic-Protestant Ecumenical Dialogue," *Marian Studies* 55 (2004): 245–68, and Edward T. Oakes, "Predestination and Mary's Immaculate Conception: An Evangelically Catholic Interpretation," *Pro Ecclesia* 31, no. 3 (2012): 281–98.

41. "Bibliography," in *The Dogma of the Immaculate Conception*, ed. O'Connor, 532–630. This page range includes the bibliography (1830–1957), the appendix to the bibliography (which details the contents of three Mariological collections), and the index to the bibliography.

42. As O'Connor notes in his "Preface," a chapter on the historical development of the dogma of the Immaculate Conception during the period "since the definition, and especially during the past fifty years" was part of the collection's original plan (xiii).

43. Ibid., ix.

44. Marie-Joseph Nicolas, O.P., "The Meaning of the Immaculate Conception in the Perspectives of St. Thomas," in *Dogma of the Immaculate Conception*, ed. O'Connor, 327–45, quote on 327.

45. Urban Mullaney, O.P., "The Immaculate Conception in God's Plan of Creation and Salvation," in *Dogma of the Immaculate Conception*, ed. O'Connor, 347–61.

46. Charles De Koninck, "The Immaculate Conception and the Divine Motherhood, Assumption, and Coredemption," in *Dogma of the Immaculate Conception*, ed. O'Connor, 363–412.

47. Edward D. O'Connor, C.S.C., "The Immaculate Conception and the Spirituality of the Blessed Virgin," in *Dogma of the Immaculate Conception*, ed. O'Connor, 413–44.

48. Mullaney, "The Immaculate Conception in God's Plan," in *Dogma of the Immaculate Conception*, ed. O'Connor, 347–61, quote on 359.

49. O'Connor, "Preface," xiii.

50. Mullaney, "The Immaculate Conception in God's Plan," 357.

51. Nicolas, "The Meaning of the Immaculate Conception," 344.

52. O'Connor, "The Immaculate Conception and the Spirituality of the Blessed Virgin," 413.

53. Ibid., 414.

54. Ibid., 421–23. O'Connor's remark that Mary "receives grace in a quasi-natural manner" (416) is interesting, especially given the controversy surrounding Henri de Lubac's *Surnaturel* (1946) [*The Mystery of the Supernatural*, trans. Rosemary Sheed (New York: Crossroad, 1998)].

55. O'Connor, "The Spirituality of the Blessed Virgin," 414, 429.

56. Ibid., 425–26, 433.

57. Ibid., 442.

58. Ibid.

59. Ibid., 444.

60. The title of the essay is thus abridged in the pages of the book.

61. For the relevant passages in Balthasar's vast corpus, see Brendan Leahy, *The Marian Profile: In the Ecclesiology of Hans Urs von Balthasar* (New York: New City Press, 2000). See also Libero Gerosa, "Secular Institutes, Lay Associations, and Ecclesial Movements in the Theology of Hans Urs von Balthasar," *Communio* 17 (1990): 343–61.

62. See Brendan Leahy, *Ecclesial Movements and Communities: Origins, Significance, and Issues* (New York: New City Press, 2011), 119–25.

63. See Hans Urs von Balthasar, "Lay Movements in the Church," in *The Laity and the Life of the Counsels: The Church's Mission in the World* [*Gottbereites Leben: Der Laie und der Rätestand, Nachfolge Christi in der heutigen Welt*, 1993], trans. Brian McNeil, C.R.V., with D. C. Schindler (San Francisco: Ignatius, 2003), 252–82.

64. John Paul II, "Message to the World Congress of Ecclesial Movements, 1998," *Laity Today* (1999): 222.

65. For a useful survey of Mariological contributions to the theology of the Catholic Charismatic Movement, which started at Duquesne University in Pittsburgh, Pennsylvania, in 1967 and quickly spread worldwide, see Reginald Alva, S.V.D., *Mary and the Catholic Charismatic Renewal Movement* (Delhi, India: Indian Society for Promoting Christian Knowledge, 2012). Among the writings Alva cites are Edward Dennis O'Connor, C.S.C., *The Pentecostal Movement in the Catholic Church* (Notre Dame, IN: Ave Maria Press, 1979); René Laurentin, *Catholic Pentecostalism*, trans. Mathew O'Connell (London: Darton, Longman and Todd, 1977); Hans Urs von Balthasar and Joseph Ratzinger, *Mary: The Church at Its Source*, trans. Adrian Walker (San Francisco: Ignatius, 2005); Hans Urs von Balthasar, *Mary for Today*, trans. Robert Nowell (San Francisco: Ignatius, 1988); and Cardinal Léon Joseph Suenens, *A New Pentecost?*, trans. Francis Martin (New York: Seabury, 1975). Suenens praises Mary as "the one upon whom the Spirit showered his graces, . . . the first Christian, the first charismatic" (197).

66. Jean Vanier, *Drawn into the Mystery of Jesus through the Gospel of John* (Mahwah, NJ: Paulist Press, 2004), 358.

67. In an interview with Fr. O'Connor on September 27, 2013, he told me that Jacques Maritain and Charles De Koninck had both encouraged him to study with Pére Thomas Philippe at Saulchoir.

68. See Kathryn Spink, *The Miracle, the Message, the Story: Jean Vanier and l'Arche* (Mahwah, NJ: Hiddenspring, 2006), 34–35.

69. For a recent biography of the latter, see Paul J. Weindling, *John W. Thompson: Psychiatrist in the Shadow of the Holocaust*, Rochester Studies in Medical History (Rochester, NY: University of Rochester Press, 2010). According to the recollection of Fr. O'Connor, René Laurentin attended Jacques Maritain's occasional seminars at L'Eau Vive. Edward O'Connor, interview with the author, September 27, 2013.

70. Edward O'Connor, C.S.C., "Preface," in Thomas Philippe, O.P., *Mystical Rose: Mary, Paradigm of the Religious Life*, trans. and ed. Edward D. O'Connor (Huntington, IN: Our Sunday Visitor Press, 1995), 8.

71. Spink, *The Miracle, the Message*, 41–42.

72. Ibid., 41, 45.

73. At the order of the Holy Office, Fr. Joseph Kentenich, (1885–1968), the founder of Schoenstatt, underwent a period of ecclesiastical exile from 1951 to 1965, when, at the conclusion of the Council, he was lauded by Pope Paul VI in a private audience and allowed to return to Germany to resume his leadership of the international Schoenstatt Work. Like Pére Thomas Philippe, Fr. Kentenich was criticized for "psychologism" in his practice of the care of souls. The standard biography is Engelbert Monnerjahn, *Joseph Kentenich: A Life for the Church* (Cape Town, South Africa: Schoenstatt Publications, 1985).

74. Quoted in Spink, *The Miracle, the Message, the Story*, 67.

75. Ibid.

76. R. Garrigou-LaGrange, *The Mother of the Saviour and Our Interior Life* [*Mariologie, La Mère du Sauveur et notre Vie intérieure*, 1941], trans. B. Kelly (St. Louis: B. Herder, 1957).

77. Thomas Philippe, O.P., *The Contemplative Life*, trans. Carmine Buonaiuto, ed. Edward D. O'Connor, C.S.C. (New York: Crossroad, 1990). See also Philippe, *Mystical Rose*, and *The Fire of Contemplation: A Guide for Interior Souls*, trans. and ed. Sr. Verda Clare Doran, C.S.C. (New York: Alba House, 1981).

78. Henri J. M. Nouwen, "Foreword," in Philippe, *The Contemplative Life*, vii–xi, at x.

79. O'Connor, "Preface," in Philippe, *Mystical Rose*, 9.

80. Philippe, *Mystical Rose*, 15.

81. O'Connor, "The Immaculate Conception and the Spirituality of the Blessed Virgin," 433, n. 39, emphasis mine.

CHAPTER 11

Anthropological and Pedagogical Implications of Mariology in the Thought of Joseph Kentenich

Danielle M. Peters

The rapid social, political, and cultural changes at the end of the nineteenth century and at the dawn of the twentieth had taken a noticeable toll on the Church. Her fortress mentality gradually lost its influence as her teaching and style in many ways failed to address or reach effectively the needs and expectations of the faithful. Yet the signs of the times were accompanied by new charisms resulting in sincere efforts—mostly by the laity—to attend to the religious and moral formation of the faithful amid secular and pluralistic realities. This revival from within led to the birth of the ecclesial movements, which in more than one way influenced the deliberations of the bishops convened at the Second Vatican Council.[1] Of the movements listed in the "International Associations of the Faithful Directory" at the Vatican website,[2] the vast majority were founded in Europe, but many have since spread internationally.[3] John L. Allen observes, however, that "many movements with a high international profile, such as the Focolare, Sant'Egidio, Schönstatt, L'Arche, and Communion and Liberation, remain largely invisible to the American mainstream."[4]

The contribution of the ecclesial communities to the deliberations and outcome of Vatican II can be summarized as "Marian prophecy," a term coined by Joseph Ratzinger, aka Pope Emeritus Benedict XVI.[5] Its characteristic is not the proclamation of something radically new or extraordinary but its ability to listen receptively and with sensitivity in order to transmit the good news authentically and attractively. With what follows I would like to present the Marian prophecy of Fr. Joseph Kentenich (1885–1968), founder of the international Schoenstatt Movement.

HISTORICAL CONTEXT

When Fr. Joseph Kentenich founded the Schoenstatt Work at the outset of the twentieth century, he was the first German founder of a religious family in the history of the Church and internationally a pioneer initiating a movement with a unique community structure, lay spirituality, and pedagogy. The movement's multiple branches of the Apostolic League are organized on a diocesan level and comprise communities of all walks of life.[6]

Two experiences during his youth marked the life of Joseph Kentenich. In 1894, when he was at the age of eight and a half, his mother entrusted him to the Blessed Virgin Mary before she had to leave him in an orphanage. This act of devotion, together with the drastic experience of the farewell, made a lasting impression on the boy. He later acknowledged that from then on Mary proved herself in an extraordinary manner as "educator of my inner and outer life."[7] At the celebration of the twenty-fifth anniversary of his ordination, he recalled: "She [Mary] personally shaped and molded me from the age of nine onwards. Usually I would be reluctant to say this but in this context it seems appropriate to explain briefly: When I look back I can say that I know no human being who had a more profound influence on my development."[8] The second momentous incident coincided "mathematically exactly" with the beginning of his novitiate in 1904.[9] The critical question that tormented him was "Does truth exist at all and how can it be perceived?"[10] He described his condition as follows: "Since my mind and soul were being divorced from what was genuinely human, earthly, and worldly, my whole person was inwardly tormented and tossed about by a total skepticism, an exaggerated idealism and one-sided supranaturalism."[11] During this profound ideological battle—which, according to his own description, brought him to the verge of insanity—there was one stable reality in his life that essentially kept him from succumbing to it.[12] Reflecting on this crisis, he wrote in 1955: "During these years (1904–1906) the soul was to a certain extent kept in balance through a personal deep love for Mary. The experiential insights I gained during these years inspired me to later formulate these sentences: The Mother of God is as it were the point of intersection between nature and supernature. She is the world's equilibrium. This means, by her being and mission she keeps the world in balance."[13] In retrospect, the seminarian realized that this crisis allowed him to share in and find the means to overcome the tantalizing torments of the modern person. Thus the conviction grew within him that God wanted to prepare and equip him through these experiences for his future ministry.

Following his ordination to the priesthood in 1910, Fr. Kentenich's first assignment led him to the minor seminary of the Pallottine Society, where he taught German and Latin. Soon his pedagogical talent became evident to his superiors, and in 1912 he was appointed spiritual director of approximately eighty-five students at the newly erected college in Schoenstatt.[14] The responsibility for the religious formation of future members of the Society of the Catholic Apostolate, the official name of the work of Vincent Pallotti, challenged him to design a pedagogical program for the young men between the ages of fifteen and eighteen, which he based on a clear cultural analysis of the historical situation in Europe. At the heart of this analysis was the observation that Christian culture was threatened by a rapidly increasing secularization accompanied by an equally accelerated dehumanization. Such a mentality, he observed, produces a gap between nature and grace, that is, between the Creator and creation. As a consequence, personal self-realization seeks only self-fulfillment, and the tendency to immanence determines largely a person's viewpoint on life.[15] In the estimation of Kentenich, these anthropological heresies disclose "the basic problem of today's time."[16] During a pedagogical convention in 1934, he clarified: "The anthropological heresy refers directly to human nature.[17] It seeks to negate, sicken, and to be hostile to the essence of human nature. I may no longer say that this heresy is brewing on the horizon of the future. No, to a great part we live already amid this heresy! Personhood is combated. Human freedom, the whole structure of human nature as it is created by God, is increasingly ruined so that in time we fall victim to mass-psychosis in a cultivated world."[18]

ANTHROPOLOGICAL AND PEDAGOGICAL ACUMEN

The phenomenon of a mass mentality, manifested in a society without tradition and culture, contributes to the depersonalization of the human being and vice versa. Already in 1948, Kentenich predicted the imminent danger of a "fateful mass production of the cloned man."[19] Most crucial for him was the circumstance that the anthropological heresy invades "all intellectual trends in and outside the Church."[20] It powerfully questions and generates a revolution against the order of being (*Seinsrevolution*), from which results a revolution within the order of action (*Tätigkeitsrevolution*). He described "the core of the disease" as "flight from God,"[21] along with "an alarming inability to build community and to love."[22] He continued: "The human person no longer finds the way to the divine and for this reason also not . . . to the human *You*. . . . Thus it happens that in spite of exterior proximity, which has been made possible and realized through technology, people increasingly are estranged to each other; likewise all exterior luxury and all improvement in today's standard of life leave them interiorly empty, spiritless, and soulless, thus profoundly unhappy."[23] He feared that education and formation without a definite ethical and religious foundation is prone to substitute God and his values with technological progress.[24] Hence he sensed that the time had come to put into practice his "innate idea," which he considered to be "the core of my soul-life,"[25] namely, the formation of the new person in the new community.[26]

THE NEW PERSON AND NEW COMMUNITY
FOR THE NEWEST TIMES

The biblical ideal of the new person posits a challenge to be realized throughout salvation history.[27] Kentenich's perception adds a unique flavor that he considered imperative at the beginning of a new era, which for him began in 1914 with the onset of World War I and the founding of the Schoenstatt Work. With his keen Marian prophecy, he perceived that these "newest times" would decisively shape the history of humanity "for the coming four or five centuries," though its symptoms might change or increase.[28] He stressed that in the present age "the new person is a personality who is independent, inspired, inwardly responsible, and inwardly free, who is joyfully ready to make decisions, who distances himself or herself equally from rigid enslavement to forms and an arbitrariness that results from being completely unattached. Hence such personalities do not claim absolute autonomy. Since they take their bearings from the ideal of the Triune God, life in all its phases of development follows the ontological laws of the same Triune God. Thus they combine autonomy with heteronomy."[29]

In view of an increasingly growing mentality among people to consciously and purposefully renounce any notion of a lasting commitment to community, Kentenich envisioned the new community in the present age to be free from every type of soulless formalism and from a mechanical, merely outward, way of living next to others. To overcome all forms of individualism and nihilism, the new community in our time, he argued, needs to attain "a deep soul-filled union: a way of living spiritually in, with, and for one another; a constantly active sense of responsibility for one another that is anchored in God, and that urges the individual member and the community towards the universal apostolate, rendering them fruitful."[30] This notion of the new person in the new community aims at assisting people living in the world without the security of convent or monastery walls to reach for everyday sanctity in the spirit of magnanimity and love.[31]

Based on his experiences and given his pedagogical endowment, Kentenich considered his task to be a "liaison between science and life."[32] Accordingly, Schoenstatt's "asceticism and pedagogy are meant to be an application of dogmatic theology, philosophy, and psychology"[33] to the concrete human condition in the here and now. Kentenich's primary intention thus was not to contribute to the theological discernment of doctrinal clarifications regarding the person and mission of Mary. Instead, he focused on amplifying the Church's teaching on the Blessed Virgin Mary in order to understand better its anthropological and pedagogical corollary for the Christian life. The key question for him was the mode of Mary's participation as Archetype and Mother in the order of redemption and its consequences for the members of Christ throughout history. He placed "the new person in the new community under the protection of Mary," mindful of her educative influence, which he himself had so powerfully experienced.[34] Reflecting on the beginnings of the movement, Kentenich asserts: "From the very beginning Schoenstatt has been a movement of education. The divinely commissioned educator has been the Mother of God."[35] How did he arrive at the notion of Mary's role as educator?

THE FUNDAMENTAL MARIOLOGICAL PRINCIPLE

In 1941, shortly before he would be apprehended by the Gestapo and eventually imprisoned in the Dachau concentration camp until 1945, Kentenich developed his understanding of the fundamental mariological principle during a retreat for Schoenstatt priests. Its formulation is adopted from Scheeben and reads: "Mary is the official and permanent associate and helpmate of Christ in the entire work of redemption."[36] The dogmas of the Immaculate Conception and the Assumption as well as the Church's teaching on Mary's sinlessness constitute the theological foundation for Mary as permanent bridal associate, or *Sponsa Christi*. Mary's perpetual virginity, as well as her divine and spiritual maternity, institute her mission as permanent helpmate of Christ. Henceforth, Kentenich's image of Mary was Christ-centered. He adhered to it even when Vatican II and post–Vatican II theology stressed an ecclesiotypical and anthropocentric Mariology, insisting: "She exists solely for his sake. There is no other reason for her existence."[37]

This original approach to the fundamental Marian principle focuses on the anthropological and salvific implications of Mary's role for the Mystical Body of Christ. In Kentenich's thought, they culminated in Our Lady's being and acting as Mother and educator of the whole Body of Christ. The theological implications of this "office" point to Mary as Mediatrix, which is taken up by *Lumen Gentium* 62; its pedagogical dimension identifies her as educator, and in the pastoral setting she is effective as the "great Missionary" or Evangelizer.[38] Schoenstatt's founder asserted that it may take time until Mary's educational office will be recognized and properly applied to the pastoral ministry of the Church.[39] In the aforementioned retreat talks of 1941, which he considered his swan song, he urged a pastoral shift from abstract analysis to an organically integrated Marian doctrine and devotion, asserting: "In the long run Mariological discussions alone will not reach their goal. The majority of difficulties are with the people who can no longer think organically or symbolically; after all, Our Lady is *the* symbol. To them the Marian world will largely remain locked."[40] Kentenich used every opportunity to impress upon his spiritual family that if Mary is our Mother in the order of grace, her foremost office is the lifelong process of birthing and forming each Christian.[41] Mary's pedagogical method, he argued, "exactly follows the rules and principles of God's educational wisdom which she became acquainted with and learned to live and love in the workshop of the divine Educator as the science of the saints."[42]

MARY'S EDUCATIONAL ROLE TODAY

As founder of an ecclesial movement, Kentenich took a keen interest in observing, studying, and teaching the specific "questions of life which the Mother of God wants to help solve in today's time."[43] He was convinced that Our Lady's timely mission as educator of God's children consists in eradicating the anthropological heresies that, in his opinion, constituted the greatest threat for the Christian image of the person and society in our age. According to his fundamental mariological principle, Mary's educational task is twofold. As associate of Christ she is the outstanding model of our union with him.[44] As helpmate of Christ she cooperates with a mother's love in the generation and formation of the faithful.[45]

Mary, Model and Educator of the Spiritual Life

When speaking of Mary as our model on the earthly pilgrimage, Schoenstatt's founder highlights in particular her sinlessness, her undivided surrender to God's will, and the fullness of her natural and supernatural life.

These ontological aspects exercise a powerful educational influence on the faithful. Hence, Kentenich considered it providential and a unique pedagogical opportunity that the last two Marian dogmas were articulated and pronounced in answer to a pressing need of humanity today.[46] For him the life mediated and generated through these teachings can be likened to a "compendium of all great Catholic truths,"[47] which should equip the mind with "a clear concept of the fully redeemed person" and "offer humanity an ultimate goal and direction for all striving and efforts."[48] In this vein, he asked his spiritual family: "Isn't it strange that the collectivistic idea of the human person figured in literature at the moment when the dogma of the Immaculate was pronounced? None of our time's images of the human person recognizes a supernatural reality."[49]

A thorough analysis reveals that Kentenich allotted the greatest part of his talks and writings to the Immaculate Conception, which for him is "the most beautiful of all Marian dogmas."[50] Anthropologically, the privilege is the prerequisite for Mary's sinlessness and assumption into heaven. Metaphysically, Mary's bridal relationship to Christ and her divine maternity are dependent on the Immaculate Conception.[51] Psychologically and pedagogically, the dogma of the Immaculate Conception is the most significant of all Marian dogmas for our time because it draws attention to the dignity and value of the human person.[52] Kentenich employs the trilogy of the Credo, Confiteor, and Magnificat when highlighting the aspects of Our Lady's pedagogical task as a model for the Christian life.[53] He argues that full acceptance of the dogma of the Immaculate Conception implies a firm Credo in the human person as the image and likeness of God in the existence of the supernatural order of grace but also in the existence of original sin and redemption. Moreover, this Credo denotes that man and woman are created by God as equal in their dignity and complementary in their manner of being human,[54] a biblical teaching opposed to the "gender hodgepodge" of our time.[55] Just as Mary was uniquely graced through the privilege of her Immaculate Conception, so is each human person, no matter his or her status in life, elevated to the supernatural order through redemptive grace, the gift of God's infinitely merciful love. God's gift to each human person signals an invitation to freely cooperate in salvation, like Mary. Thus a sincerely spoken Credo implies the belief that in and like Mary, each person is loved and graced with a unique mission, which leaves no room for any inferiority complex.[56] Men and women are to learn from Our Lady's attitude of serving as expressed in her fiat. Above all, Kentenich was adamant that in Mary, the ideal model of "feminine dignity and beauty,"[57] all confusion regarding authentic womanhood is dispelled.[58]

Notwithstanding our election as children of God, mirroring ourselves in Mary, the paradigm of the human person, entails recognition and acknowledgment of personal culpability and should result in a genuine Confiteor.[59] This "feeling of guilt" concedes the need for redemption and includes the admission of having freely deviated from the order of grace.[60] Kentenich noted that in a world where the sense of sin, guilt, and shame has weakened, the role of the Immaculate as visual instruction of the God-willed human person is crucial, although deplorably seldom recognized in contemporary catechesis. He was convinced of the *Purissima*'s pedagogical and psychological significance because "the deepest and truest longing of humanity and each individual is the paradise person."[61] Finally, Mary's Magnificat expresses optimistic realism in God's power, mercy, and faithfulness.[62] With her song Our Lady teaches us an eloquent lesson of a harmonious human-divine relationship. Kentenich observed that with one exception (cf. Luke 1:48b), "all other parts of the Magnificat . . . circle around the eternal God, around his way of government."[63] Thus it should be with the melody of our lives.

In 1941, nine years before the solemn definition of Mary's bodily assumption into heaven, Kentenich commented on the reservations expressed by some theologians regarding the dogma. For him the "hot air" produced by the vehement debate was primarily concerned with the anthropological implications for life after death.[64] In October 1950, two weeks before the solemn proclamation of the dogma, he emphasized that to a certain extent, the Church's teaching on Mary's person would now be concluded.[65] He considered this infallible doctrine a "pedagogical event" and a "synthesis of anthropology."[66] He pondered: "What does . . . the bodily assumption of the Mother of God into heaven have to tell us? Each body . . . is intended and called by God to once participate like . . . the Mother of God . . . in the glory of heaven. Obviously . . . these truths are threatened to such a degree nowadays that God had to apply the means of a dogma. And those who know life also know how the body is valued today. On the one hand the body is maltreated and on the other hand it is being 'adored.'"[67] He emphasized three pedagogically important truths implicitly revealed with the dogma of the Assumption. First, Mary's bodily assumption draws attention to the Christian understanding of the human body as the dwelling place of the Trinity.[68] Alluding to the subhuman treatment he experienced while in Dachau and in view of the idolization of the body in our time, he clarified: "It is not the purpose of self-denial to harm the body's beauty and health, to break the sacred powers of mind and body, but rather to place them in the service of the soul. Therefore mortification must be prudent and enlightened."[69] Secondly, Mary's assumption also includes the center of her feelings and *Gemüt*, implying that Mary's education and our self-education must take into account a much-neglected aspect of the spiritual life, namely, the formation of the heart.[70] Finally, the Assumpta can teach us important principles concerning the *ars moriendi*.[71] Kentenich summarized them with three imperatives: (1) Take care that your death, like Mary's, will be a death of love and longing![72] (2) Do not forget the transience of all earthly things![73] And (3) remember your glorification in heaven![74]

In sum, Our Lady's exemplary life can be likened to a book that leads heavenward.[75] Kentenich encouraged his spiritual family to frequently page through this book in order to gaze at "our model whose reflection we may and should become."[76] With her and like her, we are to make our entire life an unending *sursum corda*.[77]

Mary, Mother and Educator of the Spiritual Life

Mary's personal character as the official and permanent helper of Christ in his entire work of redemption signals her role of forming Christ in us. Accordingly, Mary's spiritual maternity comprises a distinct pedagogical dimension that, in the opinion of Kentenich, is urgently needed in the Church today. In a study composed while in Dachau he observed that "until now Mariology has dealt primarily with the relationship of Mary to God. The task of the coming centuries will be to reveal her relationship to us."[78] Speaking with theology students in Milwaukee in 1963, the year of the opening of the Second Vatican Council, Kentenich stressed that this perception of Mary is still not sufficiently known or recognized, although it is a natural consequence of Mary's spiritual maternity. If applied correctly, he argued, it will bear much fruit in the spiritual life of the individual and the community. He expressed this concern while reflecting on the so-called Marian Age, which began around 1850. Though she was highly esteemed and profusely venerated on account of her spiritual privileges, Kentenich deplored that Mary was not yet sufficiently recognized by the Church and individual Christians as spiritual Mother and educator. He certainly was not opposed to Marian devotions, but he feared that they did not suffice to change a person from within.

Toward the end of his life, Kentenich clarified his position: "I think often of the years 1950 and 1954. It seemed as if all of Catholicism was steeped in Marian devotion. But see how little depth it had! What is left of it today? . . . How little it [Marian devotion] has taken root in the subconscious life of the soul!"[79] For Kentenich, this was the crux of the sudden decline of Marian devotion and, for that matter, of a vital faith in the Church. He argued that "each of us bears a large share of the responsibility for the form that the world will take in the future. If this future . . . is to bear the resemblance of Christ, then Mary must step more into the foreground and be acknowledged everywhere as the official Christ-giver, Christ-bearer, and Christ-bringer. . . . By so doing we make our contribution, so that the coming hundred years radiantly bear the name of Mary on their brow."[80]

Mary's mission as educator points to the correlation between Marian doctrine and devotion. Concerning Marian doctrine, Kentenich adopted Scheeben's view regarding Mary's mode of participation in the order of redemption. She spoke her "Yes" to Christ, to Redemption, and to the New Covenant representatively for humanity in need of Redemption. Mary's fiat was thus not a private but a representative act and the expression of humanity's self-surrender to the Son of God. The "Yes" of the individual to Christ is therefore, though not always consciously, the individual's alignment with Mary's "Yes." Mary's task as our Mother and educator is to awaken within us a receptivity, surrender, and love for Christ similar to her own.

Kentenich reasoned that since the office given to the Blessed Virgin Mary as Mother of the whole Body of Christ is objectively "necessary for our salvation," it follows that "our love for her is also necessary for our salvation."[81] Henceforth, the fruitfulness of Mary's office depends on the individual's "reverence, love, and obedience" for and to her and finds expression in a lasting attachment to her.[82] Personal attachment to Mary sets into motion a process through which a person matures in love for God. This love, in turn, has a transforming effect, bringing about a new creation in Christ, the new person in the new community. The example of the saints teaches us that "we can never love her too intimately or be too solicitous about permitting her to shape us in the image of Christ."[83]

Genuine Marian devotion[84] includes three elements: love, imitation, and invocation.[85] In this trilogy, affective and effective love is the first and most important component. The connection between filial attachment to and imitation of Mary gradually results in a Marian attitude or demeanor.[86] Kentenich explained that "the attachment is the wellspring and soul of the attitude and the attitude is a sign of the authenticity and depth of the attachment."[87] For him, the most effective expression of a relationship to the Mother of God is expressed in consecration to her. During the Marian Year 1954 he proposed that the "Marian consecration should be the permanent possession of the church in order to impress upon the world Marian features."[88]

MARIAN CONSECRATION

Every Christian is consecrated to God at baptism.[89] Moreover, through baptism each Christian has become God's covenant partner, a relationship Kentenich said should become "the heart of the Christian life."[90] Since God is Love, it follows that the covenant relationship with Him is founded on love. Notwithstanding the theological primacy of love, Kentenich lamented that traditionally, in particular during the first half of the twentieth century, pedagogical emphasis was mostly placed on God's justice, which evoked anxiety instead of trust in his mercy. Schoenstatt's founder was of the opinion that in this regard a major shift in catechesis and education had to occur. With Thérèse of Lisieux, Kentenich maintained that our main vocation is to love, though it is also true that any vocational crisis is at its root a crisis of love. As a remedy to the crisis of love prevalent today, Kentenich suggests that "Mary will set the love in us aright, that is to transform, after her own likeness, all who have given their hearts to her into fully formed children of a singularly great and organic love of God and neighbor."[91] He argued that "because and in as much as the grace of baptism makes us children of Mary as well," our consecration at the sacrament of initiation "is objectively and in essence also" a consecration to the Mother of God.[92] He asserted: "That is the meaning of the Marian consecration as we understand it and have described it. . . . Thus, in its total structure, namely in its preparation and subsequent renewal and deepening, the consecration may be considered an important part of baptismal education. Living this consecration should be considered a means of allowing this basic relationship to grow and develop into its perfection."[93] Hence Kentenich's notion of Marian consecration as "an expression of and a means toward, and an outstanding safeguard of the covenant with God" sealed at baptism.[94]

Schoenstatt's founding on October 18, 1914, included a consecration to Mary, later called a covenant of love. Since then, everyone who joins the Schoenstatt Movement enters this covenant of love with the Mother Thrice Admirable, Queen and Victress of Schoenstatt.[95] The Schoenstatt Shrine is considered the place of the covenant and Our Lady's school of education.[96] In 1952 Kentenich reflected on the significance of Schoenstatt's covenant of love in the context of the covenant in salvation history: "The thought of the covenant is so deeply rooted in our awareness and feeling of life that we may call it without hesitation our fundamental form, our fundamental meaning, our fundamental strength, and fundamental norm. Thus far is the similarity between us and the thinking, feeling, volition, and acting of the New and Old Testaments. I do not know if there is any religious community in the modern time that can make the same statement about itself."[97] In 1966 he reminisced: "The origin of our family is . . . analogous to the origin of Christianity: a life process, a covenant of love of the Eternal Word with human nature; . . . a covenant of love of the Triune God through his exponent, the Blessed Mother . . . with our shrine and the Schoenstatt Family."[98] Following the open doors and signs of the times, Schoenstatt's founder developed a covenant spirituality and pedagogy with a particular emphasis on cultivating a healthy personal relationship to God, people, places, creation, ideas, and ideals.

Through Schoenstatt's covenant of love, a person is intimately drawn into Mary's universal organism of attachments. Within this organism

Mary, as our educator, has an integrating function that, in the opinion of the movement's founder, was not sufficiently acknowledged by Vatican II. He addressed this topic when speaking to clergy shortly after the Council: "In my opinion the Council ended where it should have started. What does that mean? The problem in our day is not primarily the liturgy, not even the Church, though it may be so under some aspects; the problem really consists in the relationship between the First Cause and the secondary causes. Unless this basic relationship is clarified along intellectual lines, practically and functionally, and unless it is lived, I think I may repeat that, humanly speaking and humanly thinking, the Church is barren and helpless in facing the heresies today."[99] In view of the drastic occurrences of modernity and now postmodernity, Mary's task as educator is "especially healing in its effect" when considering "the confusion of the times; . . . and because of the spiritual and emotional fragmentation of the modern person."[100]

A founder's "Marian prophecy" sometimes meets the opposition of the official Church. Thus it happened that on the eve of Vatican II Kentenich was separated from his foundation. He spent most of the next fourteen years (October 22, 1951–October 22, 1965) on administrative leave in Milwaukee, Wisconsin, the place assigned to him by the Holy Office. From there he followed with much interest the deliberations of Vatican II. He noted the Council's liturgical and biblical focus as a positive development but observed helplessness when drawing psychological and pedagogical applications.[101] One year before the Council's conclusion, Kentenich expressed his concern that the deliberations of Vatican II did not succeed in addressing the most pressing issues and heresies of its time. Mary's importance in and for the Church was a matter of course for him, as self-evident perhaps as her lack of importance is perceived in most theological circles today.

MARIAN PROPHECY AND THE CHURCH TODAY

The proximate period leading to the Second Vatican Council belonged to the so-called Marian Century, which began in 1830. It was characterized by the convergence of systematic reflection on the Blessed Virgin

Mary, Marian devotion, Marian spirituality, and a Marian dimension to the apostolate. The relationship between Mariology and anthropology was not addressed by Vatican II.[102] The Council did, however, succeed in abandoning the one-sided Neo-Scholastic approach to Mariology, which tended to idealize Mary and crown her with privileges. The portrayal of Mary in *Lumen Gentium* (LG) was based on the scriptural evidence of the Mother of Jesus, from which emerged other essential features of the historical person of the Virgin. Among them were her dialogical rapport with the Triune God and the Son in particular (LG 53, 56–59); her relationships in solidarity with Jesus's disciples, which continued after the Resurrection (LG 58f); and her pilgrimage of faith (LG 58), emphasizing her free and responsible adherence to the plan of God (LG 56), which moves her closer to each Christian. In addition, *Lumen Gentium* elaborates Mary's motherhood in the order of grace (LG 60–65), highlighting that she cooperates with a maternal love in the spiritual birth and education of the faithful (LG 63).

Two years after the Council, on May 13, 1967, Paul VI published the apostolic exhortation *Signum Magnum* on "Venerating and Imitating the Virgin Mary, Mother of the Church and Model of All Virtues." Article 9 links Mary's spiritual maternity to the role of any mother, who, along with "the procreation of new human beings . . . must also undertake the task of nourishing them and educating them." This statement, together with *Lumen Gentium* 63, points to Mary's pedagogical role from the onset of the Christian's existence, a reality that would later, without difficulty, find entry into the Rite of Baptism and even earlier, when the Rite for the Blessing of a Child in the Womb is administered.[103]

In 1974 Pope Paul VI promulgated the apostolic exhortation *Marialis Cultus* (MC) aimed at "the Right Ordering and Development of Devotion to the Blessed Virgin Mary." It was the first magisterial document wherein an anthropological dimension of Mariology was introduced. Paul VI argued that the "anthropological ideas and the problems springing therefrom" in our time can stand the comparison "with the figure of the Virgin Mary as presented by the Gospel."[104]

Fast-forward to the pontificate of St. John Paul II. Dubbed "Mary's Pope," he left us a rich Marian heritage, including references to Our Lady as the teacher and educator in whose school saints are educated.[105]

John Paul II observed that Our Lady's school of life imprints a "Marian dimension on the life of a disciple of Christ" that "has its beginning in Christ but can also be said to be definitively directed towards him."[106] It appears that in John Paul II the Marian prophecy of Fr. Joseph Kentenich had found an ally.

The nature of our topic asks us to transcend the speculative and theoretical realm and to propose ways in which Our Lady's pedagogical mission can be promoted. Two areas lend themselves to a timely exploration: (1) When the Christian message concerning life is threatened, how could Mary's position as educator of the spiritual life of the Christian from conception to natural birth be more actively invoked? (2) When "the Crisis of Faith and Family Life" needs to be conquered by an authentic Christian family culture, how could the maternal and educational activity of she "who believed" be better invoked within the realm of the domestic church?[107] Pope Francis has drawn attention to Mary, the Untier of Knots, citing St. Irenaeus, who was the first to employ this metaphor when combating the heresies of his time.[108] The Council fathers incorporated this notion into *Lumen Gentium* 56. Kentenich, who frequently invoked Our Lady as the Three Times Admirable Untier of Knots, was convinced that she will also dissolve the knots created by the anthropological heresies of our age.

NOTES

1. Ecclesial movements, inter alia, drew attention to a new reflection of the universal call to holiness of all the baptized (see *Lumen Gentium* [LG], chapter 5). Likewise, they contributed to the formulation of a Christian anthropology (see *Gaudium et Spes* [GS], parts 1 and 2), which in turn led the Council fathers to provide principles concerning various aspects of modern life and human society (GS, part 3). For further study, see, for example: Pontifical Consilium Pro Laicis, *Movements in the Church: Proceedings of the World Congress of the Ecclesial Movements, Rome, May 27–29, 1998* (Vatican City: Libreria Editrice Vaticana, 1999), and *The Beauty of Being a Christian—Movements in the Church: Proceedings of the Second World Congress of the Ecclesial Movements and New Communities, Rocca di Papa, May 31–June 2, 2006* (Vatican City: Libreria Editrice Vaticana, 2006).

2. The first eight of these movements date back to the nineteenth century. We can observe a steady progression of new foundations in the first half of the

twentieth century, with a peak of thirty new ecclesial communities in the 1920s, and again during the decade of Vatican II, with twenty-seven new associations.

3. See Danielle M. Peters, "The Role of Mary in the New Ecclesial Communities in the Twentieth and Twenty-First Centuries," *Marian Library Studies* 31 (2013–2014): 147–67.

4. John L. Allen, "Creative Minorities," *First Things*, June–July 2012, 61.

5. Joseph Ratzinger, "Das Problem der christlichen Prophetie: Niels Christian Hvidt im Gespräch mit Joseph Kardinal Ratzinger," *Internationale katholische Zeitschrift Communio* 28 (1999): 178.

6. The Schoenstatt Movement is part of the larger Schoenstatt Work, which includes the Apostolic League, six secular institutes, and seven federations. Cf. Jonathan Niehaus, *200 Questions about Schoenstatt* (Waukesha, WI: Lithoprint, 2002), 143, 109–10, 147–48.

7. Joseph Kentenich, "Apologia pro vita mea" (unpublished study, n.p., 1960), 87.

8. Cited in Engelbert Monnerjahn, *A Life for the Church* (Cape Town: Schoenstatt Publications, 1985), 138.

9. Joseph Kentenich, "Antwort auf Gründer und Gründung" (unpublished manuscript, n.p., 1955), 8. Joseph Kentenich joined the Society of the Catholic Apostolate, better known as the Pallottines, in 1899.

10. Kentenich, "Antwort auf Gründer und Gründung." English translation in Monnerjahn, *A Life for the Church*, 41.

11. Ibid., 45.

12. See ibid., 9.

13. Ibid.

14. Dorothea Schlickmann, *Die Idee von der wahren Freiheit: Eine Studie zur Pädagogik Pater Josef Kentenichs* (Vallendar-Schoenstatt, Germany: Schoenstatt Verlag, 1995), 42.

15. Joseph Kentenich, *Oktober Brief 1949* (Vallendar-Schoenstatt, Germany: Schoenstatt Verlag, 1970), 16, 70.

16. Joseph Kentenich, "Nordamerikabericht: Auf Dein Wort hin werfe ich die Netze aus," partially published in *Philosophie der Erziehung: Prinzipien zur Formung eines neuen Menschen- und Gemeinschaftstyps* (Vallendar-Schoenstatt, Germany: Schoenstatt Verlag, 1991), 91–158, at 129.

17. In the estimation of Schoenstatt's founder, the anthropological heresy originated in "mechanistic thinking," rampant especially in the Western Hemisphere. Its resulting analytical-mechanistic mentality habitually separates ideas from life and God from the world, as well as life processes and ideas that belong together. For example, mechanistic thinking can be observed wherever Christ is separated from his Mother. When this happens, very often Jesus Christ is acknowledged either solely as human liberator or as an abstract, far removed from the human experience. For Kentenich, mechanistic or separatistic thinking af-

fected above all two significant secondary causes: the Blessed Virgin Mary and the father figure both in the natural and the religious sense. In our time, John Paul II has drawn attention to this "serious and destructive dichotomy" in his 1993 encyclical letter *Veritatis Splendor*, 4, 88.

18. Joseph Kentenich, *Marianische Erziehung: Pädagogische Tagung 1934* (Vallendar-Schoenstatt, Germany: Schoenstatt Verlag, 1971), 192.

19. Joseph Kentenich, "May Letter 1948" (unpublished manuscript written in Nueva Helvetia, Uruguay, on May 20, 1948, at the Occasion of the Canonical Erection of the Schoenstatt Sisters of Mary as Secular Institute), 61.

20. Joseph Kentenich, "Oktober Brief 1948" (unpublished manuscript, n.p., 1948), 311.

21. Joseph Kentenich, *Das Lebensgeheimnis Schönstatts*, 2 vols. (Vallendar-Schoenstatt, Germany: Patris Verlag, 1972), vol. 2, 24.

22. Joseph Kentenich, *Maria, Mutter und Erzieherin: Eine angewandte Mariologie* (Vallendar-Schoenstatt, Germany: Schoenstatt Verlag, 1973), 396.

23. Ibid., emphasis in original.

24. See Joseph Kentenich, *Unter dem Schutze Mariens: Untersuchungen und Dokumente aus der Frühzeit Schönstatts*, ed. F. Kastner (Paderborn, Germany: Schoningh, 1939), 21–27.

25. Joseph Kentenich, "Brasilienterziat," 3 vols. (unpublished manuscript, n.p., 1952), vol. 2, 229f.

26. Joseph Kentenich, *Zur Psychologie der Jugend: Seelenführerkurs 1926* (Munster: Joseph Kentenich, 1982), 50.

27. The *new* person, in contrast to the *old* person, is described in the letters of St. Paul to the Ephesians (4:22–24) and the Colossians (3:10). In addition, Paul's letter to the Galatians (6:15) specifies that Christians, as distinguished from non-Christians, represent the *new creation*. The Pauline development of the theology of the new person was taken up by the Fathers of the Church, who further elaborated a theology based on it. For example, Ignatius of Antioch conceived the whole work of salvation as consisting of the new person who is in Christ. Through Christ's Incarnation and Redemption the newness of life is made accessible to humanity and the reign of death and sin is ended. For Irenaeus of Lyons, the Lord, who is newness, has renewed and revivified the person through the event of the Incarnation. Christ has introduced all newness in himself (cf. *Adv. Haer.* IV 34, 1). Irenaeus's theology is of special significance since it relates the renewal brought by Christ to the prophetic vision of Isaiah (cf. *Adv. Haer.* III 9). Clement of Alexandria speaks of the new person under the social aspect after the model of Christ, in whom there is no Jew or Greek, no man or woman (*Stromata* VI 6). Accordingly, the mystery of the new person is the mystery of Christ.

28. Kentenich, *Oktober Brief 1949*, 16. Cf. GS 54, which speaks of a new humanism.

29. Joseph Kentenich, *What Is My Philosophy of Education?: Study with an English Title and German Text*, trans. M. Cole (Cape Town: Schoenstatt Publications, 1990), 7.

30. Joseph Kentenich, "Schlüssel zum Verständnis Schönstatts," in *Texte zum Verständnis Schönstatts* (Vallendar-Schoenstatt, Germany: Patris Verlag, 1974), 149.

31. Everyday sanctity is one of the three dimensions of Schoenstatt's spirituality. The other two are covenant and instrument spirituality.

32. Kentenich, "Oktober Brief 1948," 39.

33. Ibid.

34. Joseph Kentenich, "Study 1954" (unpublished manuscript, n.p., 1954), 70.

35. Joseph Kentenich, "Tertianship Held in Bellavista" (unpublished manuscript, n.p., 1951), 95–97.

36. Joseph Kentenich, "Der Marianische Priester" (unpublished manuscript, n.p., n.d.), 40. For an in-depth discussion of Scheeben's fundamental Mariological principle, see Ivo Muser, *Das Mariologische Prinzip "gottesbräutliche Mutterschaft" und das Verständnis der Kirche bei M.J. Scheeben* (Rome: Analecta Gregoriana, 1993).

37. Joseph Kentenich, *Mary, Our Mother and Educator: An Applied Mariology* (Waukesha, WI: Lithoprint, 1987), 155.

38. In using "office" (*"Amt"*), Kentenich did not intend to indicate that Mary held a hierarchical office (*ordo*) in the Church. The term was used exceedingly by Leo XIII and points to the unique and irreplaceable mission of the Blessed Virgin Mary in the history of salvation. Vincent Pallotti spoke of Mary as the great missionary, and Kentenich referred to her using this title frequently. Cf. "Second Founding Document of October 18, 1939," in *Schoenstatt: The Founding Documents* (Waukesha, WI: Lithoprint, 1993), 37–80; Kentenich, *Mary, Our Mother and Educator*, 19, 33, 72; and Kentenich, *What Is My Philosophy of Education?*, 23. For Kentenich's thought on Mary as evangelizer, see his "Brasilienterziat," vol. 3, 47.

39. See, for example, René Laurentin, "La donnée dogmatique fondamentale: Marie, mere, donc éducatrice" (unpublished manuscript, International Marian Research Institute, Dayton, OH, 2003), 1.

40. Kentenich, "Der Marianische Priester," 26, emphasis in original. Regarding symbolic thinking, see ibid., 27–30. The term "swan song" is a reference to an ancient belief that the Mute Swan (*Cygnus olor*) is completely mute during its lifetime until the moment just before it dies, when it sings one beautiful song. By extrapolation, "swan song" has become a metaphor referring to the final appearance, work, or accomplishment of a person. It generally carries the connotation that the performer is aware that this is the last performance of his or her lifetime, and is expending everything in one magnificent final effort. Since in 1941 Ken-

tenich had to count on being transported to a death or concentration camp, he consciously summed up his life with what could have been his last work: "The Marian Priest." Cf. Alfred Tennyson, *The Dying Swan* (Boston, 1898).

41. Joseph Kentenich, *Exerzitien für die pars motrix et centralis* (Vallendar-Mt. Sion: Archive of the Schoenstatt Fathers, 1966 and 1967), 29–30. See also Kentenich, *Mary, Our Mother and Educator*, 367, and *Das Lebensgeheimnis Schönstatts*, vol. 2, 264; LG 61.

42. Kentenich, *Mary, Our Mother and Educator*, 184.

43. Kentenich, "Der Marianische Priester," 32.

44. LG 53.

45. Ibid., 63.

46. Cf. Joseph Kentenich, "Oktoberwoche 1950" (unpublished manuscript, Schoenstatt, Germany, 1950).

47. Ibid., 94. Cf. Kentenich, "Der Marianische Priester," 32, 82.

48. Joseph Kentenich, *Sign of Light for the World* (Constantia, South Africa: Schoenstatt Publications, 1980), 18.

49. Ibid., 17f. Kentenich alludes here to, among others, Karl Marx (1818–83), often referred to as the Father of Communism.

50. Joseph Kentenich, "Menschheitsschuld im Lichte der Immaculata" (unpublished manuscript, n.p., 1929), 4, 6.

51. Kentenich, "Der Marianische Priester," 46. Cf. Kentenich, "Oktoberwoche 1950," 161.

52. Cf. Kentenich, "Menschheitsschuld im Lichte der Immaculata," 5.

53. Cf. ibid., 3, 5; Kentenich, *Marianische Erziehung*, 148ff; and Kentenich, "Oktoberwoche 1950," 101–3, English translation in *Jewel of Purity*, a translation of Kentenich's *Vom Reichtum des Reinseins* (Waukesha, WI: Schoenstatt Sisters of Mary, 1993), 20–22.

54. Cf. Joseph Kentenich, "Hirtenspiegel (Shepherd's Mirror): Composed in the Concentration Camp Dachau," 2 vols. (unpublished manuscript, Schoenstatt Sisters of Mary, n.p., 1972), vol. 1, 363; and Joseph Kentenich, *Marian Instrument Piety: Composed 1944 in Dachau* (Waukesha, WI: Lithoprint, 1992), 110, 193.

55. Kentenich, *Marianische Erziehung*, 199.

56. Cf. Kentenich, "May Letter 1948," 7–10; Kentenich, "Brasilienterziat," vol. 1, 159–62.

57. Kentenich, *Marian Instrument Piety*, 137f, and *Marianische Erziehung*, 220, 228. The term can be traced to Heinrich Heitger, "Das Amt der Gottesmutter im Gottesreiche," *Präsides Korrespondenz*, 11 (Vienna, 1915–19), 44.

58. Cf. Joseph Kentenich, "Desiderium Desideravi: Talks Given to Seminarians between 1962 and 1963," vol. 9 (unpublished manuscript, Mt. Sion, Schoenstatt, Germany), 161, English translation in Joseph Kentenich, *With Mary into the New Millennium: Selected Texts about the Mission of the Blessed Mother*, trans. M. Jane Hoehne (Waukesha, WI: Schoenstatt Publications, n.d.), 118–19.

59. Cf. Kentenich, "Oktoberwoche 1950," 95.

60. For Kentenich this means that we not only teach theoretically about grace but try to find concrete ways to cooperate with grace in our personal lives and the lives of those to whom we minister. Cf. Kentenich, *Marianische Erziehung*, 149, and "Der Marianische Priester," 91.

61. Kentenich, "Menschheitsschuld im Lichte der Immaculata," 21.

62. Cf. Joseph Kentenich, *Aus dem Glauben leben: Sermons at St. Michael's Parish, Milwaukee, WI, between 1962–65*, 18 vols. (Vallendar-Schoenstatt, Germany: Patris Verlag, 1969–2005), vol. 10, 54.

63. Kentenich, *Aus dem Glauben leben*, vol. 13, 171.

64. Kentenich, "Der Marianische Priester," 20.

65. Cf. Kentenich, "Oktoberwoche 1950," 25.

66. Ibid., 103.

67. Ibid., 104.

68. Cf. Joseph Kentenich, *Das Katholische Menschenbild* (Vallendar-Schoenstatt, Germany: Schoenstatt Verlag, 1977), 101.

69. Kentenich, *Jewel of Purity*, 65.

70. Kentenich defined *Gemüt* as the harmony between the higher (rational) and lower (sensory) appetites. In the 1960s he used the term "affective maturity" to indicate the result of a purified and educated *Gemüt*. Cf. Joseph Kentenich, "Weihnachtstagung 1967" (unpublished manuscript, Schoenstatt, Germany, 1967), 109. Concerning the education of the heart, see Kentenich, "Der Marianische Priester," 84–87, and Joseph Kentenich, *Daß neue Menschen werden: Eine pädagogische Religionsphilosophie, 1951* (Vallendar-Schoenstatt, Germany: Schoenstatt Verlag, 1971), 58–62.

71. Cf. Kentenich, "Weihnachtstagung 1967," 102.

72. Cf. ibid.

73. Cf. ibid., 104.

74. Cf. ibid.

75. Kentenich, "Desiderium Desideravi," vol. 2, 339.

76. Ibid., 340.

77. Cf. ibid., 171.

78. Kentenich, *Marian Instrument Piety*, 169.

79. Joseph Kentenich, "Propheta locutus est: Talks Given by Father Kentenich between 1966 and 1968," 20 vols. (unpublished manuscript, Archive Schoenstatt Fathers, Mt. Sion, Schoenstatt, Germany), vol. 9, 148.

80. Kentenich, *Mary, Our Mother and Educator*, 118.

81. Ibid., 66.

82. Ibid., 44.

83. Ibid., 175.

84. It is commonly accepted that *devotio*, as an act of virtue or religion and distinguished from devotional practices, implies a stable interior disposition and

readiness to serve God joyfully and generously. Accordingly, authentic Marian devotion equips heart, mind, and will to be receptive to a deeper understanding and fulfillment of God's ways in imitation and through the intercession of Our Lady. Cf. *Catechism of the Catholic Church* (CCC), 2102, based on *Codex Iuris Canonici*, ca. 1191, 1.

85. Cf. Kentenich, *Mary, Our Mother and Educator*, 284. Kentenich cites in this context Pius XI's encyclical on the Council of Ephesus, *Lux Veritatis* (1931), 43.

86. See Joseph Kentenich, "Marianisch-Pädagogische Tagung," 1932 (unpublished manuscript, n.p., 1932), English translation in Kentenich, *With Mary into the New Millennium*, 124.

87. Kentenich, *Maria, Mutter und Erzieherin*, 281, English translation in Jonathan Niehaus, *Schoenstatt's Covenant Spirituality* (Waukesha WI: Lithoprint, 1992), 42.

88. Kentenich, *Maria, Mutter und Erzieherin*, 327.

89. See CCC, 1273.

90. Kentenich, *Das Lebensgeheimnis Schönstatts*, vol. 2, 55, English translation in Niehaus, *Schoenstatt's Covenant Spirituality*, 128.

91. Kentenich, *Mary, Our Mother and Educator*, 183.

92. Ibid., 182.

93. Ibid.

94. Ibid., 183.

95. The title Mother Thrice Admirable (MTA) originated with the Jesuit priest Jacob Rem (1546–1618), who worked as spiritual director in the renowned school of Ingolstadt, Germany, where he formed the so-called Marian Colloquium in 1595 to inspire the most motivated students to the highest aims of sanctity. With the solemn crowning of the MTA in the Schoenstatt Shrine in 1939, the title Queen was added. After Kentenich's return from Dachau and especially from exile, Mary's many victories in Schoenstatt's history were acknowledged, and on June 2, 1966, she was given the title Mother Thrice Admirable, Queen, and Victress of Schoenstatt.

96. From the original shrine in Germany, 210 exact replicas, the so-called daughter shrines, have been built around the world. There the same sacred atmosphere prevails as in the original shrine, although each of these daughter shrines has its own significant history and mission, which is articulated by the local Schoenstatt family guarding it.

97. Kentenich, *Das Lebensgeheimnis Schönstatts*, vol. 2, 58.

98. Kentenich, *Exerzitien für die pars motrix et centralis*, 1966, 72.

99. Kentenich, "Propheta locutus est," vol. 3, 129, English translation in Kentenich, *With Mary into the New Millennium*, 176–77.

100. Kentenich, *Mary, Our Mother and Educator*, 44–45.

101. Cf. Kentenich, *Aus dem Glauben leben*, vols. 13–17.

102. Nevertheless, just like Kentenich, the Council fathers were alarmed by the materialistic conception of the human person and the religious indifferentism prevalent in the nineteenth and twentieth centuries. One day before the conclusion of the Council—on December 7, 1965—they rendered a systematic account of a Christian anthropology. The Pastoral Constitution on the Church in the Modern World, *Gaudium et Spes*, reflects with great sensitivity on the anthropological dimension of theology and pastoral practice "of this age" (GS 1). Sadly, with the exception of one subtle reference to the Incarnation in GS 22, Mary is not mentioned in the document of ninety-three articles. This is especially surprising since LG praises Mary as "the most holy Virgin," in whom "the Church has already reached that perfection whereby she is without spot or wrinkle [cf. Eph. 5:27] and . . . who shines forth to the whole community of the elect as the model of virtues" (LG 65).

103. United States Conference of Catholic Bishops, *Rite of Baptism for Children: The Roman Ritual* (Collegeville, MN: Liturgical Press, 2002), and *Rite for the Blessing of a Child in the Womb; Rito de Bendición de una Criatura en el Vientre Materno* (Washington, DC: Liturgical Press, n.d.), 18–19.

104. MC 37.

105. For example, John Paul II, apostolic letter *Rosarium Virginis Mariae* (October 16, 2002), 1, 3, 14, 32, 37, 43, and encyclical letter *Ecclesia de Eucharistia* (April 17, 2003), 7, 53, 58, 62.

106. John Paul II, encyclical letter *Redemptoris Mater* (March 25, 1987), 45–46.

107. III Extraordinary General Assembly of the Synod of Bishops, *Instrumentum Laboris: The Pastoral Challenges of the Family in the Context of Evangelization* (Vatican City, 2014), 61 a.

108. Irenaeus, *Adv. Haer.* III, 22, 4.

CHAPTER 12

Virgin of Mercy

The Marian Profile in Twentieth-Century Catholicism

PETER CASARELLA

In the wake of Vatican II, recent popes have again proposed using the figure of Mary as a lens for looking at the Church as a whole. She is the lens, not the light. The lens brings more sharply into focus fundamental realities not expressed by Mary herself, for example, the redemptive power of the Cross or God's loving outpouring of Trinitarian communion into the world. In 1988 Pope John Paul II lent official status to this Marian profile of the Church in his *Letter on the Dignity and Vocation of Women (Mulieris Dignitatem)*. He wrote:

Although the Church possesses a "hierarchical" structure, nevertheless this structure is totally ordered to the holiness of Christ's members. And holiness is measured according to the "great mystery" [Eph. 5:32] in which the Bride responds with the gift of love to the gift of the Bridegroom. She does this "in the Holy Spirit," since "God's love has been poured into our hearts through the Holy Spirit who has been given to us" [Rom. 5:5]. The Second Vatican Council, confirming the teaching of the whole of tradition, recalled that in the hierarchy of holiness it is precisely the "woman," Mary of Nazareth, who is the "figure" of the Church. She "precedes" everyone on the path to holiness; in her person "the Church has already reached that perfection whereby she exists without spot or wrinkle [cf. Eph. 5:27]." In this sense, one can say that the Church is both "Marian" and "Apostolic-Petrine."[1]

In this case the Marian lens opens up a path of following Christ that can lead the whole Church from its present blemished state to the spotless perfection toward which the Church strives. The subsequent inclusion of this *theologoumenon* in the *Catechism of the Catholic Church* represents the first official sanctioning of this way of thinking.[2] The teaching unpacked in this dense paragraph had been prepared at the Council by chapter 8 of the Dogmatic Constitution of the Church, *Lumen Gentium*, principally because of its biblically guided recovery of the Ambrosian/Augustinian idea of Mary as the *typus ecclesiae*.[3] In addition, Pope John Paul II confirmed an earlier *ressourcement* of theological reflection extending back to the first half of the twentieth century. As part of our exploration of Mary on the eve of the Council, I explore in this chapter the roots of the Marian profile in this earlier period.

Mulieris Dignitatem links the complementarity of profiles (Mary-Peter) to the New Testament image of the marriage of Christ and the Church. As Andrew Lichtenwalner has recently demonstrated with true brilliance, ecclesial bride imagery is a theme well developed prior to John Paul II's inauguration on September 5, 1979, of a Wednesday catechesis on the theology of the body.[4] In fact, there is a rich tradition of reflection on the real symbolism of a Marian, bridal Church that extended from Leo XIII to Paul VI. John Paul II nonetheless marks a noteworthy shift in the characterization of the symbolism. Lichtenwalner explains the new development in Karol Wojtyła's reading of biblical bridal symbolism starting with the image from Ephesians cited above:

Ephesians 5:32 served as the basis for John Paul's most significant and developed considerations of the Church as Bride. Furthermore, according to John Paul II, the "great mystery" encompasses the mystery of Christ and the Church as well as the sacrament of marriage, and it also pertains to the life and vocation of all the baptized—

especially those in consecrated life—and even every human person. In this way, the "great mystery" became for John Paul a drama encompassing every human life, a drama to be entered and lived. *All persons are called to this drama.*[5]

The Polish pope (and former playwright) allowed the figure of Mary to shed light on the theodrama of redemption made possible by Jesus Christ.[6] No previous pope had clearly delineated the significance for all of the faithful of this drama of redemption seen through the lens of Mary.

Tucked away in the background of this development of the Magisterium lies a theological *ressourcement* carried about by Hans Urs von Balthasar.[7] Moreover, Brendan Leahy's masterful book *The Marian Profile in the Ecclesiology of Hans Urs von Balthasar* is quite revealing on this development. Leahy's work has as its point of departure the interplay that climaxed in the Second Vatican Council between the functionalist Church and its Marian "soul."[8] Leahy writes this sobering gloss on the Swiss theologian's breakthrough: "In a 'male functionalist world,' [von Balthasar] comments, there is a risk that to a large extent we have become a Church of permanent discussions, organizations, advisory committees, congresses, synods, commissions, academies, parties, pressure-groups, functions, structures and re-structuring, sociological experiments, statistics, that is, more than ever a 'male Church' lacking the Marian 'soul.'"[9] Leahy, who is now bishop of Limerick, deftly foregrounds this subtle interplay without elaborating the origins of this dynamic prior to and apart from the writings of Hans Urs von Balthasar. Leahy still confirms that a Balthasarian engine is driving the train of doctrinal development with regard to the emergence of a theodramatic Marian profile.

This chapter focuses on developments that took place before and during the years when von Balthasar began to formulate his ideas about the Marian profile of the Church. Von Balthasar was convinced that Mary as a prototype of the Church comes to the fore "by means of active testimonies from heaven."[10] He wrote this in *Neue Klarstellungen*, a book from 1979 in which he offered as evidence a string of Marian apparitions: those to Catherine Labouré (1830), Bernadette at Lourdes (1858), and Our Lady of Beauraing (1932–33) and the apparitions at Banneux (1933) and Fatima (1917). These testimonies to the earthly disclosure of an *Ecclesia Immaculata* involved the cooperation of laypersons. The "masculine hierarchy" (von Balthasar's actual term) and the Marian encyclicals written by members of the hierarchy recognize and underscore "the rightful place of woman in the Church's inmost nature."[11]

This insight confirms that a new approach is needed to understand the genesis of the Marian profile, one that derives from the confluence of popular piety and official theology without adopting the standard hagiographical approaches. Elsewhere von Balthasar refers to this approach as an attempt at "theological phenomenology."[12] Von Balthasar was convinced that academic theology could benefit from "a blood transfusion," from a consideration of the lives of saints.[13] In terms of understanding the Marian profile, he was suggesting that new sources are needed, sources that reunite the relationship between theology and sanctity in ways that are more akin to the synthetic approach of the Fathers of the Church than to contemporary theological fragmentation.[14]

In what follows, I highlight the place that this teaching began to have not just among academic theologians but within the lay apostolate.[15] I have chosen two figures who worked in von Balthasar's milieu (and, in one case, at his side) and quietly but decisively gave shape to the future emergence of the Marian profile. After a brief introduction of a few basic terms, I focus on the witnesses to a Marian profile of the Church in Adrienne von Speyr (1902–67) and Chiara Lubich (1920–2008). Together the lives of these women spanned the twentieth century. Their experiences and articulations differed slightly, but, as I shall demonstrate, both placed themselves at the foot of the Cross of Jesus Christ for the sake of spiritual maternity and generativity.

THE MARIAN PROFILE AND THE APOSTOLATE OF THE LAITY

What is the Marian profile? What, for that matter, is a profile in theology? Is it the same as what *Lumen Gentium* called a *typus* ("an exemplary realization")? Is it, as von Balthasar once averred, a "watermark" of the Church?[16] Pope John Paul II proposes in *Mulieris Dignitatem* that the Church is "both 'Marian' and 'Apostolic-Petrine'" in its profiles. Accordingly, the role of the laity in the Church is to be likened to the figure of

Mary and the role of the ordained priest to that of Peter. The Petrine profile of the Church is different from the Petrine ministry, for its *terminus a quo* is the biblical figure of Peter and not the office held by the bishop of Rome. As laity we are all called through our baptism to imitate Mary's stance of faith, and this vocation is nothing less than an empowerment of human freedom. The Marian stance enhances the dignity of all Christians—male and female, lay and clerical—who are baptized into the universal priesthood of Christ's body. Because Mary goes before us all in the holiness that is the Church's mystery as "the bride without spot or wrinkle," we are also told by the Polish pope that the Marian profile precedes the Petrine.[17]

A profile is not a strategic plan or a report prepared for an accrediting body. Most fundamentally, the "profile" is a *stance* that all the laity—female *and* male—are called to embody.[18] The *Merriam-Webster Dictionary* defines a "stance" as a term deriving from the Latin *stare* ("to stand") that was first used in the fourteenth century and signifies either "a publicly stated opinion" or "a way of standing." Both of these definitions pertain here since we are talking about a profession of faith that hearkens back to Mary standing at the foot of the Cross. The Marian profile is likewise not, at least in the first instance, a plea for more devotions, feast days, special prayers, or even the promulgation of new Marian doctrines.[19] Nor is the profile a special possession of the avowedly Marian movements. As a profile of the whole reality of the Church, it is fundamentally biblical in origin and takes as its point of departure the Marian experience of God.

This symbolic way of theologizing was quite common in the early Church but lately has fallen into disfavor. Hugo Rahner's *Maria und die Kirche* was published in Innsbruck in 1951 precisely with the goal of reviving this patristic way of thinking among the faithful.[20] In the1950s, in the wake of Pius XII's solemn proclamation of the Bodily Assumption of the Virgin, it was also not uncommon for Church leaders to link the symbolic theology of Marian piety with apostolic activity. In the mid-1950s the Belgian Cardinal Suenens addressed the Legion of Mary, a vast international outpouring of service to the poor that began in Dublin in 1925, based upon the model of the Society of St. Vincent de Paul, with these questions: "Can it be that the Holy Ghost, Who inspires at once the rediscovery of Mary and the revival of the apostolic spirit, has established no link between these spiritual currents, and that His action follows two merely parallel, or even dissimilar, courses? Should we not rather conclude that these Marian and apostolic graces move together towards one point and that the hour has come to accept and unite what, in the sight of God, belongs to the same mystery of Love: Marian piety and the duty of apostolic action?"[21] Suenens wrote this as an auxiliary bishop of Malines. He later became a prominent figure at Vatican II, participating in the drafting of *Lumen Gentium*.

Yves Congar, in his sketch of a theology of Catholic Action from 1957, also returned to this way of thinking. The ecclesial identity of the laity, he writes, is analogous to a mother's womb:

> One could express the same ideas and the same distinction in terms of the motherhood of the Church. We are accustomed to envisaging this maternity hardly at all, [as if] it only happens through the carrying out of the particular means of divinely instituted grace: sacraments, priesthood, official preaching. But Holy Scripture, the Fathers, and the facts of ecclesial life of every age teach us that all the faithful also exercise this motherhood through faith, charity, prayer, and through the entire *vita in Christo* (*in Spiritu Sancto*), with which it also worthily includes satisfaction, merit, and cooperation in Redemption. This motherhood the Virgin Mary is the first to employ, under the totally exceptional conditions of her predestination as the Mother of the Incarnate Word-Savior and of her grace. But it is *this very* motherhood that she uses for the benefit of all of humanity, she who has no hierarchical power and who is in a matter of speaking the first lay person. The Fathers never tired of showing in Mary the actualization of the spiritual maternity that they also attributed to all the faithful: "*concepit de fide*" ["she conceived by faith"], "*cooperata est caritate ut fideles in ecclesia nascerentur*" ["she cooperated out of love so that the faithful would be engendered in the Church"]. . . . [According to St. Augustine,] if we consider Christians individually and in isolation from one another, we must call them sons of the Church. If we consider them in the unity that they form through *caritas*, we must accord them the value and role of mother. As a matter of fact,

it's in this unity, in this *caritas* that souls are begotten by God, that sins are forgiven, and that sacraments bear the fruit of grace.[22]

Needless to say, it is difficult to capture the analogical relationship between God and the world in just the right terms.[23] There is the temptation to project onto God a merely finite conception of the spousal bond as well as the equally dangerous possibility of banishing the idea of divine love to a realm wholly unrecognizable to us. Cardinal Angelo Scola, for example, invokes "the strength of the principle of the *maior dissimilitudo*" within the application of the spousal analogy to the Triune God.[24] By invoking the patristic theme of spiritual maternity and its exemplarity in Mary, Congar, I believe, maintains the proper and properly analogical equilibrium.

Congar states that sacraments bear the fruit of grace. In fact, the spousal relationship of Christ and the Church is also disclosed in the celebration of the Eucharist, for this is clearly the event par excellence whereby the people of God are called to partake of a wedding feast. The ordained priest partakes in a unique fashion in the sacrifice of the Mass. By virtue of Christ's promise "Where two or three are gathered in my name, I shall be there with them" (Matt. 18:20), the community of believers also discloses a distinct manifestation of the Body of Christ. The gathered assembly brings with them a share in Christ's priesthood by virtue of their baptismal priesthood. There is also the liturgical connection between the priest's unique consecration in the Mass and the mission of service to the world by all the baptized.[25] The dismissal of the congregation, for example, is a sending into the world to enact in works of mercy the offering of praise that has been made at the altar. The Eucharistic event ("Eucharist makes the Church") is thus the total lived context for the everyday realization of the Marian profile.

We turn now to two examples of what I, following von Balthasar's clue in his book on Thérèse de Lisieux, am taking to be a theological phenomenology of the Marian profile: the lives of Adrienne von Speyr and Chiara Lubich.[26] These two lives witness to the Marian profile as it was articulated not only in academic theology but also in the new forms of theological existence that were being forged in mid-twentieth-century Catholic life.

ADRIENNE VON SPEYR: THE HANDMAID OF THE LORD
AND HER MANTLE OF MERCY

Adrienne von Speyr (1902–67) was a Swiss medical doctor. She was also a married woman and mother who converted to Catholicism under the guidance of von Balthasar and later collaborated with him in the founding of a secular institute and in several joint publications on theology and the Church. Although she had no formal theological training, von Balthasar strongly endorsed the publication of many volumes of her own writings on Scripture and Christian mysticism. Von Speyr also viewed her profession as a healing ministry that could help meet the health needs of individuals, families, and groups in the community. She understood what it means to adopt an integrated approach to professional life, one that emphasizes the interrelationship of the physical, social, psychological, intellectual, and spiritual well-being of all persons.

Von Speyr's active commitment to the Marian profile of the Church can be seen from a book containing letters she wrote that has never been published in English.[27] It consists of advice to patients and fellow counselors written in her capacity as a medical doctor, and many of the recipients were young couples either recently married or about to be married. In the final five letters she also discusses marriage and the religious life as complementary states of life in the Church. She covers timely issues like the plight of unwed mothers, concerns about dating, a young woman's apprehensions over marital sex, mixed marriages, abortion, and a miscarriage. In her advice to engaged couples, she stresses the distinction between "being in love" and the constant love nurtured through marital fidelity. The former can appear "like a game that only accompanies the seriousness of love." The latter bespeaks not only the irrevocability of the indissoluble bond but also the mystery of spousal self-giving that can be revealed in and through hardships. Von Speyr stresses even to engaged couples the real need for solitude with God and the free conversation of prayer.

In her theology of marriage, Adrienne von Speyr fused Marian availability at the foot of the Cross with what Fr. Blaise Berg calls the characteristic "matter-of-factness" (*Nüchternkeit*) of her pastoral-medical outreach.[28] In this case practical know-how in the form of service obviates the tendency already noted for Marian suffering to degenerate to a degrading form of passivity. In other words, von Speyr's mode of practical wisdom was not just spiritual but also "concrete and down to earth," and she was thus able to apply her insights as a wife, mother, medical doctor, and co-founder of a secular institute to the everyday situations of married and engaged couples.[29] In fact, few commentators on her life or works pay attention to her vocation as a medical caregiver. Von Balthasar speaks of the "complete reciprocal penetration of professional ability and fellowship with her patients (*Mitmenschlichkeit*)."[30] For von Speyr, medical expertise was not a mere instrument that she applied to her patients as objects. Her faith was integral to her medical vocation. Her solidarity with her patients and her commitment to God were as important as her technical expertise in her role as a healer. This unity also underlies the vision of the work of the Community of St. John, the secular institute that she co-founded, in the world of the professions.

The same accents are found in her book *Magd des Herrn* (*Handmaid of the Lord*), which was written in 1948 (eight years after her conversion). Johann G. Roten, S.M., reminds us that this came toward the end of her second period of engagement with von Balthasar, the period of the great dictations and of the founding of the Community of St. John.[31] Von Balthasar's book *Der Laie und der Ordenstand* (The Layperson and the Religious State of Life) was written in the same year. This joint witness of Adrienne von Speyr and Hans Urs von Balthasar gives evidence of their mutually influential concentration on the question of how laypeople participate in the mission of Christ to build up the Church *and* to bear witness in the world.

The entire witness of Mary in *The Handmaid* is predicated upon "the light of her assent." "Mary's life," says von Speyr, "is bound together by her assent."[32] All of the elements of the biblical narrative—including the Visitation, Joseph, the Nativity, the Presentation at the temple, the wedding at Cana, rejections by her Son—refer back to this more fundamental reality. The freedom of this total commitment to Christ gives rise to Mary's fruitfulness and maternal generativity. Von Speyr adds a double freedom to the Marian fiat: she not only pledges obedience to the Word but also says "Yes" to herself. "She wants to be the one who is thus given away."[33]

What does this theology of the handmaid teach us about the Marian profile? Mary has been completely expropriated into the community of the Church.[34] "Against her pureness the dross of his own [that of the member of the Church] spirit will become apparent in earnest."[35] The rosary is just one example of how the concreteness of her response offers guidance to the believer. Her contemplative stance before conception was abstract. After pregnancy and giving birth, after standing at the foot of the Cross, she becomes a model of contemplative prayer that is in touch with the anguish of the human heart.[36] At the Cross, Christ alone suffers actively and for the sake of our salvation. Mary, in communion with John, "goes into labor" as a passive recipient of that suffering. Herein lies the mystery of her generativity: "The man is exhausted and woman goes into labor: the whole appears to be negative. But if it is done in love, the pain is surpassed by joy."[37] Painting in images but with the lucidity of genuine theological reflection, von Speyr lays the foundation for a new understanding of the everyday significance of the mystery of the Cross.

How did this unusual collaboration help to spawn the theological complementarity of a Marian and Petrine profile? The "nuptial dialogue-event" (Leahy) of complementarity deserves more extensive treatment than can be warranted here, but I will focus on the *Jawort*, or free response, of Mary at the core of the event.[38] The attitude of Mary is one of "self-giving," which is centered on the event of the silence that cries out from the Cross: "The being silent at death (*Todesschweigen*) is the incalculable moment of the bearing forth and birth of the new man out of the impoverished womb of the Church that spiritually co-suffers even unto death."[39] By giving all of herself to the God who is himself suffering with humanity for the sake of humanity, Mary gives expression to the superiority of the principle of analogy over that of a sheer dialectic or the formalism of "a speculative Good Friday."[40] The stance of a cruciform Mary is also profoundly Eucharistic since her self-offering is identical to that of the entire congregation in the sacrificial meal of the Mass.[41]

The "ecclesial mediation" of Mary through her outpouring of an obedient faith to the Son of God makes possible her role as an intercessor and a mother to all the faithful.[42] This truth enlivens the faithful and has generated countless devotions, icons, and personal testimonies. One

particular iconographic tradition wove its way into the theological speculation of Hans Urs von Balthasar and Adrienne von Speyr. Von Balthasar
was very fond of using the image of Mary's protective mantle.[43] This
image was often associated with a "Virgin of Mercy." In German-
speaking countries the *Schutzmantelmadonna* was a favorite *topos* of Cistercians and Dominicans in the Middle Ages. In the imagery of the period, religious are seen kneeling under the protection of the mantle,
which is sometimes depicted as protection from the plague. What is significant here is that von Balthasar and von Speyr are proposing the same
image for laypeople today: "No one, whether he wants to or not, fails to
find room under her cloak."[44]

In "Who Is the Church?" von Balthasar says that there are three
different ways in which the image of the Church came to be centered on
Mary in the Middle Ages.[45] The first can be found in the Song of Songs
or the Letter to the Ephesians. There Mary is an idea laid up in heaven
that informs the present reality. The second ties Mary to the hierarchical
and sacramental structure of the Church, which has the unintended effect of making the Marian profile highly impersonal. The third fixes on
Mary's Immaculate Conception. In this view Mary stands as the universal womb bearing progeny, behind the sanctity of the apostles and with
them at Pentecost receiving the Spirit. German mysticism, von Balthasar
explains, internalizes the "external, imaginative presentation" and thus
"brings out the idea of the essential fecundity and apostolic character of
love (even—and especially—of silent, contemplative love)."[46] Mary is, in
essence, the teacher of the fecundity of contemplative prayer that is in
solidarity with the suffering of the world. Von Balthasar continues: "She
is seen as spreading her protective cloak over the whole of Christendom,
and making some part of her stainlessness flow out over the bride, the
Church."[47] Von Speyr writes in *The Handmaid of the Lord* that the prayer,
action, and suffering of priests and religious who choose virginity "will
be wholly enveloped by the mantel of the Mother's assent."[48] She tries
looking to her Son to bring his new friends to perfection in his Spirit.[49]
Surprisingly, von Balthasar even says that the Church can in some sense
be "re-virginized" through her mantle.[50] He concedes that this claim was
transmitted through Origen, Ambrose, and Jerome. He concludes: "This
theme would need further study."[51]

CHIARA LUBICH: THE WORK OF MARY

Chiara Lubich (1920–2008) was born Sylvia Lubich in Trent in 1920.[52] Her father was a printer and a Socialist. Her mother was a practicing Catholic. Her brother would later write against the Fascists in a newspaper sponsored by the Communist Party in Italy. In 1939 she received a vocation at the Marian shrine of Loreto to form a community named Focolare, or "hearth." Four years later she took the name of Chiara, showing her commitment to the spirituality of the Third-Order Franciscans to whose order she belonged. The spirituality of the movement sees itself even today as a gathering point for distinct Catholic spiritual traditions.[53]

Chiara Lubich exemplifies a woman entrusted with the gift of the Holy Spirit to go forth like Mary from the foot of the Cross without forgetting the total significance of the event she has witnessed.[54] In theology she contributed many profound insights. One idea closely tied to her Marian origins is that Jesus Forsaken is a key to a Christian understanding of unity. In living Jesus Forsaken, Lubich rediscovered the practice of the Christian life, the mission of the Church, and the concrete way to propose a path for peace and unity in the human family. The many countries, cities, and transnational organizations that have praised her for her social activities know she was sustained by Jesus Forsaken. Her witness integrated the practical task of sanctity with the contemplative aspect of a theological vocation. In the uniqueness of her witness, Chiara Lubich embodied a new path to theology and holiness, to theology as holiness, and to the holiness of theology.

Brian K. Reynolds in a recent study has uncovered the roots of Chiara Lubich's dedication to *Maria desolata*, Mary Desolate, in certain mystical illuminations that she received between 1949 and 1951, shortly after the birth of the Focolare Movement.[55] One set of these Marian meditations focuses on Mary as Theotokos, or Bearer of God; another deals directly with her as the *Desolata*. One utterance from the latter set is as follows: "The sons of men re-enter the most pure Womb of Mary, out of which issued the Son, so as to enter into God [*indiarsi*, literally, "to ingod"] in Mary."[56] There are many repetitions of patristic and medieval thought in Chiara's construct of a desolate Virgin.

These familiar resonances hide what Reynolds considers Lubich's "entirely new way of understanding Mary's participation in the Passion."[57] Without veering from the authentic teaching of the Church, the new accent added by Chiara Lubich was the linking of Mary's loss of biological maternity to her desolate condition in solidarity with Jesus Forsaken. In other words, the sufferings that she underwent at the foot of the Cross were other than and deeper than the suffering of a mother who had lost a child. Chiara writes:

> But what suffering she endured at the cry of abandonment of Jesus we cannot imagine. It was the moment when she would have wished to be closest to Him. But she had already lost Him as his Mother, had no right to be a Mother to Him, and faced with the passage from one Maternity to another which Jesus indicated to her, she could not complain or break down. Therefore in that moment Jesus had neither Mother nor Father. He was nothingness born of nothingness. And Mary was also suspended in nothingness. Her greatness had been her divine Maternity. Now it had been taken away from her.[58]

In sum, through Mary's renunciation of maternity she became mother of us all. There was something like a two-step process to her fiat. First she accepted being Mother of God. Then, at the foot of the Cross, she had to, at least in some figural sense, renounce it in order to become the mother of all believers and Mother of the Church. In the history of the Christian tradition, much speculation has been elicited from John 19:26–7, particularly on how the immensity of her desolation made the cruciform Mary a gate of heaven, but the idea of a two-stage process centered on her spiritual communion with Jesus Forsaken belongs entirely to Chiara Lubich.

Lubich's words, she tells again and again, come from the Spirit.[59] Who is the Spirit who has given us such abundant blessings in the person of Chiara Lubich? Who is the Spirit who speaks to us through her?[60] It is the same Spirit who speaks in us when we cry out "Abba!" by virtue of our adoption as children of God.[61] Focolarini are empowered to respond to the will of the Lord in the Spirit.[62] The spirituality of unity fostered by the movement is also one that comes from the Spirit.[63] The positive and spiritually challenging idea of being nothing before the Lord is also a radical openness to his Spirit.[64] The Holy Spirit is a teacher to those who seek to live Jesus in their midst: "The Holy Spirit was making us understand that in order to bring about Jesus' prayer 'may they all be one in the world,' it is necessary to consume in ourselves any form of abandonment, to welcome Jesus Forsaken in any disunity."[65] The same Spirit has given life to the movement to proclaim the notion of "mutual interdependence" to a multicultural, multiethnic world threatened by the atomizing, deracinating effects of unrestrained globalization.[66] In the Church we live out the truth that Love shared by the Father, Son, and Holy Spirit is the deepest and most universally available hidden reality of the world. For Lubich laypersons have a distinctive (though by no means unique) relationship to the Spirit: "Lay persons are in the condition of having to listen to the voice of the Holy Spirit; they do not have superiors who express God's will to them."[67] This place for the Spirit of Jesus Forsaken is constantly expanding. This expansion does not take place outside of the institutional Church. This spirit of unity dwells within it and lends constant support to its parishes, its universities, its bishops, and its global mission.[68]

Lubich was an immensely practical woman. For example, her concern for the means of social communication was deep and longstanding. An address she gave, "Mary and Communication," was given during a Marian year. Her emphasis even here on Mary Desolate is noteworthy.[69] She focused on the pain-filled words and horrifying event at the scene of the Crucifixion in the Gospel of John: "Woman, behold your Son."[70] This scene, she said, becomes "a little Church that stands before Jesus the head of the Church."[71] In a famous metaphor that recapitulates her entire doctrine, she writes: "If Jesus Forsaken seemed to us to be the pupil of God's eye open onto the world, we can say that Mary desolate seems to us a kind of *camera obscura* taking in all that is negative in the world."[72] In Lubichs's other writings she develops the notion of Jesus as the empty pupil of God's eye who takes nothingness into his own being for the sake of our redemption.[73] Here she extends this thought by an even further radicality to Mary's agony as a dark chamber with a slight aperture into which light enters. According to the optics of a *camera obscura*, light from outside the enclosed chamber passes through a miniscule hole and forms an image of what is outside on the back surface of the chamber. In the chamber the world appears in a completely realistic and accurate form except for the fact it is upside-down. The Mary who holds the disfigured Christ is also the one who can gaze objectively at the world in all of its disfigurement. Just as a photographic image is developed from a negative, Mary can hope for the redemption of a fallen world in the midst of her and the world's most complete agony. Jesus's mother is no Pollyanna when it comes to the state of the world. She teaches a thoroughly realistic path to love and justice. Citing Piero Coda, Máire O'Byrne writes: "This understanding of Mary and her work provides a background against which the 'feminine can be seen as fundamental not only for a complete hermeneutic of the anthropological mystery, but also for a balanced and authentic hermeneutic of the Church mystery.'"[74]

How does Mary Desolate function in everyday life? The lesson actually extends beyond people in the media. The virtues of Mary Desolate are refreshingly concrete. "Her example," Lubich writes, "will help professionals in communication see events objectively and remain firm in service to the truth even when inconvenient and sometimes at personal cost."[75] Beyond the mediation of sheer honesty and a "monument of virtue," Mary Desolate also offers "an icon of knowing how to lose."[76] Such phrases do not make the greatest advertising jingle in a world so dependent on tangible success. Apart from her Son, Mary had very little. When she lost him in his Passion, the loss was total and decisive. But she saw this loss for what it really was. The one who prepared all her life to be alone, became Mother to each of us, to the whole of the world.[77] She is an example of the true and pure communication of the Word of God as a result of her "intense apprenticeship" under her Son, one that she underwent her whole life.[78] Her love, her capacity for giving, is human, real, and maternal. It consists of a unique capacity to bear the sorrow of the world in one's heart. According to Lubich, when a mother hopes all things for her child and puts up with all the troubles involved, she sees further than others.[79]

Chiara Lubich, like Mary, spent her life undertaking a similarly intense apprenticeship. Through the witness of her life and the gift of her words, the members of Focolare—as well as anyone called similarly to abide in a spirituality of communion—live in the Spirit of Jesus Forsaken. Lubich teaches everyone touched by the Catholic communion to communicate a hope for genuine unity even where it is palpably absent.

THE VIRGIN OF MERCY AND A RENEWED
ECCLESIAL ONTOLOGY

The origins of the idea of a Marian ecclesial profile as such are quite recent and still relatively unknown in many parts of the Church. Although closely related to developments spanning the time from the Fathers of the Church to the Second Vatican Council, its recent genesis lay in the collaborative venture that marked the lives of the priest and theologian Hans Urs von Balthasar and the laywoman and medical doctor Adrienne von Speyr. I would like to draw to a close with two conclusions, one historical and one theological. Historically, it seems that there was a convergence in European Catholicism on the eve of the Second Vatican Council that gave rise to the Marian profile in the life and work of Adrienne von Speyr and Chiara Lubich. One could look to other noteworthy female models of ecclesial engagement with culture and society from that epoch (e.g., Raïssa Maritain, Gertrud von Le Fort, Alice von Hildebrand, Flannery O'Connor, Madeleine Delbrêl, Dorothy Day, and Edith Stein). The post–World War II search for compelling new forms of Catholic social life played a pivotal role in this development and allows one also to bring Simone Weil's witness and especially her book *L'Enracinement* into the company of these holy women.[80] What marks Adrienne von Speyr and Chiara Lubich as distinctive in this illustrious company is that they articulated the spiritual basis for that engagement by looking outward from the place of Mary at the foot of the Cross.

This brings me to my second conclusion. The Marian stance as configured by these three women was not only shorn of all self-deprecation but was linked directly to a mission into the world. In other words, the protection of the Virgin's mantle is not offered in order to create a hermetically sealed refuge for like-minded believers. The mantle, like the *tilma* of Juan Diego Cuauhtlatoatzin, is a shield of mercy that invites people of all backgrounds into communion and sends the same flock outward into the margins of society with new conviction and resolve. Among other things, contemplation and action are being understood in a new fashion, a topic that merits a study unto itself.[81]

These two women, as well as the others mentioned earlier, bear witness to the vitality of the Marian profile in late modernity. Moreover, the short life of this relatively new reality seems to have flourished with particular vibrancy in the new ecclesial movements. Pope John Paul II was quick to draw this connection, and Chiara Lubich, founder of the Focolare Movement, eagerly noted his approval of this characterization of the movement, which also carries the official title of "The Work of Mary."[82] The future of the Marian profile, however, need not be relegated to the ecclesial movements. By considering this aspect of ecclesial ontology through the lens of the Council's call for a theology of communion and a universal call to holiness, its fruitfulness for the whole Church can perhaps be brought to its proper fullness.[83]

Just two years before his passing on June 22, 2003, Luigi Giussani shared a letter with the Fraternity of Communion and Liberation about a recent pilgrimage to Loreto. The letter was titled "Moved by the Infinite." The core vision is Giussani's meditation on Dante's "Hymn to Mary" in *Paradiso* XXIII. Since the letter expresses eloquently the sheer attractiveness of a Marian form of existence in the Church to Dante, Giussani, and countless lay Catholics today around the globe, I can cite some of his words:

> Our Lady is the method we need for familiarity with Christ. She is the instrument that God used in order to enter into man's heart. Dante, the greatest poet of our lineage, creates a Marian theology unlike anyone else has ever done. . . . The Mystery from which creation proceeds, is sustained, and is brought to completion, is Our Lady. "Virgin mother, daughter of your Son": this verse [of Dante] indicates the total meaning of creation as acceptable to man, that is, offered to man. Thus in Mary's womb, the creator Spirit, the evidence of the Spirit, surfaced. "Fixed term of the eternal counsel": this is the word that defines the nature of the things that are. In its definitiveness it is the expression of God's creative power. That "fixed" is not a block to Mary's freedom, because the fixed term is a suggestion that comes from the Eternal that confirms God's work. Thus the first part of Dante's hymn is the exaltation of the Eternal. What has to be rekindled in our hearts and in the hearts of believers is love for Christ, for Christ who is the eternal counsel. Everything belongs to the Eternal. Fixed term of the eternal counsel: this is the final plan, the first and final plan of creation. It is an eternal counsel. It is something that resonates. It is something that is called eternity.[84]

For Giussani Mary is the fixed term of the eternal counsel *of Christ.*
This rootedness in Christian discipleship shows why the profile that
Mary imparts is much more than the Catholic version of what Goethe
termed "the eternal feminine." Giussani thus confirms in his reading of
La Divina Commedia a well-known teaching of Henri de Lubac: "The
motherhood of the Church . . . can be neither thoroughly understood
nor unreservedly accepted by anyone concerned about the full dignity of
man unless it is considered within the whole Christian mystery. . . . This
mystery is none other than that of our participation, through the grace
of Christ, in the internal life of the Divinity."[85] The Virgin of Mercy is
illumined by the light of Christ. With the protective mantle that the
dying Christ entrusts to her, we can better discern the path of discipleship that may lead us to the God of Jesus Christ. *Ecclesia de Trinitate*
("Church [comes] from the Trinity"), as de Lubac would say.[86]

NOTES

1. John Paul II, *Apostolic Letter Mulieris Dignitatem on the Dignity and Vocation of Women Promulgated on August 15, 1988* (Washington, DC: Office of
Publication and Promotion Services, U.S. Catholic Conference, 1988), 27.
2. *Catechism of the Catholic Church* (CCC) (Mahwah, NJ: Paulist Press,
1994), art. 773.
3. On this point, see the chapter in this volume by Fr. Brian Daley, S.J.
4. Andrew Lichtenwalner, "The Church as the Bride of Christ in Magisterial Teaching from Leo XIII to John Paul II" (Ph.D. dissertation, Catholic
University of America, Washington, DC, 2012).
5. Ibid., 320, emphasis mine.
6. On the philosophical dimension of this drama in the plays of the young
Wojtyła, one may consult Kenneth L. Schmitz, *At the Center of the Human
Drama: The Philosophical Anthropology of Karol Wojtyła/Pope John Paul II* (Washington, DC: Catholic University of America Press, 1993), 1–29, and Peter Casarella, "The Proper Weight of Love": What Can We Learn from John Paul II's
'The Jeweler's Shop'?," *Communio: International Catholic Review* 38, no. 4 (Winter, 2011): 621–42.
7. The reference to von Balthasar first arises in a speech that John Paul II
gave to the Curia on December 22, 1987, and appears in the official Vatican edition as "Come bene ha detto un teologo contemporaneo, 'Maria è regina degli
apostoli, senza pretendere per sé i poteri apostolici: Essa ha altro e di più'" (H. U.

von Balthasar, *Neue Klarstellungen*, Italian trans. [Milan, 1980], 181; English trans., *New Elucidations* [San Francisco: Ignatius, 1979], 196): "Mary is 'Queen of the Apostles' without claiming apostolic powers for herself. She possesses something else and something more." This citation was then incorporated word for word into *Mulieris Dignitatem* 27. The quote from von Balthasar, however, disappears when the same passage of *Mulieris Dignitatem* is cited in CCC.

8. Brendan Leahy, *The Marian Profile in the Ecclesiology of Hans Urs von Balthasar* (Hyde Park, NY: New City Press, 2000), 165.

9. Ibid.

10. Hans Urs von Balthasar, "Women Priests?," in *New Elucidations*, 195.

11. Ibid.

12. Hans Urs von Balthasar, *Two Sisters in the Spirit: Thérèse de Lisieux and Elizabeth of the Trinity* (San Francisco: Ignatius, 1992), 39.

13. Ibid.

14. Cf. Hans Urs von Balthasar, "Theology and Sanctity," in *Explorations in Theology*, vol. 1: *The Word Made Flesh* (San Francisco: Ignatius, 1989), 181–209.

15. Needless to say, lay Catholics serving in an official capacity as academic theologians were scarce in the period of the genesis of the Marian profile.

16. Peter Casarella, "Trinity and Creation: David L. Schindler and the Catholic Tradition," in *Being Holy in the World: Theology and Culture in the Thought of David L. Schindler*, ed. Nicholas J. Healy Jr. and D. C. Schindler (Grand Rapids, MI: Eerdmans, 2011), 41.

17. *Mulieris Dignitatem*, 27; CCC, 772.

18. On the "comprehensive femininity of the Church" according to von Balthasar, see Brendan Leahy, *The Marian Profile*, 119–22.

19. Leahy, *The Marian Profile*, 10.

20. Hugo Rahner, S.J., *Maria und die Kirche: Zehn Kapitel über das geistliche Leben* (Innsbruck: Marianischer, 1951). Rahner writes in the preface: "The thought that is presented in this book comes, so we would like to maintain, with particular significance at this moment because the teaching Church transmits the truth of the bodily Assumption of Mary into heaven as a proclamation and celebration of its own faith. Right now everywhere in Christendom the question—whether joyfully or with concern—is raised: 'What place is to be accorded to this dogma within the totality of truths of faith and what does this [proclamation] signify for the formation of a truly adult Christian life?'" (7). This translation is my own. The published English translation of this book is *Our Lady and the Church* (London: Darton, Longman Todd, 1961; reprint San Francisco: Ignatius, 2005).

21. Léon J. Suenens, Frank Duff, et al., "Legion of Mary: A Work of God for Our Day," Legion of Mary; accessed September 2016, http://www.pamphlets.org.au/docs/cts/australia/html/acts1287. See also Léon Joseph Suenens, *Theology of the Apostolate of the Legion of Mary* (Westminster, MD: Newman, 1954).

22. Yves Congar, O.P., "Esquisse d'une théologie de l'Action Catholique," in *Sacerdoce et laïcat devant leurs tâches d'évangélisation et de civilisation* (Paris: Cerf, 1962), 343, emphasis in original. In order to avoid any sense of abstractness in this remark, Congar also invokes in the same context the exemplary spiritual maternity and Christian witness of St. Thérèse de Lisieux.

23. See Hans Urs von Balthasar, *Heart of the World* (San Francisco: Ignatius, 1979), 39–40.

24. Angelo Cardinal Scola, *The Nuptial Mystery* (Grand Rapids, MI: Eerdmans, 2005), 238.

25. See Peter Casarella, "Eucharist: Presence of a Gift," in *Rediscovering the Eucharist: Ecumenical Considerations*, ed. Roch A. Kereszty (New York: Paulist Press, 2003), 215–19. On the vital connection between the Marian profile and baptism, see Rahner, *Maria und die Kirche*, 65–74 ("Maria am Taufbrunn").

26. For a thorough critical analysis of this category, see Virginia Raquel Azcuy, *La Figura de Teresa de Lisieux: Ensayo de fenomenología teológica según Hans Urs von Balthasar*, vol. 1 (Buenos Aires: Teologia, 1997).

27. Adrienne von Speyr, *Christiane: Briefe über Liebe und Ehe* (Lucerne: Josef Stocker, 1947).

28. Blaise Berg, "Christian Marriage according to Adrienne von Speyr" (S.T.D. dissertation, Pontifical Lateran University, Rome, 2013), 294.

29. Ibid.

30. Benediktiner-Missionare von St. Ottilien, *Missions Kalender 1972*, 58–61, quote on 58, as cited in Berg, *Christian Marriage*, 26, n. 32.

31. Johann G. Roten, "Die beiden Hälften des Mondes: Marianisch-anthropologische Dimensionen in der gemeinsamen Sendung von Hans Urs von Balthasar und Adrienne von Speyr," in *Hans Urs von Balthasar: Gestalt und Werk*, ed. Karl Lehmann and Walter Kasper (Cologne: Communio, 1989), 107–8.

32. Adrienne von Speyr, *The Handmaid of the Lord* (San Francisco: Ignatius, 1985), 7.

33. Ibid., 14.

34. Von Speyr, *Handmaid*, 149–55.

35. Ibid., 150.

36. Ibid., 161.

37. Adrienne von Speyr, *The Passion from Within* (San Francisco: Ignatius, 1988), 116.

38. Hans Urs von Balthasar, *Theo-dramatik*, vol. 3: *Die Handlung* (Einsiedeln, Switzerland: Johannes, 1980), 327–37. For a general comparison of the Marian and Petrine dimensions, one may consult Leahy, *The Marian Profile*, 129–36.

39. Von Balthasar, *Theo-dramatik*, vol. 3, 334.

40. Ibid., 333. This, in essence, is von Balthasar's Marian rejoinder to the Trinitarian theology of Jürgen Moltmann.

41. Von Speyr, *The Handmaid of the Lord*, 151: "The Church as liturgical service, the faithful as servants, and the Mother as the one expecting: all three wait together, in a unified readiness, for the coming Lord." Cf. Leahy, *The Marian Profile*, 112–13.

42. Von Balthasar, *Theo-dramatik*, vol. 3, 327–37; Henri de Lubac, *The Motherhood of the Church* (San Francisco: Ignatius, 1982), 75–84. Adrienne von Speyr writes: "When the Son commands her: 'Express in yours the essence of the Church,' he gives her no new nature, no new character; he says to her: 'Remain who you are, but be so for everyone. Remain no longer this individual woman, but become the objective idea which the Father had of you eternally in his intention to found the Church of the redeemed'" (*The Handmaid*, 149).

43. See, for example, Hans Urs von Balthasar, *Love Alone Is Credible*, trans. David C. Schindler (San Francisco: Ignatius, 2004), 80. For background on the late medieval cloak Madonna, see Angela Mohr, *Die Schutzmantel-Madonna von Frauenstein in Oberösterreich: Eine kunstgeschichtliche Betrachtung* (Steyr, Austria: Wilhelm Ennsthaler, 1983); Christa Belting-Ihm, *"Sub matris tutela": Untersuchungen zur Vorgeschichte der Schutzmantelmandonna* (Heidelberg: Carl Winter Universitätsverlag, 1976).

44. Hans Urs von Balthasar, *Mary for Today* (San Francisco: Ignatius, 1987), 73.

45. Hans Urs von Balthasar, "Who Is the Church?" in *Explorations in Theology*, vol. 2: *Spouse of the Word* (San Francisco: Ignatius, 1991), 177. Leahy refers to this theme only in passing in *The Marian Profile*, 148–49.

46. Von Balthasar, "Who Is the Church?," 177.

47. Ibid.

48. Von Speyr, *The Handmaid of the Lord*, 178.

49. Von Balthasar, "Who Is the Church?" 177.

50. Von Balthasar, *Theo-Drama*, vol. 3, 334.

51. Ibid., 334, n. 57.

52. For biographical details I rely on Jim Gallagher, *A Woman's Work: Chiara Lubich* (Hyde Park, NY: New City Press, 1997).

53. Chiara Lubich, *The Cry of Jesus Crucified and Forsaken* (Hyde Park, NY: New City Press, 2000), 112–14. See also Fabio Ciardi, O.M.I., *Koinonia: Spiritual and Theological Growth of the Religious Community* (Hyde Park, NY: New City Press, 2002).

54. Remembering in mourning is a proper, perennial, and always complex task of the Christian, a point inimitably unfolded in Cyril O'Regan, *The Anatomy of Misremembering: Von Balthasar's Response to Philosophical Modernity* (New York: Crossroad, 2014), 1–27.

55. Brian K. Reynolds, "The Virgin Mary and Creation: From the Church Fathers to Chiara Lubich," *Universitas: Monthly Review of Philosophy and Culture* 40, no. 10 (2013): 71–101.

56. Chiara Lubich, *Maria, trasparenza di Dio* (Rome: Città Nuova, 2003), 93, as cited in Reynolds, "The Virgin Mary and Creation," 82–83. The term *indiarsi*, Reynolds notes, echoes Dante in *Paradiso* 4, 28, and might have been based on that source.

57. Reynolds, "The Virgin Mary and Creation," 86–87.

58. These locutions were recorded by Lubich on October 2, 1949, and are translated here from Gerard Rossé, "La realtà dell' 'Anima' alla luce del mistero di Maria nell'esperienza mistica di Chiara Lubich," II, "La Desolata," *Nuova Humanità* 196–97, nos. 4–5 (2011): 450–53. On this theme, see also Chiara Lubich, *An Introduction to the Abba School*, with an introduction by David L. Schindler (Hyde Park, NY: New City Press, 2002), 27–28.

59. Chiara Lubich, *The Essential Writings, Spirituality Dialogue Culture* (Hyde Park, NY: New City Press, 2007), vi.

60. On the overall Trinitarian dimensions of Chiara Lubich's gift to theology, see Klaus Hemmerle, "Unser Lebensraum—Der Dreifaltige Gott: Die Gotteserfahrung von Chiara Lubich," in *Ausgewählte Schriften*, vol. 5: *Gemeinschaft als Bild Gottes* (Freiburg: Herder, 1996), 296–305.

61. See Romans 8:15.

62. Chiara Lubich, "The Beginnings," in *Essential Writings*, 5.

63. Chiara Lubich, "Two Sides of the Same Coin," in *Essential Writings*, 28. See also her "Mary in the Focolare Movement," in *Essential Writings*, 43.

64. Lubich, "Two Sides of the Same Coin," 17.

65. Ibid., 26.

66. Chiara Lubich, "The Charism of Unity and Politics," in *Essential Writings*, 265.

67. Chiara Lubich, "Holy Spirit, the Unknown God," in *Essential Writings*, 146.

68. On Lubich's approach to the Holy Spirit in general, see her "Holy Spirit, the Unknown God," in *Essential Writings*, 143–56. On the application to revitalized parish life, see Adolfo Raggio, ed., *The Parish Community: A Path to Communion* (Hyde Park, NY: New City Press, 2000).

69. See Máire O'Byrne, *Model of Incarnate Love: Mary Desolate in the Experience and Thought of Chiara Lubich* (Hyde Park, NY: New City Press, 2011).

70. John 19:26.

71. Chiara Lubich, "And the Focolare Was Born," in *Essential Writings*, 52.

72. Chiara Lubich, "Mary and Communication," in *Essential Writings*, 299.

73. Lubich, *The Cry of Jesus Forsaken*, 136.

74. O'Byrne, *Model of Incarnate Love*, 93, citing Piero Coda, "Three Keys for the Reading of *Mulieris Dignitatem*," *Being/One* 4, no. 3 (1995): 19.

75. Chiara Lubich, "The Charisms of Unity and the Media," in *Essential Writings*, 300.

76. Ibid.

77. Ibid., 302.

78. Ibid.

79. Ibid., 296. Cf. Virgilio Elizondo, *Guadalupe: Mother of a New Creation* (Maryknoll, NY: Orbis, 1997).

80. Simone Weil, *L'Enracinement* (Paris: Gallimard, 1949). The work was completed in 1943, shortly before her untimely death. The English translation appeared as *The Need for Roots*, trans. Arthur Wills, preface by T. S. Eliot (London: Routledge Kegan Paul, 1952). The witness of Weil is now comprehensively surveyed in the Cahier de L'Herne titled *Simone Weil*, ed. Emmanuel Gabellieri and François L'Yvonnet (Paris: Éditions de l'Herne, 2014).

81. Cf. Hans Urs von Balthasar, "Action and Contemplation," in *Explorations in Theology*, vol. 1, 227–40, and Pope Francis, *Apostolic Exhortation Evangelii Gaudium* (November 24, 2013), 284–88.

82. Chiara Lubich, "The Attraction of Modern Times," in *Essential Writings*, 177–78.

83. On fullness as a Marian category, see Thomas J. Norris, *Mary in the Mystery: The Woman in Whom Divinity and Humanity Rhyme* (Hyde Park, NY: New City Press, 2012), 29–49.

84. Luigi Giussani, "After the Pilgrimage to Loretto," letter of June 22, 2003, to the community of Communion and Liberation, Communion and Liberation website, http://english.clonline.org/whatiscl/default.asp?id=633&id_n=14445.

85. Henri de Lubac, *The Motherhood of the Church* (San Francisco: Ignatius, 1982), 113.

86. Ibid., 113–39.

CHAPTER 13

Mary and the Contemplatives

Thomas Merton

LAWRENCE S. CUNNINGHAM

> *Any soul who longs for a holy love for the Word should listen to her wise invitation.*
>
> —John of Ford

It is odd that in the twenty-two volumes of *The Merton Annual*, the quasi-canonical resource publishing research on the monk, not one essay appears on the mariological thought of Thomas Merton. It is odd in the sense that it is hard to think of a contemplative religious order in the Christian West that has a longer or more pronounced tradition of Marian devotion than the Cistercians in general or of a Cistercian monk in modern times who has written more on Mary than Thomas Merton.

When Thomas Merton went to Gethsemani Abbey as a postulant in 1941, he entered a community that reflected a long history of devotion to Our Lady. Cistercian spirituality nurtured a love for Mary rooted in the works of the founding fathers, especially those of St. Bernard of Clairvaux, who, it will be remembered, was the person Dante chose to address the Virgin on Dante's behalf in the *Paradiso*. The twelfth-century Cistercians were noted for their deep affective love for the Mother of God.

That affection never waned in the Cistercian tradition. The monks of Gethsemani took the name of Mary along with their religious name. Merton was known as Brother Mary Louis. They recited the Little Office of Mary each day as a prelude to the chanting of the Divine Office. Each evening they ended compline with the solemn chanting of the *Salve Regina* before receiving the abbot's blessing and retiring for the night. In addition they absorbed all of the devotional practices that reflected the changes superimposed on traditional Cistercian spirituality by the seventeenth-century reforms of La Trappe Abbey, from which they got their popular name of Trappists.[1] May processions, recitations of the rosary, and festal celebrations in honor of Mary were woven into the life of the monastery. Merton was keenly aware of that long Cistercian Marian tradition. In 1960 he finished writing a course of instruction for his novices, developed over a long period, which ran to over four hundred mimeographed pages. As he concluded these notes, he ended with this observation: "Let us rely at all times on the intercession of Our Blessed Lady whose life we imitate in our monastery. By her help, our vows will bring us deep into the mystery of Christ and the resurrection of the Lord Jesus. Amen."[2]

Merton himself was predisposed to a deep devotion to Our Lady. He had been a convert for only a few years when he entered Gethsemani, but he already had developed a strong Marian devotion. Some fifteen years after entering the monastery, he would recall an image of Our Lady of Carmel he saw when visiting Cuba before he went to Gethsemani and would write a prayer in her honor in which he addressed Mary personally: "I have never forgotten you. You are more to me now than then, when I walked through the streets reciting (which I had just learned), the *Memorare*." In that same prayer Merton would later implore Our Lady of Carmel to teach him to go beyond "this country beyond words and beyond names."[3]

The "country beyond" in Merton's vocabulary meant contemplative experience, which brings us to a question that constitutes the central issue of this chapter. It is easy enough to show that Thomas Merton was deeply devoted to Mary; his writings in both prose and poetry, as well as his journal jottings, could establish that fact with ease. It is more interesting, however, to pose this question: How did Merton understand Mary in relationship to the contemplative life in general and to his contemplative vocation in particular? Was his devotion to her merely an adjunct form of monastic devotion superadded to monastic essentials (after all, there is nothing about Mary in the early monastic rules and little in ancient literature in general), or did Merton intuit a serious link between Mary and the contemplative life? What significance should be given the fact that for his first Mass he chose the votive Mass of Our Lady?

A good place to start in order to see how Merton understood the role of Mary is a poem first published in his volume titled *The Tears of the Blind Lion* (1949). In this long poem on the Visitation, called the "The Quickening of St. John the Baptist," with the subtitle "On the Contemplative Vocation," Merton captures the moment when Mary, heavy with child, approached her cousin Elizabeth. Merton likens the unborn John "leaping in the womb with joy" (Luke 1:41) to the contemplatives hidden in their cloistered solitude: "Sing in your cell, small anchorite! / How did you see her in the eyeless dark? / What secret syllable woke your young faith to the mad truth / That an unborn baby could be washed in the Spirit of God?"[4] Merton, toward the end of the poem, makes explicit the parallel between the unborn child darkly in Elizabeth's womb and the hidden life of the contemplative: "Then, like the wise, wild baby / The unborn John who could not see a thing / We wake and know the Virgin presence / Receive her Christ into our night / With stabs of intelligence as white as lightening."[5]

It is not hard to see the point Merton urges. The contemplative is an eschatological watcher standing in hope for the coming of the Word. That Word comes in receptivity like Mary, heavy with child, visiting Elizabeth, whose unborn child receives in darkness the equally hidden Christ mediated to him by Mary. The contemplative tradition loved the notion of a person hidden from the world waiting in prayer. It is not accidental that the tradition often compared the lives of contemplatives to that of Jonah hidden in the belly of a sea monster, praying and waiting for rescue, or that model of the ascetic, John the Baptist, patient in the desert, watching for the one who was to come. Merton's poetic conceit in this poem is not unlike that written centuries earlier by St. John of the Cross, whose four-line Christmas refrain (*letrilla*) bears more than a little resemblance: "The Virgin, weighed / with the Word of God / comes down the road: / If only you'll shelter her."[6]

What Thomas Merton discovered in his devotion to Mary was a kind of template for the contemplative: a life hidden, a place obscure, a heart informed by the Word, and a capacity for wonder. The late English Benedictine Hubert von Zeller, writing on the eve of the Second Vatican Council about the ideals of the monastic life, made Merton's point in different terms: "It was not the hidden life alone, lived in the obscurity of Nazareth, which guaranteed her [Mary's] calm in the face of puzzlement and anxiety; it was her solitude of heart, her 'aloneness' with God. Only those who possess God can be truly self-possessed."[7]

There is no way, in a short chapter of this kind, to survey the ways in which Merton treated Our Lady, but one theme that does recur in various ways is the hiddenness of Mary. While contemporary writers on Mary tend to underscore her role as a "strong woman" in the line of the wisdom women of the Old Testament, the contemplatives found instruction in Mary's hidden acceptance of the Word, her fiat that ran from the Annunciation to the foot of the Cross to the coming of the Spirit at Pentecost. Merton made this point explicitly in the opening line of his essay on Mary in *New Seeds of Contemplation*: "All that has been written about the Virgin Mother of God proves to me that hers is the most hidden of sanctities."[8] This hiddenness, in Merton's construal of the matter, "is hiddenness in God and, thus, her humility and hiddenness and poverty, her concealment and solitude is the best way to know her."[9] Even casual readers of Thomas Merton will see that the sentence just quoted about humility, poverty, concealment, and solitude expresses major themes that run like a red thread through all of his writings. In that same essay he reiterates the point by praising Mary in that, in his opinion, knowledge of Christ is only speculation except when, as in Mary, "it becomes experience because all her humility and poverty, without which Christ cannot be known, is given to her."[10]

In what we have seen so far, Mary models, for Merton, the contemplative life. She takes the Word of God into her heart and ponders it (see Luke 2:19, 51). However, when Merton turns his attention to the contemplative path, its theology and its practice, there is scant mention of Mary and very little about her role in contemplation other than her exemplary modeling of what a contemplative should be. On reflection, this lacuna should not be surprising since Merton's understanding of the contemplative path puts great emphasis on the *apophatic*—that place where little is needed of words and less of images. After all, if one consults the indexes to the collected major works of St. John of the Cross, one finds fewer than six references to Mary in the whole corpus. Merton pondered this issue of images more generally in a well-known essay in which he inquired about the humanity of Christ in monastic prayer.[11] The matter can be briefly stated: Mary, in her receptivity of the Word and in her privileged place at the foot of the Cross, teaches the contemplative how to be receptive to the grace of contemplation, which is experienced without symbols or words.

That being said, one does find some sustained interest in Mary in Merton's reflections and meditations on the liturgy. Liturgy, in his construal of the matter, is not to be identified with contemplation but is the necessary matrix out of which true contemplation arises: "Contemplation is not prayerfulness, or a tendency to find peace and satisfaction in liturgical rites. They too, are a great good, and they are almost necessary preparations for contemplative experience. They can never, of themselves, constitute that experience."[12] Merton's point is that participation in the liturgy provides the attitude of adoration, the necessary language, and the orientation toward which the contemplative becomes receptive to the grace of contemplation. If one needs a parallel, the practice of *lectio* provides an analogy. One reads, ruminates, and prays in order to contemplate. *Lectio*, like liturgy (there is an intimate connection between the two), becomes the platform from which one reaches toward the pure contemplation of the Divine.

However dedicated Merton was to the contemplative path, his journey is unthinkable apart from his deep involvement in the Liturgy of the Hours and the celebration of Mass after his ordination. He also published a number of essays on the liturgy during his lifetime as a monk, which were gathered into a single volume, *Seasons of Celebration*, three years before his death.[13] His notebooks are replete with references to lines in the liturgy that give him a launching pad for further meditation.

One particular essay in that volume of liturgical essays is perhaps his most sustained monastic meditation on Mary in the liturgy. Titled "Homily on Light and the Virgin Mary," this essay traces out the biblical theme of the lamp and the light which shines from it. Drawing on the application of the sapiential images from the Old Testament used in the Marian liturgy, Merton says: "No one has ever more perfectly contained the light of God than Mary who by the perfection of her purity and humility is, as it were, completely identified with truth like the clean window pane which vanishes entirely into the light which it transmits."[14] Merton sees in Mary a rekindling of that light extinguished in the sin of Adam, now "illuminating the whole house of God, restoring meaning to all God's creatures and showing the rest of men the way to return to the light."[15]

What Merton says of Mary as the light coming from a lampstand is, in a sense, a recapitulation of his "Nativity Kerygma" written four years earlier. In that prose meditation on Christmas, Merton focuses precisely on Christ as the light of the world coming into the darkness of our sinful state, "plunging us into the Light of God shining in the darkness of the world, in order that we may be illumined and transformed by the presence of the newborn Savior."[16] This reworking of the theme of light, first applied to the one who says "I am the light of the world" and then, by liturgical application to the Woman of Revelation, underscores a foundational concern of the contemplative: the search for the Light who illuminates everything. Mary is the figure who shows the contemplative how to be the light that points to the ineffable light that is God's very self. I think it not insignificant that as an epigraph to his book *New Seeds of Contemplation* Merton wrote these Latin words: *Tu qui sedes in tenebris / spe tua gaude/orta stella matutina / sol non tardebit* (You who sit in darkness / rejoice in hope / the morning star has appeared / the sun will not delay). The morning star, in Christian piety, is Mary, who points to the Son, who, like the sun, illuminates everything. That illumination is, of course, what the contemplative experience is all about.

NOTES

1. On the Marian practices of La Trappe, see David N. Bell, "Armand-Jean de Rancé (1626–1700) and the Mother of God," *Cistercian Studies Quarterly* 48, no. 1 (2013): 39–61; Rozanne Elder, ed., *Mary Most Holy: Meditating with the Early Cistercians* (Kalamazoo, MI: Cistercian, 2003), provides a generous sample of medieval Cistercian Marian texts.

2. Thomas Merton, "The Life of the Vows," ed. Patrick O'Connell, *Monastic Studies*, vol. 6 (Collegeville, MN: Liturgical Press, 2012), 479–80.

3. For this chapter I have used the condensed version of Merton's journals edited by Patrick Hart and Jonathan Montaldo: *The Intimate Merton* (San Francisco: Harper, San Francisco, 1999), 114.

4. From Thomas Merton, *Collected Poems* (New York: New Directions, 1977), 200.

5. Ibid., 201.

6. St. John of the Cross, *The Collected Works of St. John of the Cross*, trans. Kieran Kavanaugh (Washington, DC: ICS Publications, 1991), 73.

7. Hubert von Zeller, *Approach to Monasticism* (New York: Sheed and Ward, 1960), 124.

8. Thomas Merton, *New Seeds of Contemplation* (New York: New Directions, 1961), 167.

9. Ibid., 168.

10. Ibid.

11. Thomas Merton, "The Humanity of Christ in Monastic Prayer," in *Thomas Merton: Selected Essays*, ed. Patrick F. O'Connell (Maryknoll, NY: Orbis, 2013), 150–71.

12. Merton, *New Seeds*, 9.

13. Thomas Merton, *Seasons of Celebration: Meditations on the Cycle of Liturgical Feasts* (New York: Farrar, Straus and Giroux, 1965).

14. Ibid., 164. One of Merton's earliest published poems used the theme of the window. See Merton, "The Blessed Virgin Compared to a Window," in *Collected Poems*, 46–48.

15. Merton, *Seasons*, 163–64.

16. Ibid., 107.

EPILOGUE

Pastoral Reflections

CHAPTER 14

Mary and the Church Today

James H. Phalan, C.S.C.

Fr. Brian Daley taught me that when he prepares a presentation he always includes the "So what?" factor. What I offer now might be considered the "So what" factor of the conference whose presentations are recorded in this book. What is the importance of our investigation of Marian reflection on the eve of the Second Vatican Council for the Church today? I hope my remarks will propose to you a context for our discussions as we continue to delve into the subjects related to our theme.

First, however, I confess to you that I cannot claim to be a member of the theological "academy." While at this point of my life I would be very grateful for a life given full-time to scholarship, this has not been my path. Instead I have dedicated the past twenty years to another work of the Congregation of Holy Cross committed to Notre Dame, Our Lady, namely, Family Rosary, aka Holy Cross Family Ministries. It was founded by one of the University of Notre Dame's (UND's) most famous alumni, Servant of God Fr. Patrick Peyton, C.S.C. I think it is safe to say that he and his good friend Fr. Ted Hesburgh, C.S.C., had more impact on the Church in America and the world in the twentieth century than any other UND alumni. For thirteen years I worked in Family

Rosary in Peru, and for the past seven years I have coordinated the mission internationally. My work has given me some experience of the Church in the world, some of which I now share with you in light of our conference's theme.

The very work of the theologians we looked at during this conference reminded of the Church in the decades before the Council, which taught that the very nature of mariological reflection requires an ecclesial context. At the same time, the specific topics we examine these days require us to take the incarnational aspect of Mariology seriously as well as we situate ourselves in the Church here and now, in this world in which we live. I myself was born into this Church "on the eve of the Second Vatican Council," in 1951. Like many others who attended the conference, I have shared in the vicissitudes and the renewal of the Church over the past fifty years. Trying to learn from experience, the Catholic Church in 2016 must pay attention to several events that have motivated our conversations in recent years at Our Lady's university. Specifically, the Year of Faith that the Church marked between October 11, 2012, and November 24, 2013, and the Synod on the New Evangelization that began it, formed a backdrop for this conference, together with the ongoing issue of what has come to be called the "New Evangelization."

Commemorating the fiftieth anniversary of the opening of the Second Vatican Council, Pope Benedict XVI retraced the steps of St. John XXIII by visiting the Shrine of Our Lady of Loreto so that he, too, could return to the House of Mary and place in her hands this synod and the Year of Faith. Are we to look upon this gesture as simply something quaintly pious, along with the directive for the Year of Faith published by the Congregation for the Doctrine of the Faith (CDF), which made Marian devotion a top priority? The CDF text states, "Every initiative that helps the faithful to recognize the special role of Mary in the mystery of salvation, love her and follow her as a model of faith and virtue is to be encouraged."[1] When Benedict called for all to pray the rosary frequently during the Year of Faith,[2] are we to hear this as something that of course popes do routinely—or might there have been something more subtle and deeper at play? Might Pope Emeritus Benedict and now Pope Francis, through a variety of his own gestures and words during his young pontificate, have been calling the Church, including the theological academy, to pay attention to something? Here I share some observations. They may seem to be random, but from my experience I suggest that they are representative.

My work took me to Monterrey, Mexico, for Holy Week in 2013. The local customs that make the image of Mary a constant presence in street processions and all celebrations during Holy Week were personally very helpful to me in my own contemplation of the Paschal Mystery, calling me to open the eyes of my soul to the crucial importance of the participation of Mary, and therefore of the whole Church and each of the faithful, in the work of salvation. Yet as I discussed this with a young Mexican confrere, he said that neither he nor most Mexican priests preach much about the Mother of God because they have never studied much about her.

Soon thereafter my work took me to Brazil. Once again I was very impressed as I encountered and heard numerous testimonies of huge manifestations of devotion to the Blessed Virgin Mary. In the city of Belem and several other places in the country, there are processions and Marian celebrations that attract literally millions of devotees each year. On any typical weekend, the National Shrine of Our Lady, *Nossa Senhora Aparecida*, is visited by 100,000 pilgrims, many of whom travel all night by bus from great distances. I have discussed with Brazilian confreres what people understand about Mary during these processions. Their consensus is that they know she is the Mother of God and she helps them, but the challenge is to link this faith with lived discipleship. Further, there are often questions of syncretism with various sorts of Spiritism. However, I learned that only very rarely do priests and religious preach about Mary. I heard once again that they do not do so because they have never studied much about her!

In spite of these huge demonstrations of popular piety, the religious geography of Brazil is very complex, and the need for the New Evangelization is becoming ever more real. It would seem fairly obvious that this great popular devotion to the Blessed Virgin would be a powerful source of energy for the New Evangelization; yet I have come to understand that this energy is relatively untapped. For example, as I studied the strategic plan for the New Evangelization of one diocese in the state of Pernambuco, where the Congregation of Holy Cross works, there was not one mention of Mary.

322 J A M E S   H.   P H A L A N ,   C.S.C.

Talk of great displays of popular Marian devotion may seem far away from experience in the United States. They may seem interesting as an object of sociological or anthropological study but may, at the same time, seem not to have much to do with religious experience. However, many of us who attended the conference on which this book is based are old enough to remember Catholic life in America in the 1950s, when the May procession down the main street of any town, centered around an image of Mary, was one of the big events of the year in any parish. Practices of what could be called "popular Marian devotion" were a part of the daily lives of the great majority of American Catholics. A rich variety of devotions reflected the cultures of origin of persons whose ancestors had relatively recently arrived here. The Blessed Virgin was a crucial part of a lively devotional life throughout the Catholic world. This was *not* something new. Indeed we can establish that Marian devotion was robust in the Church at least by the fifth century. I would propose that this devotion to Mary began in the apostolic church, but there is no way to either prove or disprove this because of inadequate documentation.

In more recent times, partially due to a series of apparitions of Our Lady, starting in 1830 in Paris with the apparition to St. Catherine Labouré, Marian devotion in the Catholic Church rose to a particularly high point during the century or so before the Second Vatican Council. Cardinal Suenens, one of the great figures at the Council, said that the Church was living in an "Age of Mary."[3] This great devotion to Our Lady throughout Christian history has not been, however, some popular religiosity disjointed from "real Christianity." It has usually gone hand in hand with serious theological reflection about Our Lady. Indeed the Marian element of theology has developed with a deeper reflection on the nature of Christ, the Church, salvation, conversion, and the living of the Christian life. Mary's title of "Destroyer of Heresy" has indeed proved valid;[4] one observes that ignorance or denial of the importance of the Marian dimension of the Church generally intersects with weak or imbalanced theological positions of various sorts. Henri de Lubac agreed with Karl Barth that "Marian dogma is the central dogma of Catholicism"—but Barth went on to call it "the clearest expression of Catholic heresy."[5] De Lubac wrote that it is central not in the sense "that it eclipses the dogma of the Word Incarnate, but in this sense, that it is the 'crucial'

dogma of Catholicism, that in relation to which all its cardinal propositions are elucidated."[6] The Blessed Virgin Mary is the principle and the
prototype of a human person cooperating with grace and also the principle and prototype of the Church.

Marian devotion and theology have been intrinsic parts of Catholicism since its origins. The conference represented by this book, I believe, revealed that Christian faith is imprinted with a Marian seal. However, something happened in the late 1960s, after the Second Vatican
Council, which has often been called a "collapse of Mariology" that led
to a steep decline of Marian devotion affecting the whole Catholic world,
particularly the United States, Canada, and Europe.[7] Many churches in
America were stripped of Marian imagery. New church construction
since then, in the name of being Christocentric and liturgically correct,
has practically ignored Marian elements. I have heard of numerous occasions of priests in the 1960s and 1970s forbidding the faithful to pray the
rosary, even to the point of breaking rosaries during homilies!

Should it be a surprise that Marian devotion among Catholics in
North America and Europe is now generally weak? No formal and extensive studies have yet been made of Marian devotion in America. I believe this would be an important undertaking. However, from my own
observations and conversations I propose that there has been a de facto
decline in Marian devotion that is correlative with a general decline in
daily devotion and prayer on the part of Catholics over the past fifty
years. (Before Vatican II, the rosary and other forms of Marian devotion
offered the faithful a structure for their daily spiritual lives.)

Catholics still have some intuitive sense that Mary is somehow important to their faith. However, this seems to have little definition, theoretically or practically. Universally (with perhaps an occasional exception
in the Philippines), I hear from people that they almost never hear a
homily about the Blessed Virgin or one into which Marian dimensions
are interwoven. This seems to be true even at places of Marian pilgrimage. I myself visited Lourdes seven times over seven years. I participated
in at least two dozen Eucharistic celebrations there, and, with the exception of several Masses celebrated during the Congress of the Pontifical
International Marian Academy in 2008, I never heard a homily on the
Blessed Virgin Mary. What are we to make of this great Marian silence?

Though weakened, Marian devotion is alive and now recovering from its post–Vatican II decline. While it had weakened in Catholic areas of the developing world, specifically in Latin America and Asia, it retained healthy roots and is growing. In the United States one also sees this recovery. I have heard numerous comments that the grotto of Our Lady of Lourdes here on the UND campus is at the center of the faith life of Notre Dame! Yet without proper shepherding, should it be surprising that this Marian energy occasionally takes a distorted direction as, at times, it seems to do? Nevertheless, shouldn't it be obvious that Marian devotion *ought* to be a great resource for evangelization today, for the New Evangelization? I make this proposal with no apology for my ever-deepening conviction, which comes from both personal experience and the experience of the Church through the ages, that the Blessed Virgin always has been and always should be the Mother of the Church and the "Star of Evangelization," as Blessed Paul VI called her.[8]

Such a proposition needs to be supported theologically. It needs to be rooted in the theological vision and foundation of the Christian faith of the Church and made manifest through different expressions of the life of the Church. How is it to be expressed for today? It may be surprising to some, perhaps even to some members of the theological academy, that the theologians whose work we considered in the conference paid specific attention to expressions of theological reflection in which the Mother of God plays an intrinsic, even essential, part. In so doing, they set the directions for the renewal of the much-needed Marian dimension of theology and devotion as well. The Church's Magisterium has repeatedly endorsed the appropriateness of these directions, particularly for today and specifically for the task of evangelization.[9]

Chenu, Daniélou, Congar, de Lubac, Schillebeeckx, Karl and Hugo Rahner, von Balthasar, Guardini, Bouyer, Suenens, Semmelroth, Ratzinger: these are names that stand out among the great theologians of the twentieth century. They were prominent guiding lights for the Second Vatican Council. All of them have left significant writings about the Mother of God. In some cases the number of pages devoted to Mary in the corpus of their life's work may be relatively small, yet they have continued to articulate the ancient awareness of orthodox Catholic theology of Mary's pervasive presence. Each, from his theological posture, locates Mary at the heart of the Christian mystery.

While the contributions of these theologians to contemporary theology in general and to the Second Vatican Council in particular are widely recognized, their contributions to the eighth chapter of *Lumen Gentium* are largely forgotten. It is to this chapter that we return these days, convinced that is of great benefit to the Church now.

Pope Benedict called the Church to celebrate the Year of Faith, to which the McGrath Institute for Church Life wished to contribute this Marian conference. As one studies *Porta Fidei*, the apostolic letter declaring the beginning of the Year of Faith,[10] one comes to understand that the year is really a preparation for a greater task, called the "New Evangelization." To what does this term really refer? The study of magisterial texts—from *Ad Gentes* of the Second Vatican Council through *Evangelii Nuntiandi* of Paul VI, *Redemptoris Missio* and other texts of the papacy of St. John Paul II, and those of Benedict XVI—reveals an expanding sense of the concept of evangelization. From what was once exclusively understood as preaching the Gospel *ad gentes*, to peoples who have not yet known Christ, evangelization today, specifically the New Evangelization, needs to address the proclamation of the Gospel in areas that once were largely Christian but now increasingly are not. Pope Benedict states: "Without doubt a mending of the Christian fabric of society is urgently needed in all parts of the world. But for this to come about what is needed is to first remake the Christian fabric of the ecclesial community itself present in these countries and nations."[11] The Year of Faith was meant to further the New Evangelization by taking it to local Christian communities.

It is noteworthy that for the Year of Faith Pope Benedict stressed the importance of a return to studying the documents of the Second Vatican Council. He proposed the continued relevance of the vision of the Second Vatican Council for facing the challenges to faith and to the Church today. Of course, in any age it is the Gospel itself that shapes our response to the world, but that response must be rearticulated for each generation. Just as the vision and the methodology of the theologians studied during this conference shaped the vision and the methodology of the Council, their insights can help the Church now in a significant way as well. This is specifically the case as we consider the Blessed Virgin, whose importance for the New Evangelization both Pope Benedict and Pope Francis have emphasized in no uncertain terms.

But why did the collapse of Mariology occur after the Second Vatican Council? Might it have been a "fruit"—or, rather, what some might prefer to call a product of the "sterility"—of the Council? I join my voice to those of all the popes since the Council with a resounding "No." The Council intended a renewal of Marian devotion, a fruit of the Council that has yet to come to maturity. However, the evolution of its Marian document was one of the most controversial aspects of the Council. Though some may know the story, it merits retelling here since it reveals much about the influence of pre–Vatican II Mariology. As we have noted, at the advent of the Vatican Council the Marian Movement in the Church was particularly strong. It was one of the main currents flowing toward Vatican II. At the same time, biblical and liturgical movements had long been gaining attention and promised to be major voices as Pope John XXIII was calling for *Aggiornamento*—a time of opening the windows for renewal.

There was a certain compatibility of visions between the biblical and liturgical movements as the Council looked to Scripture and to tradition to shed light on the renewal of the Church in the modern world. However, what came to be seen as a methodological weakness in the Marian Movement seemed out of sync, at least, with the biblical and liturgical thrust. While the biblical and liturgical foundations of Marian devotion could not be questioned, Marian reflection and theology seemed to have become autonomous and detached from the rest of theology, concentrating with much attention on explaining Mary's privileges.

A crucial moment in the Council came as a decision was to be made concerning the magisterial text on the Mother of God. Given the high level of importance that Marian devotion had in the Church, many assumed that a separate document would be devoted to Our Lady. However, this proposal itself highlighted the methodological question. Should there be a separate document, or should a text on Our Lady be integrated into the schema on the Church? A draft of a proposed autonomous Marian text had been prepared when this question came up for a decision on October 29, 1963. After extensive debate, the vote taken was extremely close: 1,114 in favor of including Marian teaching in the constitution on the Church and 1,074 in favor of a separate text. This meant that a new text was to be prepared to be included in the dogmatic text on the Church that became *Lumen Gentium*. The Marian text became its eighth and final chapter and was almost unanimously approved on November 21, 1964.[12]

This interesting turn of events is fairly well known and has been commented on by—among others—Council *peritus* Joseph Ratzinger.[13] He notes that while the decision of the Council fathers was necessary and correct, it was not without serious implications. While Pope Paul VI attempted to avert or soften a mariological crisis by formally declaring Mary to be the "Mother of the Church" very soon after the promulgation of *Lumen Gentium*, the apparent change in emphasis given to the Blessed Virgin contributed to some extent to what became the full-scale collapse of Mariology. Yet the Council fathers had intended for the chapter on Mary to bring about a reorientation that would help give birth to a renewal. Examining all the factors leading to the collapse of Mariology is beyond the scope of this chapter, having to do with larger issues of hermeneutics and of social and technological change in the late 1960s and since. But the result of the collapse has been that the Marian renewal is still waiting to happen fully.

The Marian text that the Council fathers did approve was meant to serve as a guidepost for that renewal, and it is clear in the writings of the post–Vatican II popes that in their estimation it is suited to this task. Note the conscious adoption of the orientations of *Lumen Gentium* chapter 8 in *Marialis Cultus* of Paul VI and *Redemptoris Mater* of John Paul II, along with the continual references to it in the work of Joseph Ratzinger, now Pope Emeritus Benedict XVI. Pope Francis concluded his recent Encyclical *Lumen Fidei* with a reflection on Mary's faith in relationship to the Church that is certainly in the same line.

The Marian reflections of the theologians who favored *ressource-ment*[14] and other theologians on the eve of the Council shaped to a great extent *Lumen Gentium* chapter 8. This text has, by and large, been insufficiently studied and deserves much more attention in order to orient Marian devotion today. It was intended to be and is, in fact, the most complete and concise summary of Marian doctrine ever offered by the Magisterium. In particular, study of the sources that shaped it is very important if one is to begin to look deeply into the doctrine it presents. Just as we can say that *Lumen Gentium* is a guidepost, so can we also say that it is a milestone to which future Marian reflection must orient itself. Correlatively, then, the Marian reflections we looked at during the conference as source texts for *Lumen Gentium* chapter 8 are in some ways guideposts as well.

Various conference presentations treated more deeply the perspectives of some specific theologians. At the same time, more general considerations of the Marian perspectives of the *ressourcement* theologians and those of other theologians writing on the eve of the Council can also illuminate their impact on the creation of *Lumen Gentium* chapter 8 and therefore on future directions for the renewal of Mariology and Marian devotion. I turn my attention now to several of these points.

First one notes a desire to look deeply and fundamentally at the role of Mary in Christian faith and theology. A particular preoccupation toward the end of the nineteenth century was to find the foundational mariological principle that would yield a unifying vision of Mary's role. We find many theologians devoting extensive discussions to this point, each from his particular theological system. These attempts originated in the desire to establish Mariology more firmly as a separate branch of theology. However, in the twentieth century, in response to the great amount of literature and devotion being devoted to Mary's titles, her privileges, and her apparitions, there was a need to ground Marian devotion once again in the corpus of theological thought.

At times this response could be called "reaction." For example, Congar could write seemingly stridently about some tendencies of thought of the Marian movement, particularly during the Second Vatican Council. He was wary of devotion that was out of control in the sense of not being founded in well-thought-out theological reflection. So much so, one might think, that he wanted to reduce Mary's place in the Church. However, his Marian perspective is clearly within the great tradition of the Church, particularly regarding Mary's cooperation with Christ in our redemption—her universal maternal role in the mediation of grace. These efforts to consider Mary from fundamental and unified perspectives, even when critical, profoundly enriched the conciliar Marian perspectives and certainly contributed to the final decision of the Council not to promulgate a separate Marian text but rather to include it in what became *Lumen Gentium*.

Further, it is most important to recognize the ongoing contribution of an apparent mariological pruning. The more fundamental and unified perspective that resulted should renew our focus on Mary's relationship to Christ, salvation history, and the Church in ways that are immensely rich for both devotion and theological reflection. Pope Benedict XVI refers to Mary as the "*nexus mysteriorum*,"[15] a beautifully evocative phrase highlighting her relationship and place in various theological and other intellectual disciplines while at the same time drawing us into contemplation of the great Christian mysteries as the Daughter of Zion, the Woman of Faith, and the Mother of God and of the Church.

Complementary to this more fundamental and unified perspective has been the *ressourcement* methodology, the "return to the sources" that became so important and at times controversial in the decades preceding the Council. It became a fundamental methodology of the Council itself, calling the whole Church to return to the sources—Scripture, tradition, and the Magisterium—to inform our proclamation of the Gospel to the world of today. Applying this methodology to the field of Mariology, which had seemed to play by its own rules, was an aspect of the shift that has not been easily assimilated. Yet at stake was not simply bringing Mariology in line with other theological disciplines but rather opening new pathways for both devotion and study. The previously dominant Neo-Scholastic theology had become a dry well, and the devotional theology common in Marian movements could be faulty, as Congar was insistent in pointing out.

As Congar, de Lubac, and others had returned to biblical and patristic sources in the decades before the Council, their studies seemed to reveal a lost Marian treasure, allowing them and us to rediscover the identity of this Mother whom we love so much. Properly understood, this methodology should not have undermined well-founded beliefs of centuries; rather it should richly complement and give new meaning to our great reverence for the Immaculate Queen of Heaven, as *Lumen Gentium* chapter 8 makes quite clear. At the same time, the *ressourcement* methodology applied to Mariology has to some extent already opened doors for ecumenical dialogue intended to bridge what has been ostensibly a seriously dividing issue for centuries. Discussing Marian devotion from the perspectives of scripture and patristic writings allows for dialogue in which we are open to listening very attentively to Protestant perspectives while remaining committed to our faith convictions.

After ten years of relative silence concerning Mary following the Council, years in which the intended Marian renewal had not at all begun, Paul VI published the Apostolic Exhortation *Marialis Cultus* (February 2, 1974), a lucid return to *Lumen Gentium* chapter 8 and a synthesis of guidelines to be drawn from it for the Marian renewal. By calling for Marian reflection and devotion that is biblical and liturgical as well as ecumenically and anthropologically sensitive, the pope offered orientations that continue to be thoroughly appropriate for today. In them I hope the voices of theologians whose work we have begun to discuss can already be recognized!

As I conclude my remarks, I turn my attention briefly to one Marian treasure that reemerged on the eve of the Council: the archetypical relationship between Mary and the Church. Many theologians, among them Congar, de Lubac, Semmelroth, Hugo Rahner, Schillebeekx, and von Balthasar, reminded the Latin Church of something of which the oriental Churches had remained much more vitally aware: that Mary is the archetype and icon of the Church. Later, Joseph Ratzinger wrote that Mary is the personal "concreteness," the "personification" of the Church.[16] I am convinced that this perspective is of particular importance today, complementing our understanding of Mary's maternal role in a profound way that resonates beautifully on doctrinal, moral, communal, liturgical, and mystical levels. However, this perspective has not yet received the attention it deserves in the life of the Church.

The fathers of the Second Vatican Council also agreed that this profound relationship between Mary and the Church was very important. Fully three paragraphs of chapter 8 of *Lumen Gentium* are dedicated to this topic, stressing that the Blessed Virgin is the complete realization of all that the Church is to be as the Bride of Christ. The Council fathers incorporate the patristic principle of her threefold relationship that de Lubac returned to the Church's memory. As de Lubac wrote: "That which is said 'universally' of the Church . . . is said of Mary 'specially' and of the faithful soul 'singularly'—that is to say, individually."[17] Recovery of this principle becomes a powerful resource for a rediscovery of what the Church is and, implicitly, who we are!

While the Council decided not to promulgate a separate document about the Virgin Mary, an act that in itself would have stressed her importance, I propose that the significance of a different symbolic gesture should not escape us. Although Mary does not have "her own text," she does occupy the final chapter of the fundamental dogmatic text on the Church. As in the case of other topics in other magisterial documents, this final turn to Our Lady was meant to stress her fundamental importance. Just as chapter 8 is something of the crowning jewel of *Lumen Gentium*, Mary is the crowning jewel of the Church. The theologians we studied during the conference wanted the Church to understand this for today. They tried to help the Church renew her understanding that Our Lady is the *nexus mysteriorum*. We have seen that they believed this to be very important on the eve of the Council. Let us try to understand them now.

In the 2013 *Civilitá Cattolica* interview with Pope Francis that drew so much attention because of the Holy Father's fresh and forthright comments, he reflected on the Church and offered a simple but penetrating statement: "This is how it is with Mary: If you want to know who she is, you ask theologians; if you want to know how to love her, you have to ask the people. In turn, Mary loved Jesus with the heart of the people."[18] I believe the pope intended for us to appreciate complementarity on several levels, including the symbolic identification of Mary and the Church. As ever, the people of God around the world love Mary and long to love her more. In this book we offer our reflections in the hope that they will help complement that desire and that love, helping the people of God today to express the identity of this Mother whom they love. At the same time we will find out who we are so as to love our Lord more and more. Holy Mother Mary, guide us and pray for us!

NOTES

1. CDF, *Note with Recommendations for the Year of Faith* (January 6, 2012), 19.

2. Benedict XVI, Angelus Address, St. Peter's Square (October 7, 2012).

3. Léon Joseph Suenens, *Mary, the Mother of God* (New York: Hawthorn, 1959), 126.

4. This ancient title was noted by St. Pius V in *Consuerverunt Romani*, the papal bull of September 17, 1569, that formally confirmed the prayer of the rosary. Cf. note 40 in the chapter of Fr. Thomas A. Thompson in this volume: "Rejoice O Virgin Mary, for you alone have destroyed all heresies. You believed the words of the Archangel Gabriel" (from *Tractus: Missae de sancta Maria in sabato II & III*).

5. Henri de Lubac, *The Splendor of the Church* (San Francisco: Ignatius, 1999), 315.

6. Ibid.

7. Cf. Cardinal Joseph Ratzinger, "Thoughts on the Place of Marian Doctrine and Piety in Faith and Theology as a Whole," in Hans Urs von Balthasar and Joseph Cardinal Ratzinger, *Mary: The Church at the Source*, trans. Adrian Walker (San Francisco: Ignatius, 2005), 24.

8. Paul VI, *Apostolic Exhortation Evangelii Nuntiandi* (December 8, 1975), 82.

9. See Pontifical International Marian Academy, *The Mother of the Lord: Memory, Presence, Hope* (Staten Island, NY: St. Paul, 2007), 69.

10. Benedict XVI, *Apostolic Letter Porta Fidei for the Indiction of the Year of Faith* (October 11, 2011).

11. Benedict XVI, *Apostolic Letter Ubicumque et Semper, Establishing the Pontifical Council for Promoting the New Evangelization* (September 21, 2010), 34.

12. A text prepared to be proposed as a schema for a "freestanding" Marian text called *Mary, Mother of Jesus and Mother of the Church* had been drafted by Rev. Carlo Balić, O.F.M. When the decision was made to incorporate a Marian text within the document on the Church and a commission was charged with the task, it was Balić, together with Msgr. Gerard Phillips, who composed the text.

13. Benedict XVI and von Balthasar, *Mary: The Church at the Source*, chap. 2.

14. A number of theologians began a renewal of theology, perhaps loosely defined as a school, that highlighted a "return to the sources," that is, the Scriptures and the writings of the Fathers of the Church; hence the name, *ressourcement*. At times it was disparagingly called the *nouvelle théologie* by opponents who criticized this trend as a rebirth of Modernism. However the theologians who began this renewal attempted in a positive way to break the hold that Neo-Scholasticim had on theology at the time. Theologians trained by the French Dominican Theology Faculty of Le Saulchoir, like Chenu and Congar, and by the Jesuit Faculty in Lyons, like de Lubac, became representatives of this methodology. They were held under great suspicion by the Vatican from 1950 to 1958, only to be vindicated by John XXIII and the Second Vatican Council.

15. Benedict XVI, *Address to the Twenty-third International Mariological Marian Congress* (Castel Gandolfo, September 8, 2012).

16. Joseph Ratzinger, *Daughter of Zion* (San Francisco: Ignatius, 1983), 67–68.

17. De Lubac, *The Splendor of the Church*, 347. De Lubac is referring to a homily of Bl. Isaac of Stella, which can be found in Jacques-Paul Migne, *Patrologia Latina* 194, col. 1865.

18. Antonio Spadaro, "A Big Heart Open to God," *America* 20 (September 8, 2013): 20.

ANN W. ASTELL, a Schoenstatt Sister of Mary, joined the Faculty of Theology at the University of Notre Dame in 2007 after serving as professor of English at Purdue University (1988–2007), where she chaired the program in Medieval and Renaissance studies. The recipient of a National Endowment for the Humanities Fellowship and of a John Simon Guggenheim Memorial Fellowship, she is the author of six books, most recently *Eating Beauty: The Eucharist and the Spiritual Arts of the Middle Ages* (Cornell University Press, 2006), and the editor or co-editor of six collections of essays. Past president of the Society for the Study of Christian Spirituality (2011–12), she currently serves as president of the Colloquium on Violence and Religion.

PETER CASARELLA is an associate professor at the University of Notre Dame and former director of the Center for World Catholicism and Intercultural Theology at DePaul University. In 2014–15 he was a Henry Luce III Fellow in Theology as well as the recipient of a sabbatical grant from the Louisville Institute for a book project titled "God of the People: A Latino/a Theology." His research publications include "Mary and Inculturation," in *A Man of the Church: Honoring the Theology, Life, and Witness of Ralph del Colle*, ed. Michel Barnes (Eugene, OR: Wipf and Stock, 2012), 265–82, and "Contemplating Christ through the Eyes of Mary: The Apostolic Letter *Rosarium Virginis Mariae* and the New Mysteries of Light," *Pro Ecclesia* 14, no. 2 (Spring 2005): 161–73.

JOHN C. CAVADINI is professor of theology at the University of Notre Dame. While serving as chair of the department from 1997 to 2010, he led the department to a top-10 position in the National Research Council rankings of doctoral programs. He is also the McGrath-Cavadini Director of the McGrath Institute for Church Life. His main areas of research and teaching are patristics, with a special focus on the theology of St. Augustine, and the biblical spirituality of the Church Fathers. He has published extensively in these areas, as well as in the theology of miracles, the life and work of Gregory the Great, catechetical theology, the theology of marriage, and so on. As director of the Institute for Church Life, he inaugurated the Echo program in catechetical leadership, the Notre Dame Vision program for high school students, the seminar What We Hold in Trust for trustees and presidents of Catholic colleges and universities, the Sustaining Pastoral Excellence program, and the Initiative in Spirituality and the Professions, among others. In addition, Professor Cavadini has served on the International Theological Commission and is a consultant to the Committee on Doctrine of the U.S. Conference of Catholic Bishops.

LAWRENCE S. CUNNINGHAM is John A. O'Brien Professor of Theology (Emeritus) at the University of Notre Dame. The author or editor of over twenty-six books, he is currently working on a volume about the theology of prayer.

FR. BRIAN E. DALEY, S.J., is the Catherine F. Huisking Professor of Theology at the University of Notre Dame and specializes in studying and teaching the theology of the Church Fathers. He has written books and articles on a variety of topics in early Christian theology, including eschatology, Christology, and the Trinity, and has recently published a volume of translations of early and medieval Greek homilies for the feast of the Transfiguration of the Lord.

PETER JOSEPH FRITZ holds a Ph.D. in systematic theology from the University of Notre Dame. He is currently associate professor of theology and Edward Bennett Williams fellow at the College of the Holy Cross in Worcester, Massachusetts. He is the author of *Karl Rahner's Theological Aesthetics* (Catholic University of America Press, 2014) and several essays on Rahner, including "Karl Rahner Repeated in Jean-Luc Marion," *Theological Studies* 73 (2012), and "Karl Rahner and Friedrich Schelling on Original Plural Unity," *Theological Studies* 75 (2014).

FR. KEVIN GROVE, C.S.C., is assistant professor of theology at the University of Notre Dame. He was ordained a priest in the Congregation of Holy Cross in 2010. He completed his seminary studies at the University of Notre Dame and his Ph.D. at the University of Cambridge in philosophical theology. His primary research is on memory in systematic theology, exploring patristic, Christological resources for considering mediation by Christ, memory, and the Church. In addition to his research on memory both ancient and modern, he also writes on Holy Cross history and the theology of Blessed Basil Moreau.

MSGR. MICHAEL HEINTZ is associate professor of systematic theology at Mount St. Mary's Seminary in Emmitsburg, Maryland. He served previously as rector of St. Matthew Cathedral in South Bend, Indiana, and director of the Master of Divinity Program in the Theology Department at the University of Notre Dame. He completed his Ph.D. in 2008 in Latin and Greek Patristics at the University of Notre Dame, and his current research includes Origen, Gregory of Elvira, and the works of Louis Bouyer.

MATTHEW LEVERING is Perry Family Foundation Professor of Theology at Mundelein Seminary in Mundelein, Illinois. He serves as chair of the board of the Academy of Catholic Theology and is co-editor of two theological quarterlies: *Nova et Vetera* and the *International Journal of Systematic Theology*. He is the author most recently of *Paul in the Summa Theologiae*; *Engaging the Doctrine of Revelation: The Mediation of the Gospel in Church and Scripture*; and *Mary's Bodily Assumption*. With Anver Emon and David Novak, he is co-author of *Natural Law: A Jewish-Christian-Islamic Trialogue*.

DANIELLE M. PETERS, S.T. D., is a member of the Secular Institute of the Schoenstatt Sisters of Mary. She currently serves as president of the Mariological Society of America and as the moderator of the Schoenstatt Apostolic Movement in Dallas, Texas. Her former assignments include research fellow at the McGrath Institute for Church Life at the University of Notre Dame, professor and coordinator of academic programs at the Pontifical International Marian Research Institute in Dayton, and employment by the Congregation for the Doctrine of the Faith. She is the author of *Ecce Educatrix Tua: The Role of the Blessed Virgin Mary for a Pedagogy of Holiness in the Thought of John Paul II and Father Joseph Kentenich* (Lanham, MD: University Press of America, 2010).

FR. JAMES H. PHALAN, C.S.C., is the director of Family Rosary International of Holy Cross Family Ministries. He is the past president of the Mariological Society of America and resides in Boston and Mexico.

FR. JOHANN G. ROTEN, S.M., is an internationally recognized expert on everything Marian. A longtime director of the Marian Library/International Marian Research Institute at the University of Dayton, he serves now as the institute's director of research, art, and special projects. He is the creator and main author of *The Mary Page*, the largest online repository of information on Mary. Fr. Roten is the principal editor of Marian Library Studies and serves as a consulting editor for *Communio: International Catholic Review*. Having served as president of the Mariological Society of America, he is currently the vice president of the French Mariological Society.

CHRISTOPHER RUDDY is associate professor of historical and systematic theology at The Catholic University of America. He is the author of two books, and his articles have appeared in such journals as *Commonweal*, *Ecclesiology*, *Heythrop Journal*, the *Irish Theological Quarterly*, and *Theological Studies*. His theological interests include ecclesiology, Vatican II, the *nouvelle théologie* and *ressourcement* movements, and the relationship of Christianity and culture. New York natives, he and his wife, Deborah, have four sons.

TROY A. STEFANO is associate professor of systematic and historical theology at St. Vincent de Paul Regional Seminary. He has published several articles, book chapters, and translations in the areas of historical theology and systematic theology. He is the author of *The Trinity in Modern Catholic Theology* (Fortress Press, forthcoming).

FR. THOMAS A. THOMPSON, S.M., is the director of the Marian Library of the University of Dayton. He contributed the final chapter, "Vatican II and Beyond," to Hilda Graef's *Mary: A History of the Doctrine and Devotion* (Ave Maria Press, 2009). He is the editor of *Marian Studies*, the annual publication of the Mariological Society of America. Among his translations is a document from the Pontifical International Marian Academy, *The Mother of the Lord: Memory, Presence, Hope* (Alba House, 2007), which presents "a review of the actual questions facing Mariology today."

CPSIA information can be obtained
at www.ICGtesting.com
Printed in the USA
LVOW09*0824110717

540767LV00001BA/1/P